cal Indicators in Market Cycles

	Changing Markets			
	Trading to Bull	Trading to Bear	Bull to Trading	Bear to Trading
:s	Excellent behavior	Excellent behavior	Excellent behavior	Excellent behavior
er of	Increasing signals to OB	Increasing frequency of OS signals	Equal number of OB/OS signals from OB skew	Equal number of OB/OS signals from show OB
ls lified	Valid signals give way to false OB	Valid signals give way to false OS	False OS to valid signals	False OB to valid signals
ls	Valid signals give way to false OB	Valid signals give way to false OS	False OS to valid signals	False OB to valid signals
m lid	Crossovers of OB/OS valid to only OS indicators valid	Crossovers of OB/OS valid to only OB indicators	Only OS area crossovers are valid to both OB/OS valid	Only OB area crossovers are valid to both OB/OS valid
wns	Can project counts to likely tops	Can project counts to likely bottoms	Cannot forecast	Cannot forecast
nd	Can see buildup of buying pressure	Can see buildup of selling pressure	Great appearance of non-trend days	Great appearance of non-trend days
ut fness id	Excellent accumulation indicators	Too late to signal volume distribution	Flattening of OBV breakouts	Flattening of OBV breakouts
nals	Excellent accumulation indicators	Too late to signal volume distribution	Flattening of OBV breakouts	Flattening of OBV breakouts
end	Reversal patterns valid	Reversal patterns valid	Reversal patterns valid	Reversal pattern valid
e	Excellent turning points	Excellent turning points	Excellent turning points	Excellent turning point
ows	Probability can be determined that this will happen	Probability can be determined that this will happen	Probability can be determined that this will happen	Probability can be determined that this will happen
	Can get you long but whipsawed first	Can get you short but whipsawed first	Whipsaw first then profits	Whipsaw first then profits

The Technical Analysis of
Stocks, Options & Futures

The Technical Analysis of

Stocks, Options & Futures

Advanced Trading Systems and Techniques

William F. Eng

Probus Publishing
Chicago, Illinois

This publication is designed to provide accurate and authoritative information in regard to the subject matter covered. It is sold with the understanding that the publisher is not engaged in rendering legal, accounting or other professional service. If legal or other expert assistance is required, the service of a competent professional person should be sought. From a declaration of principles jointly adopted by a committee of the American Bar Association and a committee of publishers.

Library of Congress Cataloging-in-Publication Data

Eng, William F.
   The technical analysis of stocks, option, & futures: advanced
trading systems and techniques/William F. Eng
     p.   cm.
   Includes index.
   ISBN 1-55738-003-1
   1. Stocks. 2. Put and call transaction. 3. Stock index futures: advanced
I. Title.
   HG4521.E58 1988
   332.63'22—dc19

88-3665
CIP

Dedication

Alden
To my father, Frank
my mother, King
my sister, Judith
Gabriele
and Martin

for their support
and devotion during the
writing of this book.

Contents

Foreword

Technical analysis today is a field that investors and traders ignore at their peril. Not in the recent memory have investment markets made price swings so frequently, even if those who play down the volatility tell us that the percentage changes in markets such as stocks are still lower than their historical averages.

That is no comfort to investors, whether they be nurses in Oregon or multi-billion dollar money managers in New York, London or Geneva. Their efforts might have been a lot simpler in the days before floating foreign exchange rates, global investment portfolios, and uncertain monetary and fiscal policies. Each of these factors now takes center stage in the minds of investors at one time or another; and when the market is tired of them, they are shunted off and replaced by some new development which the public slowly tries to understand. In a certain sense, the investment market is like a child; although there may be dozens of factors that could explain its performance, the child will only be able to name one or two. And when it grows tired of hearing about them the child replaces them with something else.

In a highly uncertain world, many people seek consolation in simplicity. They try to fix on some sure and true method for interpreting the market's behavior and block out any source of information that complicates their analysis. Others go to the opposite extreme in attempting to collect every bit of information they can. They run the risk of tying themselves up in utter confusion as they try to determine which information is correct, or most influential.

Investors and traders thus face new challenges in interpreting market behavior as a consequence of the globalization of investment. Depending on where you live in the world, your investment preferences will be mostly affected by the financial condition of your country and its currency, and if you are a money manager, by those of your clients. If a Japanese investor perceives U.S. Treasury bond yields as attractive, he may be ignoring U.S. inflation because he does not hear much about it in Japan. The Japanese is only looking at the yield on Treasuries because they appear highly attractive compared with the much lower yields on yen bonds. But the U.S. investor may be putting his money in yen bonds because he expects an enormous appreciation in the yen against the dollar, to more than make up for the relatively lower yield on the yen bond coupon.

This example illustrates how people may act on incomplete information, as well as how people can draw different conclusions from the same information. The best arbiter of the accuracy of investment information is the market itself, since it displays the actual results of investor decisions. The field of technical analysis focuses on market results in order to help the investor separate reality from desire.

Even technical analysis is complex, however, like everything else in today's world. The interpretation of market activity through technical analysis provides different clues about price behavior at various stages of the market cycle. Since a variety of methods are followed around the world today, it is necessary to be at least somewhat familiar with each one. This book not only gives a basic description of these methods, but also details their advantages and limitations. It thus provides an enormous service to not only the professional market "technicians" who may rely heavily on one or more methods for their analysis, but also to non-professionals who take their investments as seriously as they do their money, their homes and their families.

John G. Powers
South Orange, New Jersey
January 1988
Editor-in-Chief
Intermarket Magazine

Preface

Every trader or investor in stocks, futures or options needs a system to follow and predict market behavior if they have any expectation that their trading will be profitable. But no single trading system can be relied upon entirely nor can any single system be used consistently over time. Astute traders recognize that changing market conditions demand periodic reevaluation of trading techniques, systems and strategies.

The Technical Analysis of Stocks, Options and Futures was written with this very need in mind. Essentially, this is a reference book that provides specific and practical information about the various trading systems in use, their applicability and their effectiveness in a variety of market conditions.

Fifteen different trading systems have been gathered in one volume with the needs of both the beginning trader as well as the veteran in mind. Each of the fifteen systems is described, explained, analyzed, and applied to a variety of trading environments. My goal is to provide an easy-to-use reference which allows users to compare the relative strengths and weaknesses of the various systems. To my knowledge no other single source affords traders and investors the ability to compare, contrast and analyze the various trading systems.

Acknowledgments

When I graduated from college, Herbert Kipnis interviewed me for a position with his firm. He asked if I wanted to be in the securities business and I answered with a question. I asked him if I needed to carry a weapon. From those early years, I graduated from the "Kipnis school." I thank Herbert Kipnis for hiring me because he thought I was a funny guy. I am indebted to him because he knew I could make it in the business.

And a thankful word to the original Kipnis crew: Robert Stendl, the second richest Kipnis man; John Hartford who graciously holds reunions on his yacht; Billy Rosen who plays bridge as well as he trades; Gary Leason who tired and found relief in solace; Ralph (Whitey) Steffen who is smarter than he acts; Clint Riley who has found a home in Chicago; and Robert Atkins, a good and trusted friend.

I wish to express my grateful acknowledgment of the Chicago Board of Trade for allowing me into their family for 9 years of my career on LaSalle Street. In the same vein, I wish to thank the MidAmerica Commodity Exchange, the Chicago Board Options Exchange and the Midwest Stock Exchange for allowing me to become one of their members.

I would like to thank Howard Hawhee, a linguist by training, who aided me in creating this book. I would like to thank the people at Probus Publishing who worked on this book. Without their help and guidance this book would never have made it out of the trading pits.

A special word of thanks to Robert Ralph, whose action on July 19, 1982 showed another path for me. Bob, here's to you, wherever you may be. Bob, I hope what I have done in this book will help others like you to conquer their greatest fear: the fear of failure.

The following people deserve special recognition: Maynard Holt, III, developer of Relevance III software; Richard Batchelor, developer of the War-Machine; Frank Soong, developer of CTS Trend; Peter Pich, developer of Ganntrader I; and Michael Erhlewhine, developer of Bluestar.

How to Use This Book

This book is designed so that you do not have to read it all the way through to profit from its lessons. The following features ensure this:

- **A conceptual framework to orient readers to the techniques**
  Page 3 contains a general overview of the basic ideas behind all market trading, so that readers can share a common picture of each technique. A glossary follows this section, so readers can quickly refresh their knowledge of general trading terminology whenever they need to.

- **A Toolkit of Market Trading Techniques and Applications**
  The "toolkit" of the trading methods on pages 22-23 give a brief two-line description of each method in the toolkit, and a brief account of each method's application.

  The market's different phases require the trader to use the same techniques in different ways. The Toolkit Application of the seven types of markets, beginning on page 24, briefly describes what to expect and how to use each of the technical indicators in that phase.

- **A chart which keys market phases to the appropriate techniques**
  The *Master Chart and Trading Guide* and yearly charts on pages 9-15 provide a five-year bar chart of the Dow Jones Industrial averages and their respective years during which prices go through many types of market phases. A brief commentary explains the significance and major characteristics of each type of market phase. The chart also keys the various toolkit applications into the appropriate market phases.

- **A "cookbook" organization for each chapter**
  All the chapters on trading techniques are put together in the same way. Each technique's chapter contains the following sections:

  - Chapter at a glance: one-page summary of the chapter
  - Background and philosophy of the technique
  - Principles of the technique's functioning
  - How to set up and maintain the technique's indicators
  - How to trade with the technique
  - Practical trading examples with the technique
  - When to apply the technique
  - Where to find out more about the technique

The above divisions let you rapidly retrieve just the information you need at the moment, allowing you to make intelligent comparisons among several or many of the techniques.

This book's modular structure also allows you to have several different kinds of reference books at your fingertips:

- The beginning student of market trading techniques who wants a general feel for the hows and whys of trading might read just the "Background and Philosophy" section of each chapter at a first pass, or perhaps only the corresponding template section. A second reading for this same person might include the "Principles," "How to Set Up and Maintain " and "How to Trade" sections. A person with more experience might just want to follow the "How to Trade" and "Trading Examples" sections.

- A very experienced trader might focus on the "Trading Examples" sections and the sections on "When to Use This Technique." The more experienced trader can also use the "At a Glance" sections as a quick refresher.

Besides the traditional bibliographical references, the "Where to Find Out More" sections give readers electronic and textual information sources, some of which are just a phone call away.*

Finally, a word about the Risk Management chapter: read that chapter. The best trading techniques in the world will not save traders from ruin if they do not have an idea of how to manage and invest their funds, and they will remain afloat with even the worst trading techniques if they have an intelligent risk management system in place.

*My own organization, Financial Options Consultants, offers extensive on-line information on trading and trading techniques to those who own personal computers with telecommunications capability (that is, a modem). Our address is:

Financial Options Consultants
Department B, Suite #314
780 South Federal
Chicago, Illinois 60605, USA

Our computer phone line number is 312/922-3626, and it is accessible 24 hours a day, seven days a week. Set the computer modem to 8 data bits, no parity, 1 stop bit and full duplex to access the information correctly. Overseas callers can access the United States telecommunications network through packet switching systems.

1

Master Chart and
Trading Guide

A Conceptual Framework
for Studying Trading Techniques

Three basic elements predict market behavior: **Price, Time,** and **Volume.**

Beginning traders tend to use mostly price-oriented techniques. After all, the whole point of trading is to buy at a low price and sell at a high price, so why concentrate on anything else? Those who have this philosophy, therefore, will concentrate on techniques which look at where price has been in order to predict where price is going.

All "price-sensitive" techniques use only one kind of data: the recent past history of prices. Users of these techniques manipulate this data in various ways to identify the current price trend and also to pinpoint when the trend might be about to end or when the trend may have been broken.

True, the trader's final objective is price—but other factors determine price.

The more advanced traders recognize this and therefore try to bring other factors to bear upon a decision to buy or sell. The most obvious market factor besides price is the amount of trading, or volume. This can signal how serious the market is about a price or what the large and influential trading concerns' intentions are toward the market.

The completely seasoned traders, who perhaps have been around so long that they can "sense" market moves without actually being able to explain them, have a longer perspective on the market. They realize that what happens in the market today, this week, or this month, is influenced in part by a very long-frame context—by tendencies and events which may play out over a number of years. In short, the fully-experienced traders see the market in a time-related frame of reference. These traders turn to time-oriented, cyclic, pattern-recognition techniques.

It is perhaps inevitable that beginning traders' philosophies will go through the above three stages. However, if they recognize them, it may be possible for them to shorten their stay at the first stages and become more sophisticated traders more quickly than they would have without this book.

Brief Primer On the Basic Concepts
Used in This Book

Note: The discussion in each of the individual chapters assumes that readers are familiar with the information on the following pages and understand the terms in the glossary for this section. Included here are some things that a trader usually thinks about when looking at any kind of chart, regardless of the method. However, many of these concepts belong properly to general, systematized charting techniques as explained in Chapter 11—Basic Charting Techniques, so a basic chapter to read before the others would be that chapter.

The Meaning of Price Level

The main concern of a trader is what price is high and what price is low.

Which Price to Use on the Bar Chart?

On the master chart the price during each period is represented by a line with tics intersecting it. Each of these lines is called a "bar," and so the traditional market chart is often referred to as a "bar chart."

The bar represents the entire range of that time period's prices, while the tic to the left represents the day's opening price, and the tic to the right represents the day's closing price. Thus at point A on the accompanying Master Chart, year 1982, the bar extends from the 910 price level to about 950. A tic, not represented on the chart, on the lower left of the bar indicates the opening price, while the tic on the upper right of the bar shows a closing price at arount 946.

Trading methods which analyze the markets may follow the day's highest price (the top of the bar), its lowest price, and its opening and closing prices. Closing price is the one which most methods usually use.

How High Is the Top—How Low Is the Bottom?

The question of what price is high or low is a relative one. Traders recognize this when they talk about market tops and bottoms, for when they do this they always have some period of time in mind. The simplest form of top or bottom is a price which is higher than both that preceding or following it, or lower than both preceding or following prices. Such tops and bottoms are also called "local" tops or bottoms. The vast majority of the techniques discussed in this book employ this concept in one way or another when they analyze price. Points B and C on the Master Chart (Figure 1-1) indicate examples of a local top and bottom. A market "tops out" when its price reaches levels where it has rarely, if ever, been and then descends and does not come back up. Similarly, a market "bottoms out" when its price falls to levels where it has rarely, if ever, been and then rises and does not fall back. These events are called "market tops" or "market bottoms."

During the whole period covered by this chart (Figure 1-1), there is one "market top," which the market reached two months before the infamous market crash of October 19, 1987 (the second point D). There was a major market bottom on August 9, 1982 (point E).

Direction and Nature of Price Moves

A period when prices are generally rising is called a "bull market."

"Bear market" is the name for a period when prices are generally falling.

The areas bracketed by F and G on the chart are bullish and bearish areas, respectively. Albeit the bearish area at G is a quite transitory phenomenon.

When the market is moving more or less steadily up or down, we say that it is a "trending" or "running" market.

Although price never stands still, it can go up and down in the same range without much net price change for a period of time. When this happens, the market is said to be a "trading" market. The area indicated at H in the Master Chart (Figure 1-1) shows a trading market.

When price has large swings up and down in a short time period, we say that it is "volatile" or exhibiting "high volatility."

Describing Significant Price Moves: Breakouts

When price moves away from older established levels, bounded by a high and a low price range, we say that it "breaks out."

Many methods described in this book look for the "breakout of a price top" or the "breakout of a price bottom." This means that price has formed a top, gone down, and then, on its way back up, it has exceeded the price level of the previous top. On the downside, price forms a bottom, goes up, and on its way back down, it goes through the previous bottom. Points I and J show breakouts of a top and a bottom, respectively.

Significant Price Moves: Resistance and Support

Many methods also talk about price either maintaining or breaking "resistance" or "support" levels.

A resistance level is a supply level that a trading method traces on the price chart somewhere above current price levels. Different methods will have different ways of determining this line, but the basic idea is that there is some resistance in the market which does not allow price to get above the resistance line. If price does manage to break through the resistance line, then most methods signal that this is an event with important consequences.

A support level or support line is exactly the same as a resistance level, except that it is placed below current price levels, and a breakdown would occur if the price went below the support line.

J and K of of Figure 1-3, Master Chart for year 1983, point to two examples each of support and resistance lines, respectively. Support and resistance lines can be diagonal sloping lines downward or upward.

Elementary Trading Concepts

Positions and Exposure

Whenever traders have a stake in the market they are said to have a "position." Their "exposure" is the amount of money they would stand to lose at any one moment if they had to get out of the market then. For instance, if a trader bought stock in a company at $30.00 a share and the price went down to $25.00, then the exposure would be $5.00 a share. Of course, he or she could lose the full amount of $30.00 if the company declared bankruptcy, but exposure refers to immediate market risk and not risk due to bad judgment of company fundamentals.

Going Long or Short

It is possible to do two things, with a market: buy it or sell it.

The most obvious chain of events is to buy something and then sell it.

If traders sell it for more than they bought it, they take a profit. If it sells for less, they take a loss. Buying with intent to sell later is "going long" or "taking a long position."

A second alternative traders have is to sell something before they have it, then buy it in the future. They make money if the price goes down. Brokers will take care of the details of how this can be done (stocks require upticks for short sales to be executed; futures and options have no restrictions). All traders have to do is enter the order. Selling in this way is "going short," or "taking a short position," or "selling the market short." Traders end their short position by buying: they "cover their short."

With some trading methods, the best approach is to go long, wait until it is time to sell, and then sell. Then some traders wait until they see an opportunity to sell short, ultimately covering their short, and so on. When they cover a short or when they sell out a long position, they "close out their position."

Other trading methods work better (and potentially make more money) if traders "flip" or "double up" their positions. That is, they are always in the market, because the minute they close out a long position (by selling it out), they go short. As soon as they cover their short, the traders go long in the same breath.

Prior to the development of the options markets it was impossible for the smaller trader to make money in static markets. Only the firm traders could make money in static markets, and this was due to the fact that they could shift money invested in stocks to other instruments which paid them for the time value of money, namely, interest-bearing instruments. However, with the options markets, this area of investment was opened wide for the smaller investor and speculator.

The market value of a stock or futures contract has three component parts: time value of money to hold the instrument, volatility component which caused the instrument to move or not move in price, and the actual value of the instrument as an investment. The former price movement play was now further separated into plays on volatility, plays on time value and plays on price movement (which was always there). No longer was the investor tied to a muddled type of play: he could now be more precise in determining what component part he wanted to speculate in through the options market.

If traders wanted to take advantage of decreasing volatility, they could sell options and watch the premiums erode. On the other hand if their analysis called for increasing price movements, then they could design strategies in options which make them exposed to volatility only. The strategy sophistication level increased with the advent of the options markets.

In a static market, traders can now design spread strategies which will take advantage of decreasing volatility. Instead of owning volatility, time value and intrinsic value, they can sell options short (sell options naked), and watch the option premium deteriorate because there is no change in the underlying cash or futures instruments' prices. When these traders cover their naked options positions, they will have accrued profits attributable to time value decay since options do expire and volatility decreases due to decreased market movement. Their risks, apart from the exposure of intrinsic value risk which is evident in all market positions, may be multiplied manifold if their price forecasting techniques are flawed. The volatility factor may increase a slight amount if the underlying instrument moves, but because of their leveraged positions whereby they take large short positions in volatility their position can expose them to huge liabilities if the options premiums expand geometrically to compensate for increased volatility. Witness what happened in the October 1987 stock market crash: the 500 point drop in one day caused volatility to explode overnight. Traders who were short volatility, even in near-out-of-the money call options, saw the premium value explode, and their equity took massive amounts of drawdowns.

Buy, Sell, and Stop-loss Orders

All trading techniques are designed to give the trader actual buy and sell "signals," or indications that it is a good time or price to buy (or cover a short) or sell (or go short). Some methods also show at what future price traders should start to buy or sell. Brokers need to know when their clients have such price levels in mind so they can automatically make the transaction when price breaks that level.

Prudent traders also realize that even the best technique can get them into losing situations. These traders use "stop-loss orders." A stop-loss order is placed below the price of an entry order or above the price of an exit order. If the price goes against them, their brokers have an automatic order to close out the position when price reaches that stop-loss level, handing the traders a small, controlled loss. In this way, they avoid nasty surprises and control their exposure.

Figure 1-1 Master Chart

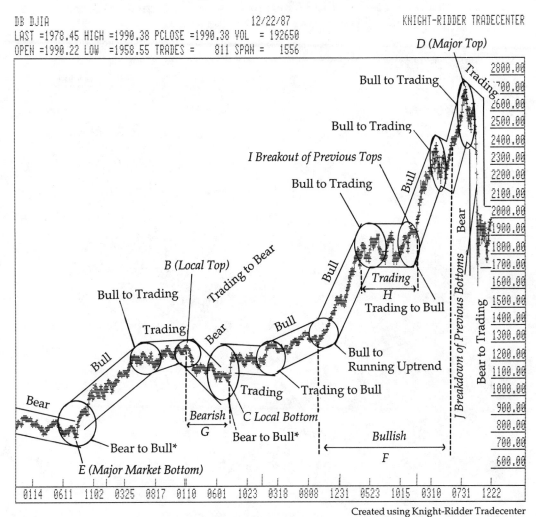

Created using Knight-Ridder Tradecenter

Daily bar chart for Dow Jones Industrial Averages from January 14, 1981 to December 22, 1987, a span of 1556 trading days from a low of 780.00 to a high of 2750.00

*Denotes lack of transition market, the trading market, and shows tremendous strength.

Figure 1-2   Master Chart A
Bear to Bull Market—Detailed Chart of Dow Jones Industrial Averages
Time Span: 1-4-82 to 12-31-82

Created using Knight-Ridder Tradecenter

Figure 1-3   Master Chart B
Bull to Trading Market—Detailed Chart of Dow Jones Industrial Averages
Time Span: 1-3-83 to 12-31-83

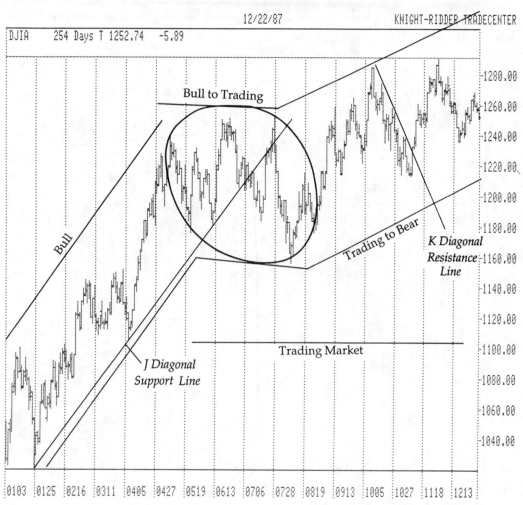

Created using Knight-Ridder Tradecenter

Figure 1-4 Master Chart C
Trading to Bull Market—Detailed Chart of Dow Jones Industrial Averages
Time Span: 1-3-84 to 12-31-84

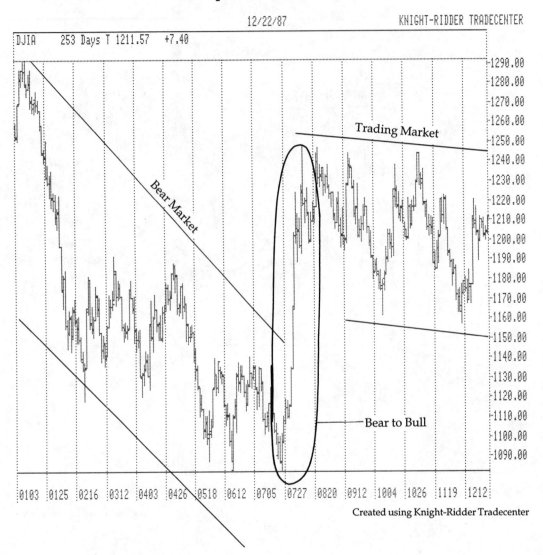

Figure 1-5   Master Chart D
Trading to Bull Market—Detailed Chart of Dow Jones Industrial Averages
Time Span: 1-2-85 to 12-31-85

Created using Knight-Ridder Tradecenter

Figure 1-6   Master Chart E
Bull to Trading Market—Detailed Chart of Dow Jones Industrial Averages
Time Span: 1-2-86 to 12-31-86

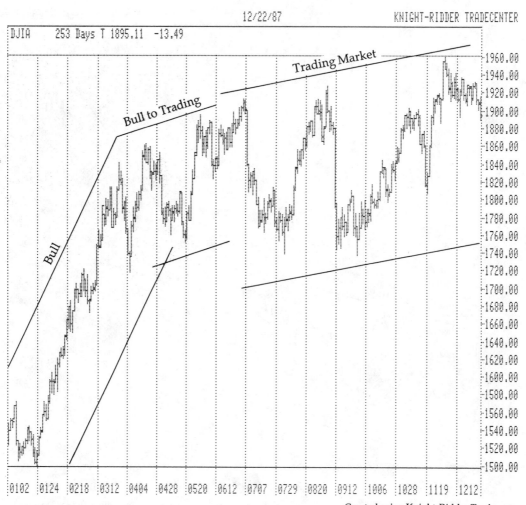

Created using Knight-Ridder Tradecenter

Figure 1-7 Master Chart
Market Cycles—Detailed Chart of Dow Jones Industrial Averages
Time Span: 1-2-87 to 12-22-87

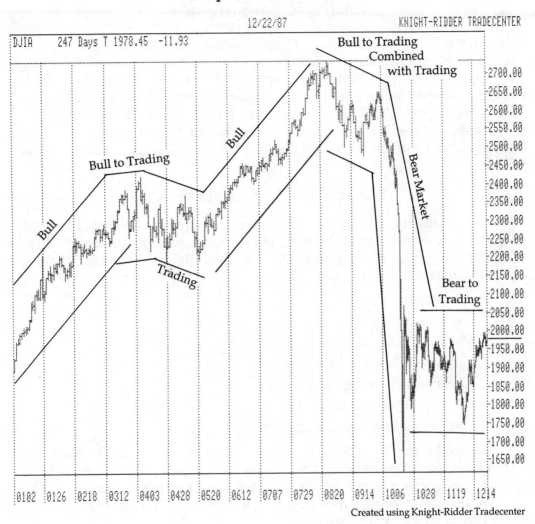

Created using Knight-Ridder Tradecenter

The Master Market Cycle Locator Chart and How to Find the Right Techniques for the Right Situation

The Master Market Cycle Locator Chart shows weekly Dow-Jones prices from August 1982 to November 1987. It covers a bull market cycle, from the market bottom of August 12, 1982 forward through a bull market (September 1982 to August 1987) to the market top on August 21, 1987, including the ensuing crash in October 19, 1987 and the beginning phases of a new bear market.

Various phases and sub-phases of the market are marked on the chart. The significance of this labeling is discussed in the following section about the Toolkit.

The Trader's Technical Toolkit

The techniques discussed in this book are not all equally well-suited for trading all the phases of a market. Therefore, the techniques are grouped into one "toolkit" (see pages 24-29) which can be applied differently to each of seven possible market situations:

- Trading market
- Bull market
- Bear market
- Trading to bull market transition
- Trading to bear market transition
- Bull to trading market transition
- Bear to trading market transition

The toolkit employs all the techniques discussed in this book. The seven "Toolkit Application" sections at the end of this chapter give a concise idea of how to employ each technique in each of the seven possible market situations.

For detailed information on how to employ each technique, of course, it is best to read its respective chapter.

Long-term and Short-term Traders

The trader with a long-range view of market events will want to use the "top-down" trading approach. That is, he or she will think of the market more in broad cyclic terms, and therefore let the cyclic tendencies govern, to some extent, the individual trades. The shorter-term, price-sensitive techniques, more appropriate for that particular market type and the techniques which are more appropriate to longer-range, cyclic events are listed in Table 1-1.

The trader with shorter-range goals will use a "bottom-up" trading approach, focusing more on the techniques which work well for individual, short-term trades. Such a trader may bring in broader, longer-range considerations later, perhaps as a way of confirming suspicions about the market's short-term behavior.

Traders should think of the first approach as a general with a picture of the whole battlefield situation, ordering his soldiers to take up individual positions. The second approach is from the point of view of the soldier, unaware of the grand strategy, who is interested in surviving and winning in each individual confrontation. If traders wonder which kind of trader to be, they should just remember that more soldiers than generals get killed in battle.

The following table shows how to arrange the techniques hierarchically from "top to bottom," that is, from the techniques with longest perspective to those with the shortest.

Table 1-1 Conceptual Application for Techniques in the Toolkit

Top/Down

View market cycle in Elliott Wave terms
Apply astronomical charts for cyclic time reversals
Input Gann's price, time, and volume analysis
Perform conventional charting analysis

Use OBV and Tic Volume analysis in accumulating markets	**OR**	Use Moving Averages in distributing markets

Apply swing charts and point-and-figure charts
   to filter price moves
Apply Stochastics, Percentage R, Oscillators,
   and Relative Strength Price-Sensitive Indicators
Use Market Profile Pattern analysis to enter the
   market correctly on an intraday basis.

Bottom/Up

Master Market Cycle Chart

The Purpose and Nature of the Master Market Cycle Chart

To use this Master Cycle Chart effectively, traders must first locate themelves in the market cycle: where is the market cycle currently? Then work backwards to determine where the market has come from. From this perspective they can use the analytical tools provided in this book to determine where the market will be a day, a week, or a month from today. They will then have an idea of current market action fixed in their minds and will be able to quickly recall the market from memory. This means that they can bring this mental picture of the current market cycle to bear on any trading analysis they are attempting. They will thus have a historical reference point with which to gauge market action.

How to Use the Ideal Market Chart

The following chart approximates the first part of an ideal market cycle. A market, whatever it might be, moves from a **trading range** situation (lettered A) to a **bull market** (lettered B), through another **trading range** (lettered A) situation and into a **bear market** (not completely shown on the Master Chart). (Figure 1-1) After the bear market is finished, the cycle begins again.

Figure 1-8   Ideal Market Chart

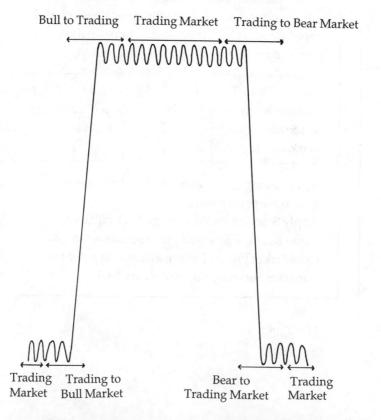

Bull to Trading   Trading Market   Trading to Bear Market

Trading   Trading to   Bear to   Trading
Market   Bull Market   Trading Market   Market

Taking Advantage of the Market Cycle's Transitions

Bull markets and bear markets behave similarly to each other. Trading markets also behave in similar fashion. The transitional phases between these three main market types, however, show great differences in behavior, based on what sort of markets precede and follow them.

The ability to recognize and take advantage of these transitional differences really makes or breaks the professional trader's career. This ability to discern what technical tools are applicable and which ones aren't, which ones will give out false signals, and which ones won't, separates the run-of-the-mill trader from the professional.

Different Uses of the Same Techniques

Different market cycle phases determine different uses of the same techniques. Therefore, the Market Cycle is classified into separate sections and will show how each of these phases differs minutely and how traders can apply the trading tools and techniques correctly to their own trading during each phase.

Table 1-2 Breakdown of Perfect Market Cycle

Market Type	*Qualification*
1) Trading market:	Neither bear nor bull
2) Trending market:	Bull
3) Trending market:	Bear
4) Changing market:	Trading to bull
5) Changing market:	Trading to bear
6) Changing market:	Bull to trading
7) Changing market:	Bear to trading

Each phase of the Market Cycle behaves differently and all the technical indicators will emit characteristic signals.

Characteristics of Market Cycle Phases

Characteristics of the Trading Market

The trading market occurs most of the time. In an overall market cycle, the trading market occurs about 60% to 70% of the time. This segment of the market action is characterized by trading volume which is lower than at other times and by a tight price trading range. The price will move up to a maximum, sell off, trade to a lower level and settle there for several days. Then the price moves again to the upside, encounters selling at the upper end of the range, and sells off to the lower end of the range. Then the cycle repeats again.

Exchange Members Make Money in Trading Markets...

Other factors also distinguish trading from other types of markets. Members of the exchanges make the bulk of their profits in these markets. As members of an exchange they pay minimal commissions (members of the New York Stock Exchange, for example, pay only $0.06, or lower, per share traded) and can buy and sell for small but consistent profits. Outside speculators must pay anywhere from $0.25 to $0.60 per share traded. In the futures markets, non-members pay from $15.00 to $60.00 per trade; members of futures exchanges pay a maximum of $5.00 per trade. Hence, non-members cannot trade markets where small fluctuations are the rule, i.e. trading markets, and make consistent profits due to the cost of commissions. Non-members must trade in markets with price action which can, first, overcome the factor of commissions costs, and secondly sustain enough of a one-directional move to show profits, i.e. trending markets. Institutional firm traders (traders employed by insurance companies trading desks and bank trading desks), because of the sheer size of their transactions can negotiate their commissions costs—the threat of moving business away from current brokers is enough for these brokers to reduce their commissions charges to institutional traders. With $6.00 per futures contract, these institutions can speculate in these markets for razor thin profits, roles to which exchange members were once privy.

...But the Public Does Not

Trading markets make money for floor traders, but not for the public participating in the markets. Even though it is much easier to predict selloffs after rallies and rallies after selloffs in a trading market than in a trending market, the actual movements are not enough to overcome the cost of commissions and slippage on order executions.

Options Can Bring Profits in a Trading Market ...

By moving away from strict cash and futures trading instruments into the realm of options, traders can profit even in trading markets. An option is a contract authorizing the owner to buy or sell a particular stock (or futures contract if a futures option) at a certain price for a limited period of time. The stock in question is called the underlying security. Options are further divided into two types: calls or puts. A call option allows the owner to buy the underlying security at a fixed price during a fixed time period; a put option allows the owner to sell the underlying security at a fixed price during a fixed time period. The options market serves many functions (hedging, risk insurance, arbitrage), one of which is to offer traders a mathematical play onthe cost of carrying cash or futures instruments. One way to make profits in trading markets using options is to sell calls and puts premiums and then wait for them to expire, becoming worthless because of time decay and diminishing cost of carry charges.

...But Know When to Stay Out of the Options Market

Premium sellers make profits this way eleven months out of the trading year; the twelfth month will result in losses of tremendous size, disproportionate to the eleven months of gains. The trick is to determine which month out of the twelve not to sell premiums.

Characteristics of Trending Markets

There are two types of trending markets: bull markets or bear markets. Both of these trending markets are characterized by the same feature: prices traverse great distances in a short period of time. The move is violent and is in one direction. These one-directional moves may or may not be accompanied by high volume. For a better grasp of the volume factor in this stage of the market movement, refer to the Elliott Wave section to see how volume behaves in the various types of upmoves and downmoves.

Bull vs. Bear Markets

There are many subtle differences between the behavior of bull trends and bear trends which would require too much detail to explain here. However, one remarkable distinction is that bear market trends are fast and brief and cover great distances in a short period of time. True bull markets, however, are slow and long-drawn out affairs, covering great price distances and taking much more time to develop. Uptrends that are relatively quick and brief and also cover great distances in a short period of time are not true bull markets, but rather reactions in bear markets. Awareness of this fact should help the trader in determining whether or not an upmove is a true bull market or rather a reaction in a bear market.

Big Money Makes Money in a Bull Market

Big and heavily capitalized traders who pyramid their positions have a decided advantage in massive bull trends—the markets go in one direction and take a long enough time to do it so that the traders can continually add to their long positions. In bear markets, however, the smaller trader makes a little money very fast: the market does not stay at one price long enough for the trader to add more to the short side. The downtrend is quick and fast—if traders aren't positioned early to the downside, they won't be able to get into a short position when the collapse occurs.

Changing Markets

Many years of observation, analysis and refinement reveal the distinguishing characteristics of the four types of changing market: 1) the trading market changing to bull market; 2) the bull market changing to trading; 2) the trading market changing to bear market; and 3) the bear market changing to trading.

Table 1-3 The Toolkit of Trading Techniques

Price-Sensitive Techniques

Moving Averages—Gives the general trend of price based on its recent behavior and tell when the trend has been broken.

Relative Strength—Measures the strength left in a price trend by comparing number of up and down days over a recent timeframe.

Percentage R—Compares a day's closing price to a recent range of prices to determine if a market is overbought or oversold.

Oscillators—Measure the momentum of a price trend based on recent price behavior.

Stochastics—Combines indicators like moving average and relative strength to measure overbought and oversold tendencies.

Point-and-Figure—Plots trends and reversals in price movement and then gives buy/sell signals based on recognizable patterns.

Basic Charting—Techniques for recognizing common price movement patterns and gauging market movements.

Swing Charting—Provides rigid entry and exit signals based on recent price history.

Time-Sensitive Technique

Astronomical Cycles—Use the cyclicity of celestial events to identify cyclic patterns in market behavior.

Volume-Sensitive Techniques

Market Profile®/ *Liquidity Date Bank*®(also price sensitive)—Compares price and volume at intervals with recognizable price distribution patterns.

Tic Volume—Similar to On-Balance Volume, but looks at the volume and directions of individual trades.

On-Balance Volume—Discovers "smart money's" moves by balancing the volume of days with rising prices against falling days.

Composite Methods

Elliott Wave—Uses rules of cyclic market behavior and pattern formations to predict future price levels, trends, and reversal points.

Gann Analysis—Compilation of a battery of time, price, and volume indicators to enter and exit positions.

Table 1-4 How to Use the Toolkit of Trading Techniques

Price-Sensitive Techniques

Moving Averages—Gives very good signals in a trending market, but can whittle away profits in a trading market.

Relative Strength—Confirms other methods in trading markets. Users have to keep adjusting the scale in trending markets.

Percentage R—Gives good signals in trading markets, but users should always confirm them with some additional methods.

Oscillators—Can confirm other techniques and indicate whether market is overbought or oversold and should be sold or bought.

Stochastics—Accurate for predicting trading market lows and highs.

Point-and-Figure—Gives acceptable results most of the time, but can be unreliable in strongly trending markets.

Basic Charting—Gives general framework for interpreting most other techniques. Volume analysis is an offshoot of basic charting.

Swing Charting—Works in trending markets. Combine longer and shorter period charts to avoid choppiness in trading markets.

Time-Sensitive Technique

Astronomical Cycles—May give traders an idea of the market's general disposition. Confirm its clues with other techniques.

Volume-Sensitive Techniques

Market Profile®/Liquidity Data Bank®—Works well for the trader whose positions last for only a few hours and can predict market objectives under certain conditions.

Tic Volume—Same observations apply as for On-Balance Volume. Does not work well in a market with no big players.

On-Balance Volume—Gives good advance warning of when the market will move off the bottom, but is late on tops.

Composite Techniques

Elliott Wave—Use other techniques to confirm the times and price levels it predicts for major market events.

Gann Analysis—Use to determine when time, price, and volume indicators intersect. Offers critical continuation or reversal point in time or price.

The Trading Toolkit Applications

Traders can apply the toolkit of trading techniques to each of the market phases discussed above.

The Master Chart (Figure 1-1) shows where the appropriate toolkit could be used with greatest effectiveness.

The tables on the following pages describe the proper way to apply the toolkit's techniques to different market situations. Note that the toolkit contains all the technical analysis methods described in this book. What differs within the toolkit is the way in which the trader must apply the various methods.

Table 1-5 Trading Market Toolkit Application

1) *Moving Averages*—Fade breakouts
2) *RSI, %R* and *Oscillators*—Sell overbought, buy oversold
3) *Stochastics*—Sell crossovers to downside and buy crossovers to upside
4) *Astronomical Cycles*—Can show beginning and end of trading range
5) *On-Balance Volume and Tic Volume*—Useless as forecasting indicators but can be viable as confirming indicators
6) *Market Profile*®—Sell the highs and buy the lows
7) *Elliott Wave*—Verifies the existence of trading market via flat-type corrections classification and shows possible end of trading range
8) *Gann Analysis*—Whipsaws unless trader backs away with timing indicators. Swing charts would be useless here

Table 1-6 Bull Market Toolkit Application

1) *Moving Averages*—Buy the upside crossovers
2) *RSI, %R* and *Oscillators*—Buy oversold indicators and ignore the overbought indicators
3) *Stochastics*—Buy the crossovers to the upside; do not sell crossovers to the downside
4) *Astronomical Cycles*—Not applicable during actual bull move upwards
5) *On-Balance Volume* and *Tic Volume*—Useless as forecasting indicators, but viable as confirming indicators, since OBV curves would continually display new breakout highs
6) *Market Profile*®—Buy selloffs to the lows and add to positions on upside breakouts to new highs
7) *Elliott Wave*—Buy breakouts of previous highs
8) *Gann Analysis*—Buy breakouts of swing charts and accumulate positions

Table 1-7 Bear Market Toolkit Application

1) *Moving Averages*—Sell the downside crossovers

2) *RSI, %R* and *Oscillators*—Sell the overbought indicators and ignore the oversold indicators

3) *Stochastics*—Sell the crossovers to the downside; do not buy crossovers to the upside

4) *Astronomical Cycle*—Not applicable during actual bear moves downward

5) *On-Balance Volume* and *Tic Volume*—Too late for forecasting, and non-effective as confirming indicators

6) *Market Profile*®—Sell rallies to the highs and add to positions on down side breakdowns to new lows

7) *Elliott Wave*—Sell the breakdowns of previous lows

8) *Gann Analysis*—Sell breakdowns of swing charts and add to short positions if possible

Table 1-8 Trading Market Changing to Bull Market Toolkit Application

1) *Moving Averages*—If traders are fading the false breakouts in the trading market, one trade will finally go against them for a greater than normal loss (short in a bull market). This will signal to them that the markets are about to change.

2) *RSI, %R* and *Oscillators*—If traders have been selling overbought and buying oversold they will find a trade which will show a loss even though they sold the overbought signal (short in bull market). This will signal to them that the markets are changing.

3) *Stochastics*—Traders must buy all crossovers from the oversold conditions and not execute trades on overbought signals.

4) *Astronomical Cycles*—Traders can forecast with accuracy the possible action reversals well in advance of other indicators.

5) *On-Balance Volume* and *Tic Volume*—Accumulation can be observed and hence eventual upside price breakouts can be forecasted with high accuracy.

6) *Market Profile*®—Trading range breakouts can be accurately predicted with congestions and various anticipatory analyses of patterns.

7) *Elliott Wave*—The theory will show a possible breakout to the upside. Cautiously buy at the trading range for an impending move and aggressively buy when the price breaks into new highs moving above the trading range high.

8) *Gann Analysis*—Traders will get chewed up in the trading markets with many false breakouts, but once the market starts up, they will have adequate buy signals to pyramid (if they so choose) more and more positions. Square of time and price charts will disclose possible reversal points to anticipate.

Table 1-9 Trading Market Changing to Bear Market Toolkit Application

1) *Moving Averages*—If traders had been fading the false breakouts to the upside and false breakdowns to the downside in a trading market, they would find their last trade to be a disproportionate loss (long in a bear market). There really isn't much chance to recoup this loss because the breakdown is fast and severe. It is best not to fade the markets on the buy side using moving averages after the markets have had a severe runup going into a trading range market.

2) *RSI, %R* and *Oscillators*—If traders had been selling overbought and buying oversold indicators in a trading market, they would suffer a large loss on the last trade. Traders would also find a growing number of oversold indicators and a diminishing number of overbought signals using standard parameters. This signals an impending change in the state of the market condition.

3) *Stochastics*—Crossovers from the overbought side to the downside are more valid than crossovers to the upside from the oversold level.

4) *Astronomical Cycles*—Pure timing cycles would allow traders to anticipate important market reversal points in advance of actual time reversal dates.

5) *On-Balance Volume* and *Tic Volume*—These two indicators are unreliable for forewarning traders of impending weakness. The best that traders can expect from these indicators is a flattening of the OBV pattern, implying a possible, but not certain, breakdown. The prices would drop dramatically and then the volume indicators would indicate a breakdown, after the fact.

6) *Market Profile*®—The technique would allow traders to see a congestion area forming and give traders the most likely direction of the breakdown. They could sell rallies to the highs, with no new highs, and continue to sell on breakdowns to the new lows.

7) *Elliott Wave*—In Elliott Wave corrections, traders have a one-in-two chance that the correction could possibly turn into a bear market sell-off (a *zig-zag* instead of a flat correction). However, in the formation of this correction traders cannot tell until they approach the forecasted event that the correction could turn into a bear market correction instead of a flat correction. If the market turns into a bear market correction they only have to sell into new lows and maintain a short position to profit from the move downwards. If, however, it turns into a flat correction, they will find themselves selling the bottom. Elliott Wave analysis does offer an inkling about what type of correction traders can expect, based on the existence of alternative patterns prior to the one currrently under examination.

8) *Gann Analysis*—When in the trading market, this technique's entry signals would whipsaw traders: selling lows and buying highs. However, once they saw the market go into a tailspin to the downside, the Gann entry techniques would get them short on the right side. The time

charts and anniversary date charts would allow them to anticipate important reversal days and time periods well in advance.

Table 1-10 Bull Market Changing to Trading Market Toolkit Application

1) *Moving Averages*—Price finally crosses the moving averages to the downside after leading the averages from above. If traders didn't buy the price breakout to the upside, traders mustn't do it now but, instead, start to fade the upside breakouts carefully and fade the downside breakdowns.

2) *RSI, %R* and *Oscillators*—After a solid series of bad overbought signals in the bull market, traders finally find more oversold indicators appearing. As the trading market continues, oversold and overbought indicators become equal in number. The fact that the numbers even out indicates the complexion of the market is changing from uptrend to trading.

3) *Stochastics*—In the bull trend upwards, the crossovers from overbought were more often than not false signals and the crossovers from oversold, if they occured, were valid buy signals. Now, as the market flattens out, traders will find the crossovers from either side to be valid and can also initiate positions with profitability.

4) *Astronomical Cycles*—This technique will allow traders to forecast with high accuracy the possible action reversals well in advance of other indicators.

5) *On-Balance Volume* and *Tic Volume*—This technique fails when you try to use it to forecast imminent price breakdowns. These cumulative volume indicators would not begin to signal distribution until price deterioration was well underway. The best signal that could be emitted would be a flattening of the price trend signal.

6) *Market Profile*®—The trading range, when using this technique, would easily give way to running markets to the downside. The strict Market Profile® technician would also find clues and indications as to the probable direction and approximate timing of the imminent breakdown. The timing forecast would not be predicted as far in advance as the astronomical cycles, since the timing sensitivity would be market condition sensitive.

7) *Elliott Wave*—According to strict Elliott Wave tenets, this application does not exist per se: A bull market turns to a bear market upon its completion. Elliott Wave would not consider the existence of trading to bear market designation, but bull to bear immediately. Yet, traders can observe that the two types of corrective markets alternate with each other: if a previous correction was one of two types (flat or zig-zag) then the second of the set will be the alternate type to the first. In this way, traders can predict something about the nature of this market phase.

8) *Gann Analysis*—Trading markets would whipsaw the Gann trader continually. As the trading market ends, the strict Gann trader would find himself in a completely bearish position. Using Gann time cycle techniques would have narrowed the time period in which the start of the actual price decline could possibly begin.

Table 1-11 Bear Market Changing to Trading Market Toolkit Application

1) *Moving Averages*—When the market changes to a trading market from a bear market, the moving averages will no longer lag as far behind the actual price or shorter moving average as was the case in the preceding bear market. Traders can now expect a flattening out of the moving average curve to correspond with the flattening of market prices. If they continued to sell the breakdowns and defer from buying as before, they would be continually whipsawed (instead, they should sell the breakouts and buy the breakdowns).

2) *RSI, %R* and *Oscillators*—In the bear down trend traders would have an overwhelming number of oversold signals and a dearth of overbought signals. They could have adjusted the overbought parameter to the downside to give themselves, in effect, "overbought" signals to initiate short positions on. At the changing point, the number of oversold and overbought signals begin to equal each other in numbers. They could sell the overbought and buy the oversold with confidence at this point.

3) *Stochastics*—During the bear market, crossovers from the oversold side were less valid as buy signals than crossovers from the overbought side were as sell signals. They will now appear equally valid as the trading market appears.

4) *Astronomical Cycles*—Can accurately forecast the possible action reversals well in advance of other price-sensitive indicators.

5) *On-Balance Volume* and *Tic Volume*—The OBV curve and Tic Volume flatten out after the bottom price is made, thereby giving traders an after-the-fact confirmation of the end of the down move, but not a reliable anticipatory signal.

6) *Market Profile*®—Moving from a downtrend to a trading market, Market Profile® would have signalled the low price during the move, but would not have signalled the traders that a trading market had begun until well after the fact. They could possibly have anticipated the end of the bear downmove and the beginning of the trading market with lesser accuracy.

7) *Elliott Wave*—The "bear move down" would have been an impulse wave down and the trading market would have been a corrective wave to this. Once traders have determined which of the three impulse waves (1, 3, or 5 of an impulse 1-2-3-4-5, or even in a larger dimension: a or c of an a-b-c correction) they were in the process of completing they would have a better idea of what type of correction was beginning.

8) *Gann Analysis*—At the end of the bear down trend, they would have amassed a nice profit using the entry techniques offered to the Gann type trader (they would have been short). However, going into the trading market and staying in the trading market would have surely caused whipsaw losses. If traders had additionally used time cycle analysis techniques, they would have sat out the trading market.

Glossary of Common Trading Terms

Accumulation—Volume-based trading systems assume that "smart" or "big" money begins to quietly buy up an issue when the price is still low. Thus, cumulative volume rises while the price is still low, and price can be expected to begin to rise in the near future. *See* **Distribution**.

Anticipatory Indicator—A trading technique which predicts market events in advance. *See* **Confirming** and **Execution Indicator**.

Bar, Bar Chart—A bar chart shows the development of price over time in a market. Each vertical bar represents a single trading period, and it extends from the lowest to the highest priced trade during that period. A small tick to the left shows the price of the first trade, and a tick to the right shows the price of the last trade made during that period.

Bear Market—A market in which the general tendency is for price to move downward.

Bottom—A point in time or price when price is lower than prices either before or after that time.

Bottom Out—The point in time or price at which a bear market reaches its lowest price, or market bottom, and a reversal of the general market trend can be expected.

Break Out—Happens when price has been staying within certain limits, and finally breaks through those limits, going either significantly higher or lower.

Break Down—When price breaks out in a downward direction.

Bull Market—A market when prices are generally rising.

Buy Order Limit—A price level which a trader determines. If price passes that level, the trader automatically buys into the market. A trader may leave a standing order with a broker regarding buy levels.

Close Out—Happens when a trader liquidates a market position.

Call Option—A call option is a contract which allows the owner to buy a fixed number of underlying security of futures contracts at a fixed price for a fixed time period.

Confirming Indicator—A market trading technique which does not predict price moves, but rather confirms after the fact that they have happened. See **Execution** and **Anticipatory Indicator**.

Congestion—This term describes a period in the market when price seems to be "bottled up" in a narrow range of values, without a break upwards or downwards.

Cover Short—When a trader closes out a short position.

Distribution—Certain trading systems like On-Balance Volume assume that "smart" or "big" money begins to quietly sell an issue when the price is still high. Thus, volume rises at this point, and price can be expected to drop in the near future. *See* **Accumulation**.

Double-Up—When traders close out a position they immediately initiate an opposite position. *See* **Flip**.

Entry Signal—A signal given by a trading technique showing at what price or when a trader initiates a position in the market.

Execution Indicator—A market technique which generates signals telling the trader either when or at what price level to buy, sell, or close out positions. *See* **Confirming** and **Anticipatory Indicator**.

Exposure—The amount a trader would stand to lose on a position if that position were closed out at that moment.

Fade—A trader "fades" an indicator by doing the opposite of what a normal interpretation of its signals would dictate. This is not the same as ignoring the indicator, because the trader actually takes action based on the indicator.

Flip—When a trader closes out a position and simultaneously opens the opposite position, that is, covers a short while going long at the same time, or closes out a long position while going short at the same time. *See* **Double-Up**.

Local Bottom—A bottom that is not necessarily of major significance, formed when one period's price level is below the preceding and succeeding periods.

Local Top—A top that is not necessarily of major significance, formed when one period's price level is above the preceding and succeeding periods.

Long—A position in the market which a trader initiates by buying into the market, hoping to sell at a greater price. The trader is said to "go long" or "be long" in the market.

Market Bottom—A bottom of major significance that only happens once in many years. At a market bottom, the price reaches levels which it rarely, if ever, has reached before, and after the bottom, it rises without returning to the bottom. A market bottom signals the end of a bear market.

Market Top—A top of major significance that only happens once in many years. At a market top, the price reaches levels which it rarely, if ever, has reached before, and after the top, it falls without returning to the top. A market top signals the end of a bull market.

Overbought—A market is overbought when it appears that buying activity has been going on for longer than the market can continue to support. Therefore, price is too high for market conditions and a market top or a local top is near.

Oversold—A market is oversold when it appears that selling activity has been going on for longer than the market can continue to sustain. Therefore, price is too low for market conditions and a market bottom or a local bottom is near.

Position—An investment in a market. A trader "has a position" if he or she has bought or sold and can lose or gain money by exposing his or her capital to risk.

Put Option—A put option is a contract that allows an owner to sell a fixed number of underlying security of futures contracts at a fixed price and a fixed time period.

Resistance—A price level which is above the current range where price is moving. A resistance level may be determined by various analysis techniques and represents a level which price is not expected to go above. If price does break out above this level, then this is a significant event, which different techniques interpret in different ways. A resistance level can be a diagonal line which follows price upward or downward and projects into the future, or it can be a horizontal line which gives an absolute limit to the top. *See* **Support.**

Running Market—A market where price is generally going either up or down, as opposed to a trading market. This is also known as a trending market.

Sell Order Limit—A price level chart which a trader determines. If price passes that level, the trader automatically sells the market. A trader may leave a standing order with a broker regarding sell limits.

Short—A position in the market which a trader initiates by selling what he or she does not own but can borrow, hoping to buy at a lower future price.

A trader who has done this is said to "go short" or "be short" in the market.

Stop-Loss Order—A price level which a trader determines after taking a market position. The stop loss order will be below the price at which the trader initiated the long position (a sell stop) or above the level at which the trader initiated the short position (a buy stop). If price passes the stop-loss point, the trader will automatically close out his or her position for a loss. A trader may specify stop-loss orders to the broker, to be carried out automatically without the trader's express instruction.

The reason for stop-loss orders is to automatically limit the trader's potential losses in a bad trade.

Support—A price level which is below the current range where price is moving. A support level may be determined by various analytic techniques and represents a level which price is not expected to go below. If price does break down below this level, then this is a significant event, which different techniques interpret in different ways. A support level can be a diagonal line which follows price downward, or upward, and projects into the future, or it can be a horizontal line which gives an absolute limit on the bottom. *See* **Resistance.**

Top—A point in time or price when price is higher than prices either before or after that time.

Top Out—The point in time or price at which a bull market reaches its highest price, or market top, and a reversal of the general market trend can be expected.

Trading Market—A market situation that happens when price moves equally up and down for a period without showing a strong tendency to move in one direction or another. The opposite of a trending or running market.

Trending Market—A market where price is either going up or down, as opposed to a trading market. This is also known as a running market.

Volatility—The relative size of price swings. When price goes up and down over broad ranges in a small time span, volatility is high. When price is sluggish over a long period of time, volatility is low.

Whipsaw—A trader gets whipsawed when the techniques he or she is using give many buy and sell signals in a small price range, without follow through in the predicted direction. This usually causes the trader to lose money.

Behavior of Technical Indicators in Market Cycles

OB = Overbought
OS = Oversold

	Trading Markets	Trending Markets		Changing Markets			
		Bull	Bear	Trading to Bull	Trading to Bear	Bull to Trading	Bear to Trading
Moving Averages	Many false breakouts and whipsaw action	Valid breakouts and continuous confirmation	Valid breakouts and continuous confirmation	Excellent behavior	Excellent behavior	Excellent behavior	Excellent behavior
Relative Strength	OB/OS indication excellent	Skewed number of signals to more overbought	Skewed number of signals to more oversold	Increasing signals to OB	Increasing frequency of OS signals	Equal number of OB/OS signals from OB skew	Equal number of OB/OS signals from show OB
Percentage R	OB/OS signals are valid	False OB signals valid. Use modified OS	False OS signals valid. Use modified OB	Valid signals give way to false OB	Valid signals give way to false OS	False OS to valid signals	False OB to valid signals
Oscillators	OB/OS signals are valid	False OB signals valid if using modified OS	False OB signals valid if using modified OS	Valid signals give way to false OB	Valid signals give way to false OS	False OS to valid signals	False OB to valid signals
Stochastics	Crossovers OB and OS are valid	Crossovers from OS only are valid	Crossovers from OB only are valid	Crossovers of OB/OS valid to only OS indicators valid	Crossovers of OB/OS valid to only OB indicators	Only OS area crossovers are valid to both OB/OS valid	Only OB area crossovers are valid to both OB/OS valid
Point-and-Figure	False breakouts whipsaw action	Valid breakouts	Valid breakdowns	Can project counts to likely tops	Can project counts to likely bottoms	Cannot forecast	Cannot forecast
Market Profile®	Normal distribution	Can observe and tell upside breakouts	Can observe and tell downside breakdowns	Can see buildup of buying pressure	Can see buildup of selling pressure	Great appearance of non-trend days	Great appearance of non-trend days
Tic Volume	Very good accumulation indicator	Can use to possibly pyramid	Valid signals but because of briefness hard to pyramid	Excellent accumulation indicators	Too late to signal volume distribution	Flattening of OBV breakouts	Flattening of OBV breakouts
On-Balance Volume	Very good accumulation indicator	Too long to use to pyramid	Valid but impractical signals	Excellent accumulation indicators	Too late to signal volume distribution	Flattening of OBV breakouts	Flattening of OBV breakouts
Bar Charts	Valid, recognizable pattern	Valid, recognizable trend lines, channels	Valid, recognizable trend lines, channels	Reversal patterns valid	Reversal patterns valid	Reversal patterns valid	Reversal pattern valid
Astronomical Cycles	No good	Not applicable	Not applicable	Excellent turning points	Excellent turning points	Excellent turning points	Excellent turning point
Elliott Wave Theory	Hard to show beginning and end—just that it is occurring	Can project market to take out previous highs	Can project market to take out previous lows	Probability can be determined that this will happen	Probability can be determined that this will happen	Probability can be determined that this will happen	Probability can be determined that this will happen
Gann Analysis	Whipsaws	Long for the upmove	Short for the downmove	Can get you long but whipsawed first	Can get you short but whipsawed first	Whipsaw first then profits	Whipsaw first then profits

Price Sensitive Indicators — Moving Averages, Relative Strength, Percentage R, Oscillators, Stochastics, Point-and-Figure

Hybrid Indicators — Market Profile®

Volume Sensitive Indicators — Tic Volume, On-Balance Volume

Time Sensitive — Bar Charts, Astronomical Cycles

Composite — Elliott Wave Theory, Gann Analysis

Micro Analysis

Macro Analysis

2
Moving Averages
Where Do We Go Now?

Moving Averages at a Glance

Background and Philosophy of Moving Averages

Derived from some of the first computer applications in World War II, moving averages were used to predict the real destination of enemy aircraft taking evasive paths. As used by traders, the moving average technique smooths out daily price fluctuations into a trend indicator.

Principles of Moving Averages

A moving average is formed using the closing prices of a pre-determined period of days. Each day's moving average is a number representing the average price for those numbers of days. Moving averages are normally plotted against daily closing prices in order to detect crossovers of the moving average by price lines. An exponentially smoothed moving average (ESMA) takes into account all prices since the indicator was initiated, successively reducing each previous day's weight by a pre-determined factor (usually between .1 and .75).

How to Set Up and Maintain Moving Averages

1) Choose the moving average period length in days, **p.**
   - **p** should be close to a cycle length of the market.
   - **p** should vary inversely according to the sensitivity desired for the indicator.
2a) For exponentially smoothed moving averages only: choose a smoothing factor (0-1). The more volatile the market, the less the factor should be.
2b) For regular moving average: After **p** days have passed, get the average of the last **p** days' closing prices
3a) For ESMA:
   day 2's moving average = day 1 price + smoothing factor X
   (where X = day 2 price - day 1 price)
3b) For regular moving average:
   today's moving average =
   $$\text{yesterday's price} + \frac{(\text{today's price - price of } \mathbf{p} \text{ days ago})}{\mathbf{p}}$$
3c) For ESMA:
   Today's ESMA =
   yesterday's ESMA + factor × (today's price - 1st ESMA)

How to Trade with Moving Averages

- Buy signals are given when prices break above the moving average line or above a channel, determined by moving averages, of daily highs and lows.

- Sell signals are given when prices break below the moving average line or below a channel determined by moving averages of daily highs and lows.

When to Apply Moving Averages

Traders should use moving averages in highly volatile or trending markets when there are crossovers of the shorter average, (if multiples are used), or the price line, (if only price lines are used). In stable trading markets the moving average crosses back and forth over the shorter average and creates whipsaw situations. By using with techniques which indicate market trend traders can determine whether or not to employ moving averages. Moving averages also confirm breakout indicators.

Glossary for Moving Averages

Channel—An area on a price bar chart bounded by the moving average lines for daily highs and daily lows.

Crossover—An event which happens on a moving average price bar chart when the various moving average lines intersect each other or the price line. Technicians use crossovers to signal price based buy and sell opportunities.

Exponentially Smoothed Moving Average (ESMA)—A moving average which gives diminishing weight to days further and further into the past. The weighting factor is an exponentially decreasing fraction.

Lagged Moving Average—A moving average which is recorded on the price chart under the price of several days ago. This is thought to compensate somewhat for the fact that the moving average is an indicator of past activity.

Moving Average—An indicator which the technician usually plots on the same chart as price and which is the daily average of prices (systematically: highs, lows, close or combinations of all three) over a fixed period.

Period—A fixed number of days which the technician chooses over which to average prices to obtain the daily moving average. Periods can vary greatly, depending on market volatility and the trader's timeframe.

Price Line—A line drawn to connect all high prices to high prices, low prices to low prices, or close prices to close prices. The most commonly used price lines are those drawn to connect closing prices.

Weighting Factor—A fractional number used in Exponentially Smoothed Moving Average computation. As the ESMA progresses through time, each previous day's moving average is given less and less weight by multiplying it by the weighting factor.

Background and Philosophy of Moving Averages

World War II brought high-speed planes, the invention of sophisticated tracking systems such as radar, and therefore both the need for and the possibility of predicting an enemy plane's future position. Techniques were developed for quickly plotting known positions at given intervals of time and smoothing out the (possibly evasive) motion of the plane to predict the probable destination of the plane.

The need for quick calculation in order to react to a rapidly changing target stimulated computer research and led to some of the first electronic calculating machines. By the end of the 1940's computing machines were finding their applications in business, and many of the first uses were adaptations of the original military uses.

One of the business uses to which these original military applications were adapted was the attempt to predict the trend or final objective of a market tendency. This, of course, mirrored the attempt to predict a flying object's path by averaging its momentary positions to obtain a smooth path toward its supposed destination.

By the late 1950's the technique of moving averages had become one of the leading and, for that time, most advanced methods of analyzing market trends. The 1960's and 1970's saw a number of quite rigorous research projects and books written on the moving averages, exploring the subject in detail and working out its possible variations and the relevant mathematics.

Researchers exhaustively explored possible scenarios for using moving average techniques. The ability to examine hundreds of possible market scenarios and compare various moving average techniques was a product of something else that the World War II airplane path prediction technique had helped to create: the electronic computer.

Although it is quite possible to compute a moving average by hand, the various techniques require either the storage of market data over a certain period, several computations (which, according to the technique used, might require calculation of logarithmic functions), and the periodic repetition of calculations. All these functions are well-suited to mechanization, and they are all used in the moving average technique, at least in part due to the fact that moving average techniques were born along with the modern electronic computer.

In brief, a moving average technique is based on the idea that a market tends to trend in the same direction as it has been going. Therefore, if we can look beyond the erratic behavior of individual moments in the market cycle, we may be able to "smooth" their common tendency together and see where things are headed in general. Armed with analysis of where the market is trending, the technician should then be able to determine whether the market is generally trending upward or downward, despite perhaps one or two days' evidence to the contrary, or whether a significant reversal in the trend has just occurred, which the technician can determine by seeing if certain limits which the current trend has established are broken.

Principles of Moving Averages

Simple Moving Average

The Simple Moving Average is the average price over a fixed period of days, computed as follows:

$$\text{Day n's moving average} = \frac{(\text{Day n-1's price}) + (\text{Day n-2's price}) + \ldots + (\text{Day 1's price})}{\text{Total number of days}}$$

Then, the moving average for the next day, or day n + 1, is found by still taking the same number of days' moving averages, but moving everything up a day:

$$\text{Day n+1's moving average} = \frac{(\text{Day n's price}) + \text{Day n-1's price} + \ldots + (\text{Day 2's price})}{\text{Total number of days}}$$

A trader keeps track of moving averages on the same chart as price. The moving average line, in contrast to the price line, will appear "smoother" and, though it still follows the price line's general ups and downs, it will do so with an additional lag. It will not be as violent in its swings, and will therefore stay more or less close to the middle of the general range of prices.

When price begins to pick up, the moving average line will first be crossed by the price line and then trail the price line, creating a "crossover." When price begins a falling trend, the price line will appear to cross over the moving average line from above.

Some Refinements on the Straight Moving Average

Exponentially Smoothed Moving Average (ESMA)

This technique was the original moving average technique used in World War II to predict the position of enemy airplanes. It takes into account all previous positions, but less recent positions are given progressively less weight.

The weighting factor is based on an exponential power of some base fraction, such as 1/10. This particular technique also takes into account all days since one began counting, but the earliest days have negligible weight because the factor is so tiny. Each earlier day's weighting factor is just another power of that fraction, so that, if 1/10 were used as the fraction, the most recent day's weighting factor is 1 (1/10 to the zero power), the second most recent day's is .10 (1/10 the first power), the third most recent day's is .01, and so on. If the base fraction had been 3/4 instead, then the weights for first, second, and third days would have been 1, 3/4, and 9/16, respectively. This type of moving average turns out to be easier to calculate than the general case of the weighted moving average, because all we have to know are the current price, the last exponentially smoothed value, and the base weighting fraction. These are then employed in the following equation:

Today's exponentially smoothed moving average =

Yesterday's ESMA + (weighting fraction) × (today's price - first ESMA)

Synchronizing Moving Averages with Prices

Since the moving average is a cumulative indicator, it reacts sluggishly to daily changes and therefore major reversals will not register with it for a few days (assuming some kind of weighted moving average, or at least an unweighted one which uses just a few days). In order for a moving average to indicate more clearly on the chart what is happening each day, it is possible to lag the moving average behind prices on a chart by a fixed amount, say one to three days. This will force the moving average line to adhere more closely to the price line and if there are crossovers then it will cross over much quicker than if it was not pushed backward. This will then show us exactly the trend crossover on that day.

In addition, exponentially smoothed moving averages will get out of step a little more each day, since the base fraction or smoothing constant tends to drag the average back slightly. To resolve this problem keep track of the lag daily, treating it as a series to be exponentially smoothed by the same base fraction, and then add it onto the original equation for exponentially smoothed weighted averages to provide the correction needed, which should improve as the series continues.

How to Set Up and Maintain Moving Averages

Choose the Moving Average Period Length for Regular Moving Averages

Traders should take two things into account in determining the moving average period: the sensitivity they desire and the average market cycle.

- Practical consideration: What will this moving average be used for? If it is to track day-to-day movement for short-term trading then of course the number of days should be shorter in order to reflect shorter-term trends, whereas if it is for institutional investors or investing mutual funds, a six-month period or more may be more useful. (In this last case, one may choose to determine price other than on a daily basis, perhaps weekly, and track longer period moving averages on a daily basis.) The complete technician will of course keep several moving averages with, say, periods of 3, 5, 10, 20 and 30 days.

- Cyclical considerations: If the particular market phenomenon being tracked is known to go through more or less predictable cycles, then it is necessary to choose a period which does not "mask" the cycle by smoothing it out. For instance, if a certain commodity goes through a monthly demand cycle, then a moving average which used a period with a magnitude on the order of one month (say, 25 to 35 days) would show a constant tendency to change neither up nor down, because by averaging the entire range of possible values with every computation, the result would be somewhere in the middle every time. For this particular commodity, if a trader wanted to see the local ups and downs within the cycle, he or she should use a shorter time frame to see the local trends. If, however, the trader were interested in where the long-range trend was over several cycles, then it might be better to choose a number of days which corresponded more closely with the length of the cycle.

How to Choose Each Day's Prices

Each trader figuring moving average must choose what "Day X's price" will be. It should always be the same: the opening price, the closing price, the high, the low or some systematic function of these.

Choosing a Smoothing Factor: Exponentially Smoothed Moving Average

The desired degree of sensitivity of the moving average helps determine what the smoothing factor should be. The greater the smoothing factor, the more sensitive the indicator. This is because larger smoothing factors give more weight to recent days, thus making this particular moving average follow price more closely and so causing more potential crossovers.

Striking the First Average: Regular Moving Average

All the days in a chosen averaging period must be passed before it is possible to compute a first moving average. To determine moving average for a five-day period, wait until the fifth day to start the analysis. At that point, simply take the average of the days of the previous period:

$$\frac{\text{sum of last } \mathbf{P} \text{ days}}{\mathbf{P}}$$

Strike the First Average: Exponentially Smoothed Moving Average

In contrast, ESMA can be computed as soon as the start of the second day of the averaging period. It will be the first day's price plus the product of the smoothing factor and the difference between the first and second day's prices:

day 1's price + smoothing factor × (day 1's - day 2's price)

Continual Computation: Regular Moving Average

It isn't necessary to keep track of lots of price levels for past days in order to be able to maintain the moving average. Simply add yesterday's price to the quotient of the difference of today's price and the price at the beginning of the period, and the period length:

$$\frac{\text{yesterday's price + (today's price - price } \mathbf{P} \text{ days ago)}}{\mathbf{P}}$$

Continual Computation: ESMA

Find this by adding yesterday's ESMA to the product of the smoothing factor and the difference between today's price and the very first ESMA:

yesterday's ESMA + (factor × (today's price - first ESMA))

Chart the Moving Average Along with Price

Charting the moving average along with price will show where the moving average intercepts the price trend.

How to Trade with Moving Averages

General Trading Rule

The moving average can be used as a line indicating a trend. When the trend is broken by price movement, it is time to take action. Thus, if the moving average is broken to the downside, it might be time to sell. If price breaks the moving average on the way up, a trader should go long.

Making the Rule Less Sensitive

Delaying Response

Again, it is important to determine what price is being used: opening, closing, daily high, daily low or a daily average of any systematic combination of open, close, high or low prices. The exact specification of which price traders use can be incorporated into the rule they use. In order to not make the rule so hair-trigger sensitive, for instance, traders could specify that the average be broken on the downside by several daily closes and on the upside by several daily closes. This would make momentary crossings a little less likely to register.

Another possibility is to delay taking action on a signal for a number of days, and wait in the meantime to see if the price re-crosses the average line. If it does, then traders have just witnessed a false breakout and should not take any action yet.

The same effect can be achieved in lagged moving averages by implementing multiple closing days to signal trend reversals rather than one day's price crossovers to signal trend reversals.

Using Bands to Dampen the Trading Signals

Another way traders can keep the moving average technique from emitting signals wildly everytime the market jiggles is to widen the line on the charts with an upper and lower band surrounding the moving average line. Only when the band itself is crossed do traders enter a buy or sell signal. This procedure then allows for minor fluctuation within the band and possibly several crossovers of the moving average of closes without traders having to spring into action each time.

Traders can determine a band in the same way as the moving average, the difference being that they modify the moving average line with a positive or negative factor to obtain the band's upper and lower limits, respectively. The most commonly used upper band and lower band are averages of the daily highs and the averages of the daily lows, respectively.

With the introduction of bands, traders now have three averages: the upper limit, the lower limit and the moving average line itself. The crossing of the upper and lower limits by price can be used as additional buy and sell signals, respectively. If traders extend the range of this band by making the band wider, it then gets to a point where they must use price moving to extremes bounded by the bands as *counter trend* execution points and not as pro-trend breakout points.

Using Multiple Moving Averages

It is possible to use a combination of moving averages which use greater or lesser spans of days for calculations (or smaller or greater base fractions for smoothing factors, if traders are using exponentially smoothed moving averages). In the case of two or more moving averages, one may use a number of rules:

- The faster moving average, one of shorter time periods, can be treated as the price in the basic rule given at the beginning of this section and can be used to indicate immediate trends.
- Take the crossing of two average lines by the price as a sell or buy signal in the direction of the crossover, and the crossing of only one of these lines as a closeout signal to a previously open position.

Trading IBM Stock Using Moving Averages

This chart covers about two years (520 trading days) from mid-August 1985 through mid-August 1987. The moving average line itself starts in the second week on November 1985 (89 days must pass before the first average can be determined). IBM stock traded in a range of an approximate $173.00 high to a low of $112.00, a range of $61.00.

At the start of this chart in August 1985, the moving average line just trails price. Even though it appears that an upside crossover has just occurred, the prudent trader will err on the side of caution and not enter the market for lack of a definitive signal.

The ensuing development of the chart may make the trader regret not entering a position. Even so, traders should resist the temptation to put on a trade the next time the situation appears. True, traders who get rich overnight do this sort of thing. These same individuals also get poor overnight with much more regularity.

The first clear sell signal happens in late February of 1986, when price crosses the moving average line to the downside, giving a sell signal.

Immediately the chart shows many buy-sell signals in a very narrow, almost static price range. A trader won't make any money trading this chart at this time. The lucky ones break even after commissions. This is what we call getting "chopped to death" by the moving average.

Finally, things begin to thin out in late May 1986. The system emits a sell signal (A), then a buy in early June (B), which nets a very slight profit.

Another sell signal on about June 11 (C) indicates the first significant profit, which traders take on the buy signal (D) of September 5. The sale occurred around the $150.00 level and the buy occurred at the $143.00 level.

Figure 2-1 Trading IBM Stock Using Moving Averages

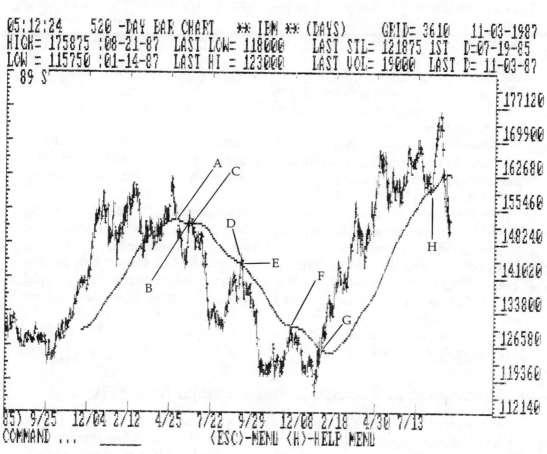

Created using CTS Trend Software

Another sell signal almost immediately follows (E), so once again the traders go short. They ignore the two grazing approaches of the moving average to price in mid-November 1986 (F), then take a profit on the short position and also go long (G). The sale occurred at $141.00 and the purchase occurred at $125.00.

They emerge from the January 1985 bottom with a crossover at $125.00, and go long (G) around January 20, 1987.

Their long position rides comfortable all the way up to the crossover in July, when they sell and go short (H) at $155.00.

Almost immediately, they cover their short and go long for a small loss (H). It looks to be another good trade, as price again shoots above the moving average line, carrying their long position along with it. Profits cumulated to be $53.00 ($7.00 + $16.00 + $30.00).

As the example shows, the moving average length of 89 days of closing price was too sensitive in the trading markets causing traders continually to be in and out of the markets. Once a clear trend was established, first down from point C, and then up at point G, they were able to sustain nice profits. The trading range just before point B was the problem period. They could have faded the moving average crossovers up to this point and sold at upper level crossovers and bought on lower level breakdowns—an oscillator. As other chapters will demonstrate there are ways to modify the moving averages to get oscillating signals of overbought and oversold.

Trading Options Exchange Index Using Moving Averages

This is a chart of 500 days' duration which averages the last 123 days' prices. A long averaging period shows the smoothness of the moving average line. The OEX moved from a low of 180.00 to a high of 329.50, or a gain of 149.50 points in the 500 days from September 1985 to July 1987.

Trading cannot begin at the point the moving average starts, at A, because traders need a moving average-price crossover, which does not happen until around mid-July of 1986. Since the price crosses the moving average line from above (B), they have a sell signal. There is an immediate reversal to a buy signal (C), with a slight loss, then a sell (D) with a slight profit. A buy at E gives them another slight loss (assuming they maintain constant, "flipping" positions).

The traders sell at the F crossover for their first perceptible profit, although this, too, is slight. Another buy signal at G also would give them a slight profit if they had flipped from long to short at F.

H gives them another sell signal, followed rapidly by I's buy and another slight loss.

Figure 2-2   Trading Options Exchange Index Using Moving Averages

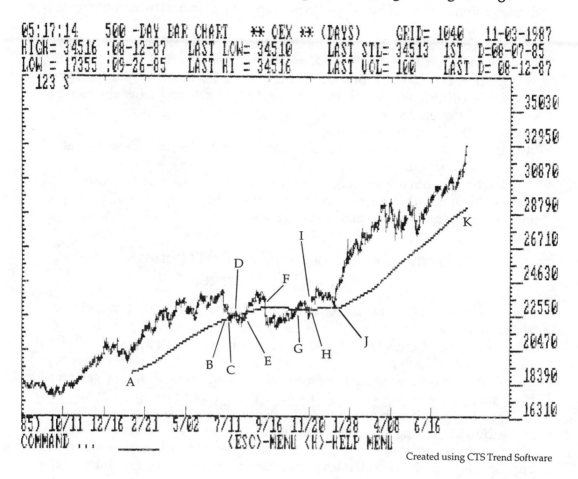

05:17:14   500 -DAY BAR CHART   ** OEX ** (DAYS)   GRID= 1040   11-03-1987
HIGH= 34516 :08-12-87   LAST LOW= 34510   LAST STL= 34513   1ST   D=08-07-85
LOW = 17355 :09-26-85   LAST HI = 34516   LAST VOL= 100   LAST D= 08-12-87

COMMAND ...   ____   <ESC>-MENU <H>-HELP MENU

Created using CTS Trend Software

To date, they have been in the market at least eight times and paid their dues in commissions. They are getting "chopped up" in a narrow-ranged trading market.

However, at point I they enter long positions and the market is headed up. A slight risk occurs at point J where the price reacts back to the moving average line, but does not break it to the downside, which would then warrant a sale of their longs and an additional short sale to follow the moving average crossover. The traders stay long now as price rises steadily through the end of the charting period (K).

After some very frustrating chewing around, the traders are headed toward a solid profit.

Clearly, the moving averages will get traders in and out of the markets continually and with disastrous consequences if they happen to be trading in non-trending, trading-type markets.

Trading September 1987 S&P 500 Futures Using Moving Averages

This moving average is for a shorter period of time (195 days' duration and a 34-day period) and it is easier to actually see the crossovers of price on the moving average. In this time period, the index moved from a low of 232.00 to an approximate high of 337.00. The fact that it is also for a moving average period of 34 days means that the average moving line will not be far away from price before giving a crossover signal, if and when they turn down.

The average starts plotting right in the middle of the prices of late 1986 and early 1987, giving at least six alternating buy and sell signals (A). Traders come out of the area at A short, and therefore the upward crossover at B is a buy signal. Price then accelerates above the moving average for almost three months, and our profits accumulate steadily.

At C (late March 1987), traders receive a sell signal and sell out their long position. If they also flip to a short position they will be short at point C and need to cover this short at point D, for a loss.

Point E gives traders a crossover to the downside and shows a nice-sized profit, only to turn into a loss at point F, which is a false crossover to the upside, thereby causing them to cover their short and also go long. It then goes straight down and traders have to go short after they sell out their long. The whole period covering points C to J is choppy and traders will doubtless see all their profits whittled away.

They will probably come out of this period losing about 1/4 to 1/2 of their gains on the trade from B to C.

Figure 2-3   Trading September 1987 S&P 500 Futures Using Moving Averages

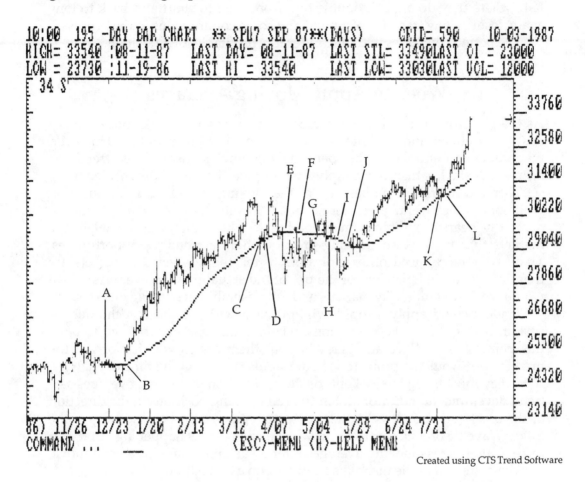

Created using CTS Trend Software

Traders emerge long from point J, and it is clear sailing until they reach K-L, where they do a quick double flip, from long to short and back to long again, losing a few fractions of a point and some commissions in the process.

The period concludes with the trader in a profitable long position.

When to Apply Moving Averages

As the preceding examples show, moving averages work well once a trend has been defined and indicate when the trend has been broken. However, much time and effort must be spent making sure that a real new trend has been established, rather than simply a feint upward or to the downside.

Therefore, perhaps the best use of the moving average is in conjunction with some other techniques, not so much to filter out the valid signals in decidedly bearish or bullish markets, but to filter out the times when the markets that traders are tracking are not offering trending opportunities. Traders therefore, need other indicators to tell them when the markets are trending or not, independent of the use of the actual moving averages which would work well in *trading* markets and fail miserably in *trending* markets.

Traders could apply a top-down approach with this basic technique by first analyzing the market conditions: where is the market supposed to be at this point? Elliott Wave analysis will help them assess whether or not the market itself would be prone to violent impulse moves at the time of analysis. If so, they must be on the lookout for the application of moving averages as a trend development indicator and initiate all opening positions in the direction of the breakouts. Conversely, the moving average could be used to give the Elliott Wave theoretician a tip about when a change was happening. That is, if price starts to cross moving averages after a sustained one-directional move, one can assume that the market is heading into a correction.

A moving averages technique might best be used on a trending type of market which is based on some sort of predictable cyclical variation. Moving averages respond sluggishly to price changes and there are problems in determining whether breakouts are genuine or not. The sluggishness of the moving averages can be mitigated by shortening the averaging period, i.e. instead of using a 123 day moving average, use a 34 day moving average; instead of using a weekly moving average, use a 6 hour moving average, etc. However, traders can never really know at what point the market is, hence, they must use moving averages of any length with great initial care. After observations of market patterns and behaviors, they can either start to lengthen the period or shorten it, to create enough sensitivity to engender valid crossovers. The sooner that traders can ascertain this, the faster they will be able to use this indicator. This last problem can be solved, of course, with some techniques which require waiting, but hindsight is not always a trader's most affordable luxury.

On the second point, that of false breakouts, it would seem that highly volatile but essentially static markets would wreak especial havoc on a trading system which was based on moving averages. As the trading examples presented show, moving averages give traders too many signals whenever the market pulls out of a steady upward or downward trend. There is nothing wrong with the many signals, but it is impossible for a trader to make profitable trades with them. There is no market follow through—the market action which makes money. The trader using moving averages tends to get "chopped to death" in the trading market.

When the market starts to behave like this, a trader can improve performance with moving averages through the use of bands or multiple moving averages, both of which will de-sensitize the moving average to whipsaw indications. However, if a trader is applying moving averages alone, and the market decides to stay in a trading range for a long time, he or she may be sitting it out for a long time. Markets which are not in a decidedly bullish or bearish trend would not be very good candidates for a moving average approach.

Where to Find Out More about Moving Averages

As mentioned in the first section of this chapter, several major studies of moving averages were done in the 1960's and 1970's. In addition, there are a number of fairly recently issued books containing comprehensive sections on moving averages.

Books and Periodicals

Brown, Robert. *Smoothing, Forecasting & Prediction of Discrete Time Series.* Englewood Cliffs, New Jersey: Prentice-Hall, 1963. Specifically discusses exponentially smoothed moving averages.

Donchian, Richard D. "Donchian's 5- and 20-day Moving Averages." *Commodities Magazine.* December 1974. The original source on a popular technique for using two moving averages at once.

Dahl, Curtiss. *Consistent Profits in the Commodity Futures Market.* Cincinnati, Ohio: Tri State Offset Company, 1960.

Dahl, Curtiss. *Consistent Profits in the Commodity Futures Market—Addendum.* Cincinnati, Ohio: Tri-State Offset Company, 1961.

Davis, R.E. and C.C. Thiel, Jr. *A Computer Analysis of the Moving Average Applied to Commodity Futures Trading.* West Lafayette, Indiana: Ouiatenon Management Company, 1969. Authors test a variety of moving average systems on various commodities markets.

Drew, Garfield. *New Methods for Profit in the Stock Market.* Boston: Metcalf Press, 1955. An early exposition of moving average methods.

Dunn, Dennis. *Consistent Profits in June Live Beef Cattle.* West Lafayette, Indiana: Dunn & Hargitt, 1972. This was a study done as a test of Taylor's system. *(See reference below about Taylor).*

Kaufman, Perry J. *Commodity Trading Systems and Methods.* New York: John Wiley & Sons, 1978. Contains a substantial section on moving averages with detailed theoretical and practical discussion.

Keltner, Chester W. *How to Make Money in Commodities.* Kansas City: The Keltner Statistical Service, 1960. Contains a section which gives a full description of a moving-average system with a band.

Maxwell, Joseph, Sr. *Commodity Futures Trading with Moving Averages.* Santa Clara, California: Speer, 1974. Applies literally hundreds of possible moving-average systems to pork-belly trading and evaluates them.

Taylor, Robert Joel. "The Major Price Trend Directional Indicator." *Commodities Magazine.* April 1972. A complete moving average system which has been fairly widely used. (*See reference above to Dunn.*)

Turner, Dennis and Stephen H. Blinn. *Trading Silver—Profitably.* New Rochelle, New York: Arlington House Publishers, 1975. The authors applied several moving average systems to the silver market.

Software to Run on the IBM Personal Computer

Chart Trader Plus—Interday charting package with the following: median lines, Fibonacci lines and spheres, recursion lines, percentage retracements, simple moving averages with bands, oscillators, relative strength index, on-balance volume, %R, cycle intervals, and parallel channels. Investor's Toolkit Ltd., Summit, IL 60501.

Computrac—Interday charting package has the following studies: moving averages, rates of change, oscillators, ratios and spread, RSI, stochastic, On-Balance volume, moving average convergence divergence, point-and-figure, etc. Chart zooming, trend lines and parallel channels, cycle analysis with Fourier analysis. Computrac, Inc., New Orleans, LA 70175.

CTS Trend—A software package which is a basic miniversion of Tradecenter. It creates many different types of studies. Including realtime studies. CTS Trend, Newark, NJ 07974.

Dow Jones Market Analyzer Plus—Interday charting with the following: moving averages, trading bands, volume oscillators, support/resistance lines, RSI, trend and parallel lines, speed lines, point-and-figure charts, split screen. Dow Jones Software, Princeton, NJ 08540.

MetaStock—Interday charting package has graphics, but primitive hardcopy features. Many moving averages, trading bands, parallel channels, linear-regression lines, cycle-interval lines, On-Balance Volume, RSI, positive/negative volume and relative-performance ratios. Computer Asset Management, Salt Lake City, UT 84126.

Quickplot—Interday charting package creates daily, weekly or monthly charts, with moving averages of all types, trend lines and parallel channels, oscillators and RSI. This is a basic program without advanced studies. Commodity Systems, Inc., Boca Raton, FL 33432.

Relevance III™—Interday charting package which creates above-average screen graphics and the finest hardcopy charts available using regular computer equipment. Performs many advanced studies and has the only available Elliott Wave ratio analysis program. Holt Investments, Nashville, TN 37238.

Telescan Analyzer—A front-end interday charting package which accesses only their own database of 7000 stocks and 150 market indices. Data retrieval cost: 50 cents peak hours, and 25 cents off peak access. Telescan, Inc., Houston, TX 77042.

WarMachine—A software package created by WarMachine for both the IBM PC and the Apple MacIntosh microcomputers. The package is designed to run on two floppies or less. Newer versions require more overhead memory. This package does realtime charting with Lotus Signal quote machine and can be used to create day to day bar charts. *WarMachine*, Chicago, IL 60660.

3

Wilder's Relative Strength Index

Apples and Oranges

Wilder's Relative Strength Index at a Glance

Background and Philosophy
of Wilder's Relative Strength Index

RSI is an overbought/oversold indicator that tries to predict price reversal points and also attempts to provide an index for comparing any market investment with any other, no matter what the market. It therefore ties in well with broad-based position management strategies.

Principles of Relative Strength Index

RSI includes a reckoning period over which Up and Down closings are averaged, usually 14 days, and an average both of Up closings and Down closings over that period. The ratio between Up and Down closing averages is known as the market's Relative Strength. The total of both averages, divided by the Up average, gives a percentage which is the final RSI indicator. This percentage is taken as an indicator of how much strength is left in a trend. An RSI value above 70 indicates an imminent top and a sale upon subsequent retracement, and an RSI value below 30 indicates a bottom. Retracements from *double tops* or *double bottoms* are more significant from above the 70% level or below the 30% level.

How to Set Up and Maintain a Relative Strength Index

1) Choose an averaging period. The norm is 14 days, but should be shortened for more volatile or very short-cycle markets and lengthened for the opposite cases.
2) Keep track of the previous 14 days of Ups and Downs (a day's Up or Down is 0 if the day's change was of the opposite sign from the previous day).
3) Figure an average of both the Ups and Downs, respectively.
4) Relative strength = Up average/(Up + Down averages)
5) Normalized RS = 1+RS
6) RSI = 100 - (100/Normalized RS)
7) Subsequent daily Up and Down averages =

$$\frac{\text{Previous day's average}/13 + \text{today's Up or Down}}{14}$$

(assuming the period size is 14)

How to Trade with a Relative Strength Index

When RSI moves into overbought territory the first time is a warning to be aware of overbought conditions; a sell signal occurs upon a subsequent retracement away from the overbought area. The converse holds for oversold territory. Better confirmations of overbought/oversold conditions is the occurrence of multiple tops and bottoms: sell when RSI breaks below the tops above 70, and buy when RSI moves above the bottoms above 30.

When to Apply a Relative Strength Index

Relative Strength Index responds best in trading or sluggish markets. In trending markets (bullish or bearish), traders must use only half the signals: overbought or oversold in the direction of the main trend. In a bull market, they should buy the oversold signals and ignore the overbought signals. Unfortunately, oversold signals rarely occur and traders will have to move their threshold line to above 30%, instead of below 30%, to get valid RSI oversold signals. Apply the same concept in bear markets, where traders get many more oversold signals than overbought signals. They need to use pattern recognition techniques/cycle indicators to show when RSI signals are confirming indicators.

Glossary for Wilder's Relative Strength Index

Averaging Period—The period over which Ups and Downs are averaged for determining relative strength. 14 days is the normal length.

Down—The amount by which each day's price closes below the previous day's closing (given as 0 if the closing is higher).

Normalized Relative Strength—1 + the day's Relative Strength.

Relative Strength—The percentage ratio between the average of Ups and the sum of the average Ups and Downs over the chosen averaging period.

Relative Strength Index (RSI)—A measure of how much "strength" or likelihood of continuity is left in a trend. It is a number between 1 and 100 and is found by subtracting 100/Normalized Relative Strength (see above) from 100. This number can then be used to compare the issue with the RSI's of other investments.

RSI Multiple Bottoms—An important trading indicator in RSI analysis, which happens when RSI bottoms more than once below the 30% mark without having risen above that mark in the intervening rally. Should be taken as a buy signal.

RSI Multiple Tops—An important trading indicator in RSI analysis, which happens when RSI peaks more than once above the 70% mark without having fallen below that level in the intervening retracement.

Up—The amount by which each day's price closes above the previous day's closing (given as 0 if the closing is lower).

Background and Philosophy
of the Relative Strength Index

J. Welles Wilder's Relative Strength Index (RSI) uses a structure and a philosophy similar to those of oscillators: the index is used to test for overbought and oversold conditions, and it depends on an averaging technique over past prices. However, Wilder's RSI seems more firmly rooted in the calculus-based concept of the derivative as a measure of tendency and momentum than are the oscillator techniques. It therefore claims to be more responsive to changes in the rate of change and therefore able to predict rather than simply confirm important price breakouts.

RSI is also more complicated to calculate than a straight moving average or oscillator (though this should matter little to the trader with computerized assistance). This added complexity points up a refinement: this technique is called relative strength index for two reasons: one is that it shows the relative strength of price gains to losses, and the other is that the RSI can be used to compare any two markets or commodities, or the same market or commodity at two very different times. This is because RSI contains a procedure for normalizing its results on a 0 to 100 scale in a very precise fashion unlike the rather arbitrary scale that one might choose for moving average trendlines or an oscillator's oversold/overbought indicators. RSI was designed this way because it commits to a total trading strategy. With this feature, RSI allows one to meaningfully compare different items in one's portfolio and decide where to make the next play based on potential profitability.

Principles of the Relative Strength Index

The RSI uses three fundamental variables for its reckoning:

- The average of all Up closes over a given period
- The average of all Down closes over that same period
- The length of the period in days over which these averages are taken

The ratio between Up closes and Down closes is known as the issue's or commodity's "Relative Strength." This Relative Strength, or RS, needs to be converted to some universal form so that it can be compared with other issues, other markets, and with itself over time (when price ranges or volatility might be different). This universalized indicator is what we call the Relative Strength Index, or RSI. RSI will use as its base the combined strength of Ups and Downs and will then express the percentage of weight which the Ups have relative to the Downs. In other words, if average Ups and average Downs for the same period on a given day are both say, 0.25 then the RSI will be 50% (average Ups make up the same amount as do Downs of the sum of average Ups and Downs). If average Ups are 0.30 and average Downs are 0.20, then RSI is 60%, and if average Ups are 0.10 and Downs are 0.30, then the RSI is 25%. We can see from the way in which this indicator is set up that it will be sensitive to any change in a price trend.

In general, an RSI of 50% means that average Ups and Downs have the same relative strength; that they balance each other out. If the RSI falls below 50%, this means that Downs are more powerful than Ups, and if it is above 50%, then Ups are stronger than Downs.

What this translates into is an index of how much strength is left in a trend. If price has been downtrending and the RSI rises violently on a price bottoming action, signalling that Downs are losing out to Ups, then the technician should look for some kind of reversal, for the downtrend appears to be weakening. If the RSI moves above 70 while in a major uptrend, then a major top may be imminent. If the RSI goes below 30 in an abrupt sell-off, while a major trend is still rising, a major top may have formed.

How to Set Up and Maintain Relative Strength Index

Deciding on a Period Length

Fourteen trading days has proven to be a good average period length for calculating RSI. The actual period length traders use will depend on their perception of the market's volatility and their knowledge of any inherent cycles in that market.

If there is some sort of weekly (7 days) or bi-weekly (14 days) cycle going on in the market, or if the market appears to be dipping wildly up and down over several weeks' time, then 14 days may be too long a period.

Cycles take time to complete and if the market appears sluggish, more than 14 days should be considered. Of course, if this is happening the market might really not be in a trading range, and is perhaps undergoing long-term accumulation and is readying itself for an upmove. In this case, the trader should perhaps keep the indicator up to date, but wait to apply it until the market shows signs of more volatility—the RSI indicator is really designed for static or congested markets.

Keeping Track of Daily Ups and Downs for One Initial Period

Before traders can do anything else, they must accumulate enough Ups and Downs to strike the first average. This will take the length of one period as determined by them in the first step. For each trading day of this initial period, note whether the day's price closed higher or lower than the previous day's. If higher, note how much higher and write it down in the Ups column. If lower, note the difference in the Downs column.

Initializing Average Ups and Downs

To find the initial average Ups traders need to add the Ups and divide the result by 14. They do the same with the Downs. There will be less than 14 of each, but they still divide the result by 14, since the value of the Up or Down for a day in which there was none is taken to be 0. This operation has to be performed only once, when traders first set up the RSI for a given market. After that they can use the shortcut described below.

Determining RSI

Once the day's average Ups and Downs are calculated traders can determine the RS (Relative Strength) by dividing the Ups average by the Downs average. The next step is to normalize RS by adding 1 to it. Then they divide 100 by the normalized Relative Strength. Finally, they subtract this result from 100.

This figure is the Relative Strength Index (RSI) for that day: that is, the percentage which the average Ups bear to the whole strength of Ups and Downs combined.

How to Determine Average Ups and Downs after the First Time

It is not necessary for traders to sum 14 separate days and then divide the result by 14 for each Up and Down average, once they have obtained the first set of averages. On all subsequent days they can:

1) Multiply the previous day's average by 13.
2) Add today's Up or Down, respectively, onto this number (add 0 if the change was of the opposite sign).
3) Divide the result by 14.

This is the new average for the day, and traders can compute the RSI from the two averages so obtained using the procedure given above.

This is similar to how one computes a moving average after the first average has been struck, and it saves lots of tedious calculation (or some computer execution time, at least).

How to Trade with Relative Strength Index

On the assumption that traders are in a trading market rather than a trending market, they can observe the following behaviors of the RSI:

- If the index rises above 70, an intermediate top is usually imminent, according to the concept behind the RSI.
- If it dips below 30, they may expect an intermediate bottom.
- Reversal of a rally is very probable when the Index peaks above 70, falls, recovers, and then fails to rise to its former level before heading downward.
- Reversal of a selloff is signalled by the inverse pattern taking place around the 30% level: the index bottoms below this point, rises, and then returns down again, but not as far as before.

Critical buy and sell points can be determined during one of the RSI reversal patterns just mentioned:

- The sell point on a rally reversal pattern is the value at which the index begins its upward recovery. An actual sell signal is given when the Index once again passes this point on its second time down.
- Conversely, a buy signal occurs when the Index breaks above the first downturn point established in the downtrend reversal pattern discussed above.

Figure 3-1 Trading Algoma Steel Stock Using RSI

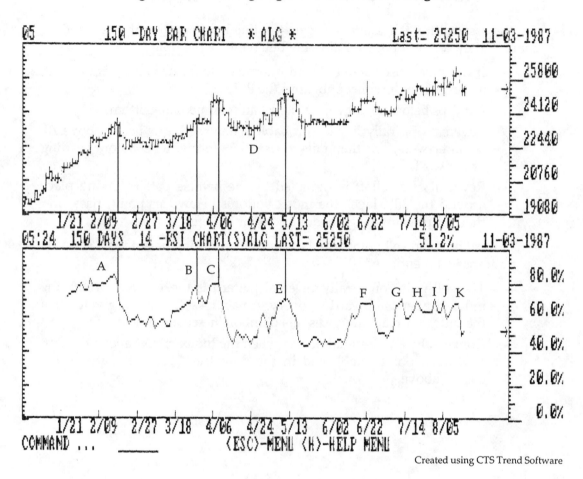

Created using CTS Trend Software

Trading Algoma Steel Stock Using RSI

This chart covers 150 days, or a little more than half a year, from December 1986 to August 1987, in which the price moved from a low of $19.00 to a high of $26.00.

Lines at the recommended 70% and 30% levels, show that there are a few sell signals and no buy signals. The three peaks at A are not sell signals, but the eventual move down below the 70% level is a sell signal. The sale takes advantage of the stock's several points selloff, but the RSI does not register a buy signal using the strict 30% oversold area—none appears. This is a cue that perhaps the stock itself is extremely bullish and is not capable of creating oversold values for traders to either go long or cover their shorts with the conventional RSI parameter.

Four months into the chart (points B and C) the first double peak appears with its intermediate valley just breaking the 70% level. If traders take point C as significant, they see in retrospect that they have a very good local sell signal. Notice, however, that there is no corresponding buy signal to take advantage of the low price at point D. True, the indicator is down, but nowhere near the 30% oversold level.

Points E through K all represent places where RSI just grazes the 70% level. By holding to the two-peak rule, traders could take points E, G, I and K as sell signals. But it is better for them to ignore these unless there is deep penetration within the 70% zone and ultimate retracement below the 70% level.

Figure 3-2   Trading August 1987 Heating Oil Futures Using RSI

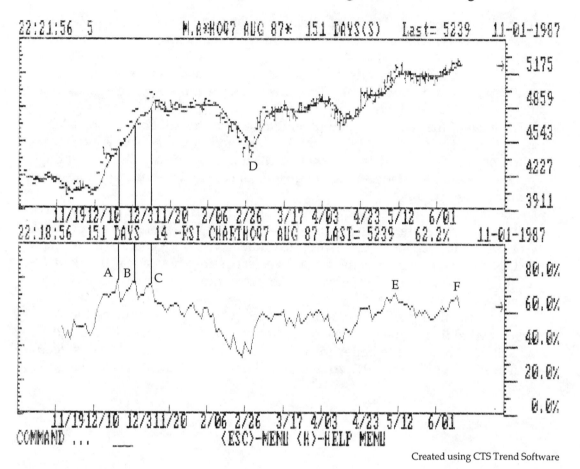

Trading August 1987 Heating Oil Futures Using RSI

The August 1987 Heating Oil contract spans October 1986 to June 1987, or about nine months. Price of the oil contract ranges from a low of $0.39 to a high of $0.52. There are three over-70% peaks at A, B and C, and by the rules set forth for applying RSI, the second peak at B should give a sell point. The existence of a triple top in the RSI formation implies that once the RSI curve starts to head down traders should have a very valid sell signal. In fact, once the RSI curve breaks below the 70% level the sale at point C creates a substantial profit: sale was at the $0.49 level and the price eventually bottoms out at the $0.43 level.

Traders could still make money with the RSI if there were some buy signal when the price reached D, but the indicator is nowhere near 30% at that point. In fact, it never gets very low in the whole chart, just as in the previous example.

The chart shows us that despite the fact that prices drop precipitously, they create no RSI buy signal using the 30%-70% conventional parameters; could the parameters be wrong? Yes, if traders do not know that they can readjust the 30% oversold ever so slightly to, perhaps, 35%, thereby creating a situation where there is an oversold condition. What traders can see by slightly adjusting the RSI is that the market in this example is not in a trading range but a trending situation, moving decidedly upwards.

If traders count E and F as peaks above 70%, then F is another sell signal. Though they don't know what will happen in the chart's continuation, this looks reasonable. F is at the highest price on the whole chart. The price rise is suspiciously flat, however, and may indicate that they sold too early.

Figure 3-3 Trading Dow Jones Industrial Averages Using RSI

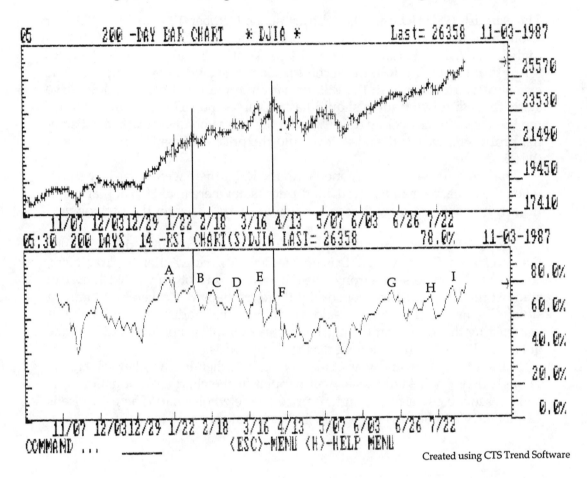

Created using CTS Trend Software

Trading Dow Jones Industrials Averages Using RSI

This example is for the Dow Jones Industrials Averages from October 1986 to July 1987, a span of 200 days in which the averages moved from a low of 1740.00 to a high of 2570.00.

After waiting almost four months, traders get their first sell signal at C. B is not a sell signal because, even though it is the second of a pair of peaks above 70, the intervening low does not go below 70. Similarly, E gives them another sell signal and, after some pause, G another, then I. The sell signals are considered false signals because as soon as one sells, the RSI rallies back into overbought territory, 70%.

Finally, at point F, the final sell signal appears and the RSI curve erodes. This is in the midst of the strongest bull trend in the averages, from A-E. Selling netted losses as the averages move into new highs. At point F, the actual Dow average selloff nets little profit. No buy signals are in sight, as the RSI stays above 40% for the entire period.

Observe carefully that had traders used oversold values of 40% or less, instead of 30% or less, they would have oversold values that signalled purchases that eventually netted handsome profits: the first time around November 10, the second around May 15.

When to Apply Wilder's Relative Strength Index

RSI was designed for, and is best at, spotting definite tops, bottoms and reversals with their corresponding signals. Of course, these signals are clearest and also bring the most profit in markets which are trendless and are neither moving substantially down nor up.

Again, the quick reversal is RSI's forte. In trending markets, traders should apply the overbought and oversold indicators with caution. Traders modify their overbought parameters downwards in severely downtrending markets and modify their oversold parameters upwards in severely uptrending markets. Unfortunately, traders don't know that they should do this at the time that this is happening. What they notice at the time is that the oversold indicators do not forecast oversold situations and the overbought indicators do not forecast overbought situations very well.

As with all indicators which seek to allow the trader to take advantage of tops and bottoms, RSI does not work well in markets not characterized by pronounced tops and bottoms. In congested markets, the oversold and overbought indicators are valid. However, the ensuing moves in these markets do not create enough profits to offset the risks and trading costs involved. Indeed, a trader who relied exclusively on RSI would be doing nothing during "congested" periods, since the small difference between Ups and Downs would keep the indicator around 50 and well away from the upper and lower reversal and buy/sell indicators.

Traders should, of course keep the indicator up to date during periods of accumulation or flat price periods, but it would be best for them not to actually trade on RSI until frequent breakouts above 70% and below 30% begin to occur once again.

In general, the thing which RSI most lacks (as is true with all purely trending techniques) is some way of determining when to apply it. Therefore, the question is, how does one determine what type of market one is in: trading or trending?

The use of an Elliott Wave-type analysis or some kind of cyclic approach can help traders determine when to bring RSI into play. This shortcoming of RSI also suggests that it could be complemented nicely with volume-type techniques which work better in accumulating, flat market situations than in distribution markets.

Where to Find Out More About Wilder's Relative Strength Index

Books and Periodicals

The main source of information about Wilder's Relative Strength Index is Wilder's own book, *New Concepts in Technical Trading Systems,* Trend Research, P.O. Box 450, Greensboro, North Carolina 27402, (1978).

The book is very explicit about what one should do to use the method and is replete with examples, exercises and technical explanations at various levels of sophistication. RSI is only one of several new and old techniques which Wilder presents in great detail in the book which, on the whole represents a detailed, conscientious exposition of a trading and money management system.

Software to Run on the IBM Personal Computer

Chart Trader Plus—Interday charting package with the following: median lines, Fibonacci lines and spheres, recursion lines, percentage retracements, simple moving averages with bands, oscillators, relative strength indes, on-balance volume, %R, cycle intervals, and parallel channels. Investor's Toolkit Ltd, Summit, IL 60501.

Comptutrac—Interday charting package has the following studies: moving averages, rates of change, oscillators, ratios and spread, RSI, stochastic, on-balance volume, moving average convergence divergence, point-and-figure, etc. Chart zooming, trendlines and parallel channels, cycle analysis with Fourier analysis. Computrac, Inc., New Orleans, LA 70175.

CTS Trend—A software package which is a basic miniversion of Tradecenter. It creates many different types of studies, including realtime studies.CTS Trend, Newark, NJ 0774.

Dow Jones Market Analyzer Plus—Interday charting with the following: moving averages, trading bands, volume oscillators, support/resistance lines, RSI, trend and parallel lines, speed lines, point-and-figure charts, split screen. Dow Jones Software, Princeton, NJ 08540.

MetaStock—Interday charting package has graphics, but primitive hardcopy features. Many moving averages, trading bands, parallel channels, linear-regression lines, cycle-interval lines, on-balance volume, RSI, positive/negative volume and relative-performance ratios. Computer Asset Management, Salt Lake City, UT 84126.

Quickplot—Interday charting package creates daily, weekly or monthly charts, with moving averages of all types, trend lines and parallel channels, oscillators and RSI. This is a basic program without advanced studies. Commodity Systems, Inc., Boca Raton, FL 33432.

Relevance III™—Interday charting package which creates above average screen graphics and the finest hardcopy chart available using regular computer equipment and has the only available Elliott Wave ratio analysis program. Holt Investments, Nashville, TN 37238.

Telescan Analyzer—A front-end interday charting package which accesses only their own database of 7000 stocks and 150 market indices. Data retrieval cost: 50 cents peak hours, and 25 cents off peak access. Telescan, Inc., Houston, TX 77042.

Relevance III™ *Software's Trend Series* includes modules for Wilder's Relative Strength Index and Modified RSI. Inquiries may be directed to 888 Lakemont Drive, Nashville, TN 37220.

4

Williams' Percentage R
Gravitation Towards the Mean

Williams' Percentage Range at a Glance
Background and Philosophy of Williams' Percentage Range

Williams' Percentage Range (%R) uses the price range over a given period of time to establish a center of gravity and then tries to spot relative overbought and oversold areas from this center as market turning points.

Principles of Percentage Range

Percentage R takes the highest and lowest closing prices within a given time period in the past as its range. The most recent day's closing price is then located within the range, its distance from the top of the range being expressed as a percentage. It is this percentage which forms the Percentage R indicator.

How to Set Up and Maintain Percentage Range

- Choose the time period over which to reckon a price range.
- The period should be at least five trading days, and half the length of an identifiable market cycle. The period will vary with each trader's market timeframe.
- Track price for one period. At this point users can begin determining the range for each day (highest and lowest prices in last period).
- Subtract the day's closing price from the range high and take the result as a percentage of the range to obtain %R.
- Continue this procedure, plotting %R at the bottom of the price chart.

How to Trade with Percentage Range

Traders should use moves below 95% in a bull market as potential buy signals, and moves above 10% in a bear market as potential signals to sell. The actual percentages used as threshold levels can be modified and adjusted to reflect the overall bullishness or bearishness of market action.

When to Apply Percentage Range

Percentage R is most effective in trading markets with defined cyclicity and in trending markets without a reputation for cyclic moves. Traders should not use %R by itself for it will give false signals in trending markets. But they can use %R as a confirming technique with trend-following and time reversal-prediction techniques. It can be used alone in trading markets, but this is not recommended if one is to generate consistent projects.

Glossary for Percentage Range

Percentage Range (% R)—A market analysis technique which compares a given day's closing price with the range of closing prices over a given period. Proximity to the top or bottom of this range expressed as a percentage gives buy or sell signals.

Period—A fixed number of days (usually at least 5) over which the price range is figured.

Range—The difference between highest and lowest closing prices for the chosen time period.

Background and Philosophy of Percentage Range

The "R" in Percentage R (abbreviated as %R) stands for "Range," and the main idea behind %R is to use rallies to the top or selloffs to the bottom of the foregoing period's price range to get sell or buy signals.

Inherent in the concept behind the creation of %R is a belief of "gravitation towards the mean." First, a center of market action is defined, in this case the range of the period's high and low price. Then, there is a comparison of the current day's price, in relation to that period's range. If the current day's price is near the high of the period's range the system assumes that the market is currently overbought and is vulnerable for a selloff. If current day's price is near the low end of the period's range, the system assumes that the market is currently oversold, and is vulnerable for a rally.

The system is not without potential error. Some traders assume that once a trend is in motion, it stays in that direction until it does otherwise. Percentage R assumes that once a trend is set in motion, it is highly probable that it is due for a correction.

Unlike the other price-sensitive indicators mentioned in this book, the actual numbers indicating overbought and oversold are 0% at the top of the range and 100% at the bottom of the range, exactly opposite are other overbought and oversold indicator levels. Like most price-sensitive indicators, this type of numeric analysis must be used intelligently.

All this suggests, of course, that %R might work well in conjunction with some of these other methods. In fact, it is not a stand-alone technique, and it is necessary to use some sort of trend formation indicators along with it in order to take advantage of its buy and sell signals.

Principles of Percentage Range

The %R technique uses three simple variables:
- A period of time over which to define the range
- The highest price within that period
- The lowest price within that period

In this aspect, then, %R is similar to a moving average in that it constantly updates its reference period with each new day.

The %R figure is derived daily from these three variables in the following fashion:
- The Range between highest and lowest prices is found by subtracting the lowest price from the highest.

- The distance of the daily price below the top of the range is then expressed as a percent of the total range distance. For example, if traders are going to use a six-day range and if the highest price is 70, the lowest 50 and today's price is 52, then today's %Range figure is 90 (at 52 today's price is 18 below the six-day high and the range size is, 20 so one can see that 18 is 90% of 20).

The %R indicator generates valid overbought and oversold signals in trading markets. However, the indicator can be modified to be used successfully in both bear and bull markets; the %R indicator is used to spot only buy signals in a bull market and only sell signals in a bear market. Thus, by itself it is not intended to give us a complete picture of the market's trend, but only of possible turning points for long and short positions. It is therefore imperative to use other methods in conjunction with %R for a full-blown trading strategy. Moving averages or Elliott Wave would be good choices to use as trend indicators to determine whether one is currently trading in a bull or bear market.

How to Set Up and Maintain Percentage Range

Choosing a Period

To begin trading with %R traders need to determine first how long a period they will use for their range. This will depend to a large extent on the general nature of the market they are trading in and also on the particular secular circumstances in that market—whether it is presently undergoing a lot of volatility or not.

In markets with more or less predictable cyclic changes such as agricultural commodities, the period should be shorter than any appreciable fraction of the cycle, e.g., a period which is a half or a quarter of the cycle length, so that the cycle will not be "dampened out" and the high and low figures simply become cyclic highs and lows.

The more volatile a market, the shorter traders will want to make the period they use for their range, because the center of market action is shorter. Periods of less than five trading days are not of much use in any case.

The length of period will also depend to some extent on what sort of game traders wish to play: how long-range do they want their plays to be? The longer they are willing to sit with a trade, the longer their period can be.

For a market of average volatility, a good period would be ten days.

Setting Up the Indicator

Traders must now begin to keep track of price on a daily basis, noting the daily highs and lows on a bar chart. Once they have charted the same number of days as are in their period they can begin to keep daily %R figures. These are best tracked on the same chart as price, at the bottom, however. Traders can use a strip of even width at the bottom of the chart, for they will be graphing percentage not price figures or any derivative of them, and therefore will never go below 0% or above 100%. It is sufficient to make the strip big enough to clearly distinguish increments of 10% or less.

To determine the day's %R indicator traders should look over the last period defined by the day and find the period's highest high and the lowest low price. The difference between these two gives traders the absolute range value. They then subtract today's closing price from the high which they have just found and divide the result by the range determined in the previous step.

The number obtained is the day's %R indicator and it should be graphed in the area reserved for it at the bottom of the graph.

Other Indicators

Along with %R, traders should keep at least one other trend-type indicator, whether that be some variety of moving average, a thorough knowledge of which Elliott Wave cycle the current market is in or another indicator. This is most conveniently plotted on the same chart as %R and will most probably be superimposed on the price lines themselves rather than the %R indicator line.

How to Trade with Percentage Range

Percentage Range is essentially a technique for determining signals for buying oversold signals and selling overbought signals in trading markets. If, however, traders find themselves in decidedly trending markets, then they must skew their trades to the direction of that general trend. If they are in a bull market, they must sell the oversold signals and if they are in a bear market, they must buy the overbought signals. To determine when they are really in a bear or bull market traders will need other indicators. These should be indicators of trends, like moving averages, or market cycles, like Elliott Wave and Gann analysis.

Percentage Range sell signals work poorly in a bull market. Of course, the tendency of %R will be toward the high side, touching 0% (overbought) during a bull market, as price exerts upward pressure in relation to preceding days and therefore stays toward the high end of the price range. A fall below 95% should be considered a buy signal in these circumstances.

In order to improve their track record with this indicator traders could refine the buy signal by requiring that the indicator touch 100% (tremendously oversold) and stay below the 95% limit for at least half the length of their %R period. Then, when the indicator does move above 95% again, they know that this is indeed a believable signal rather than a flash in the pan. This additional filtering of the signal should help them in picking more profitable trades.

The inverse use for %R indicators is selling in a bear market. Traders can pretty much invert what has just been said about buying in a bull market to see how they would use it, substituting 0% on the overbought scale for 100% on the oversold side.

Trading September 1987 Swiss Franc Futures Using Percentage Range

This example runs 100 days, from April 1987 to August 1987. The Swiss Francs went from a low of $0.65 to a high of about $0.70 and then to a new local low of $0.63.

At point A traders get a doubtful buy signal (the indicator just barely penetrates the 80% area before swinging back). As it turns out, it is a valid buy point because the price of the franc goes from $0.66 to about $0.70.

Point B, which actually touches the 0% line signals a sale and traders take a loss on this trade as the price goes higher. A clue to this incorrect trade can be seen in the above paragraph—note that price moved from $0.66 to $0.70 after the price of $0.66 registered an 80% Percentage R figure.

Price has actually risen when point C's sell signal comes through and at point D is the highest it ever gets. Following the overbought signals, traders will sell at all three signals, B, C and D, realizing losses until the third signal, at D, which actually signals a valid sale at the top of the move for the Swiss Francs. This emphasizes strongly that traders mustn't give too much credence to overbought signals from Percentage R in bull markets!

Heeding point E's buy signal—of course, this is after the market has topped out and is decidedly bearish—would make traders a profit if they had sold at points D, C and B. But it is a gross trading error to sit with such losses from trades initiated at points C and B, into new highs around May 1, 1987.

The indicator at F just nicks into the overbought area. If traders heed its signal, then the corresponding sell signal takes place at a top. G gives them an appropriate buy signal at the bottom, and H indicates another well-timed sale at a price top.

Although the signals are well-defined, the spread between the purchase at I and the sale at J is disappointing, though perhaps still profitable.

Figure 4-1   Trading September 1987 Swiss Franc Futures
Using Percentage Range

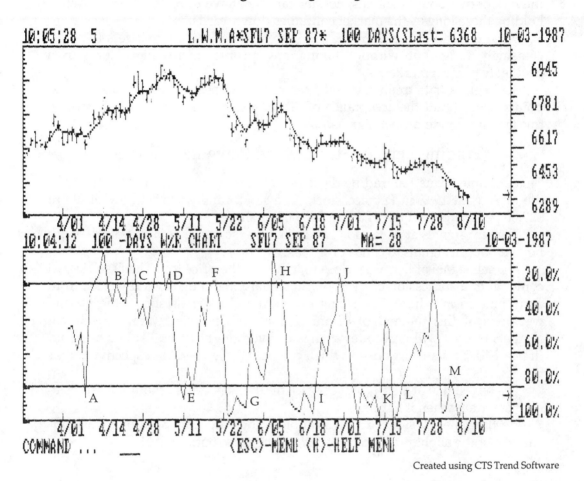

Created using CTS Trend Software

K, L and M all provide successive buy signals which do correspond to local price bottoms, but not only can traders not sell out their longs, based on the lack of overbought signals, neither can they have unrealized profits while holding these longs—the market continues downwards.

So, at the end of the chart the %R system is encouraging traders to go increasingly long, but without taking any profits; increasingly long in a decidedly bearish market.

An intermediate trend reversal from bullish to bearish takes place around points D or F, and the acceptance of %R buy signals has to be readjusted to this fact to provide proper signals.

Trading Pepsico Stock Using Percentage Range

This example spans 100 trading days, from the end of March, 1987 to the middle of August 1987 in Pepsico stock. The stock ranges from a low of about $29.00 per share to a high of about $40.00 per share.

The buy signals at A, B and C all indicate exact price bottom points—with no overbought signals to cause profit taking.

The sell signal at D is very close to, if not at, the price top. The D sell signal comes after a succession of overbought signals spanning several weeks, from early June to mid June. The string of overbought signals shows the glaring weakness of this method of technical analysis. In strongly one-directional markets traders will encounter strings of overbought (if bullish) or oversold (if bearish) %R values, none of which can be validly used as respective sell or buy signals.

The buy signal at F still catches price on the way down, though F seems to hit it squarely when it happens.

Heeding the sell signal at G would put traders in some position to take advantage of the slight profit to be had from the price bottom at H.

Figure 4-2 Trading Pepsico Stock Using Percentage Range

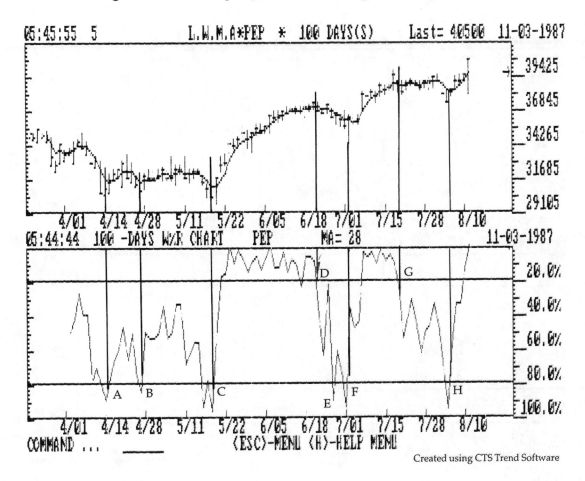

Created using CTS Trend Software

Figure 4-3   Trading S&P Cash Index Using Percentage Range

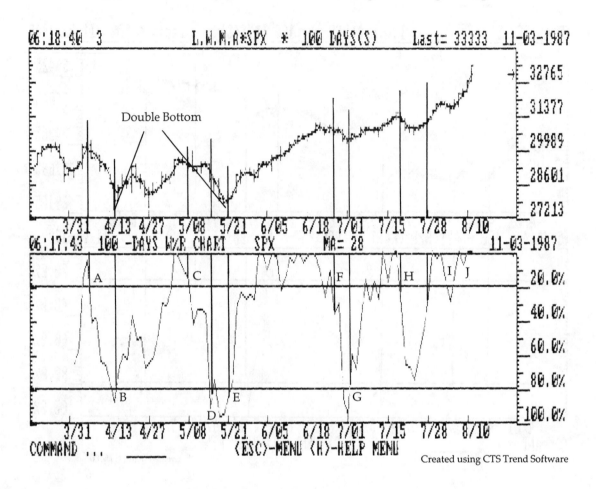

Created using CTS Trend Software

Trading S&P 500 Cash Index Using Percentage Range

The S&P 500 Cash Index trades for 100 days from the end of February 1987 to the early part of August 1987 are shown in this example. The price double bottoms around the 272.50 level and goes to new highs months later at the 328.00 level.

Points A and B provide a nicely-timed pair of sell-buy signals. The strict %R trader would have capitalized on this pair of valid signals.

C's sell signal catches the next top well, but the corresponding buy at D is timed just a bit early for optimum profits to be made. Additionally, point E goes lower than point D and would have served as a better oversold signal. The nuance to the professional trader would have been this: an imminent major bottom is near.

E's buy signal, however, coincides exactly with price bottom and is complemented nicely by F's accuracy in marking the sale at the top. The actual move from the point F sale is slight and shows a minimal profit. Perhaps the trader should view this as a bull trend up and ignore overbought signals? G points to a minor bottom. If traders purchase here, H will show them at exactly what point to cash in, for it points directly to the top.

Point I gives another sale indication, and there is a small top there—too small, however, to realize profits.

As the chart ends, it looks as if the indicator is just about to break above the 20% level again, providing another sale signal. Should this sale signal (overbought) be heeded? Since price has gone quite high at this point, traders might expect a fairly profitable play here. See other techniques in the book which forecasts price reversal points in time.

When to Apply Percentage Range

Traders who are fairly familiar with and confident of the market's general patterns and directions use %R carefully. As mentioned above, %R serves primarily to give overbought and oversold signals from a center of gravity point, depending on the market trend traders are currently in. The validity of these signals, of course, depends on traders being sure about whether they are in a trending market, bull or bear, or a trading market.

In grossly bullish markets, traders must skew their indicators to ignore the overbought indicators and act on the oversold indicators.

In bearish markets, they skew their indicators to ignore the oversold indicators and act on the overbought indicators.

Since correct application of the technique prescribes one action if there is a bull market and another if a bear market, traders must know whether they are in a bull or bear market in order to use it.

In trading markets with very tight ranges or during long periods of accumulation traders can use the indicator with a high degree of accuracy. However, potential profits are limited because of the shortness of the countermoves: trading markets just do not generate enough one-directional movement to offset costs of trading.

Since the method assumes signal points at the 95 and 10 %R levels, markets whose price pattern is relatively level can trigger this indicator. The range will be very narrow over any given period because the market is in a trading mode, and the 95 and 10 %R areas may only be a short period of time apart—that is, nothing very significant—and therefore the "signals" they give probably won't have much meaning.

If the market changes so rapidly that traders don't realize there has been a change in tendency they will, of course, be reading the wrong signals for %R indicators. They will be oversold in limit up situations and overbought in limit down situations. Using a little common sense here would allow their trading capital to last longer.

As mentioned before, %R was not really designed to stand on its own and, therefore, it is necessary to use other techniques in conjunction with it to do serious trading.

The main way to combine %R is with a trend following method, such as Moving Averages and Elliott Wave cycle analysis for determination of what wave the market might be in.

Where to Find Out More
About Williams' Percentage Range

Books and Periodicals

The main source of information about William's Percentage R is Williams' own book, *How I Made One Million Dollars Last Year Trading Commodities*, (Monterey, California: Conceptual Management, 1973, 2nd edition). This book also contains good general advice for the beginning trader.

Software to Run on the IBM Personal Computer

Chart Trader Plus—Interday charting package with the following: median lines, Fibonacci lines and spheres, recursion lines, percentage retracements, simple moving averages with bands, oscillators, relative strength index, on-balance volume, %R, cycle intervals, and parallel channels. Investor's Toolkit Ltd., Summit, IL 60501.

Computrac—Interday charting package has the following studies: moving averages, rates of change, oscillators, ratios and spread, RSI, stochastic, on-balance Volume, moving average convergence divergence, point-and-figure, etc. Chart zooming, trend lines and parallel channels, cycle analysis with Fourier analysis. Computrac, Inc., New Orleans, LA 70175.

CTS Trend—A software package which is a basic miniversion of Tradecenter. It creates many different types of studies, including realtime studies. CTS Trend, Newark, NJ 07974.

Quickplot—Interday charting package creates daily, weekly or monthly charts, with moving averages of all types, trend lines and parallel channels, oscillators and RSI. This is a basic program without advanced studies. Commodity Systems, Inc., Boca Raton, FL 33432.

Relevance III™—Interday charting package which creates above-average screen graphics and the finest hardcopy charts available using regular computer equipment. Performs many advanced type studies and has the only Elliott Wave ratio analysis program. Holt Investments, Nashville, TN 37238.

5

Lane's Stochastics
%K, %D and %D-Slow

Lane's Stochastics Technique at a Glance

Background and Philosophy of Lane's Stochastics

This method was developed by Dr. George Lane. Its involved and tedious calculations makes automation, such as a spreadsheet on a personal computer, almost indispensable. At the heart of the method lies the paradoxical assumption that one can predict the market's "random walk."

Principles of Lane's Stochastics

This method uses a total of four indicators, combining Relative Strength with Moving Average methods:
- %K, an unsmoothed RSI
- %D, a five-day moving average of %K
- %D-Slow, a longer-period moving average of %K
- A moving average of %D-Slow

How to Set Up and Maintain Lane's Stochastics

- Reserve two 0-100 scale bands on a price chart
- Calculate each of the four above indicators and plot them on the scale bands

How to Trade with Lane's Stochastics

Look for overbought/oversold indications and confirming crossovers of one indicator by another for respective sell/buy signals.

When to Apply Lane's Stochastics

Lane's Stochastics works well in trading market situations with no discernable trends and in accumulating or distributing markets. In bullish or bearish trending markets traders may use Lane's Stochastics with caution once the trend is established. Traders should use it with techniques which indicate market volatility and with techniques which indicate whether the market is distributing, accumulating, trending, etc.

Glossary for Lane's Stochastics

Crossover—When the faster of two indicators which are plotted together overtakes the slower. Crossovers usually give potential buy-sell indications.

Overbought/Oversold—Terms indicating that a trend has "topped" or "bottomed" out because price has reached an extreme relative to previous prices. In Lane's Stochastic technique, this is usually taken as being at the 80% + level for overbought and the 20% – level for oversold.

%D (Percentage D)—A five-day moving average of %K, usually plotted together with %K.

%D-Slow (Percentage D-Slow)—A moving average of %D, usually plotted together with a moving average of itself.

%K (Percentage K)—An unsmoothed Relative Strength Indicator of daily closing price, usually plotted with %D.

Background and Philosophy of Lane's Stochastics

Lane's Indicators and the Computer

George Lane has compiled a complex of indicators for the markets which combine the smoothing traits of moving averages with an overbought/oversold indicator, thus rolling trend indicators and overbought/oversold indicators into one.

It is safe to say that this complex of indicators would not have been devised if not for the electronic computer. Just as moving averages came from a technique born alongside the computer, so Lane's Stochastics is a product of the revolution in the use of personal computers in everyday economic analysis and business applications. To calculate the necessary indicators for this technique would be a tedious and perhaps error-fraught task if one were to do it by hand, and, indeed, it is hard to imagine someone even having the idea for something like Lane's Stochastics without a PC at hand and some software package such as Lotus *1-2-3* or *Symphony*, or *Excel* for the MacIntosh.

The Paradox of Predicting a Random Walk

"Stochastic" functions are those which are said to generate random results or which are intended to analyze random numerical output. Thus, the term would seem to indicate that these indicators are tools for analyzing the "random walk" of market phenomena. As such, this term points up a central dilemma of market prediction techniques: are market actions really random? If they are, why do such techniques assume implicitly that there is some sort of predictability here? Even more disturbingly, why do they actually seem to work many times?

Stochastics then represent one more link in the long chain of market techniques which try to have their cake and eat it too: here is a very basic assumption of randomness. This basic randomness, if it is true, means that whoever does correctly forecast imminent market moves will be more or less alone and very lucky: that is the cake.

The fact that there are techniques to try to anticipate this random behavior seems to show that there is somehow a way to predict chance events: this is eating the cake one has.

What is really basic here is the fact that no one knows for sure whether or not the market is random. The only certain thing is that no technique is based on the assumption that it is, even one calling itself "Stochastic."

Principles of Lane's Stochastics

A Combination of Relative Strength Indicators and Moving Averages

The trader who knows relative strength-type techniques (such as Wilder's Relative Strength Index, discussed in an earlier chapter) and who knows how to set up moving averages already knows the two basic conceptual building blocks behind the market stochastics. In brief, stochastics represent a first and second-order moving average of an *un-smoothed* relative strength indicator.

The First Indicator: %K, the Un-smoothed Relative Strength Index

"Un-smoothed" relative strength indicator (see chapter on Relative Strength Index) means one which has not had the smoothing factor which Wilder uses factored in. The biggest difference in appearance between an un-smoothed and a smoothed relative strength indicator is that, whereas the smoothed one will appear to trend smoothly back and forth between upper and lower limits, the un-smoothed one will jump up and down abruptly with frequent bottoming and topping out. This is because the un-smoothed indicator reflects the fact that today's price might in fact be the highest or the lowest in the range—a fairly common occurrence—and therefore the relative strength indicator, which is really a range indicator, will spend some considerable portion of time at the very top or the very bottom, respectively.

This un-smoothed relative strength indicator, which Lane calls "Percentage K," or %K for short, is therefore more sensitive to short-term fluctuations. When used with some other steadier derivative indicator on the same scale, it can yield a multitude of signals. A trader's interpretation will depend on the status of that other indicator. Percentage K, then, is simply an indicator of today's closing price in relation to the price range over a period chosen by the technician.

The Second Indicator: %D, the Five-day Moving Average of %K

This steadier derivative indicator, Percentage D, or %D, is a moving average of %K, usually chosen to be a five-day period. The Stochastic technician uses the position of the %D indicator to filter out a lot of the %K crossover signals, paying attention to them only when %D signals an overbought or oversold condition as verified by the market action pursuant to the indicator.

The Third Indicator: %D-Slow, a Moving Average of %D

Percentage D-Slow is a kind of second derivative of this dual indicator system. It is termed "slow" because, as a moving average, its period is longer, thus making it less responsive to daily price changes. Concretely, its period is the same as that chosen for the %K range period. Percentage D-Slow is, therefore, an even more conservative benchmark for overbought or oversold than the original %D, since it takes a stronger price move for the indicator to climb up into the overbought area or descend to oversold.

The Fourth Indicator: A Moving Average of %D-Slow

Moreover, %D-Slow is the more sprightly of the two indicators, for the second indicator used to signal possible buys and sells against %D-Slow is a moving average of it. This moving average is usually selected over a shorter period of time than the %D period in order to give it some pep and provide enough signals for the trader.

Summary

This is an extremely complex system with at least four different layers of indicators: the current price range, a normalized relative position within that range (%K), the moving average of that relative position (%D), the moving average of that moving average (%D-Slow), and finally another moving average based on top of that (%D-Slow Moving Average).

How to Set Up and Maintain Lane's Stochastics

Summary

1) Calculate %K
   a) Choose a period, **p**, and compute the range of closing prices over **p**
   b) Divide today's closing price by the range of **p**
   c) Multiply the result by 100 and plot on upper band
   d) Adjust range computation with each new day
   e) Then determine %K and plot as in b,c, and d

2) Calculate %D
   a) Average the first five %K's
   b) Subsequently, multiply previous %D by 4/5 and add 1/5 of today's %K. Plot with %K

3) Calculate %D-Slow
   a) For the first day, choose a period, **p**, and average first **p** %D's
   b) Subsequently, multiply previous day's %D-Slow by (p-1)/**p** and add (1/**p**) × today's %D. Plot on lower band

4) Calculate the Moving average of %D-Slow

    4) Calculate the Moving average of %D-Slow
        a) Choose a period, **p** (usually shorter than **p** for %D-Slow), and average first **p** %D-Slow's to get first day's moving average
        b) Subsequently, multiply previous day's moving average by (**p**-1)/**p** and add (1/**p**) × today's %D-Slow. Plot on lower band.

Setting Up the Chart

As with all indicators which are intended to provide trading signals, the best place to chart Lane's Stochastics is on the same chart where price information is kept.

Since Stochastics is based on daily closing prices, traders may want to show only closing prices on their charts.

The lower portion of the chart (below where prices normally penetrate) is the best place to set up Stochastic indicators. This area should be a horizontal band high enough to clearly distinguish four different sub-areas running horizontally across the price sheet within the main band. The bottom line of the main band will represent 0 and the top line, 100. Traders should draw one band across the middle equidistant between 0 and 100, and two other bands which should correspond to 20 and 80, respectively.

Setting Up %K

Choosing a Period

First, traders need to choose a period of days, **n**, over which to take the range for highest and lowest prices. Generally, the more volatile the market the shorter they will want to make their time period. Otherwise, their indicator will turn out to be too sluggish in relation to the market's movement and they will miss the plays. A good starting value for **n** would be five days, and if this appears to be giving a lot of false signals they can lengthen it, or if they seem to be getting cut out of the action, they may even try shortening it to four or three.

Performing Initial Computations

Once traders have decided on a value for **n**, the number of days in their range, they plot the closing prices for the first **n** days in the main part of their chart.

Then they find the high and the low closing prices over this period.

They compute the range of prices over **n** days by subtracting the low from the high.

Computing the First %K Value

- Take the current day's closing price
- Subtract the low price for the last **n** days from this price

- Divide this difference by the range period's which is already determined
- Multiply the result by 100 to obtain %K

Note that the first %K value will correspond to the nth day since the chart began. Before this nth day, no valid %K values are calculable.

Computing Subsequent %K Values

- "Slide" the attention period up each day, so that the past **n** days are always under consideration
- Make necessary changes in the periodic high and low values as the days covered by the period of length **n** progress
- Re-compute the range, if necessary, to reflect new highs and lows
- Now compute the day's %K as above

Setting Up %D

- After the first five %K's have been computed begin computing %D

Computing the First %D Value

- Average the first five days' %K values. This is the first %D. Note that at **n + 5** days into charting is when the first %D value can be computed

Computing Subseqent %D's

- On all subsequent days, the new day's %K gives the new %D value simply by multiplying the previous day's %D by 4/5, and then adding on 1/5 of today's %K. Note that this is standard moving average technique. See the section on moving averages for a justification of this method

Plotting %K and %D Together

Both %D and %K should be plotted on the reserved 0-100 scale on the chart, and crossover points and high and low points should be compared with the day's closing price.

Setting Up %D-Slow

Computing the First %D-Slow

- To set up the first %D-Slow, traders must wait **n** days after the first %D has been set up, or **n+5** days since the first %K was set up, or **n+n+5** days since they first began keeping their closing-price chart
- The first %D-Slow is found by averaging the first **n** %D values

Compute Subsequent %D-Slow Values

- Subsequent %D-Slow values are found by multiplying the previous day's %D Slow by $(n-1)/n$, then adding the result onto today's $\%D/n$

Setting Up the %D-Slow Moving Average

Choosing a Period for the %D-Slow Moving Average

- First, traders must select a period, p, for their new moving average. This is best determined on a shorter-term basis than the %D-Slow and %K n-value. For normal volatility, choose about three days to every five days of n. For greater-than-normal volatility, choose shorter periods (this makes the moving average more sensitive to the more intense activity of a highly volatile market), and for lesser-than-normal volatility, choose longer periods (otherwise, the low volatility combined with a fast-reacting moving average will give many false signals).

Computing the First Value for the %D-Slow Moving Average

- Once traders have chosen the number of days p for their moving average, they can compute the value for the first day. They must wait one period-length p of %D-Slow results, then take the average of the first p %D-Slow values for the first moving average figure. Note that at this point, they are now $n+n+5+p$ days into their project, and it is therefore this long that they have to wait before they can get the whole system set up.

Computing the Subsequent Values for the %D-Slow Moving Average

- Thereafter, they will find new moving averages by taking the previous day's moving average, multiplying by $(p-1)/p$, and adding the result to today's %D-Slow$/p$.

Tracking %D, %K, and %D-Slow

All of these indicators can and should be kept on the same chart, preferably at the bottom of the main chart where traders track prices, and on the same 0-100 scale below them. Besides the 100 and 0 lines, the 80-level and 20-level lines should be drawn as well, since, as in the next section shows, these are significant points for the use of these indicators.

Traders may want to keep the indicators for %K and %D on one part of the chart (the upper band) and the %D-Slow and its moving average on another (the lower band), since all those indicators in one small space can get rather confusing, especially with the erratic swings of %K, which tends to fill up the space with a web-like confusion of lines.

How to Trade with Lane's Stochastics

Overbought/Oversold Indications and Crossovers

The two basic points which the trader should look for in stochastic indicators are the aspects taken from the two elements contributing to stochastics: relative strength and moving averages. These major aspects are overbought/oversold indicators, which come from the relative strength side of the board, and crossover signals, which come from moving averages. Traders should first look for overbought/oversold indicators and, once these are signalled, should look for crossovers by the slower indicator of the faster one in these areas. These crossovers will give possible buy and sell signals.

Percentage D Above 80% or Below 20%, with Crossovers of %K

Generally, a %D above 80% shows an overbought condition in the market, and a %D below 20% shows an oversold condition. When the %D indicator is between these two benchmarks, it does not have that much to say.

Above 80%, watch for %D crossing over the %K indicator from below/behind. This means that the average has caught up with the daily indicator, which shows that the latest prices are outpacing earlier ones. In combination with the overbought indication, this makes it a very wise time to sell.

When %D dips below 20%, watch for %D crossing over %K from above/behind. The converse of what to expect from crossovers above 80% holds for crossovers below 20%. They show that the average has dipped down to the level of the daily indicator, indicating that recent prices are falling faster than earlier prices, which is a rate which would be hard to sustain for any long period of time, and so provides an unmistakable buy indicator upon the crossover to the upside when accompanied by a strong oversold signal.

Percentage D-Slow Above 80% and Below 20% with Crossovers of Its Moving Average

Percentage D-Slow and its moving average can be treated in much the same manner as %K and %D: watch for %D-Slow to top 80 or undercut 20 for overbought/oversold indications, respectively; and watch for crossovers by the moving average to get specific buy and sell indications.

Crossovers in the Middle Range...

The one difference between these last two indicators and the first two would be that, since they are more smoothed out, taking more effort to show bought and oversold conditions, the trader might also pay attention to crossovers within the 20% to 80% range.

A %D-Slow indicator and its moving average tend to give legitimate buy-sell signals with almost every crossover, and not just those above 80 or below 20. If this untidiness bothers some traders, they might want to shorten **n**, the period for the %K range and for the moving average represented by %D-Slow. This should make %D-Slow a little more jumpy and bring it into the overbought/oversold regions more often.

...But Not Necessarily in a Trading Market

In a trading market, that is one in which there is neither a strong bull or bear trend, weak buy and sell signals do not work out so well, if and when they appear. (More often than not there are valid overbought and oversold signals, demarcated by crossover above 80% and below the 20% boundaries.) This is due to simple market logic: since a bull market is dominated by upward price movement, even a weak oversold (i.e., one not in the 80% oversold area) will give legitimate countertrend direction. Conversely, since a bear market is dominated by the downtrend, even weak overbought signals should be heeded (that is, signals which are not necessarily below the 20% oversold area). It follows from this that, in a market dominated by neither a strong uptrend nor a strong downtrend, weaker signals will have little meaning. Traders should, therefore, ignore them and concentrate just on crossovers above 80% for sell signals and crossovers below 20% for buy signals.

How to Discern a Trading Market

On-Balance Volume, Elliott Wave, and Gann trading systems all give the trader indications of what kind of mode the market is in at the moment: either trading or trending. Using these methods together with stochastics will then allow traders to know whether or not to pay attention to the weak crossover signals (those between the 20% and 80% levels).

How to Trade with Lane's Stochastics

The examples and a trading technique for stochastics are ones provided and suggested by the programmers of *Relevance III* ™ software in their source materials (see reference at the end of this chapter). *Relevance III* ™ assumes that one uses %D-Slow as the main indicator (since it is the final refinement of the others) and takes its crossovers with its own moving average as signals.

There are four kinds of crossovers marked on each price chart:

- Upper crossovers which occurred when the indicator was in the overbought area (80%+). These are marked with a letter of the alphabet.

- Upper crossovers occurring when the indicator was not in the over-bought area. These are marked with a letter of the alphabet followed by a number.
- Lower crossovers occuring when the indicator was in the oversold area (less than 20%). These are marked by a number.
- Lower crossovers occurring when the indicator was not in the over-sold area. These are marked by a number followed by a letter of the alphabet.

These indicators give very accurate signals of local tops and bottoms in market price, but there are two problems which consistently come up when using this method:

- The first problem is in deciding which signals to follow of the four types listed above. The weak signal crossovers (between 20% and 80% levels) should not be heeded in a trading market, while weak buy signals can be used in a bull market and weak sell signals in a bear market.

- The second problem consists in being able to act quickly enough on signals to enter or close a position, since the indicators are based on daily closing prices and one must therefore trust that the next day's opening will still be in line with the previous day's closing. See the summary section for these examples below for a possible way to improve on this situation using Market Profile® or Liquidity Data Bank® methods.

For the sake of simplicity, the following examples assume a mechanical trading procedure that does not take the above possibilities into account. All action is based on a strict buy-sell signal from %D-Slow crossovers with its moving average. Closing prices will determine the signals, and traders act on the signals at the following day's opening.

Figure 5-1A   Trading December 1986 Swiss Franc Futures Using Lane's Stochastics

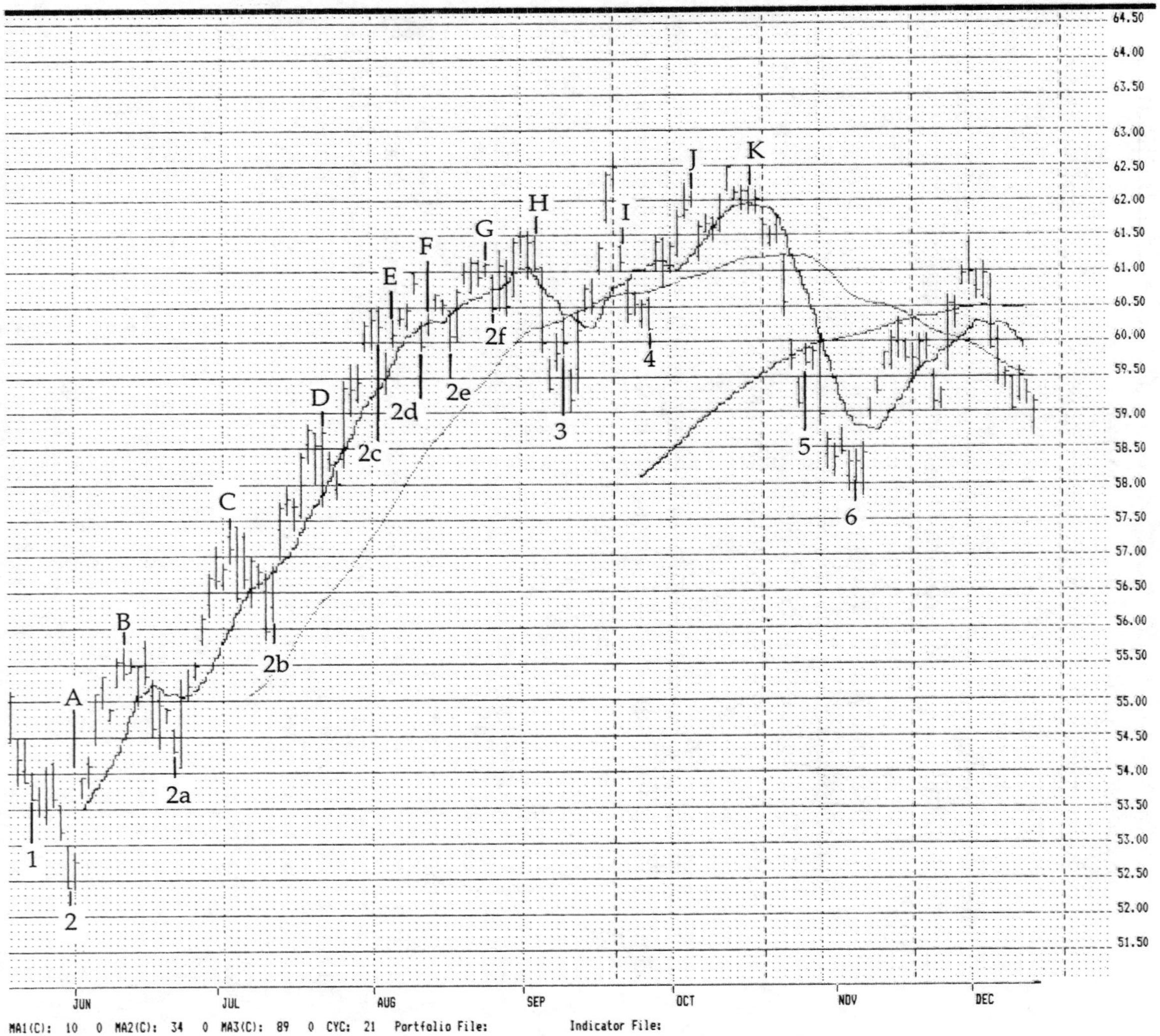

Created using Relevance III™ Software

Figure 5-1B

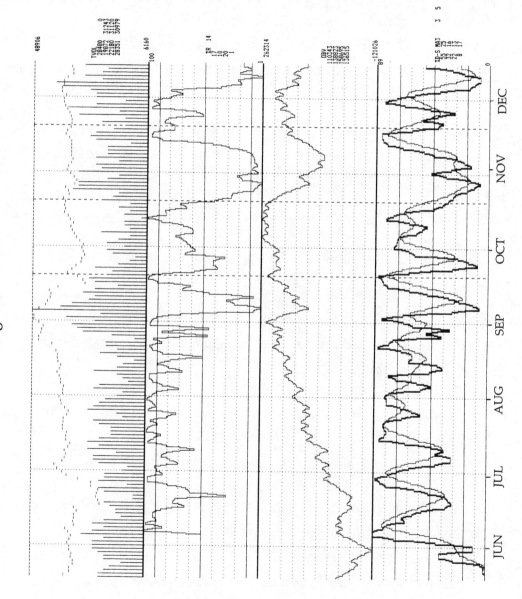

Trading December 1986 Swiss Franc Futures
Using Lane's Stochastics

The following example covers a 150 day period that the December 1986 Swiss Franc Futures contract traded from May 1986 to November 1986. The Swiss Franc moved from a low price of about $0.53 to $0.625.

Signal	1	Buy the next day's opening price at $0.5315.
Signal	A	Put in an order to sell the next day at any price above where the position was initiated. The price is not reached all day.
Signal	2	Ignore this signal because of the long position.
Signal	B	Put in an order to sell the next day, to complete the first trade successfully at $0.5555 for a net favorable spread of $0.024.
Signal	2a*	The next day's opening price is $0.5450; initiate another long position at that level.
Signal	C	Following the sell signal causes us to sell the next day at the opening price of $0.571, for a net profit on a spread of $0.026.
Signal	2b*	Buy the next day's opening at $0.5651.
Signal	D	Sell the next day's opening at $0.5855 for a net profit of $0.0204.
Signal	2c*	Buy the next day's opening at $0.6000.
Signal	E	Sell the next day at $0.606 for a net profit of $0.006.
Signal	2d*	Buy the next day at $0.603.
Signal	F	Sell (only two days later) at $0.605 for a net profit of $0.002.
Signal	2e*	Buy the next day at $0.603.
Signal	G	Sell the next day at $0.6065 for a profit of $0.0035.
Signal	2f*	Buy the next day at $0.6077.
Signal	H	Liquidate the next day at $0.6095 for a profit of $0.0018.
Signal	3	Buy the next day's opening at $0.6045.

*Asterisk indicates weak indications because the indicator never actually reached beyond the oversold or overbought paramaters.

Signal	K	With no open position at the moment (the last signal was also a sell), go short at the next day's opening price of $0.6200.
Signal	5	Close out the short, pessimistically, at the next day's opening price of $0.5985. This still leaves a profit of $0.0215.
Summary		By consistently missing the very top or the very bottom, since the indicator shows only at the day's very end that the extreme had been reached, traders still manage to consistently make profits by always trading the next day's opening. Notice that the indicators are able to give good signals all the way up in a trending market. As the price zig-zags upward, the indicator allows traders to take profits at each turn. Though not spectacular as individual trades, the traders are consistent. The traders made a total profit of $0.0995 points.

Figure 5-2A Trading January 1987 Soybeans Futures Using Lane's Stochastics

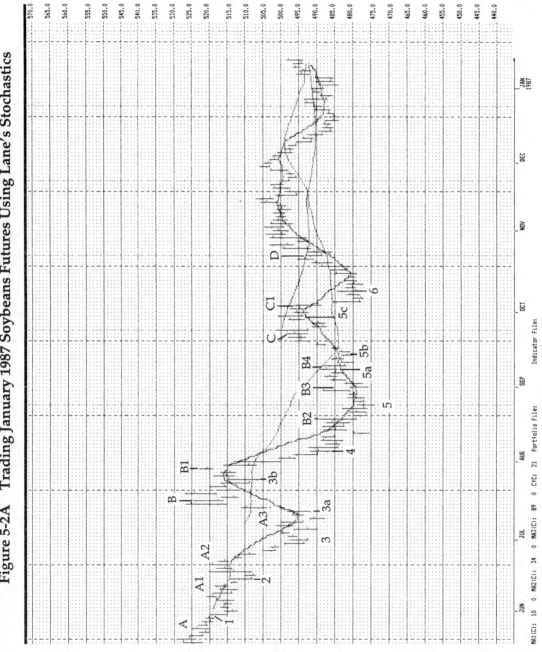

Figure 5-2B

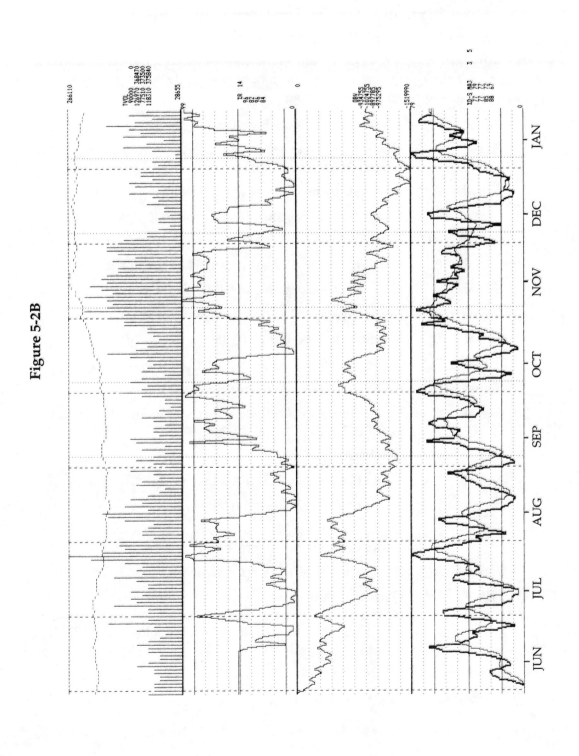

Trading January 1987 Soybean Futures
Using Lane's Stochastics

The following example is from the January 1987 Soybean futures contract from June 1987 to November 1987, in which soybeans traded from a low of $4.75 to a high of $5.30 in a span of 180 days.

Signal	A	Go short at the next day's opening of $5.21.
Signal	1	Close out the short at the next day's opening of $5.16, for a total profit of $0.05 points.
Signal	A1*	Go short the next day at $5.14.
Signal	2	Cover the short at $5.075 for a profit of $0.065.
Signal	A2*	Go short at $5.10.
Signal	3	Cover the short the next day at $4.95 for a profit of $0.15.
Signal	A3*	Go short at the opening of $4.97.
Signal	3a*	Cover the short at $4.965 for a profit of $0.005.
Signal	B	Go short the next day at $5.15.
Signal	3b*	Cover the short the next day at $5.15 for no profit.
Signal	B1*	Go short the next day's opening at $5.151.
Signal	4	Cover the short at the next day's opening of $4.90 for a profit of $0.251.
Signal	B2*	Go short at $4.795.
Signal	5	Cover the short at $4.77 for a profit of $0.015.
Signal	B3*	Go short again the next day at $4.795.
Signal	5a*	Do not cover the short today, because the price is never low enough to show a profit.
Signal	B4*	Because of the already open short position, do nothing.
Signal	5b*	Once again prices do not go low enough to make a profit on the open short position. If traders are on the wrong side of the market, they may take out a loss at $4.82, for a total net loss of $0.025.
Signal	C	Go short the next day at $4.95.

*Indicates weak overbought or oversold signals.

Signal   5c*   Cover the short at $4.94, for a profit of $0.01.

Signal   C1*   Go short again the next day at $4.80.

Signal   6   There is not enough drop in price to cover the short. The price has gapped down between the time of the short signal and the time to make the short sale, making it hard to work the technique for this particular play.

Signal   D   Take no action on the already short position.

Summary   At the end of this period, it looks like the traders have gotten on the wrong side of the market (i.e., they're short and the price is rising). Perhaps Signal D is a good place to take losses rather than to sit tight and hope for a miracle. If traders do so at the end of the day after signal D, they may just break even on this last trade.

               A non-trending market which zig-zags for a net change close to zero can wreak havoc on this system. It works much better in trending markets, as shown in the first half of this example or in the previous example. Also, a lot of the problem would disappear if traders were able to tell whether a trending market was upon them and then trade only the strong signals (above 80 and below 20).

Summary for Examples

The method is accurate for predicting market lows and highs. However, because it depends on closing price, it sometimes gives bad signals because the day after the buy or sell signal is given may gap upward or downward in the direction of the signal. Traders have two choices: either ignore these signals when the next day's opening is completely out of the signal day's range; or use a method like Market Profile® or Liquidity Data Bank® to try spotting a day's closing price. This would help them predict in advance when a day's closing price will give them a crossover signal and therefore allow them to position themselves properly during that very day rather than afterwards. Traders can also precalculate the theoretical crossovers and their derived overbought and oversold indicators by calculating for hypothetical closing prices which would create these situations. This is best done on a personal computer.

When to Apply Lane's Stochastics

Stochastics should work very well in markets with a relatively predictable cyclicity. In such a situation, the overbought/oversold indicators can be used as is without modifications. Traders can judiciously choose the period for the various moving averages so the moving averages will coincide with cyclic highs and lows.

Stochastics itself is a technique for dealing with cyclic markets—so it is almost begging the question if one only uses cyclic indicators when there are indications of cyclicity!

Traders can also cautiously use the indicators in trending markets or running markets. Caution is the word here because in trending markets there are overabundances of false signals in the direction of the trend. Traders may modify the parameters to be more sensitive to extreme and opposite conditions from the main trend. They should not heed these indicators in volatile or irregular markets. The overbought and oversold signals that such indicators might give are valid signals, but the direction of the countermoves are so minimal that for all practical purposes no profits can be accrued. Markets which are about to change direction from whatever it was before are also the most difficult markets to make profits from.

Stochastics are best used in combination with other techniques which give some general indication of market volatility and those which tell what mode the market is in. These other indicators should then tell traders, in accord with what has been said in the preceding two sections, whether or not to heed signals from Stochastics. As the Examples section shows, a non-trending or trading market does not fit well with this technique.

The examples section also shows that this method can sometimes work to a trader's disadvantage in a more volatile market, since he or she depends on closing price for signals, and sometimes a day's closing price will be nowhere in the range of the next day's price movement. There is a suggestion of how to deal with this problem in the summary paragraphs of the "Trading Examples" section above. It is only with such things in mind that one can fairly judge what this complex of indicators is saying.

112

Where to Find Out More About Lane's Stochastics

George, Lane, Ph.D., Investment Educators, P.O. Box 2354, Des Plaines, Illinois 60018. Dr. Lane is one the originators of the Lane's Stochastics complex of indicators.

Software to Run on the IBM Personal Computer

Chart Trader Plus—Interday charting package with the following: median lines, Fibonacci lines and spheres, recursion lines, percentage retracements, simple moving averages with bands, oscillators, relative strength index, on-balance volume, %R, cycle intervals, and parallel channels. Investor's Toolkit Ltd., Summit, IL, 60501.

Computrac—Interday charting package has the following studies: moving averages, rates of change, oscillators, ratios and spread, RSI, stochastics, on-balance volume, moving average convergence divergence, point-and-figure, etc. Chart zooming, trend lines and parallrel channels, cycle analysis with Fournier analysis. Computrac, Inc., New Orleans, LA 70175.

CTS Trend—A software package which is a basic miniversion of Tradecenter. It creates many different types of studies, including realtime studies. CTS Trend, Newark, NJ 07974.

MetaStock—Interday charting package has graphics, but primitive hardcopy features. Many moving averages, trading bands, parallel channels, linear-regression lines, cycle-interval lines, on-balance volume, RSI, positive/negative volume and relative-performance ratios. Computer Asset Management, Salt Lake City, UT 84126.

Relevance III™—Interday charting package which creates above average screen graphics and the finest hardcopy chart available using regular computer equipment. Performs many advanced type studies and has the only available Elliott Wave ratio analysis program. Holt Investments, Nashville, TN 37238.

6

Oscillators
Overbought and Oversold Reversal Indicators

Oscillators at a Glance

Background and Philosophy of Oscillators

Although older than moving averages, the oscillator technique has many similarities to moving average techniques. Instead of looking at price breakouts from average lines, it examines overbought/oversold conditions from a price viewpoint.

Principles of Oscillators

An oscillator gives a measure of how much momentum is left in a price swing, momentum being the measure of how much the price has changed over a fixed period of time. This momentum is usually expressed as a number between -1 and 1, and is the result of the the price change over the chosen time period divided by the maximum possible price swing over a period of that length. Usually, a number above .75 or below -.75 is considered to signal conditions of "overbought" (if positive) or "oversold" (if negative), because the price has gone to almost its full possible extent.

How to Set Up and Maintain Oscillators

1) Determine the period length for measuring momentum
2) Set up a horizontal strip below the price section of the price chart with a vertical scale from -1 to 1
3) When the number of days in the period have passed, subtract the first day's price from today's price and divide the result by the maximum possible price move in one day
4) Record the result on the -1 to 1 scale
5) For each successive day, subtract the price of one period ago from the day's price and repeat the computation and graph entry

How to Trade with Oscillators

The strategy is to sell when overbought and buy when oversold. Traders may make the system less sensitive by lagging the signal behind penetration of the overbought/oversold areas, or waiting until the indicator has just passed out of these areas before taking action.

When to Apply Oscillators

Traders cannot use this technique by itself. It is best for traders to use it in highly volatile markets with large price swings and fast turnarounds, as long as price can be expected to stay within some identifiable range. They should not use it when maximum price range cannot be clearly identified. It can be used carefully in trending markets, as the frequency of signals will be skewed in the direction of the main trend. Oscillators are a good check on volume-based techniques and other time cycle techniques.

Glossary for Oscillators

Acceleration—A measure of the change in velocity.

Mid-line—The horizontal line on an oscillator chart which marks the division between negative and positive momentum.

Momentum—Velocity of price change over the momentum period.

Momentum Index—A running chart of daily momentum fluctuations on a given momentum period. The values of the chart are normalized so that they range between -1 and 1.

Momentum Period—A set period over which the technician figures each day's momentum.

Overbought—The condition at the top of a market, when demand has begun to give ground to supply and positive momentum begins to slack. Thought to signal an imminent selloff.

Oversold—The condition at the bottom of a price drop, when supply has begun to give ground to demand and negative momentum begins to let up. Thought to signal an imminent rally to the upside.

Oscillator—A momentum index which is used to predict overbought/oversold conditions in the market.

Velocity—The amount by which price changes over time.

Background and Philosophy of Oscillators

Those already familiar with moving averages know that one problem with them is their inability to predict reversals. True, the moving average gives traders some possibility of knowing when to react to a price move based on the recent history of the price, but it still leaves traders in the dark as to whether a price which breaks the moving average is really a reversal, a previous main trend or just another false breakout.

Some of the additional modifications of the moving average which might help to reassure traders that a price move is really a reversal before they commit their position to that particular move are: use of bands with upper and lower limits, or two moving averages with different periods (see moving averages chapter). Even so, traders are still depending on purely positional information (the sum of discrete past positions) to give them information about time and direction.

In order to make the moving average more useful, traders need some indicator inherent in the motion of the prices which will tell them how much movement is really left in a certain direction before a definitive reversal: that is, how close a rally or selloff is to being "played out" and how much upward or downward force a tendency still has left in it. This would then definitely help traders to decide whether or not something which crosses the moving average line is a valid signal or just a false breakout.

Although the oscillator techniques might seem to logically follow moving averages, they were actually developed first, before World War II. In general, an oscillator is easier to calculate and so perhaps the appearance of oscillator techniques was not as dependent on the computer.

Oscillator techniques may either be used on their own or in conjunction with more "positional" techniques such as moving averages in order to predict just when a trend might be about to reverse.

If moving averages are based on the idea of an object (originally, an airplane, but for traders, the price) which is definitely going somewhere but whose goal is masked by its individual motions, then oscillators are based on the idea of a trajectory. A projectile which follows a path known as a trajectory maintains a constant forward motion, but climbs more rapidly when it first leaves the ground, slowing gradually until it reaches the peak of the trajectory, at which time it literally stops movement and reverses direction and then increases in speed until it reaches the ground again.

Since a projectile only goes up and comes down once, traders might try, instead, to think of a roller coaster. A roller coaster is at its slowest in relation to up-down motion either when it is at the top of a crest or at the bottom of a trough. It is changing its motion from up-down to down-up, or vice versa. Once it leaves the top (or bottom), it picks up speed until it is about half-way up (or down) the slope. For the rest of its climb (or descent) it gradually slows down until it reaches the top or bottom, and then the whole process is repeated again, but in the opposite direction.

The cycle of price follows the same pattern as a roller coaster ride: once prices have hit bottom a recovery begins and gradually picks up momentum as more investors and speculators get on the bandwagon. As the prices rise more and more some investors get nervous and others begin to decide that it is time to take profits or that, after all, the trend cannot go on for ever, and they begin to sell.

The rise begins to slow, and finally it "tops out," perhaps remaining relatively stationary for a day or two or perhaps abruptly beginning its downward slide. The falling curve steepens as those who are still long in the market come to their senses and begin trying to liquidate their positions quickly. Eventually, the price gets low enough that people who have stayed with the position all this time see no point in unloading now and those who got out earlier now start to buy the bottom. The downslide slows, stops, then starts to take on upward momentum again, and the cycle repeats itself.

Oscillators are techniques for trying to predict how fast the market is moving with the idea that this velocity, like the roller coaster example, will be related to how close the immediate trend is to being played out. If traders know this, then they are forewarned and can adjust their positions accordingly. If the market is moving rapidly, then it is still in the middle of a trend. If it is slowing down, then it is approaching a reversal point; a reversal of the trend.

Thus, oscillators and moving averages tend to complement each other. The latter pays attention to where price is and where price is coming from but gives few clues as to what specific changes mean or when direction will really be changed. Oscillators, on the other hand, may tell little about specific location of prices on a chart or how these locations tie together but they will tell when to expect a probable change in direction.

Principles of Oscillators

Overbought/Oversold

Since oscillators basically look at market momentum, two common concepts used by those who employ oscillators are overbought and oversold. These two terms refer to the condition encountered when market momentum is slowing down near the top or bottom, respectively, and the trend is ready for a reversal. Another signal that may come before this, and which an oscillator can also give traders, is an excessive velocity. Such activity cannot last, and in all probability it signals that an overbought or oversold situation is imminent.

Velocity/Acceleration

In order to use an oscillator, the first step is to construct and use a momentum index. By using several physics concepts, those of velocity and acceleration, traders can refine their treatment of oscillators. Velocity is, of course the speed with which something moves, in this case price, and it is used here to mean the number of points per period which a price indicator changes (10-2/3 points in two days means a velocity of 5-1/3 points a day). Acceleration is the rate at which the velocity changes, a sort of *velocity* of velocity. Thus, if price increased four points one day and eight points the next day, acceleration would be four points per day per day. (Recall that gravitational acceleration is "32 feet per second per second", that is, that a speed of 32 feet per second is added on to the original speed every second).

Acceleration can be negative, even though velocity is positive. For instance, price could increase four points in one day and two points the next day. Acceleration would then be -2 points per day per day; that is, price would be decelerating and might be approaching a complete standstill and thus an imminent turnaround. Anyone who is familiar with the calculus will recognize these as first and second derivatives of an equation of motion.

Of course, the price is not determined by an equation (if it were, traders would need only a simple computer program to do all their trading for them!) It is beyond the scope of this chapter to discuss how one might go about fitting price trends into equations of motion and thus calculating first and second derivatives. However, to find out more about this topic, readers might want to consult Kaufman (1978, pp. 95-99) (see this chapter's section on Where to Find Out More).

Momentum Index

Momentum, as it is used here, is simply the velocity of price change over a given time period. Traders customarily refer to several price momenta, each relating to the number of days over which they figure the change. A three-day momentum would simply be today's price less the price three days ago. Momentum might be zero after a given period if the prices of today and the first day of the momentum period were the same. However, there would very possibly be some internal momentum within that period. If, for example, price were 62 on day 1 and 62 on day 10, there would be 0 momentum for the ten days. However, price might have gone up and come back down over those ten days, so that the intermediate days would show some momentum value among themselves.

A momentum index is usually charted separately from price, unlike moving averages. To determine the format of the chart (what the highest and lowest values and the mid-line should be), we must first determine the momentum period, then determine what the maximum possible change is over that period.

How to Set Up And Maintain Oscillators

Determining the Momentum Period

As with moving averages, traders do not want to choose a period which will "mask" the phenomena they are interested in. Perhaps the best way to determine what the oscillation period should be is to determine the approximate length of a cycle of the scale the traders are interested in. The best period for a given trader and market, however, should be found by testing through trial and error.

In general, a shorter period will give a chart with more overbought or oversold signals, whereas a longer period will give a smoother chart with less erratic movement and therefore less sensitivity as well.

Setting Up the Momentum Chart

The oscillator itself should oscillate between values of +1 and -1. So, the highest and lowest possible price levels must be scaled down so that they are represented by these values. Thus, if the greatest possible move in one day is $0.33 and the oscillator period is ten days then the greatest possible ten-day change would be 10 x $0.33 or $3.30. Traders, therefore, set up a chart whose top is +1 (corresponding to +$3.30) and whose bottom is -1 (corresponding to a negative value of $3.30). Before they enter any movement on the chart they will first divide it by $3.30. If they find a rise of $1.10 between ten days ago and today, they would mark the position +0.33 on the chart under the heading for today's date (1.10/3.30 = 0.33). If there was a fall in price of $1.65 then they would have marked -0.50 on the chart (-1.65/3.30 = -0.5).

Notice that the software package for the trading examples which are presented later in this chapter does not refine the oscillator in this way, but simply presents the unnormalized scale.

To make the chart useful, traders must define what they mean by "overbought" and "oversold" for this market. That is, when does the momentum change start to tell them that the market is being prepared for a turnaround?

This will be based on the traders' experiences, and on trial and error. Once they have determined what momentum level signals overextension of the market, they mark these levels on the chart. Thus, if .75 and -.75 seemed like reasonable overextension signals, they would draw two lines across the chart at these respective levels. These are the lines they will use for signals in their trading method.

Other Ways to Track Oscillators

This is essentially the technique traders use for determining and tracking oscillators. They often track moving averages in conjunction with oscillators. However, oscillators are not tracked on the same chart as prices, whereas moving averages are, since moving averages are on the same scale as prices but oscillators use a -1 to +1 scale. One way to keep them together is not to track the oscillator as such, but to track simply the momentum. This would then be just the price change over the selected period, without adjusting it to the oscillator scale.

Another variation on the oscillator would be to smooth it out, using techniques similar to those used for moving averages. This will have the effect, as it does with moving averages, of keeping the oscillator from reacting oversensitively to insignificant changes in market momentum. However, it may then be too insensitive to ever swing into the overbought/oversold zones. In order to remedy this, traders must readjust the limits of these regions on the chart in toward the zero- or base-line so that the smoothed-out oscillator will still intersect them.

How to Trade With Oscillators

Basic Rules for Using an Oscillator

The upper bound (overbought indicator) can be used in various ways to signal the trader to go short. The different ways one can use this boundary basically have to do with timing: enter the position as soon as the overbought indicator is broken to the downside, or a given number of days after it has stayed oversold, or when the oscillator crosses it going back down. These second two types of strategies are, of course, to insure less sensitivity to false signals.

The lower bound (oversold indicator) can then be used in an inverse fashion to the upper bound to signal the trader to take a long position when it crosses the median line to the upside.

One way to interpret the oscillator chart is to to watch for the oscillator to move from one half of the range to the other half, crossing the 0 mid-line. Once the crossover is made, then it is considered to be signalling overbought if in upper half and oversold in the lower half. Traders could initiate trades at this point, but very carefully.

Figure 6 -1 Trading Motorola Stock Using Oscillators

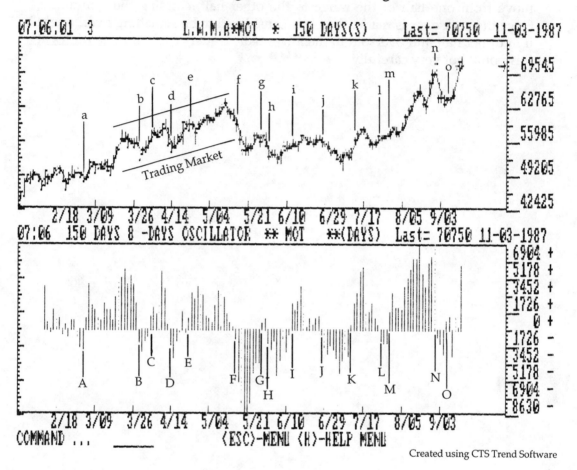

Created using CTS Trend Software

Trading Motorola Stock Using Oscillators

The oscillator indicators for this chart are for the 150 trading-day period from mid-January 1987 through the end of September. The particular software package used to print this indicator does not use a normalized -1 to +1 scale, but the crucial 80% overbought and 20% oversold ranges are clearly distinguishable (emphasized with horizontal lines).

There are two important areas to watch in oscillators: the zero line in the middle and the two extreme overbought and oversold areas at the top and bottom.

At point A, Motorola is trading at about $49.00 around February 1987. This is a signal to buy Motorola. The oscillator has just started moving from below the zero line to above it. Buying at $49.00 insures a profit until the first sell point, B, when the oscillator goes below the zero line. This corresponds with a price of about $52.00. However, from point A to B there is no overbought signal, which would have occurred had the oscillator reached near the 1.00 level; this would have helped traders to start looking out for signs of weakness and they would have unloaded the stock.

From points B to E traders encounter an after-the-fact trading market. It is trending upwards, but is still a trading market bound by upper ranges and lower ranges, both oscillating into higher and higher prices. Here, the overbought and oversold oscillators would have been ignored by professional traders. Profits accrued by following the signals would have been minimal at best.

Once out of this gentle upsloping trading market, traders encounter an oversold signal at F. Going long at this level shows losses as the entry price of $59.00 gives way to selloff lows to about the $50.00 level. At point G, traders get their overbought signal and sell out their long, at $56.00. Selling out at the bottom of the swing, $50.00, or the overbought signal at $56.00 would have meant losses either way.

Since the start of this example, there have been no overbought or oversold signals generated by movement of the indicator touching 1.00 or touching –1.00 (80% oversold and 20% overbought). All signals to date have been generated by the crossing of the 0 mid-line.

At point G traders get a diminuitive overbought signal and go short, on the way down. At point H they get a crossover of the 0 line and get an oversold signal. They cover their short or at least go long; hardly worth the effort of the trade.

Point I indicates overbought followed by point J oversold, a sale followed by a buy. Traders scratch another series of trades which offer no profits, but commission costs and market risk.

Point K shows overbought, but the price goes higher. If the traders had gone short at point K, they would have an oversold signal at L, causing them to buy their short in . . . at higher prices or at least for a scratch. Meanwhile, the price of the stock had moved from a low of $49.00 to a high of $57.00.

The example continues while the market is in a runaway stage to the upside. Here traders get an 80% or better overbought oscillator (touching +1.00 on the normalized scale). At period L they have an oversold signal and go long. At M, they get an oversold signal—should they go short? Yes! They had used this signal before as a sell signal and managed to scratch all their trades, so why shouldn't they use it now? Their equity gets a bit damaged: the stock runs from about $57.00 level at M to a high of $70.00 at N. In between M and N, they never get an oversold signal to cover their short. There is no scratch in this series of trades, but losses.

Where can traders use this indicator? The oscillator actually touches +1.00, or over 95% around the end of August 1987. This is a definite oscillator sell signal. The price is at the $70.00 level. This is one of only two extreme signals in 150 days (The oversold signal between periods F and G isn't discussed because it didn't make any money, but traders need to pay attention to this one because it could have lost them a lot of money) and it comes right at the top! Unfortunately, the previous crossover of the 0 line indicates an oversold condition at point M, and they just had to go short. What timing! One right signal out of 14 signals is a terrible ratio on which to base one's trading career.

In retrospect, this example shows really bad signals. The losses are not extreme and are mostly scratches. Since this is the case, traders can't use this oscillator as a fade indicator, by executing the signals exactly the opposite way they were intended to be used, because they would only get back to a scratch situation.

Trading New York Averages Index Using Oscillators

In practice, oscillators don't work by themselves. The following example shows just how badly traders might do if they relied only on such indicators.

This chart covers 150 trading days, or a little more than half a year. The New York Averages Index goes from a low of about 133.00 to a high of 170.00. Notice on the bottom oscillator chart that there are only two penetrations of the 80% and 20% momentum areas; one apiece.

For this example, ignore the crossovers of the 0 line from either side of overbought or oversold. By carefully analyzing the results of using the first crossovers of the 0 line from the opposite side as indications of extremes, one can observe that profitable trades were not to be found. Instead, filter out the signals more stringently. Use only 80% overboughts and 20% oversold.

Figure 6-2 Trading the New York Averages Index Using Oscillators

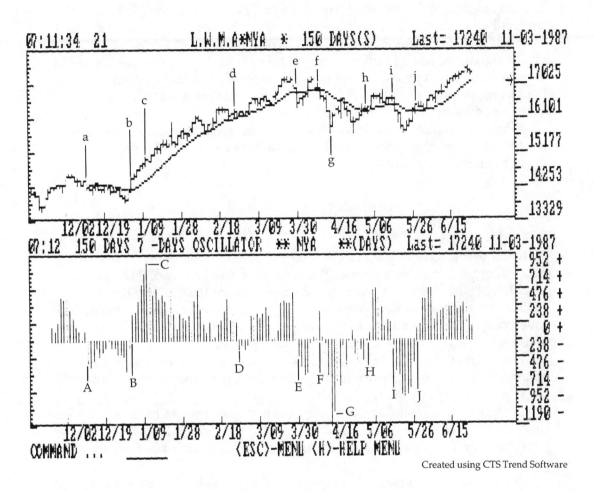

Created using CTS Trend Software

Two Signals

The first signal, at C, is saying "overbought," i.e., a sell signal. It is true that price is higher than what it had been recently (this is essentially what an oscillator can measure). Unfortunately, for anyone going short at this point based on the signal, the strong bull market just takes price higher for many months. The oscillator gives no clue about what to do. The price moves from the overbought signal price of 150.00 all the way up to 170.00, without ever generating a similar counterpart oversold signal.

When the oscillator finally does give an "oversold" indication (G), it is at least in a local price valley—but still far above the original sell point.

In brief, this is a disaster.

Trading September 1987 Swiss Franc Futures Using Oscillators

As in the previous example, the chart covers 150 days and gives only two signals throughout the entire period. The price goes from a low of $0.62 per franc to a high of $0.70 back to a low of $0.62 from January 1987 to July 1987.

Traders lost very little money applying oscillators to the Swiss Franc. The "overbought" indicator at A occurs when price is relatively high. The traders take a short position at $0.66, on the way up to $0.68.

The market then backs away to $0.64, and a valid oversold signal is generated at point B, or a price of $0.64. There is a depression low on the oscillator, but it barely reaches the 20% oversold level.

Traders now go long, at $0.64, after covering their short for a profit. This time, the market moves up to $0.70 around the previous B level without ever generating an overbought signal for them to sell out their position and take profits.

The second "overbought" indicator tells them to sell at around price point B. The signal is not quite what they would have wanted because it does not touch the 80% overbought line, but traders give themselves a bit of a leeway here—otherwise this technique won't generate good signals. This is a nice trade. Traders go long at $0.64 and now have an overbought signal at point C to unload it. They sell at $0.70 and take a nice-sized profit signal at $0.70.

At D they receive a strong oversold signal—do they buy? Yes, they adhere to the signals. And they do generate slight profits. Point E misses being an absolute oversold condition (therefore, they should have bought) by just a bit, but the market went down after that signal.

In conclusion, this technique needs to be used carefully because the valid signals generated are few and far between.

Figure 6-3   Trading September 1987 Swiss Franc Futures Using Oscillators

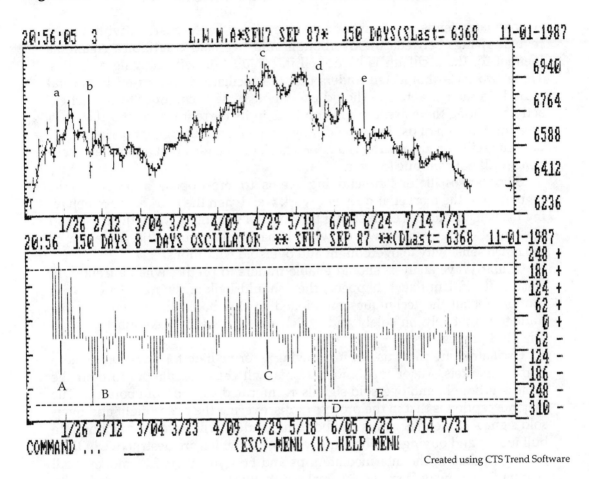

Created using CTS Trend Software

When to Apply Oscillators

An oscillator tends to assume a certain cyclicity in the market, with almost regular swings between the overbought and oversold conditions. Again, as mentioned, the oscillator is used well in conjunction with moving averages. These two facts should tell traders that the oscillator is best used in neutral periods in the market. One should use Elliott Wave techniques to predict exactly how long the market might continue in its current trend, and then rely on a combination of oscillators and moving averages during that period.

An oscillator, in general, is a good check on the idea that a long-term tendency will not continue forever.

Since an oscillator's functioning seems to presuppose a certain cyclic regularity in the market, it does not work well when the market is not behaving in such a fashion, i.e., in strong bear or bull situations when the trend still has lots of energy left. However, when behavior is more erratic, there can be too much sensitivity to overbought and oversold conditions.

Elliott Wave analysis should enable traders to predict when a trend will exhaust itself. Until such happens, they should look at their oscillators with caution. Of all the techniques mentioned in this book this is the one that traders cannot rely on solely and which must be used in conjunction with other techniques.

Oscillators are most useful in showing intermediate tops and bottoms in trading markets. Major tops and bottoms will cause oscillators to emit the same overbought and oversold signals as intermediate tops and bottoms. The major exception is that in the process of discovering the overbought and oversold signals at the major tops and bottoms, traders will have been selling into bull moves and buying into bear moves, both of which are destructive to their trading capital. In the intermediate tops and bottoms, there is a move, small as it might be, away from the reversal point and they can capitalize on it with a reduced level of risk.

Oscillators can be used in trading markets or cautiously used in trending markets with reversal indicators which use time cycles or volume analysis. If traders use derivative techniques to signal overbought and oversold areas which are solely reliant on price sensitive data, they would be getting oversold and overbought values at the same time that their oscillators would most likely signal their overbought and oversold values. Traders must use other indicators that do not rely on price sensitive data.

Where to Find Out More About Oscillators

Books and Periodicals

Indicator Digest. Palisades Park, New Jersey 07650. Publishes frequent studies with ideas for the use of oscillators.

Floss, Carl W. *Market Rhythm.* Detroit, Michigan: Investors Publishing Company, 1965.

Gartley, H.M. *Profits in the Stock Market.* New York. 1935. Still probably the most comprehensive handbook on oscillators ever published.

Hurst, J.M. *The Profit Magic of Stock Transaction Timing,* Englewood Cliffs, New Jersey: Prentice-Hall, 1970. Presents a system combining moving averages and oscillators in a cyclic analysis of market activity.

Waters, James J. and Larry Williams. "Measuring Market Momentum." *Commodities Magazine.* October 1972. An exposition of the two authors' own oscillator system, known as the A/D (Accumulation/Distribution) Oscillator.

Software to Run on the IBM Personal Computer

Chart Trader Plus—Interday charting package with the following: median lines, Fibonacci lines and spheres, recursion lines, percentage retracements, simple moving averages with bands, oscillators, relative strength index, on-balance volume, %R, cycle intervals, and parallel channels. Investor's Toolkit Ltd., Summit, IL 60501.

Computrac—Interday charting package has the following studies: moving averages, rates of change, oscillators, ratios and spread, RSI, stochastics, on-balance volume, moving average convergence divergence, point-and-figure, etc. Chart zooming, trend lines and parallel channels, cycle analysis with Fourier analysis. Computrac, Inc., New Orleans, LA 70175.

CTS Trend—A software package which is a basic miniversion of Tradecenter, It creates many different types of studies, including realtime studies. CTS Trend, Newark, NJ 07774.

Dow Jones Market Analyzer Plus—Interday charting with the following: moving averages, trading bands, volume oscillators, support/resistance lines, RSI, trend and parallel lines, speed lines, point-and-figure charts, split screen. Dow Jones Software, Princeton, NJ 08540.

Quickplot—Interday charting package creates daily, weekly or monthly charts, with moving averages of all types, trend lines and parallel channels, oscillators, and RSI. This is a basic program without advanced studies. Commodity Systems, Inc., Boca Raton, FL 33432.

Relevance III™—Interday charting package which creates above-average screen graphics and the finest hardcopy chart available using regular computer equipment. Performs many advanced type studies and has the only available Elliott Wave ratio analysis program. Holt Investments, Nashville, TN 37238.

Telescan Analyzer—A front-end interday charting package which accesses only their own database of 7000 stocks and 150 market indices. Data retrieval cost: 50 cents peak hours and 25 cents off peak access. Telescan, Inc., Houston, TX 77042.

7

Point-and-Figure
Pure Abstraction
of Price Moves

Point-and-Figure Technique at a Glance

Background and Philosophy of Point-and-Figure Technique

This technique was used at the beginning of the modern trading era and is perhaps the most purely price-based of all trading methods, since there is nothing else it takes into account.

Principles of Point-and-Figure

Point-and-figure charts track price moves of a given size, known as a box size. Box size can vary with market volatility and price level, as well as with the trader's timeframe. Upward price moves are tracked by a series of X's, downward moves with O's. Reversals between series of X's and O's happen when price has gone in a new direction for a given number of boxes (known as the reveral criterion), and they signal important market events.

How to Set Up and Maintain Point-and-Figure Operation

1) Determine box size and mark a piece of graph paper with the entire price range for the issue being followed.
2) Determine number of boxes in the reversal criterion.
3) When the issue has moved the size of one reversal criterion *or more,* mark X's if rising, or O's if falling, on the graph in the appropriate place.
4) As long as box moves continue in the same direction, keep putting the same symbol below (if falling) or above (if rising) previous ones in a lengthening vertical line.
5) When the direction of box moves changes, begin the same procedure with the opposite symbol one box *to the right* of the charted vertical line.

How to Trade with Point-and-Figure

Point-and-figure uses many of the same basic patterns as conventional bar charting methods, as well as sudden breakouts known as catapults. Traders can use the same rules for interpretation of breakouts as they use with basic bar chart analysis. Measurement rules apply as well, most notably the "three times retracement," which predicts that the extent of a new price direction after a major bottom will be three times the length of the previous opposite trend. Stops and buy orders are placed on point-and-figure charts in the same way as on bar charts.

When to Apply Point-and-Figure

Traders should use point-and-figure in markets not dominated by volume trading with a price range which is fairly constant and well-defined when they wish to filter out time and observe straightforward wave formations. It is also helpful in markets with cyclicity and in markets with erratic and wide price ranges. Traders should not use point-and-figure in markets where volume indicators are crucial to forecasting reliability. Supplement point-and-figure with volume-based techniques, and use it as a confirmation tool to supplement cycle pattern-recognition patterns.

Glossary for the Point-and-Figure Technique

Box—The area of a point-and-figure chart into which the technician places one X or O, representing a given amount of price increase or decrease.

Box Size—The amount of price increase or decrease represented by a box on a point-and-figure chart.

Catapult—A pattern found on a point-and-figure chart when a string of X's or O's breaks far above or below the previous price range.

O—The mark which the technician puts into a box on a point and figure chart when price decreases by one box size. The mark goes below the previous mark if that mark was an O, or to the right of the previous mark if it was an X.

X—The mark which the technician puts into a box on a point-and-figure chart when price increases by one box size. The mark goes above the previous mark if that mark was an X, or to the right of the previous mark if it was an O.

Background and Philosophy
of Point-and-Figure Technique

Although its cousin, the bar chart, is more well known, the Point-and-Figure chart dates back to the inception of modern market analysis: the first published account of their use dates from before the turn of the century.

Point-and-figure charting isolates just one aspect of market activity: price change, and its imminent reversal. No reference is made to time factors or to volume of trading. A very weak volume analysis can be applied to point-and-figure technique: the greater the congestion in a point-and-figure chart, the greater the volume activity. How a trader can make good use of this fact is another matter.

It would be wrong to suppose that the pioneering technicians who used point-and-figure charts were simply unsophisticated or too primitive to appreciate the other aspects of market activity. The founder of modern technical analysis, Charles Dow, is reported to have used point-and-figure techniques and the quantity of serious writing on the subject has remained appreciable up to the present.

It would be nearer the truth to state that those using point-and-figure techniques simply wish to abstract price information from the technical data so that they can concentrate on it alone before looking to other indicators.

This implies that point-and-figure techniques should be supplemented by techniques which take other market factors of time and volume into account. Studies of real-world trading have shown that point-and-figure technique can by itself yield respectable and consistent profits.

Another characteristic of this system is that point-and-figure's signals are unequivocal. Because it abstracts or, in a sense, "digitizes" price information, there is never more than one way to read its signals. Thus, the system is a way to learn trading discipline. If traders do not follow point-and-figure signals when using the method, they know that they do not have sufficient discipline to be successful traders, because with point-and-figure users either follow the method to the letter or they really aren't using it at all.

Principles of Point-and-Figure Technique

Boxes

"Box size" refers to the minimum price move with significance for the point-and-figure technique. Boxes are plotted on quadriculated graph paper, with each vertical graph division representing one point-and-figure box. Therefore, a box size of five points would mean that ten marks on a point-and-figure graph would represent a 50-point range.

More advanced traders will consider varying box size as price enters new ranges. If the overall price range begins to rise, then the proportional amount of price represented by one box will shrink and the indicator will become too sensitive, cluttering the chart with many false signals. Conversely, if the overall price falls and box size stays the same, box size will be proportionally larger than it was before with relation to price. This means that the overall system will be less sensitive to market fluctuation.

A further consideration for changing box size is the amount of volatility in the market, that is, the rapidity of the price changes. If price changes very rapidly with violent reversal swings, the system should be relatively less sensitive to the same size move at the same price as compared with a more well-behaved market. This sensitivity adjustment can again be accomplished by increasing box size for less sensitivity.

Finally, box size depends on what time frame is of interest in the trading system. If a longer term is desired then box size should be larger because sensitivity to minor fluctuations will be less desirable.

Box size can usually be determined by taking some percentage of total price at a given level. As the amount of price range taken in by this percentage varies over time, so should the box size vary as well. The percentage itself should depend on the timeframe of the trading system, becoming greater for a longer timeframe.

A usual box size is somewhere between 2% and 3% of actual market price.

Reversal Criteria

Traders must decide how many boxes the price has to go in the opposite direction before changing columns and starting a column of the opposite type of figure. Traders usually use from one to three boxes as their reversal criteria.

In general, the greater their timeframe and the more they are willing to risk, the greater will be their number of boxes needed to signal reversals. The greater risk is evident because the actual market price will have to move a greater amount, in the opposite direction of their position, to signal reversals.

The Graph of Price Moves

A point-and-figure chart looks like a series of vertical strings of X's and O's placed next to one another from left to right on the graph. There is no horizontal scale because time is not taken into consideration in point-and-figure technique, and horizontal motion on the graph simply reflects the number of price reversals that have taken place since the beginning of the graph.

Each X or O fills one box on the chart. An X represents a price increase the size of one box while an O represents a decrease. A string of X's represents a period when the price increased without falling at any time by at least one reversal criterion and, inversely, a string of O's represents a period when the price decreased without rising at any time by at least one reversal criterion.

Thus, the first O immediately to the right of the top of a string of X's represents a downside reversal, while the first X to the right of the bottom of a string of O's represents an upside reversal.

The strings of X's and O's collapse price trends over time into single-dimensioned bars on the graph. This is really the same information a bar graph shows, but with the time factor and some of the detail taken out. It should, therefore, be no surprise that significant patterns exist on a point-and-figure chart paralleling the patterns that technicians look for in basic bar charts (see the chapter on basic charting techniques and patterns).

How to Set Up and Maintain a Point-and-Figure System

Keeping Point-and-Figure Charts

Setting Up

Determining the Box Size

Technicians' experience will tell them what a significant change in price would be for their trading strategies. The term "box size" refers to the size of increment to which the analysis should be sensitive. Box size will be determined mostly by the time frame which is important to the technicians and also by the volatility of the market. It will thus vary over fairly long periods of time to adjust for changing volatility.

Because point-and-figure techniques are quite popular, various services offer periodic recommendations for the box sizes to use for specific markets. In general, box size should be increased at higher price levels and decreased at lower ones.

Determining the Reversal Criterion

The reversal criterion normally varies from one to three boxes. If technicians want a lot of trades and are in a market which is not trending too steeply, then one box is a good reversal criterion. If, however, they have a longer time-frame and do not want to be bothered by many signals which will get them into short-lived positions, then they should use a larger reversal criterion, such as three. In general, any size greater than three will get them into trouble, because it will increase their risk of missing important market signals and having to take a loss well into the wrong side of a trend.

Waiting for Price to Give a Box Move ...

If traders find themselves waiting very long for a valid point-and-figure chart signal, then they should consider reducing the box size and thereby increasing price sensitivity.

...Then Writing in the Appropriate Symbol ...

If the move was upward, traders should write an X at the appropriate price level's box on the left-most column. If the move was downward, they should write an O.

...and Continuing to Track Price

As long as price continues in its initial direction, traders enter in the same symbol each time a new box's level is broken by the price. When price goes the other way, they should see if it goes as far as the predefined reversal criterion. If it doesn't, then they ignore the move and wait for a new box to be broken into in the same direction as before.

Changing Columns and Symbols When a Reversal Occurs

If, however, price continues in the opposite direction for a distance equal to the reversal criterion, traders must then shift one column to the right on the chart and, starting at the place where the criterion was fulfilled, begin putting symbols of the opposite sign (O if the new tendency is downward, X if upward) in the appropriate direction and at the appropriate price levels.

Maintaining the Point-and-Figure Chart

From this point on, traders basically need to follow the last two steps mentioned above: continue to add boxes in the direction of the trend, checking for reversal points. When they find a reversal has happened they switch columns and begin plotting in the opposite direction and with the opposite letter from the price level where they recognized the reversal.

How to Trade with Point-and-Figure Charts

The signals used to trade point-and-figure charts are derived largely from signals for classic bar charting methods—except that with point-and-figure there are only two or three technical facts to watch.

Point-and-figure is truly an abstraction of price-based methods, even abstracting the types of signals that traders need to recognize to be able to use the technique. Traders need to look at the following basic indicators when they trade with point-and-figure:

- *Breakouts of double tops and bottoms of the same sign:* When traders see a column of O's or X's not leaning on a larger column of opposite sign just to the left then they should look for an ensuing column of like sign to break past it. When this happens, they have a strong signal from the market—to buy when it is a string of X's or to sell when it is a string of O's. The further apart the first and second columns are, the stronger the signal. The more columns which are broken past at the same time, the stronger the signal

Figure 7-1

```
    X                                    X
  X X    ⇐Breakout of a single top      XO
  X X                                    XO
OXOX                                     XO   X
OXOX                                     XOX XO
OXOX                                     XOXOXO
OXOX                                     O OXO
OXO                                      O O O
OXO     Breakout of a double bottom⇒ _____ O
OX                                           O
O                                            O
O
```

- *Penetration of support/resistance lines:* Support and resistance lines are determined by two observations:
  - *Reversal points:* Since the first box after a reversal is always set off from the previous column by the number of boxes in the reversal criterion, the tops of these two boxes determine angular lines of support and resistance which one can extend across the rest of the chart.

Figure 7-2

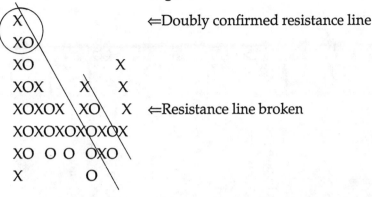

⇐Doubly confirmed resistance line

⇐Resistance line broken

- *Multiple tops and bottoms:* these determine horizontal support and resistance lines.

Figure 7-3

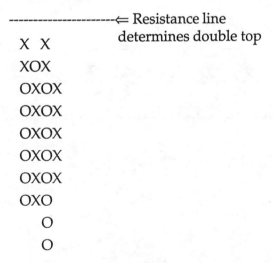

⇐ Resistance line determines double top

Both types of lines gain more significance if they are confirmed again by a column of like signs which refuses to cross them or just touches them.

The more significant the line, the stronger the signal to buy or sell once it has been broken. The weaker lines (ones which are only determined by two columns) can be taken as signals to get out of a trade when the profits have run for a long time and traders are becoming anxious about closing out the trade.

Figure 7-4 Trading June 1987 Deutsche Mark Futures Using Point-and-Figure

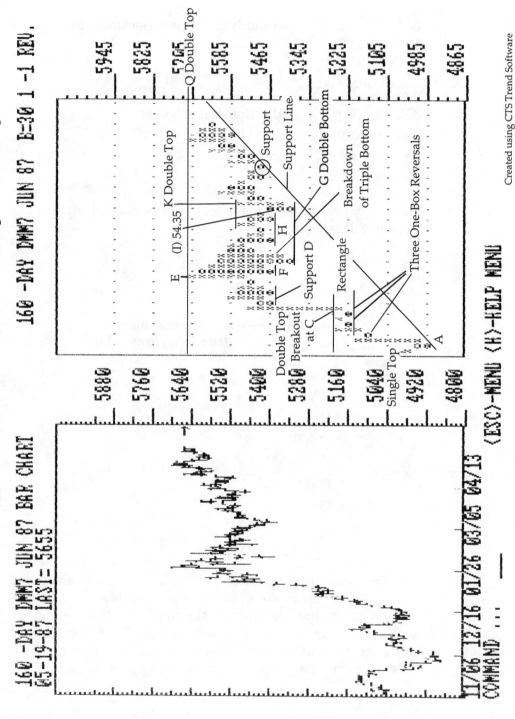

Trading June 1987 Deutsche Mark Futures
Using a Point-and-Figure System

This chart covers 160 days of June 1987 Deutsche Mark futures from November 6, 1986 through May 19, 1987. The scale on the right-hand side indicates the value of the Deutsche Mark in 10,000th's of a dollar, so that the 5465 level, for instance, indicates 54.65 cents. The price moves from a low of $0.49 to a high of $0.56. The box-size for the point-and-figure chart is 30, or .3 cents, and the chart uses a one-box (not a three-box) reversal.

To help readers understand how a point-and-figure chart appears in relationship to a conventional bar chart, a bar chart of the same period under study is included with the point-and-figure chart. With this comparison the waves and congestions take on more meaning in the point-and-figure chart.

After some initial indecisive moves an up-box, or X, is entered at the 5045 level. An immediate reversal takes the chart two O boxes down to the 4985 level.

This first column of O's establishes a local bottom upon its reversal. Traders, therefore, define a support level at 45 degrees to this bottom, marking a line along this angle from that point.

Even though the next rise in price goes quite far, to a level approaching catapult dimensions, there are still no definite buy signals because this rise breaks only a very questionable single top.

There is a brief reversal. In order for it to give traders a sell-short order, the O's would have had to extend below the 45-degree line drawn from the first reversal point. As it is, there is only one box of O's. A one-box X reversal happens, and another one-box O.

When the next X happens traders can define a rectangle, recognizable from standard bar charting practice. Bar charting rules tell traders that there could very possibly be an upside swing out of the rectangle. This does indeed happen (C). That there will be a sustained trend is also confirmed by the fact that this second X takes out the double top just defined by the two brief upside reversals.

Traders can take this as a strong buy signal and initiate a long position at this point, at a price level of 5285.

This position is handsomely rewarded by the ensuing unbroken rise in X's, then a brief two-box correction, another, shorter rise, and a longer correction (D) which, however, fails to exceed the former.

Because this second correction right went below the O's to its left, it should be considered a local bottom. Traders should take a breakdown of this bottom as a sell signal.

A small rise, a pause for one box's worth of O, and then the X's jump to new heights (E) before a rather long downswing which just reaches the same level as the previous bottom. (F) is a triple bottom and if this triple bottom is broken it is definitely the pre-signal for a sell-off.

An upward rally of X's precedes a long slide downward, past the double bottom, and so traders close out their long position, taking profits at the 5405 level (G). Since they purchased at 5285, their profit spread is 120, or 1.2 cents. The weakness of point-and-figure is shown here. The approach made it very difficult for traders to sell it near the top because they could not get a tight enough reversal signal. They could, if they maintained a continual point-and-figure approach to market entry and exit, have taken the data at the top and made the box sizes smaller and the reversal points tighter and forced point-and-figure patterns to appear.

At this point, traders can see that the high so far on the chart (E) represents a local top, so they draw a 45-degree angle downward from it. This will represent a resistance level, and if they haven't gotten a buy signal before it is broken, they should definitely heed it when it breaks out.

Continuing with the chart, price pulls back up, but not as far as the resistance line. A series of fairly short ups and downs inches toward the original bottom support line, which would be a strong signal to sell short, and the bottom established at 5405 (G), where traders also took profits. If the chart breaks either one of these, traders should take it as a short-sell signal.

Among these short movements, there is a double bottom defined at 5465 (H). One X up, and then the bottom is broken, so traders should go short at 5435 (I). Price holds firm just around the level where they had closed out their long position before (G), creating a strong double bottom, and so a new support line (G).

The X's which reverse on this local downtrend go far enough to define a double top at 5555 (K) and also touch the 45-degree support line already defined. Based on these facts, traders buy more against this major 45 degree support line.

A two-O reversal, and then another column of X's breaks simultaneously above the top of the last X's (L). Based on this, traders go long again at 5555.

O's define a weak double bottom at 5495, but then X's and O's begin a ratchet-like move upwards, traders can hold onto their long position.

They are still long at the end of this period, with a nice profit. As long as traders watch their sell signals, there is no risk in this long position, because the market price has moved considerably above the initial 45 degree support line. There is an assured profit at this point of at least 30, or .03 cents, which will only grow as the support line moves upward into the future.

The massive double top at around the 5705 level appears to be on the verge of being broken—on the upside. By looking at the total pattern one can discern the development of an ascending right triangle—very bullish—bounded by the 45 degree support line and line Q, across the double tops.

The trading was profitable and point-and-figure analysis generated enough sell and buy signals that you can safely use this approach of filtering out unwanted time noise and price noise to see market essentials: price action.

Figure 7-5   Trading IBM Stock Using Point-and-Figure

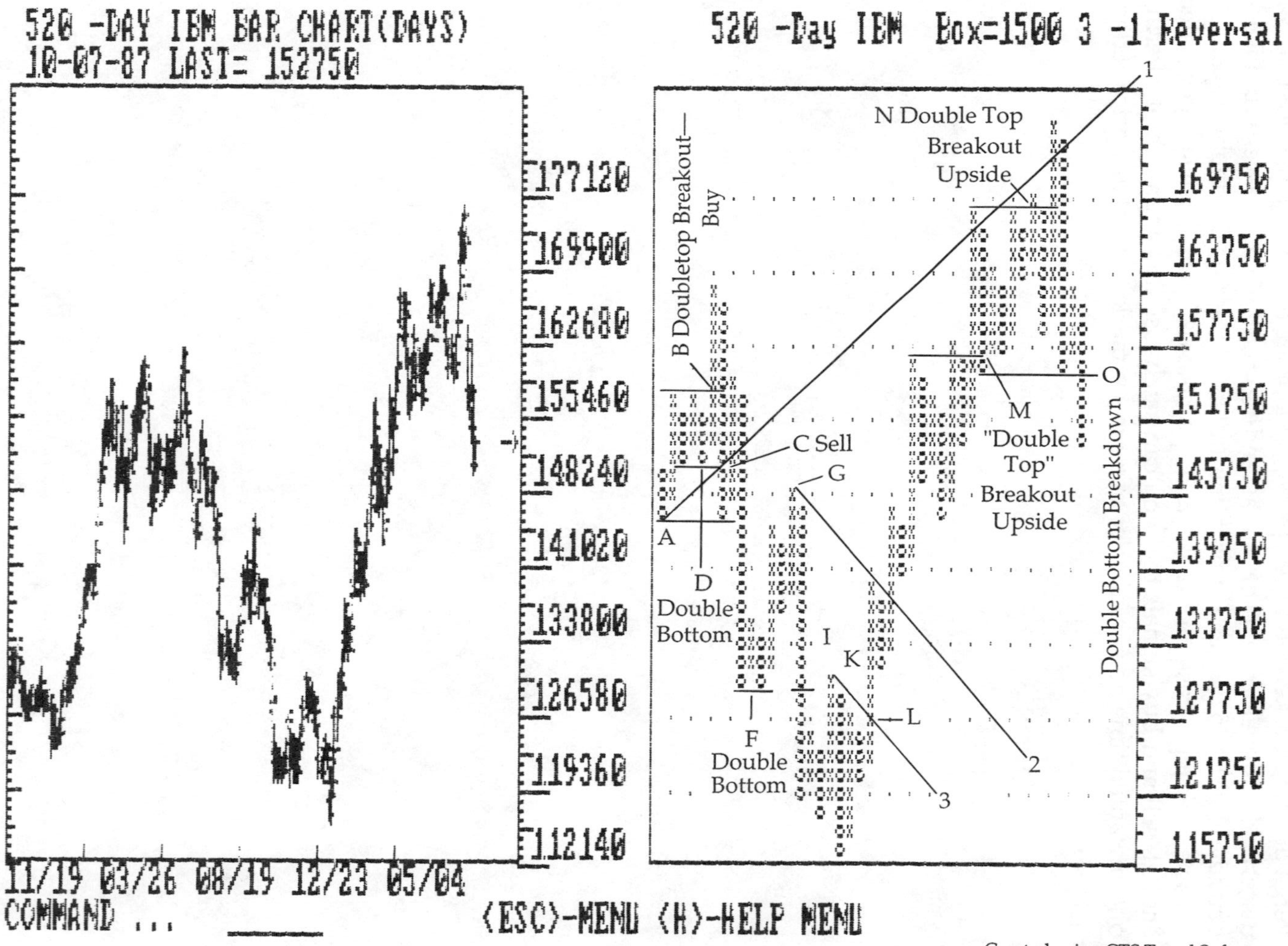

Created using CTS Trend Software

Trading IBM Stock Using a Point-and-Figure System

This point-and-figure chart covers 520 days of trading of IBM stock from November 1986 through October 7, 1987. The scale is in 1,000th's of a dollar (e.g., 139750 = $139.75), and the box size is 1500, or $1.50. The stock traded in a range of $113.00 low to a high of $173.00 per share.

When the initial three downward O's reverse (A), traders draw their first 45-degree support line upward (1). The upward reversal pattern of X's then reverses to a shorter string of O's, and the second column of X's defines a double top with the previous column of X's. The following column of O's likewise forms a double bottom with the previous column. This double bottom/double top formation thus forms a rectangle in standard chart interpretation manner.

Normally this rectangle will be broken in the direction it was entered—to the upside. This, indeed, happens at point B, and so traders enter a long position at $156.25.

Price rises and then reverses, but without a clear sell signal. However, at point C it breaks the original 45 degree support line and so traders now sell at $147.25, for a loss of 9000 ($9.00).

A signal to sell short also comes at point C, when price breaks the earlier double bottom at $147.25. Although there is an upside reversal shortly thereafter, no buy signal occurs, so the traders hold onto this short. The ensuing drop goes past an even stronger double bottom (D), and this might even be taken as a signal to go short further. Price forms a double bottom at F, then heads back up without, giving any buy signals. Traders stay short. The price moves up to an intermediate high at G, $145.75, but then starts to back off. Traders are still short at the C level, $147.25.

Price breaks down below its previous double bottom (I) and traders enter another short position at $128.25. Price falls steadily, recoups slightly, falls a bit further, then jumps back up to K without any clear buy signals.

The next downward plunge increases profits on all the traders' short positions and sends them looking for an excuse to take profits. The resistance level defined by the reversal at K gives a 45-degree line. When price breaks this on the way up, traders will take profits. This it does shortly (L), and they take profits at $127.75, for a very nice gain on this series of trades.

There are no actual upside breakouts of doubletops to signal traders to go long. Strict adherence to the point-and-figure charting approach would not have gotten us long on the move up from the bottom, $115.75, to the ultimate high of $173.00.

At M and N there are upside breakouts of two doubletops and traders could go long. Eventually, the stock drops past O, a double bottom, and head lower. On October 20, 1987, the stock trades below 10800 per share.

This whole series of trades was profitable. The risk, however, was in trying to limit losses when the market actually did start to reverse. This technique offers traders insights into the major trends but cannot tell them when the market is ready to top out or ready to bottom out.

Trading Options Exchange Index Using a Point-and-Figure System

This is a 500-day chart with a scale in 100ths of a dollar (so that 33355 = $333.55). The box size is 5.00 and a reversal is formed when there is a $15.00 move in the opposite direction. The chart tracks the Index from December 1985 to May 1986, in which the price moves from a low of 170.00 to a high of approximately 330.00.

Though the chart begins with a strong upward catapult, this in itself is not enough to tell traders to buy, since there is no point of reference for this price move.

At A traders finally get a very strong buy signal with the breakout of a double top. They go long at 24355.

Price obligingly marches on up, then enters a rectangle-like congestion area. Traditional charting methods indicate it will be slightly more likely that price will break out of the rectangle to the upside. There is a moment of doubt that this will happen as price makes a double bottom at B. It then, however, refuses to fall beyond this point and, in fact, gives an extremely bullish signal at C by breaking a well-defined triple top.

This is a signal for traders to add onto their already long position, or at least to hang on tight to the position they have.

At the end of this charting period traders haven't taken any profits because everything went straight up. If, however, they assume the standard risk management rule for stop-loss orders, then they will not let more than ten percent of the value erode before selling. Since price now stands at 34355, this means the lowest selling price would be at approximately 31000. Since they bought in at 24355, the assured profit at this point is about 6650, or $6.65 per index.

Please note that the point-and-figure patterns of breakout tops and bottoms are more noticeable if box sizes are larger and the tracking period longer. However, the risk in doing this is high because of the box sizes needed to form a reversal pattern—a pattern that will affect an execution of the trade.

Figure 7-6   Trading Options Exchange Index Using Point-and-Figure

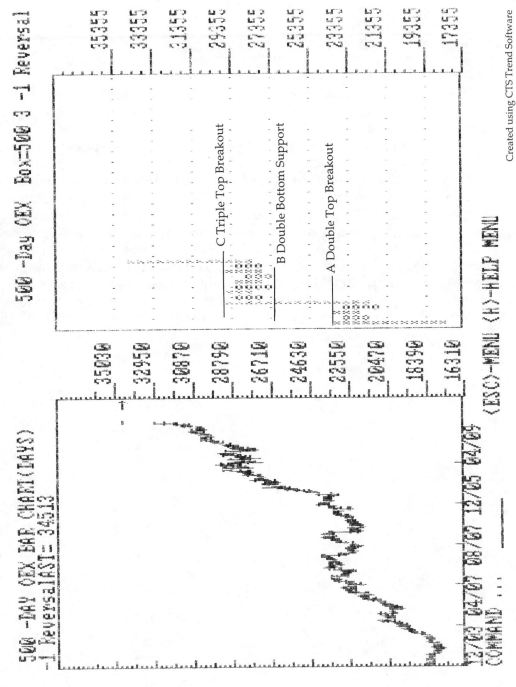

Created using CTS Trend Software

When to Apply Point-and-Figure Charts

Point-and-figure charts work well in any trading situation where it is advantageous for traders to mask out the passing effects of high volatility in a narrow price range. If the market is trading or gently trending, point-and-figure techniques give good signals.

As the examples show, point-and-figure charts may not give enough signals in a strongly trending market to allow traders to get out of bad trades in time to cut losses short.

Use point-and-figure charting techniques with traditional price-following techniques that are based on bar charts. The point-and-figure approach can often clear needless "noise" from the bar chart and show clearly where the market is headed—information which might be masked by wild but unimportant price swings in a volatile market.

The patterns formed with this approach are based on traditional charting methods (see chapter on conventional bar charts). Point-and-figure charts are helpful in filtering out unwanted and extraneous waves and corrections in Elliott Wave analysis. Oftentimes, the constant up and down jiggles of Elliott Wave analysis interfere with a correct analysis of wave formations. However, by filtering the market's bar chart and movements through the point-and-figure strainer, waves clearly stand out.

Where to Find Out More About
Point-and-Figure Techniques

Books and Periodicals

Cohen, A.W. *How to Use the Three-Point Reversal Method of Point and Figure Stock Market Trading*. Larchmont New York: Chartcraft, 1972. This is the standard work in point-and-figure charting.

Davis, Robert Earl. *Profit and Profitability*. West LaFayette, Indiana: Robert Earl Davis Publisher,1969.

DeVilliers, Victor. *The Point-and-Figure Method of Anticipating Stock Price Movements*. New York: Trader Press, 1966 (1st Edition, 1933). This is the work upon which most of what is known today was based.

Dines, James. *How the Average Investor Can Use Technical Analysis for Stock Profits*. New York: Dines Chart Corporation, 1972.

"Hoyle," *The Game in Wall Street and How to Play it Successfully*. 1898.

Schulz, John W. *The Intelligent Chartist*. New York: WRSM Financial Service Corporation, 1962.

Thiel, Charles and Robert Earl Davis. *Point-and-Figure Commodity Trading: A Computer Evaluation*. West LaFayette, Indiana: Dunn & Hargitt, 1970.

Wheelan, Alexander. *Study Helps in Point-and-Figure Technique*. New York: Morgan, Rogers and Roberts, 1962. This is also a classic work in the field of point-and-figure charting.

Wyckoff, Richard D. *Stock Market Technique Number One*. New York: Wyckoff Associates, Inc.,1933.

Zieg, Kermit C. and Perry J. Kaufman. *Point-and-Figure Commodity Trading Techniques*. Larchmont, New York: Investors Intelligence, 1975.

Software to Run on the IBM Personal Computer

Computrac—Interday charting package has the following studies: moving averages, rates of change, oscillators, ratios and spread, RSI, stochastics, on-balance volume, moving average convergence divergence, point-and-figure, etc. Chart zooming, trend lines and parallel channels, cycle analysis with Fourier analysis. Computrac, Inc., New Orleans, LA 70175.

CTS Trend—A software package which is a basic miniversion of Tradecenter. It creates many different types of studies, including realtime studies. CTS Trend, Newark, NJ 07794.

MetaStock—Interday charting package has graphics, but primitive hardcopy features. Many moving averages, trading bands, parallel channels, linear-regression lines, on-balance volume, RSI, positive/negative volume and relative-performance ratios. Computer Asset Management, Salt Lake City, UT 84126

8

Tic Volume
Tracking Big Money's Moves

Tic Volume at a Glance

Background and Philosophy of Tic Volume

Tic volume analysis cumulates all volume-factored trades of stocks or futures as defined by intraday price changes from previous transactions. Implicit in this analysis is the assumption that volume activity precludes price activity.

Principles of Tic Volume

This method uses two indicators of intraday activity, cumulated over the course of a trading day:

- Volume of each transaction, either shares or contracts
- Price of each transaction

How to Trade with Tic Volume

In accumulating markets where price activity shows no movements, look for upside breakouts of tic volume charts. In distributing markets look for tic volume breakdown as confirmation of price breakdowns.

How to Set Up and Maintain Tic Volume

- Start trading day with second trade after the opening volume transaction.
- Cumulate all associated volume per trade as defined by upticks or downticks.
- Chart cumulative number and look for appearance of breakout patterns.

When to Apply Tic Volume

In stock trading where limited volume activity is displayed, use tic volume analysis. In futures trading where volume per transaction is not displayed, use actual number of price changes to create *hybrid* tic volume analysis.

Glossary for Tic Volume

Accumulation—A condition occurring in falling markets when smart money begins picking up stocks or futures under cover of small trades, and which signals that a bottom has been reached and a breakout is imminent.

Confirming Indicator—An indicator belonging to a minor or ancillary price prediction technique which serves to confirm signals already given by other techniques.

Differential Activity Volume (DAV)—A daily indicator used in tic volume technique which is derived from the difference between the number of upticks and the number of downticks.

Distribution—A condition occurring in rising markets when smart money begins dumping stock in order to take profits, and which signals that a top has been reached and a breakdown is imminent.

Downtick—A trade which takes place at a lower price than the immediately preceding transaction.

Leading Indicator—A signal given by a major market analysis technique which forecasts future price movements or market actions.

Smart Money—A group of investing institutions and individuals which tic volume theory claims exists and which both manipulates and foresees major market trends, thus positioning trades to its advantage. This group moves quietly, but its actions can be detected by volume techniques such as tic volume.

Tic Volume—A market technique which attempts to uncover the moves of smart money by determining its trading activities through volume-monitoring methods.

Trend or Trending Market—Market condition which is obtained when prices are steadily rising or falling.

Uptick—A trade which takes place at a higher price than the immediately preceding transaction.

Background and Philosophy of Tic Volume

Tic volume techniques represent an attempt to refine price analysis by inputting volume data analysis. Tic volume analysis discriminates between "blocks" of trades within each day's figures and focuses only on larger sized trades. Implicit in this type of analysis is the assumption that volume activity foretells price activity and that large volume activity is a sign of smart money moving markets.

Tic volume analysis attempts to quantify basic tape reading techniques. Tic volume practitioners choose an arbitrary size of trades under which they ignore the results. This is normally 100 shares, although it is instructive to use higher cutoffs as well. Following the major assumption that smart money trades in larger sizes and with greater activity, trades of 100 shares or less are considered to be transacted by the smallest and less informed public. Thus, tic volume figures for the trading day do not take into account the smaller trades. In the case of trading instruments where volume is not denominated in shares but in contracts traded, the analysis is different if and when one is able to sustain the actual contracts traded per price reported.

Tic volume technicians keep a cumulative daily running total based on the price direction of every trade, the volume of that individual trade, and the price difference from the last trade.

The tic volume analyst believes in the existence of a small, moneyed elite trading group which is privy to information not available to the trading public. He or she also believes that this group regularly manipulates prices in order to accumulate stocks or futures at lower prices and distribute them at higher prices and that, if one can detect what this group is up to, one can profit by it.

The advocate of tic volume technique reasons that there are a lot of market players other than the larger, informed interests, and, in fact, that "big" or "smart" money needs these players to keep things going and to cloak its own accumulation and distribution strategies. Therefore, one must dig a little deeper into the daily figures to see what the "big boys" are really up to.

Principles of Tic Volume

The heart of tic volume technique is the tabulation of the activity of large block trades through the Differential Activity Values line, or DAV. This indicator is usually graphed on a chart together with prices complete for comparison purposes.

The DAV is determined each day by calculating "upticks" and "downticks." Upticks are all those shares traded at a greater price than the previous trade, and downticks are all those shares traded at a lesser price than the previous trade. Shares traded at the same price as the previous trade are not taken into account.

Smaller trades are not counted. It has been found that trades of under 100 shares usually wash each other out and since the whole purpose of this method is to detect the accumulation and distribution of stocks by large buyers it makes sense to disregard these trades.

In addition, some traders will not take the first transaction of the day into account, since it represents pent-up orders which have accumulated overnight without benefit of the open market.

The difference between total upticks and total downticks represents the net volume gain or loss of the issue during the day, and this net volume is then divided by some convenient factor (usually 100) to give a manageable index number.

This index number can be used to detect when accumulation and distribution are going on in large blocks. It will often happen that what looks like an advance on heavy volume (which on-balance volume, (see chapter on on-balance volume) would count as an "Up" day) will be a neutral or even a negative day for tic volume, and, conversely, what looks like a negative or neutral day on on-balance volume may turn out to be a strong advance day for tic volume. What is crucial is the overall direction of this tic volume or on-balance volume curve.

In general, on-balance volume is more tied to price, because, in the final analysis, it depends on the day's closing figure to determine whether there will be a rise or a drop in the indicator.

Tic volume, on the other hand, does not have this limitation and therefore can show what may be happening behind the scenes. This is especially true in what would be known as an "accumulation" phase of an issue, when price seems flat for long periods of time. It is important to watch for large-volume transactions on the uptick during such periods, since this may indicate important accumulation by "smart money" in preparation for some maneuver which will raise the price.

Unfortunately for tic volume, distribution does not need the same cloak-and-dagger techniques, and so the large volume trading triggered by big money's decision to distribute can be done with many small trades, since now the public is eager to buy. Therefore, by the time tic volume tracking gives notice of large distribution volume, prices will usually have already dropped considerably, thus making the distribution indicator simply a confirming indicator rather than a useful trading tool.

In a running market (one heading up or down), tic volume may indicate what strength is left in a trend and therefore give some advance notice of turning points.

How to Trade with Tic Volume

Traders can use tic volume techniques to confirm or strengthen their impressions about where price is headed. As with on-balance volume, however, it would be difficult to trade on this indicator alone. After all, the bottom line for the trader is price, and tic olume measures something else. Of course, that "something else" is linked to price, and it supposedly is linked to something connected with price manipulation. Therefore, tic volume is definitely something one should set up in conjunction with other trading techniques.

To set up a DAV line, traders need to look very closely at the particular issue they are trading and keep track of all transactions reported. This, in itself, is a lot of work, but that is what tic volume techniques require. The presupposition behind tic volume is that traders have only a dozen issues or so that they can watch regularly.

It will not do to watch many issues and, when traders find interesting stocks or futures with other indicators, begin to track it on tic volume. This does not work, simply because volume indicators will behave differently for different stocks. For some, any volume activity at all may signal some major change in the direction of the issue, while others customarily trade on heavy volume every day. Thus, traders must be familiar with the typical behavior of each issue in order to comfortably use tic volume techniques with it, and this familiarity can come only from long and detailed observation.

How to Set Up and Maintain Tic Volume

Assuming a trader has chosen an issue which deserves tracking from the perspective of volume, the first order of business will be to set up a bar chart for price. This bar chart is used to record the DAV.

At the close of a day's trading traders must have a list of *all* transactions in the order they occurred, the price at which each occurred, and how many shares were in each transaction. Then they follow these steps:

1) Throw out every transaction at 100 shares or less, as well as the day's first transaction
2) Compare every remaining transaction with the previous one. If it is at a higher price than the one before it, annotate it as an "uptick." If at a lower price, a "downtick," and if the same, "unchanged"
3) Total all the shares on upticks and write this down
4) Do the same for all shares on downticks, writing the result directly below the total upticks

5) Subtract the downticks total from the upticks total to get the differential in shares

6) Divide the result by 100, to get the DAV index value

7) Plot the DAV index somewhere on the same line where the day's price is recorded in to get a feeling for what the DAV line is doing relative to price

Once this indicator is established over a few weeks, traders may begin to use it. Traders will encounter the following four generic situations:

Accumulation (High DAV)

- *Price rising*—This is the perfect mixture of signals for accumulation.
- *Price dropping*—This is divergence of price movement and volume accumulation and can be used with a high probability of accumulating more positions in the face of price erosion. However, traders should be careful of this situation because they can easily continue to buy when the DAV line abruptly reverses and starts to *confirm the downward price trend.*
- *Price static*—This is a situation which shows that price will eventually catch up with the upwardly trending DAV line and show an opportunity to buy at below "market" value.

Distribution (Large Negative DAV)

- *Price rising*—This situation hardly exists because the distribution based on price erosion will be confirmed by the reversal of the DAV line to the downside. Note well that DAV act only act as a confirmation of a bear trend and not *forecast* the beginning of a bear trend.
- *Price dropping*—This is the ideal mix of indicators: price and DAV lines are heading downwards.
- *Price static*—This situation rarely exists. Distribution of issues is performed over a wide price range due to the inability of the insiders to unload to all participants of the unsuspecting buying group at one fixed price; distribution occurs at a range of prices, hence prices cannot remain static.

Neither Accumulation nor Distribution (DAV with Neither Large Positive nor Negative Value)

- *Price rising*—Most indicative of a short squeeze or any market condition where supply of the issue is decreasing at a rapid rate. New buyers of that issue must adjust the price higher to obtain supply.

- *Price dropping*—this situation cannot exist for long and must eventually turn into DAV line heading downwards to confirm the price erosion.
- *Price static*—most likely to be found at the bottom of markets, immediately after a long sustained selloff. This stage occurs before a start of an upwardly sloping DAV line indicating accumulation.

It should be emphasized again that this is an ancillary method: it should not be used as a main trading technique. Therefore, any buy or sell signals generated in this way should be compared with other methods, and possibly with what traders know about the issue itself. They should verify what the news is, especially that which they know to be open to manipulation by those having an interest in the issue. For instance, if there is a lot of negative publicity, the price will drop, yet with signs of high accumulation, this would mean that the "smart money" interests probably feel the stock has hit bottom and are now loading up on it in preparation for its upcoming climb.

In general, as noted above, all volume indicators are better as buy signals than as sell signals. Therefore, never wait for confirmation at the top from a volume indicator before deciding to sell: it will be too late by the time the confirmation comes around and price erosion of the trader's equity would have ensued.

Volume-related techniques work best over long periods of time. Therefore, tic volume investments which are intended as growth investments could work especially well.

The best strategy would be to get into reputable, but inactive issues which are underpriced and show evidence of long-term accumulation through volume and other indicators. They may stay that way for years, but eventually those who have been accumulating must start moving the price up, if only to recoup their original investment, which will have been considerable with the added cost of carry.

It is appropriate at this point to mention an analytical technique that has not been discussed anywhere else before and which should help predict the approximate price objectives of issues which have undergone long periods of accumulation and which are now moving upward: the carrying cost of the money required to accumulate them over the years.

If accumulation has taken place over a long period of time traders should be able to use the interest rates in effect over this time period to compound the periodic accumulation purchases and arrive at some sort of factor expressing the present value of all money invested in relation to the payments necessary to purchase the issue. This factor when multiplied by the average accumulation price, should indicate a *minimum* upside price objective for the issue. If the climb itself takes place over a long period of time, then this time period must also be taken into account when compounding to obtain the final factor, the ultimate price objective.

Trading Example with Tic Volume

This example is duplicated from the volume, *The Art of Tape Reading: Ticker Technique*, written by Orline D. Foster in 1935. The revised edition, copyright 1965 by Investor's Publication, contains revisions and chapters added by Don Worden, (editor of Worden Tape Reading Studies), and Herbert Liesner (publisher of Tape Analyst for Indicator Digest, Inc.). This volume is out-of-print and this chapter must suffice to explain this unique approach to volume analysis.

The example displays the cumulative DAV's for the stock of Monsanto Corporation from September 1963 to the end of December 1963. No other examples of this analytical approach exist.

The chart displays Monsanto stock price with three indicators: volume, DAV's and On-Balance Volume (OBV) on a daily basis.

Please note that from points A to B, on the OBV curve, distribution or volume breakdown occurs. However, the DAV curve is sloping upward indicating continued accumulation. The detailed analysis of the DAV numbers indicate that the downward price activity is not being confirmed by the volume accumulation figure. Additionally, the more generalized volume accumulation number, OBV, is giving false signals.

From early September to the end of the example, the DAV curve continues upwards, while OBV first shows topping out action at the end of September and early October. While price is reflecting distribution and the OBV curve flattens out, the DAV curve shows continued accumulation.

When price initially tops out at $61.00 and backs off to the $55.00 level, OBV flattens out. Meanwhile DAV charges onto new highs. The divergence of price and, minimally the OBV curve from the DAV curve indicates that intensive accumulation is being performed by insider trading activity. Eventually the price bottoms out in late November and early December and charges from a bottom price of $55.00 to an all time high of $66.00.

The amount of data required to cumulate the DAV curve necessary to arrive at a chart for current trading activity is time consuming and need to be performed manually since there are no computer programs to perform this analytical technique.

Figure 8-1   Trading Monsanto Using Tic Volume

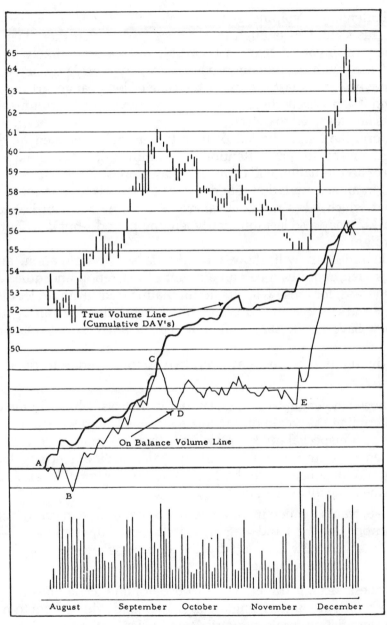

Courtesy of Investor's Press Publications from Orline Foster's
The Art of Tape Reading: The Ticker Technique (1965, pg. 69).

When to Apply Tic Volume Techniques

Technical attention to volume, generally takes the moves of "big money" into account. This should be enough to convince traders that there is something more long-term involved than an hour-by-hour scalper is likely to be interested in. Those with deep enough pockets to play the big money games are also those who can outlast others for the sake of long-range, greater ultimate gains—and it is precisely these players whose moves the tic volume and OBV techniques are designed to detect.

Therefore, the longer period of time traders are interested in, the more they might want to pay attention to volume-related techniques, since strategies of accumulation will come into play more strongly.

Often, in an accumulation-markup-distribution cycle, it is the accumulation period which takes the lion's share of the time and can last for many years. Markup may also last for a fairly lengthy period—but distribution happens overnight.

A little reflection will show why this is so: accumulation, and often markup as well, requires a certain amount of discretion and quiet action in order to succeed, for those who are accumulating don't want to let the cat out of the bag and cause a mad rush for their issue, thereby raising the price before they have accumulated enough to make a worthwhile play for themselves.

Once distribution begins, however, two factors operate to cause price to drop rapidly:

- Those who engineered the play in the first place have gotten out first, skimming the cream off the top, so to speak, and so will no longer be as circumspect about the play, since they are out of it now. (They may even have an interest in hastening the decline, since perhaps they would like to get prices back down to their original levels and try the same thing all over again.)

- Also, fear is a much more powerful motivation than greed: those who jumped on the band-wagon over the markup period in twos and threes will now leap off by the dozens when they see a definite downtrend developing.

Given these facts, if traders want to use volume techniques it is wise to find stocks which are undergoing accumulation and which seem to have fairly long accumulation-markup-distribution cycles, rather than those which seem well-advanced into the markup phase, or which seem to have short, more erratic cycles of accumulation and distribution.

It is also important to apply volume-related techniques on well-capitalized issues. Though this is true of any trading technique in general, it is especially true of this type of technique, since under-capitalized issues probably would not attract big money in the first place and therefore these techniques would have little data to analyze or would give meaningless results.

The converse of what was mentioned in the previous section applies here:

- Tic volume is of little use for shorter periods of time. Over less than a week's time it is utterly meaningless.

- Tic volume also does little good once the issue is out of the accumulation phase, for the downswing tends to happen before it can give traders a clear enough signal for them to act. It is better to depend on other indicators in this situation.

- Neither does this technique function well in a typically erratic market or in issues which are under-capitalized (both these facts are signs of little participation by large investors).

Where to Find Out More About Tic Volume

There is only one mention, in all documentation, about this approach to volume analysis. This work is Orline D. Foster's *The Art of Tape Reading: Ticker Technique*, republished in 1965 by Investors' Press, Inc., Palisades Park, New Jersey 07650. The revised 1965 edition contains additional materials by Herbert Liesner, market analyst, investor and trader, who was at that time on the technical staff of *Indicator Digest*, and Don Worden, editor of the *Worden Tape Reading Studies*. Aside from this one volume, there are no other references currently available to readers to add to their knowledge of volume analysis.

Likewise, there is no software currently available for microcomputers that can track tic volume on this basis.

9

On-Balance Volume

Accumulation and Distribution

On-Balance Volume at a Glance

Background and Philosophy of On-Balance Volume

On-balance volume (OBV) tries to detect hidden accumulation/distribution of stocks initiated by "smart money" in anticipation of price breakouts.

Principles of On-Balance Volume

On-Balance Volume has techniques both for the market as a whole and for individual issues. This chapter concentrates on techniques for individual stocks or commodities. The primary indicator, on-balance volume, is a running balance of daily accumulation (positive) and distribution (negative). Up or Down designators show OBV breakouts, and the Field Trend indicator of Up-Down tendencies can be Doubtful, Falling, or Rising. Confirming indicators are velocity and relative volume per eighth of a point or minimal price increments in instruments other than stocks.

On-balance volume looks for agreement between OBV direction and price for bullish indicators, and disagreement for bearish indicators. The Up-Down and Net Field Trend indicators give OBV direction trends, and the other indicators can help refine and pinpoint OBV indications and determine the general bull or bear trend.

How to Set Up and Maintain On-Balance Volume

Initiate a daily table of price and total trading volume. Keep track of OBV after each day's data has been received. Use Up and Down notations when there are OBV breakouts, and make field trend notations of Falling when clusters of Up and Down zig-zag lower, Rising when zig-zagging higher, and Doubtful when neither Rising nor Falling patterns predominate.

How to Trade with On-Balance Volume

Buy an issue only on evidence of accumulation (high OBV) at a low price. Sell, if possible, on clear signs of distribution at a higher price. Use Net Field trend to determine the general market trend.

When to Apply On-Balance Volume

On-balance volume is always appropriate in accumulating markets. It works especially well in markets dominated by a mix of large professional players and smaller uninformed traders. On-balance volume does not work well in a market with no "smart money" players or in very short-term trading frameworks. on-balance volume gives confirmation of the predictions accumulation patterns. It also helps indicate the significance of doubtful signals in such methods as moving average or Market Profile® .

Glossary for On-Balance Volume

Accumulation—Describes volume which occurs on a day that has a price increase.

Designators—Up or Down notations written beside a day's OBV when that figure tops a previous high or goes below a previous low.

Demand Volume—Same as **Accumulation.**

Distribution—Describes volume which happens on a day that has a price decrease.

Field Trend—Rising, Falling or Doubtful notations written when cluster-patterns of Up and Down designators have been zig-zagging downward, upward, or in neither direction, respectively. If cluster patterns are zig-zagging upwards the Field Trend is rising. If the patterns are zig-zagging downwards, then Field Trend is falling. If the Up-Down designations are not in gear with each other, then the Field Trend is doubtful.

On-Balance Volume—The total volume traded in a day, subtracted from the previous day's OBV if price closes down, or added if price closes up.

Relative Volume Per Minimal Trader Fluctuation—A refinement on OBV which measures how much volume change has occurred in relation to price swing. When relative volume per minimal fluctuation decreases, it can be an early indication that OBV may soon be indicating a top or bottom.

Spring Principle—Used to measure "tension" in a stock (likelihood that it will have a reversal) based on how many times it has reached 100% velocity (capitalization turnover) and how close cumulative OBV is to 100% of stock capitalization. This is not applicable to futures and options where there is no base capitalization to work from.

Supply Volume—Same as **Distribution.**

Velocity—Cumulative volume of an issue traded since its last major top/bottom, expressed as a percentage of that issue's capitalization.

Background and Philosophy of On-Balance Volume

This method was originally developed for the stock market, however, as with most technical indicators, practitioners modified the technique and applied it to futures and options.

Joseph Granville, the modern creator of on-balance volume techniques, makes the basic assumption that the marketplace is divided between "smart money" and "the general public." Smart money is able to, more or less, surreptitiously accumulate stock issues at low prices. It then drives the price up, continuing to buy for the first half or two-thirds of a bull market, holds for the last third, and sells at the top. Again, it does so without the general public noticing that massive distribution is taking place, and this does not affect price until the smart money is out of the market and the general public rushes to sell. Once this distribution has taken place, the price weakens and a bear market ensues. Because the general public does not notice this accumulation/distribution tendency it tends to be on the wrong side of the price most of the time.

For OBV analysis to be effective, such a relation between smart money and the general public is necessary, because the smart money must have someone to buy from and sell to in order to make its profits. That someone is the run-of-the-mill uninformed investor.

The major motivation of the on-balance volume technique is the attempt to uncover smart money's hidden accumulation and distribution patterns before the price break happens. Informed technicians with the proper analytical tools can discern and use these patterns. These informed technicians are those not dazzled by price as the primary indicator of market behavior, but who are willing, rather, to look at what drives price—volume.

On-balance volume skirts the border of that other vast territory of market analysis which this book does not deal with: fundamental analysis. Fundamental analysis, is that technique which traders use to look at other indicators besides simple numerical market indicators in order to arrive at their decisions. These indicators might include general news about the economy, world and national politics, relative financial soundness of corporations whose issues are being traded, news about the weather affecting agricultural commodities and, in general, just about anything that could conceivably affect the market—but which market technicians look upon as being largely irrelevant and misleading.

On-balance volume is a technique which allows its practitioners to take advantage of the "inside knowledge," possibly of a fundamental nature, in the possession of large concerns and investors. On-balance volume allows technicians to do this without having to obtain this "inside knowledge," themselves. Rather, OBV is a kind of technical barometer of informed fundamental knowledge and insight. Granville referred to the OBV technician as a "parasite" of smart money.

Little interest should be shown for what it is that makes smart money smart, or who the smart money investors are. All that matters is that smart money's moves ultimately determine price, and therefore a technique which reveals these moves will be all the technician needs. This approach constitutes an almost a contrarian philosophy, since Granville admits that smart money appears to use some of the more visible indicators of market action, price, as covers for accumulation or distribution of stock.

Principles of the On-Balance Volume Technique

Three Major Components in On-Balance Volume Analysis:

1) The Primary On-Balance Volume Indicator

The on-balance volume indicator itself is a daily running indicator of whether a stock is undergoing net distribution or accumulation.

If a stock closes higher than the previous day's closing, then the day's volume is said to be *accumulated* or *demand* volume.

If a stock closes lower than the previous day's closing, then the day's volume is considered to be *distributed* or *supply* volume.

The day's on-balance volume figure is derived from the previous day's OBV total, plus today's figure, if demand volume, or less today's figure, if supply volume.

2) Designations and Clusters

A day bears an Up designation if its OBV shows a break toward the upside, that is, if the day's OBV is higher than the last OBV high point.

A day carries the Down designation in the opposite case, that is, if OBV is lower than the last OBV low point.

Two or more Ups or Downs without an intervening day of the opposite sign are called a "cluster." After four clusters have been encountered, the trader observes the trend of OBV clusters, known as the "net field trend."

3) Field Trend

At the end of a cluster, the net field trend is called "rising" if the net field trend has been undetermined or doubtful and there are four clusters in a pattern of Ups, then Downs, then Ups, then Downs, or if the net field trend is already rising and does not become doubtful (see below).

At the end of a cluster, the net field trend is called "falling" if the net field trend has been undetermined or doubtful and there are four clusters in a pattern of Downs, then Ups, then Ups, then Downs, or if the net field trend is already falling and does not become doubtful (see below).

The net field trend becomes "doubtful" when

a) The net field trend has been falling and an Up betters the previous cluster of Ups

b) The net field trend has been rising and a Down goes below the previous cluster of Downs

c) The net field trend has been doubtful and there have not yet been enough Up-Down clusters to determine whether the trend is rising or falling

Two Minor Components of On-Balance Volume

1) Velocity

Velocity is the percentage relation between cumulative volume and total capitalization of a stock, such that a complete turnover of the issue's stocks would be 100% velocity. When both velocity and OBV as a percentage of total stock issues become very large, there is a great strain on rising price.

(Velocity and OBV/capitalization percentage figures can be kept daily alongside the indicators already mentioned.)

2) Relative Volume per Minimal Fluctuation

This indicator compensates somewhat for the fact that the OBV indicator does not take into account that heavy or light volume may bear a different relation to price change at different times. This indicator is simply the day's volume divided by the minimal fluctuations that that particular issue can make (i.e., in stocks, 1/8, in bond futures, 1/32). This indicator can be listed alongside the OBV cumulative numbers.

How to Set Up and Maintain On-Balance Volume

Initial Requirements

Traders must have a source of information on the daily prices and volumes of the stocks they are interested in. They should begin keeping track of these and the OBV derivative indicators on a large sheet of paper with about 15 vertical columns.

In the leftmost column, they put the first date which they intend to observe. Next to it they mark the day's closing price and next to that the volume
traded. On this first day, traders put the day's volume in the OBV column to
the right of volume traded.

On the second day, they can actually derive one indicator, OBV. If the
day's price is not different from the previous day's, they copy the same
amount down for OBV. If it is different, they subtract daily volume from the
previous OBV if the closing price has fallen and add it on if price has risen.
They record the result down under the day's OBV.

On the third day, traders can begin looking for Up-Down designators.
They repeat exactly the same steps as for day two for price, volume, and OBV
then compare today's OBV figures with OBV for the two previous days. If the
middle day of the three being compared has a volume figure below or above
both the others, this is a beginning bottom or top with which to make subsequent comparisons. Traders should have columns for "Most recent bottom"
and "Most recent top." These may not get filled right away at the start of their
analysis, but eventually traders will have both figures and be able to check
them daily for updating.

On subsequent days, after traders have figures for most recent top and
most recent bottom, they can watch for breakouts above and below these two
numbers, respectively. When there is a breakout above the most recent top,
they should enter "Up" in the seventh, or "Designator" column. When there is
a breakout below the most recent bottom, they enter "Down." Of course, the
breakout figure should then become the new most recent top or bottom
figure.

Traders will have to wait until they have a series of two or more designators of the same sign, followed by an opposite designator, before defining
the first "cluster" of designators. Once they have four clusters, they can examine the sign of each. If the clusters go in the pattern Up-Down-Up-Down,
traders can assign a field trend indicator of Falling in the final column. If the
pattern is the opposite, then the field trend indicator will be Rising.

Traders continue in this fashion, and will not change the field indicator
until they see evidence to the contrary. If the field trend is falling, it will
remain falling even though there may be several Up clusters during that
time—if none of these Up clusters' final volume levels exceeds the previous
Up cluster top.

Conversely, if the field trend is rising, it will remain rising even through
several Down clusters—if none of these Down clusters' final volume levels
breaks below the previous Down cluster bottom.

Once the upward or downward trend has been broken, however, traders
can then mark the field trend status as Doubtful. The Doubtful designation

will continue if both Up and Down clusters do not begin to move in the same direction as indicated by the breakout. Until they do, the trend continues to be Doubtful. Once the trend begins to move, wait for the tell-tale four-cluster zig-zag before marking the field trend as Up or Down.

Plotting Supplementary Indicators

If traders want to do the OBV technique properly, then they may also want to keep columns for the following indicators:

Total Capitalization

This does not need to be kept every day, as long as the total number of issues of the stock remain constant. Just a single notation in the upper left-hand corner of the sheet would be sufficient.

Velocity

This applies only to the Rising trend portions of the chart. From the time the Rising trend begins (traders will have to back-date this, since they can't know this at the very time it begins), traders can keep a column with a total of *cumulative* volume, not *on-balance* volume. Cumulative volume simply adds today's volume figure (regardless of price) to yesterday's cumulative figure.

Velocity is then the day's cumulative volume figure divided by the total capitalization of the stock and written as a percentage. This can be written next to the cumulative volume column.

On-Balance Volume as a Percentage of Total Capitalization

This final column to the right is simply the day's OBV figure divided by total capitalization and expressed as a percentage. This mathematical calculation can only be performed when tracking stocks.

How to Trade with On-Balance Volume

There are many special situations to consider when using OBV techniques, making this far from a mechanical trading system. The best way to explore this complexity is to start with the simplest, most basic situation, and then begin to qualify that situation with exceptions and special considerations.

Base Case: Buy Accumulation, Sell Distribution

The most fundamental rule of OBV trading is never to buy a stock, no matter what price indicators might show, unless there is clear evidence of accumulation of that stock at low prices, as shown by OBV analysis. The lower price and the greater the evidence of accumulation, the greater the opportunity for an eventual upward move in price and the more bullish the OBV technician will be. A steadily increasing OBV at a price which has been held down for a long period of time is the ideal situation for this base-case rule.

Conversely, evidence of heavy distribution at high prices or after a sustained rise in price should make the OBV technician eager to sell, for it indicates that the price will be plummeting as soon as smart money has unloaded its supply at the desired high price.

First Qualification: Watch the Field Trend Patterns

The basic rule, however, doesn't give traders a clue how to tell whether a stock is really undergoing accumulation or distribution, or how to predict when accumulation or distribution might begin or cease, so they might better anticipate and understand what they see the market doing. On-Balance Volume can take its own dips and leaps, just like price, without necessarily meaning that there has been a switch to accumulation or distribution.

The net field trend indicator (based on the Up and Down designators) helps traders eliminate whipsaw trading based on passing fluctuations in the OBV. It is a sort of swing-pattern (see chapter on Swing Charts) indicator that helps traders evaluate local tops and bottoms in the context of longer-term considerations of where price and volume are headed.

In general, the four-cluster Up-Down-Up-Down pattern, defining a Falling field trend, should warn traders to keep away from purchasing a stock. It means the stock is under distribution and that smart money is getting out.

The Rising field trend, on the other hand, should signal a buy opportunity.

The Doubtful trend gives traders ample warning that the field will change from Rising to Falling or vice versa, and therefore should allow traders to position themselves with anticipation.

Qualification on Field Trends—Width of Volume Band

Sometimes even the refinement of the field trend indicator can be too skittish and the technician who follows it, alone, will bolt from the smart money herd because a rising issue has entered a Falling field trend. Anticipating the need to correct for this, the technician should also check on the width of volume change when recognizing a Rising or Falling trend. If the change in OBV from beginning to end of the the Up-Down clusters is not great in relation to the absolute amount of OBV on balance, then this field trend may not change. If on the other hand, OBV changes dramatically from beginning to end of the Up-Down clusters, then the trader would recognize that a possible reversal is imminent. Of course, this caveat is not hard and definitive, but a rather subjective caution to the traders who are using this technique.

Worksheet Showing On-Balance Volume Calculations

The following is partial worksheet data for a stock, XYZ, which was tracked with the OBV technique:

Date	Price	Volume	OBV	Designation	Field Trend
1	37.00	13,500	-15,000		Falling
2	37.63	5,100	- 9,900		Falling
3	37.75	14,100	4,200		Falling
4	37.63	14,200	-10,000		Falling
5	38.00	40,200	30,200	Up	Falling
6	38.50	10,300	40,500	Up	Falling
7	39.63	18,000	58,500	Up	Falling
8	39.50	16,200	42,300		Falling
9	39.50	19,400	42,300		Falling
10	39.38	13,800	28,500		Falling
11	39.88	24,700	53,200		Falling
12	41.00	48,900	102,100	Up	Doubtful
13	40.38	21,600	80,500		Doubtful
14	40.00	18,900	61,600		Doubtful
15	40.88	18,900	80,500		Doubtful
16	40.75	26,300	54,200	Down	Doubtful
17	41.00	14,000	68,200		Doubtful
18	40.88	16,100	52,100	Down	Doubtful
19	40.88	18,300	52,100	Down	Doubtful
20	40.75	35,000	17,100	Down	Doubtful
21	42.00	55,700	72,800	Up	Doubtful
22	43.63	58,500	131,300	Up	Rising
23	44.75	77,000	208,300	Up	Rising
24	45.00	82,800	291,100	Up	Rising
25	45.88	77,200	368,300	Up	Rising
26	46.38	78,800	447,100	Up	Rising
27	47.25	38,900	486,000	Up	Rising
28	48.13	91,900	577,900	Up	Rising
29	47.63	126,600	451,300		Rising
30	48.63	91,300	542,600		Rising
31	49.25	142,300	684,900	Up	Rising
32	50.00	121,800	806,700	Up	Rising

This example specifically shows Designation changes from Up to Doubtful to Down to Doubtful to Up, Field Trend from Falling to Doubtful to Rising.

Figure 9-1 Trading Motorola Stock Using On-Balance Volume

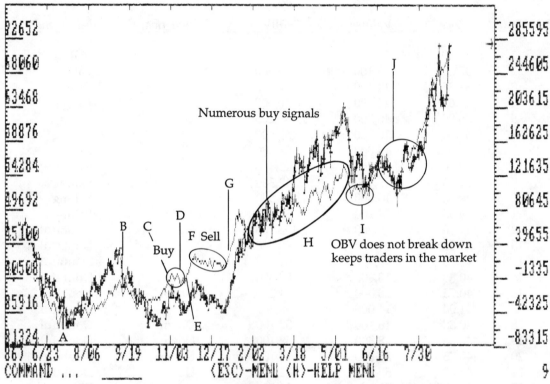

Trading Examples with On-Balance Volume

A Note about the Examples:

Most computer services which currently chart on-balance volume do not go into the fine points of Up, Down, Rising And Falling indicators, contenting themselves with showing the raw numbers representing on-balance volume.

These examples show the information a trader would get from one of the services.

When OBV is charted on a daily line-graph, traders can follow its breakouts of tops and bottoms, taking them to be an abstraction, or short-hand, for the more complex computations necessary to follow the full-blown OBV system.

Trading Motorola Stock Using On-Balance Volume

This example is 333 days of Motorola stock trading in which the price moved from a low of around $32.00 per share to a little under $72.00 per share. On-balance volume moved from positive to negative, and proceeded to cumulate to the positive side, while price went slightly lower and eventually charges onto new highs.

The first minor buy signals occur in the small breakouts after point A. No really dependable signal occurs, however, until point C, which breaks the top at B. This would signal a buy.

There is a sell signal which is really too weak to be heeded at D (a low followed by a second low) followed immediately by a buy signal at E breaking above the tops formed at D.

The area is a distribution area, so in OBV this is a sell signal.

At G, the OBV indicator moves beyond all previous OBV highs on the chart and so is a strong buy signal.

Area H contains numerous minor buy signals as both price and the OBV indicator edge steadily upward.

At point I, the stock tops out. OBV tests its previous bottom here and at J, but holds—so it is not a sell signal. Then, OBV begins to rise along with price.

This last development is interesting. Even though pure price-following techniques would have dictated a sale at the breakdown before point I, OBV holds firm. This insistence of OBV that the rally is not over would have paid off, because it would have kept traders on board for the dramatic rise at the end of the charting period.

In the first part of the charting period, OBV shows accumulation and correctly advises traders to buy—whereas price-sensitive indicators such as moving average would have whipsawed them back and forth between buy-sell signals, or would have indicated nothing at all. However, this example

Figure 9-2 Trading General Motors Stock Using On-Balance Volume

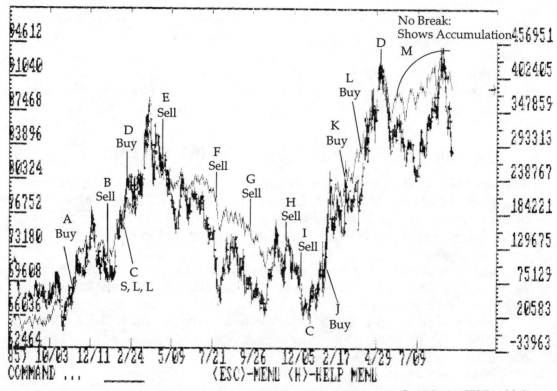

shows OBV at its best—giving buy signals and telling traders when to expect a rise to continue.

Where OBV fails is in the amount of warning it will give traders that a significant breakdown is near. Notice that the end of this chart shows both OBV and price going strong. Price might fall soon after this charting period ends, but OBV will probably not forewarn traders to do anything about it.

Trading General Motors Stock Using On-Balance Volume

This example is 520 days of trading in General Motors stock in which the price moved from a low of around $54.00 per share to a little under $94.00 per share. On-balance volume moved from positive to negative, and proceeded to cumulate initially to the positive side, with prices following upwards, then price moved down followed by the on-balance volume deterioration. Price bottomed out and on-balance volume abruptly reversed offering no significant indications of accumulation.

On-balance volume may work a little better for distribution when dealing with a traditionally less volatile stock, such as GM, because blue-chip stocks traditionally move sluggishly away from market tops—perhaps giving OBV enough time to get in a warning before the stock itself drops.

At point A, OBV goes above the previous tops and therefore gives traders a buy signal (in retrospect, OBV indicates that acculmulation was going on).

Point B gives traders a sell signal, because its low takes out previous local lows. If they had gone short, it would have been an unlucky move. Immediately thereafter, at C, there is another buy signal

Point D's OBV takes out a previous high, for another buy signal and then OBV and price begin an extreme climb.

After price tops out, traders get a good sell signal at E, even though it is *after the top*. Since price does not erode too fast here, the signal still lets them get out on time. Then points F through I all show continual erosion of OBV, giving continual sell signals as price drops. Volume-price lag lessens throughout this move. At the H and I points, price has held but OBV continues to fall. This may indicate that this market is regarded as being more price sensitive than some others, among many participating traders who buy only as a function of price.

J gives a buy signal because it takes out a previous OBV high.

The K period gives a sell signal, which hurts traders, because a new buy signal at L, preceded by rapid price rise, continues onward and upward through the end of the charting period.

The same observations about the previous example also apply here: OBV holds (in fact, here it goes up) while price drops. This shows accumulation even while price is falling. Heeding OBV helps traders weather a temporary setback in the stock's price and therefore get in on the continued rise.

Figure 9-3　Trading Standard and Poor's Index Using On-Balance Volume

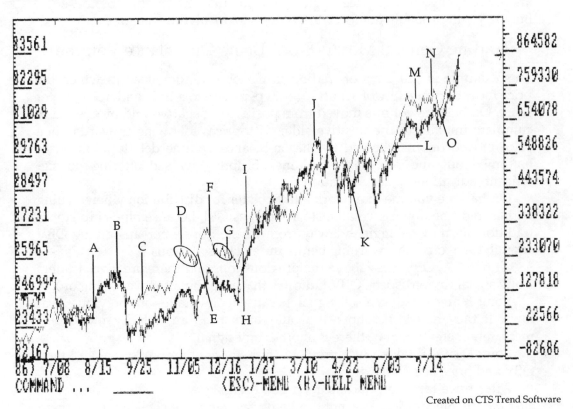

08:13 300 -DAY ON-BAL. VOL. CHAR** SPX **   10-07-1987
LAST Vol= 847032 ;08-11-87

Created on CTS Trend Software

Trading Standard and Poor's Index Using On-Balance Volume

This example is 300 days of trading for the Standard & Poor's cash index using on-balance volume. Price moved from an approximate low of $222.00 to a high of $335.50. On-balance volume showed continual accumulation to the upside.

At point A, OBV takes out a previous high and so gives a buy signal.

At point B, both price and OBV top together, so OBV provides traders with a valid (and, for OBV tops, unusually timely) sell signal.

Point C indicates that a previous double top has broken out, giving another buy signal. Point D gives a cluster of sell signals, breaking below a previous bottom.

Point E breaks above the tops formed during D, giving a buy signal.

F shows a breakdown off a high. The reversal in itself is not a sell indicator, but it warns traders that something might be around the corner. G then gives another cluster of sell signals.

However, H immediately provides traders with another warning signal that there might be another reversal (takes out the tops of G), and I then provides them with the actual buy signal (takes out the high of F).

All the way up between I and J, traders have a series of buy signals.

J tops out, and then at K OBV backs away from making new lows. Price continues down, but OBV tells traders to hold.

Again, OBV carries traders over a temporary dip in price, going on to new buy signals at L. A small sale indication occurs at M, and a buy indicator at N.

O defines a new OBV bottom, and provides a warning level to see if OBV will break it the next time around. However, the price and OBV simply continue upwards.

Figure 9-4A Modified Tic Volume/On-Balance Volume Trading Example with IBM

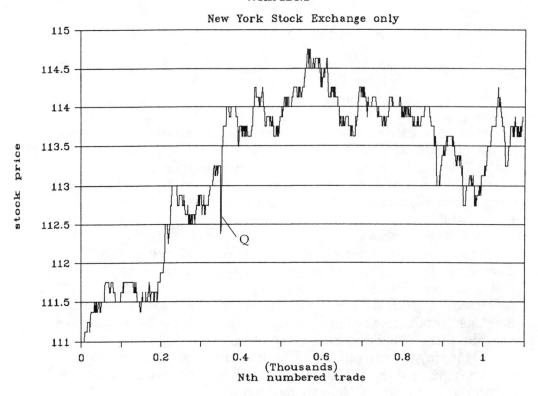

New York Stock Exchange only

Figure 9-4B

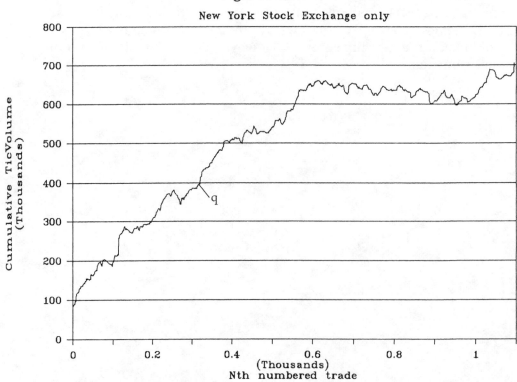

New York Stock Exchange only

Modified Tic Volume/On-Balance Volume
Trading Example with IBM

The following example illustrates modified tic volume/on-balance volume (TV/OBV) analysis for IBM stock on December 9, 1987. Total volume for all New York Stock Exchange trades in IBM was 1,806,100 shares. The price ranged from a high of 114.875 and an opening low price of 111.00 per share. For the purpose of this illustration all data was provided by MarketData services and all off-exchange (Midwest Stock Exchange, Pacific Coast Stock Exchange, ITS, and third market transactions) transactions were deleted from the charts to allow for more concise analysis.

Tic volume and on-balance volume were melded together and redefined as TV/OBV for this detailed analysis. Each trade's size was added or subtracted to a cumulative number regardless of whether or not there was a previous uptick or downtick. If there were no changes from the previous trade, the decision to add or subtract the latest trade to the cumulative figure was arrived at by going as far back as was required to determine the next earliest price change, either uptick or downtick. In conventional OBV analysis technicians add or subtract only the volume that was associated with either an uptick or downtick. The author's analysis indicated false signals based on the conventional OBV approach: the very detail that was used to analyze a day's trading data causes greater need to remove variations. The parameters of trade size ranged from a low of 100 shares per trade to a high of 83,600 shares. Using conventional analysis could eliminate high volume trades if the higher volume trades were transacted at no uptick or downtick from the previous trade, i.e. an equalizing tick.

Chart 9-4A displays prices as a function of numbered trade. Note that a dip at point Q (349th and 350th trade) was a drop from $113.250 on two trades to $112.375 (3300 shares) and $112.50 (2000 shares). These two trades were keypunched wrong at the New York Stock Exchange itself, but for purposes of keeping analysis pure they are retained here to keep the continuity of trades. Please note that price opened at $111.00 and steadily moved up to $114.875, the high of the day, before backing off to around the $113.00 level.

Chart 9-4B is the chart to concentrate on. It displays the total cumulative TV/OBV for all New York Stock Exchange transactions in IBM stock. There are a total of 1095 separate transactions for a total volume of 1,806,100 shares. For the purpose of this analysis, all trades, even those of 100 shares, were integrated into the analysis. Since IBM is a stock heavily dominated by institutional and Chicago Board Options Exchange member hedging activities, the number of 100 share trades numbered only 165 out of a total 1095 trades for a total volume of only 16,500 shares. The rest of the trades ranged in size from 200 to 84,600 shares (which was traded on the opening block). The 165 trades of 100 shares each are incorporated individually into the cumulative volume.

Chart 9-5A onwards contain detailed analysis of the TV/OBV of IBM transactions.

Chart 9-5A displays IBM prices from the 1st trade to the 200th trade. The price ranges from an opening low of $111.00 to a high of $111.875 and cumulative volume ranges from an opening low of 84,600 to a high of 306,200 shares.

Note the TV/OBV breakouts at points A, B, C, D and F, in Chart 9-5B; each of these breakouts to the upside indicates the accumulation of the stock had concluded and that the stock is being marked up.

The previous TV/OBV high prior to Point A is 155,900 shares on the 37th trade of the day at price of $111.50. TV/OBV sells off to a low of 151,500 shares while price dips down to only $111.375. TV/OBV then shoots up to 164,000 on the 45th trade of 9000 shares at $111.50. The 164,000 TV/OBV takes out the previous high of 155,900. This signals the first TV/OBV breakout buy price of $111.50.

TV/OBV then backs off to 163,100, establishing a support point. This sets up another upside breakout indicated by Point B, where TV/OBV takes out the 165,200 previous high with a high of 166,400 on the 52nd trade of 3,000 shares at $111.50. Please note traders are seeing continuous breakout highs of TV/OBV while the price of the stock remains steady between $111.375 and $111.50.

At Point C, total TV/OBV cumulates to a high of 202,100 on the 75th trade of 5000 shares at $111.75. The immediate high is on the 69th trade of 200 shares at $111.75, TV/OBV of 197,200 shares. On the 79th trade of 500 shares at $111.75, the highest TV/OBV for the day is achieved, 204,100 shares.

From the 79th trade, the price remains locked in a trading range of $111.50 low and a high of $111.75. TV/OBV starts deteriorating and sells off to a low of 186,000 on the 98th trade of 3800 shares at $111.50. This low takes out the previous TV/OBV low of 187,100 shares which occurs on the 73rd trade of 100 shares at $111.625. (This is an immediate sign telling traders that this accumulation process was not strong.) This takeout of the previous low of the 73rd trade is a signal that if it is taken out again from a higher TV/OBV number, then traders must liquidate longs and possibly go short. Price is still in the $111.50 range to the $111.75 range, so liquidating at this point would create a scratch situation.

From the 98th trade low TV/OBV of 186,000, the TV/OBV cumulates again and at Point D takes outthe previous high which is made on the 79th trade, 204,100 TV/OBV. Point D signals continuous strength since the TV/OBV is at 208,000 and price is at $111.50 on a trade of 3800 shares. This

Figure 9-5A

for 1st trade to 200th trade

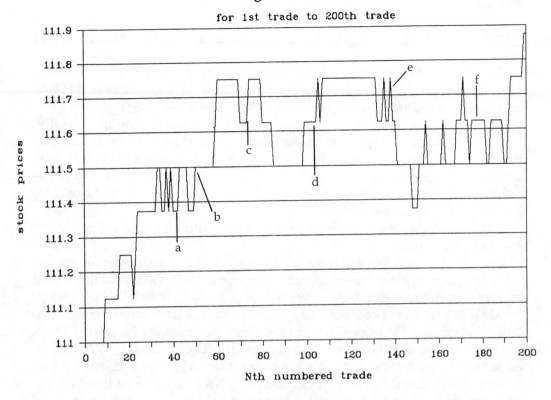

stock prices

Nth numbered trade

Figure 9-5B

from first trade to 200th trade

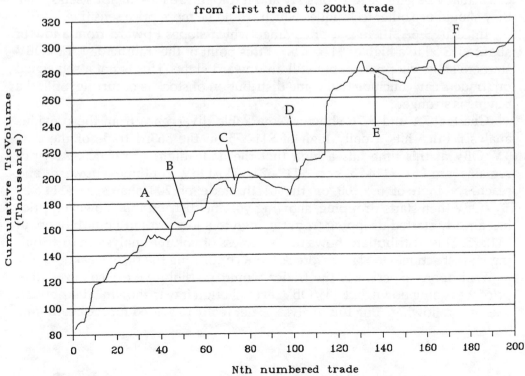

Cumulative TicVolume (Thousands)

Nth numbered trade

continuous new high in TV/OBV should strengthen traders' resolve to stay long.

TV/OBV continues onto new highs, first taking out the 208,000 TV/OBV to eventually go up to 287,300 on the 129th trade of 100 shares at $111.75. Price is still locked in a trading range of $111.75 and a low of $111.50.

At Point F, which is a very bullish takeout of a double top in TV/OBV, 284,000, (184th trade) traders now see price follow the intensive volume accumulation that had been signalled, and also confirmed, earlier at Points A, B, C, D and F. Price follows volume shortly. Price now charges upward from the trading range to a high of $113.00, first made on the 227th trade of 2000 shares. (see Chart 9-6A and 9-6B.)

Charts 9-6A and 9-6B display Points G, H, I, J and a trading range market with an upward bias.

Each of the respective analyses can be applied but here the details are left out. Suffice it to say that the breakouts on continued TV/OBV new highs lead the way for price to move up.

At Point J traders encounter a dip in price. As was later confirmed the two trades that created the price dip were keypunch errors at the New York Stock Exchange. Please note however, that because this is cumulative TV/OBV, no sell signal was generated with this inadvertent dip. Here traders can see that no false signal was given and might consider this a strength of the analysis. However, because of the nature of this type of volume analysis no sell signal can actually be generated so quickly and if traders are looking for a sell signal, they should use other techniques which would be more price sensitive.

In Chart 9-6A, there is a price range which slopes upward from a low of about $113.50 to a high of $114.375. At this point of the trading day, TV/OBV starts to show choppiness, but still an upward slope. This is not a sell signal but traders can conclude that some distribution of stock is occurring. Still, the buying is stronger.

Charts 9-7A and 9-7B show a remarkable divergence from the previous analysis. Price hits a daily high of $114.75 on the 563rd trade of the day. TV/OBV at this time hits a high (not the daily high) of 618,000. As price remains around $114.75 and $113.625, TV/OBV continues upward and reaches a high of 659,200 on the 611th trade of 200 shares at $114.625. TV/OBV then starts dropping, showing volume distribution. However, price has already started dropping from the high to a low around Point L of about $112.75. This distribution shows the weakness of volume analysis in distributing market action—too late to forecast, but confirming the price weakness.

With more experience, the trader would possibly have recognized that price was going down, but TV/OBV, even though it was showing distribution was not following. But this analysis is not really provided for the beginning trader.

Figure 9-6A

for 201st trade to 550th trade

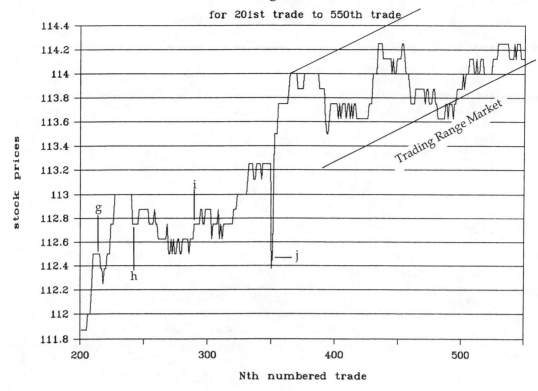

Figure 9-6B

for 201st to 550th trade

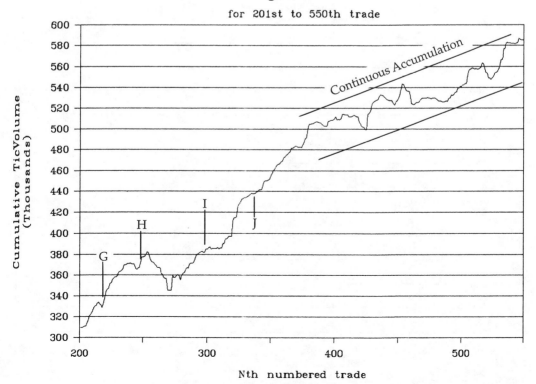

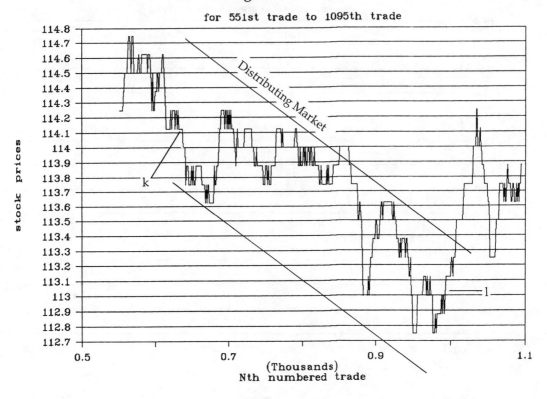

Figure 9-7A

for 551st trade to 1095th trade

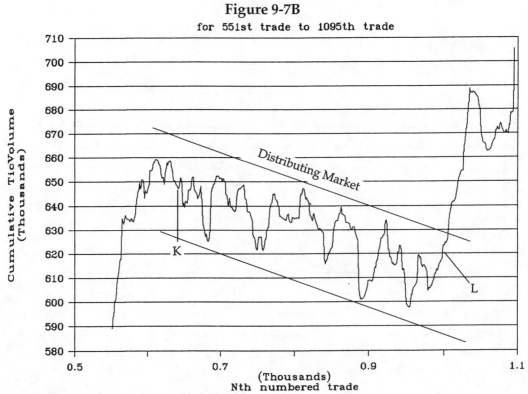

Figure 9-7B

for 551st trade to 1095th trade

At Point L, towards the end of the trading day at the 939th trade of 4300 shares at about $113.00, a rush of accumulation comes into the market. TV/OBV charges into new highs and takes out the previous high of 659,200 and closes with TV/OBV standing at 705,300. Looking strictly at this type of TV/OBV pattern, one might have concluded that there was buying, not necessarily accumulation, towards the close price of $113.875. The last 150 trades continue upward.

The next day, the price of IBM touches a high of $114.50, but closes lower. The trade deficit came out in the opening and surprised everyone with its bearishness.

When to Apply On-Balance Volume

On-balance volume can be used to good advantage whenever one is dealing with a market situation in which there are "smart" moneyed players. This is an excellent tool for the trader with a mid- to long-term timeframe.

Since OBV's basic premise is that "smart money's" moves are the ones to be followed, it is reasonable to assume that uninformed traders may not behave according to OBV standards, and the indicators in such cases would merely reflect herd instinct, or uninformed buying.

On-balance volume takes many weeks, even months, to develop, and therefore is of little use to those who trade on short timeframes or in volatile markets where tops and bottoms come too frequently. Despite this fact, OBV can be used as an important confirmation/non-confirmation for other methods which do use shorter timeframes. For example, Market Profile® daily patterns can be uncertain at times (see chapter on Market Profile®). Knowing the broader context of a market's underlying trend can sometimes help resolve doubts about where the pattern is heading. As a further example, a short-term moving average technique sometimes gets into a situation where the crossover indicators just graze each other. OBV could tell traders whether a real breakout was imminent or whether to ignore the grazing signal. Besides supplementing shorter timeframe techniques, OBV can supplement some of the longer-range cyclic recognition techniques. OBV might help traders decide at what point an Elliott Wave pattern had peaked or bottomed, just as Elliott Wave impules waves might tell whether an OBV volume breakout was real or not.

On-balance volume, as a trading technique is used best in situations where price is not immediately reflecting accumulation pressures. This is directly attributable to the fact that the strength of market buying or selling is not reflected in price first, but volume first. Even before price goes up, the supply of stocks or futures must be accumulated and diminished. It is only when the supply of stocks or futures is diminished that we find price moving up to reflect both increased demand and decreasing supplies at higher prices.

On-balance volume does not work in distributing markets because stocks, more so than futures, are not distributed in a tight price range, but in a broad range of prices. Accumulation takes place in narrow ranges and distribution takes place in wide price swinging markets. Graphic OBV charts at tops of markets, even though they would show erosion and hence distribution, would be far too late in giving a sell signal—price would have broken down much earlier. The weakness of OBV as an indicator in distribution is not a flaw of this approach, but rather a by-product of the market stage that traders find themselves in—bear markets and its price drops do not last as long as those in bull markets.

A note on the application of OBV techniques to futures analysis is warranted here. Since volume disclosure is a required adjunct of this analysis, OBV cannot be applied legitimately to futures analysis techniques. Additionally the volume figures that are disclosed by the futures exchanges are subject to great interpretation. Certain futures trade in new and old contract months. In rare cases the prices of the contracts and new contracts can settle on either side, one season's contract settles higher and the next season's contract settles lower. In such cases traders do whatever they think they must do without throwing off their cumulative totals. In cases like these the mandatory rule is to keep this "error" constant throughout the cumulation of these numbers, that is, if it is agreed that only the front end contracts be considered then it must be carried throughout the calculations.

Where to Find Out More About On-Balance-Volume

Books and Periodicals

Foster, Orline D. *The Art of Tape Reading: Ticker Technique.* Revised and edited by Dr. Robert H. Persons, Jr., with additional material by Don Worden, and Herbert Liesner, Palisades Park, N.J.: Investors' Press, Inc., 1965.

Granville, Joseph. Granville's *New Strategy of Daily Stock Market Timing for Maximum Profit.* Englewood Cliffs, N.J.: Prentice-Hall, Inc., 1976. This is the classic work in OBV analysis.

Software to Run on the IBM Personal Computer

Chart Trader Plus—Interday charting package with the following: median lines, Fibonacci lines and spheres, recursion lines, percentage retracements, simple moving averages with bands, oscillators, relative strength Index, on-balance volume, %R, cycle intervals, and parallel channels. Investor's Toolkit Ltd., Summit, IL 60501.

Computrac—Interday charting package has the following studies: moving averages, rates of change, oscillators, ratios and spread, RSI, stochastics, on-balance volume moving average convergence divergence, point-and-figure, etc. Chart zooming, trend lines and parallel channels, cycle analysis with Fourier analysis. Computrac, Inc., New Orleans, LA 70175.

CTS Trend—A software package which is a basic miniversion of Tradecenter. It creates many different types of studies, including realtime studies. CTS Trend, Newark, NJ 07974.

MetaStock—Interday charting package has graphics, but primitive hardcopy features. Many moving averages, trading bands, parallel channels, linear-regression lines, cycle-interval lines, On-Balance Volume, RSI, positive/negative volume and relative-performance ratios. Computer Asset Management, Salt Lake City, UT 84126.

Relevance III™—Interday charting package which creates above-average screen graphics and the finest hardcopy available using regular computer equipment. Performs many advanced type studies and has the only available Elliott Wave ratio analysis program. Holt Investment, Nashville, TN 37238.

Telescan Analyzer—A front-end interday charting package which accesses only their own database of 7000 stocks and 150 market indices. Data retrieval cost: 50 cents peak hours and 25 cents off peak access. Telescan, Inc., Houston, TX 77042.

10

Market Profile
Familiar Patterns
in Statistics

Market Profile Techiques at a Glance

Background and Philosophy of Market Profile

Market Profile is based on the belief that markets are the place where price adjusts to value over time: equilibriums are established until unbalanced. The Market Profile technician recognizes the different typical adjustment patterns.

Principles of Market Profile

The day is segmented into half-hour periods with letters of the alphabet representing each segment. All prices traded during one segment receive that segment's respective letter. There are three basic patterns that develop (see charts in Set-up section):

- *Trend days*—Distribution pattern falls into earlier and later clumps of value, showing an overall bowed shape. Price action is steady in one direction.
- *Non-trend days*—Price action goes nowhere and the day' pattern resembles an amorphous lump.
- *Normal days*—Opening price action can quickly cover a wide range and then retraces. Over the entire day price tends toward the center of the day's range.

How to Set Up and Maintain Market Profile

- *Decide on strategy*—Either sell the top and buy the bottom, or sell breakdowns while buying upside breakouts.
- *Decide on timeframe*—Market Profile will serve long-term traders as an indicator for use with other methods. Short-term traders can use Market Profile as the primary method.
- *Begin charting*—Traders set up a vertical base-line (*auction line*) to the left of their chart covering full range of prices for the day. They enter each half-hour's letter opposite every price level covered in that period.
- *Trade on the information*—During a *normal* day can take advantage of one of the extremes earlier in the day or of a later irregularity away from the indicated final objective. During a *non-trend* day they should not initiate new trades but use information as a longer-term indicator. During a *trend* day, they should try to position themselves early and then ride the trend to the end of the day. Market Profile may be used long-term to confirm market strength.

How to Trade with Market Profile Techniques

Since this technique is basically a short term trading approach to market analysis, it can be applied independently of the actual long term market trend. Hence, this technique is usable in all markets: bull, bear and neutral. When using this technique traders must be aware of the longer term trends. Otherwise the effectiveness of the use of this technique is diminished, i.e. buying trending days up in long term bear markets can be profitable, but the effort to obtain these profits are great. It would be better for traders to wait for a trend day down to initiate sell positions when they find themselves in long-term bear markets.

When to Apply Market Profile Techniques

Use Market Profile as a confirming indicator or warning flag with long-term techniques. Trend days show breakouts or market strength. Non-trend days show underlying weaknesses of the major trend and impending reversals.

Glossary for Market Profile

Auction Line—A vertical line on the left-hand side of a daily chart. The first half-hour's price-trading range of high to low prices is entered here. Future price moves into new price territory is also entered here and will compose the auction line's continuation.

Distribution Pattern—A knot of half-hour letters appearing on a daily chart, indicating sustained action around that price range.

Liquidity Data Bank®—A Market Profile distribution with further details on volume traded at each price level. Volume is further broken down into local trader volume and hedger volume.

Normal Day—A day in which the distribution pattern resembles a pot belly. During the opening periods, price ranges widely and retraces. This oscillation settles down as the day progresses and price tends toward a closing objective at around the midpoint of the day's range.

Market Profile—A statistical distribution of price activity over discrete time intervals which form bell-shaped profiles. The implication is that certain statistical distributions occur with greater frquency than others.

Profile—The visual shape of a daily chart.

Non-Trend Day—A day in which no clear distribution pattern emerges and whose profile resembles a large clump.

Tails—The two extreme ends of a normal day Market Profile chart.

Time-Price-Opportunity Count—A counting of frequency of distributions of price occurrences as defined by letters above and below a center line. Evaluation of the balance allows for further evaluation of the Market Profile directional implications.

Trend Day—A day in which the profile resembles a bow shape, due to two (and rarely three) distinct distribution patterns. Price moves slowly but steadily in one direction.

Value Area—A clustering of trade activity around a range of prices. The narrower the range and/or the greater the clustering of trades the greater the significance of that price level. *See* **Distribution Pattern.**

Background and Philosophy of Market Profile

Market Profile represents a body of analytical information about the behavior of the market which the trader is free to use in whatever manner or within whatever framework he or she pleases.

The thing that makes Market Profile so useful to the trader is its conceptual coherence. That coherence does, in fact, imply some sort of underlying framework with its own assumptions about the nature of the market. For one thing, its very existence means Market Profile assumes that the market follows certain daily patterns which can be codified and recognized. Furthermore, this recognition is based on certain assumptions about what price represents, assumptions which have been well articulated by Market Profile's creator, Peter Steidlmayer.

Price and Time: The Market's Way of Adjusting to Value

Steidlmayer sees value as being the constant medium within which the market for anything moves, be it a stock, commodity or other tradable issue. Value, however, can only be manifested through market acceptance, which is basically indicated by market volume, not price. The value is expressed or becomes "liquid" through the play of price over time. The market is constantly adjusting to changes in value and to over- or under-pricing.

Learning to Recognize the Common Patterns of Value-Adjustment

By monitoring these adjustments in price over time, that is, in value, traders can see the underlying value adjustment patterns, learn to recognize them, and take advantage of the ensuing price changes. It is this feature of pattern recognition of daily prices on an hourly basis which defines the Market Profile technique.

Principles of Market Profile

Plotting Price in Half-Hour Segments

The Market Profile technician segments the daily market into half-hour price ranges, assigning successive letters of the alphabet to each half-hour segment. The price action in each half-hour segment is then plotted on a chart big enough to show a day's price range. Every price reached in a given half hour receives the period's corresponding letter next to it. If that price level already has the letter from another half-hour period entered, then the technician simply enters the current half-hour's letter immediately to the right of the one already there.

Three Types of Price Pattern

There are three basic patterns which define any day in terms of price activity:

- *Trend days* show a significant change in the price level from the beginning to the end of the day;
- *Non-trend days* show no tendency toward any price objective and no large price range;
- *Normal days* show a tendency for the price to oscillate with progressively less amplitude as the day goes on, closing at a point about midway between the day's upper and lower extremes.

Significance for the Short and Long Terms

The main use traders can make of this information is to try to recognize the type of day which is developing in the early hours of the trading day and thus establish short-term positions. They might also use this information in conjunction with some other, longer-term trading scheme to yield information about trends and longer-range strength and weakness.

The Market Profile itself, established by Peter Steidlmayer at the Chicago Board of Trade, is an approach of viewing market supply and demand during the course of the trading day. Liquidity Data Bank® contains information to supplement this basic technique, giving more detailed volume breakdown information for each half-hour's activity: small trader and large trader activity at all price levels. At the moment, the Chicago Board of Trade is the only exchange to provide such information for the longer term.

Volume is critical in making more informed analysis of market activity.

How to Set Up and Maintain Market Profile

No Set-Up Computation—But More Homework Needed

Starting to trade with this method is both simpler and more demanding than those other methods which require some sort of indicator/trend line to be kept. On the one hand, there is no preliminary computation or set-up to be done. On the other hand, there is a lot of homework to be done first, as well as a lot of charting during the day, since this is essentially an intraday charting method which can be extended into a longer time frame.

Deciding on Strategy and Timeframe

Traders must first decide which strategy they will use on the different types of days and work out some sort of disciplined personal system for trading these different market patterns. There are two general trading strategies to choose from—sell the top and buy the bottom, or buy breakouts and sell breakdowns.

Use Over the Shorter Term

Traders may decide to use Market Profile as a short term, hourly strategy, in which case it can be their primary tool to create daily patterns in the first hours and, thus, forecast their strategy. Traders should decide on and test personal approaches to Market Profile information if they plan to use the method short-term. Steidlmayer stresses that every trader's personality is different and, therefore, different traders will use different trading approaches that help them to maintain personal trading discipline while maximizing profits.

Longer-term Use of Market Profile

Market Profile may be used long-term in two ways: 1) by charting the progress the market over period involving many days or months, so that Market Profile is simply a type of indicator which supplements some trend-following, strength indicator or 2) as a volume-determining or pattern-recognizing method.

Get the Necessary Information

Traders may select a data service which gives Market Profile information. They must also decide what other information will be relevant to the Market Profile approach.

Traders can set up their own charts without special Market Profile information services by reformatting a regular 30-minute bar chart. If they do this, traders must decide what to do about gaps in price information (such as prices where no trades occurred during the particular half-hour time segment).

Once they have prepared themselves in these ways traders may chart a day's action as follows:

Setting Up a Chart with the Full Possible Price Range

Before the day begins, traders should set up a chart which will show a range giving the entire spectrum of possible price ranges during the day. The chart should use as its height the possible price range and should be wide enough to accommodate as many units as there are half hour segments in the day. (It would only be necessary to go this wide in the extreme case that the price was in the same range during the entire day and so every half-hour segment at that level would be occupied.)

Traders should draw a vertical line on the left-hand side of the chart. Whenever a price is reached for the first time during the day in one of the half-hour periods, the letter for that period should go on that line. This line is called the *auction line* by Market Profile technicians.

Using a Letter of the Alphabet for Each Half-Hour Period

Traders assign a letter to each half-hour during the day that the market they are tracking is open. This will be the same every day and so needs to be done only once. Thereafter, traders just keep a small chart handy for reference when they plot price action. After a while, of course, they will know this by heart and so won't even need the reference chart. As an example, a market open from 9:00 to 4:00 would have half-hour letters that looked like this:

Figure 10-1

Letters	Time Brackets
A	9:00—9:30
B	9:30—10:00
C	10:00—10:30
D	10:30—11:00
E	11:00—11:30
F	11:30—12:00
G	12:00—12:30
H	12:30—1:00
I	1:00—1:30
J	1:30—2:00
K	2:00—2:30
L	2:30—3:00
M	3:00—3:30
N	3:30—4:00

Charting Every Price Level Reached in Each Half-hour Segment

During the day, for each price level occupied by the market, traders note the half-hour segment by writing the appropriate letter for that segment at the price level. If the price fluctuates a lot during a half hour, then that particular letter will appear in many places on the chart. Traders should end up with something that looks like the figures in the next few pages.

Sample Charts For Market Profile

Figure 10-2

Normal Day Profile

```
D
D
D J
D EH I  J  K
D EF HI  J  K
D EF G HI  J  K
D EF G HI  J  K
D EF J  K
D
D
```

Figure 10-3

Non-Trend Day Profile

```
D E
A B C D E F  J  K
A B C D E F  G H I J K L
A B C D E F  G H I J K L M
A B F G H K  L M
A B F H L M
A
```

Figure 10-4

Strong Trend Day Profiles

Profile Type 1   *Profile Type 2*

```
                                 L
                                 L
                                 H L
                                 H J K L
A B C                            H J K L M
A B C                            H I J K L M
A B C D E                        G H I J K L
B C D E F                        G H I J K
C D E F G                        G
C E F G                          G
C F G H                          F G
F G H                            F G
G H I                            F G
H I                              B D E F G
H I   K L                        B D E F
I J K L                          B C D E F
I J K L M                        A B C D E F
I J K L M                        A B C D E F
I J K L M                        A B
I J K                            A B
                                 A
                                 A
                                 A
                                 A
```

How to Trade with Market Profile

Come Well-Prepared—This Technique Is Not for Novices

To successfully trade with the Market Profile technique, traders need to have made the preparations noted in the preceding section.

These preparations are especially emphasized for this technique, because they include certain matters of personal discipline which are easy to overlook: traders must become familiar with the daily pattern types and define a personal trading style or strategy before embarking upon Market Profile trading. Otherwise, they will simply muddle through and drift along with each day's trading without a clear sense of where they are headed. In other words, Market Profile is not the best technique for beginning traders to use.

It is, indeed, an extremely powerful and accurate weapon in the trader's arsenal, but it is likely to backfire if the user doesn't know the kind of game he or she is hunting and what its habits are.

Learn to Recognize the Profiles of Distribution Patterns

The most important things for traders to know are the typical daily patterns, as given in the figures below. These three types of patterns are distinguished from each other by the type and arrangement of distribution pattern they show. A distribution pattern is a visual cluster of many half-hour letters together in the same area on a daily chart. These distribution patterns form clumps on the chart. The variation in thickness between a clump and a more sparsely-frequented price range makes a certain profile stand out. The typical profiles of the various distribution patterns are what give the Market Profile technician the power to literally recognize how the day is "shaping up" at a glance.

Trading the Normal Day

Recognizing the Pattern for a Normal Day

A normal day pattern occurs about 65-75 per cent of the time. During a normal day, the price begins by probing both high and low levels at first, but gradually, as the day wears on, succeeding prices tend to cluster more and more around a central value more or less midway between the high and low. Part of a typical normal day "profile" is shown below. Profile refers to the shape finally formed by the right-hand line of half-hour price notations on the Market Profile chart. If traders were to trace a normal day's profile, it would look like a pot belly, with the last hours sticking out toward the middle of the range on the right and the first hours extended up and down on the left.

Figure 10-5

Normal Day Profile

```
D
D
D J
D E HI J K
D E F G HI J K
D E F G HI J K
D E F G HI J K
D E F J  K
D
D
```

The trick, of course, is to be able to determine within the first few hours of the market's opening whether it is a normal day or something else. Remember that the first hours are represented by the first letters of the alphabet. If traders see a wide range covered by the price in the first several periods, followed by retracements, then they have received the classic signal for a normal day. To further confirm that a normal day is developing, traders should wait to see if a distribution pattern, or the value area, seems to be forming toward the middle of the range covered in the opening periods.

The trading day's final price objective is going to be around the middle of the distribution pattern.

Trading a Normal Day: Two Basic Options

It is up to the individual trader to do what he or she wishes with this insight. However, traders would be wise to follow one or perhaps both of these options:

- *Option I*—They could wait for an anomalistic later period, such as J in the (sample illustration). As the half hour represented by the letter J shows, the market does not trend with strict mathematical regularity, and this type of irregularity, combined with the trader's knowledge of the general trend, will make profitable trading plays possible. The trader can wait to enter longs in long term bull markets by buying at the lower half of the "belly," and not selling at the upper half.

- *Option II*—They could take advantage of one of the extremes of the early hours. Traders can do this well if they can determine fairly early that they are in a normal day. Traders can buy the lower half and cover in the middle; or they can sell at the top half and over in the middle. They should make sure to religiously liquidate their position at the day's end if they decide to make such a play, trusting that the market will follow the pattern and close around a central value, and therefore at a point favorable to their position.

Trading the Non-Trend Day

Recognizing the Non-Trend Day's Pattern

A non-trend day has the following typical profile:

Figure 10-6

Non-Trend Day Profile

```
D E
A B C D E F J K
A B C D E F G H I J K L
A B C D E F G H I J K L M
A B F G H K L M
A B F H L M
A
```

That is, its profile resembles an amorphous lump.

Trading Strategy for a Non-Trend Day: Use Caution

On a non-trend day, it is best for traders to stay out of the market if they rely on short-term trading as their bread and butter and if they have no other indicators than Market Profile for their short-term trend indicators.

A non-trend day's price movement is rather desultory and there is nothing in the first hours to indicate exactly where the final price is going to end up nor is there any clear directional tendency in the whole day. The day's aggregate price notations just hang together in an amorphous clump.

Using a Non-Trend Day as an Indicator for Longer-Term Positions

The non-trend day is not a total loss, however. It might tell those looking at long term trades that the day's range is not too indicative of any trend. Rather, the day's middle price range should be taken as its representative price.

As an indicator of general confusion or uncertainty, such a day might well indicate the weakening of the dominant tendency in the market or even herald an imminent reversal point: there are evenly matched buyers and sellers at this narrow ranged point.

Since a non-trend day occurs only about 10% of the time, traders will not have to deal with it more than about twice a month in any given market. When it does occur, they should pay attention to the signals it is giving for the longer-range trends.

Trading the Trend Days

Recognizing the Trend Day's Typical Patterns

The trend day is the most spectacular day as far as trading opportunities go. Unfortunately, it can also be the most deceptive. As the typical profiles on the next page show, a trend day need not open with a quick run of prices over a wide range. Rather, it can inch slowly and steadily in the same direction all day, or it can start slow and end with a rapid rush. This can catch many traders off guard, since they are looking for a normal distribution day which occurs abut 70% of the time and expect to see a large incremental change in any one time period, and so let the market's steady march lull them into inactivity.

The Double-Bow Shaped Pattern

For both Strong Trend Profile Patterns, there is a spurt around the middle of the trading day which separates the ranges of the earlier hours from the ranges of the later hours.

The typical profile shape for the trend day is bowed. Market Profile technicians call this a *double distribution pattern* due to the appearance of an earlier and a later distribution pattern during the same day, whereas the normal day's distribution pattern looks like a pot belly and the non-trend day shows an amorphous lump. On rare occasions, a trend day's profile will develop a triple distribution pattern instead of a double.

Type 1 Trend Days

A trend day with Profile Type 1 advances in very small increments, forming a cluster in the earlier hours, then a longer run in the middle hours, and a smaller, more spread-out cluster in the closing hours.

Type 2 Trend Days

Profile Type 2 is somewhat more spectacular. The price ranges for each time period and for the day as a whole are wider, and the direction taken by the ranges tends always in the same direction. Again, there are two clusters of price range in the earlier and later hours.

Figure 10-7

Strong Trend Day Profiles

Profile Type 1   *Profile Type 2*

```
                              L
                              L
                              H L
                              H J K L
A B C                         H J K L M
A B C                         H I J K L M
A B C D E                     G H I J K L
B C D E F                     G H I J K
C D E F G                     G
C E F G                       G
C F G H                       F G
F G H                         F G
G H I                         F G
H I                           B D E F G
H I K L                       B D E F
I J K L                       B C D E F
I J K L M                     A B C D E F
I J K L M                     A B C D E F
I J K L M                     A B
I J K                         A B
                              A
                              A
                              A
                              A
```

Strategy: Stake a Position Early and Ride It to the Day's End

Provided a trader can recognize a trend day quickly enough in the early hours, the strategy is simple: establish a position on the proper side of the trend, and ride it to the end of the day.

Significance of the Trend Day to Longer-term Traders

For the longer-term trader, a trend day can either simply confirm a trend that longer-range indicators are showing, or it can provide evidence of a breakout. Volume measures supplied with the more detailed Liquidity Data Bank® information can tell traders how strong the trend is and what it might or might not foretell. Volume is the final indicator of whether or not a newly-achieved price level is accepted or not, by current market conditions. If volume is high at one end, then one could expect price to work around that area more before it moves away from that area.

Trading March 1987 Treasury Bonds Using Market Profile

This example came from the trading activity for bond futures on December 22, 1986.

After the first 2-1/2 hours' trading, we see the following price spread for the first five half-hour periods of the day. Modest ranges are defined in each half-hour, with each range creeping slightly upward over the previous ranges. According to Market Profile practice, this has all the earmarks of a classic trend day to the upside:

Figure 10-8

99	25/32	E		
99	24/32	E		
99	23/32	E		
99	22/32	D	E	
99	21/32	D	E	
99	20/32	C	D	
99	19/32	C	D	
99	18/32	C	D	
99	17/32	C	D	
99	16/32	B	C	
99	15/32	B	C	
99	14/32	B	C	
99	13/32	A	B	C
99	12/32	A	B	
99	11/32	A	B	
99	10/32	A	B	
99	09/32	A	B	
99	08/32	A	B	
99	07/32	A		
99	06/32	A		

Recall that, during the first half of the day, the first of two distribution patterns should fill out on the bottom side of the trend day's bow-shaped pattern. Traders should wait another hour to see if this will happen:

Figure 10-9

99	26/32	F G
99	25/32	E F G
99	24/32	E F G
99	23/32	E F G
99	22/32	D E F G
99	21/32	D E G
99	20/32	C D E G
99	19/32	C D
99	18/32	C D
99	17/32	C D
99	16/32	B C
99	15/32	B C
99	14/32	B C
99	13/32	A B C
99	12/32	A B
99	11/32	A B
99	10/32	A B
99	09/32	A B
99	08/32	A B
99	07/32	A
99	06/32	A

It does, indeed, look like this is going to happen somewhere around price level 99-22/32. Since the trend day should close considerably higher, traders now initiate a long position at the close of period G (the end of the sixth half hour) and, with a fair degree of confidence, sit back to watch their profits accumulate through to the end of the day.

The classic pattern is followed closely—a distribution pattern does form through periods G through K between the price levels of 99-26/32 and 99-20/32.

During period K, the breakout happens, and prices in that period shoot upward to 100-6/32. Period L defines a smaller range at the top, and the day closes with period M's prices within the range of period L, thus filling out a smaller distribution pattern at the top and completing the bow or double-curve pattern.

Since traders decided to liquidate at the end of the day, based on the morning's perception of where the market was headed, they would have a profit which would be the difference of the price in the M range where they liquidated and the price in the G range where they made the decision to buy.

Figure 10-10

100	06/32	K
100	05/32	K
100	04/32	K L M
100	003/32	K L M
100	02/32	K L M
100	01/32	K L
100		K L
99	31/32	K L
99	30/32	K
99	29/32	K
99	28/32	K
99	27/32	K
99	26/32	F G K
99	25/32	E F G K
99	24/32	E F G I J K
99	23/32	E F G H I J K
99	22/32	D E F G H I
99	21/32	D E G H I
99	20/32	D E G H I
99	19/3	C D
99	18/32	C D
99	17/32	C D
99	16/32	B C
99	15/32	B C
99	14/32	B C
99	13/32	A B C
99	12/32	A B
99	11/32	A B
99	10/32	A B
99	09/32	A B
99	08/32	A B
99	07/32	A
99	06/32	A

Having bought at G period, 99.22, traders can sell their position out at around the close, M period or 100.02, for a nice intraday trading profit of 12/32 of a bond point.

Notice in this example—and this is very important—traders should not initiate a position on the first indication of a typical pattern. Rather, they wait for further confirming information before staking anything on their hunch.

Trading June 1987 Treasury Bonds Using Market Profile

This trading example came from bond futures trades for March 27, 1987.

Notice that the reporting service and software uses different letters for the same periods, preferring to start the trading with the letter E and running up through the letter Q. Variations can exist as long as they are standardized.

During the first 2-1/2 hours (E through I), there is a less-than-classic pattern—indication seems to lean toward a trend day to the upside, as there are modest ranges and there also appears to be some upward creep. However, the upward motion is not consistent, as periods H, J and K do not break any new ground on price. Also, the width of the distribution pattern is already too much for this to look like the beginning of a trend day: non-trend and normal days, to a lesser extent, tend to pick up this kind of knotted mass, and not trend days. Traders, therefore, cautiously diagnose either a normal or a non-trend day. A normal day is more likely, because there does seem to be some concentric motion toward a definite price objective around the 100-15/32 level or so. What traders should expect after period K would be the formation of a short "tail" to the upside, "balancing" the tail formed to the downside during period E, from 100-11/32 to 100-8/32. This double tail would then form the base over which the day's price range would gradually contract.

Figure 10-11

100	20/32	I J	
100	19/32	I J K	
100	18/32	I J K	17 TPO
100	17/32	F I J K	
100	16/32	F G H I K	
100	15/32	E F G H I K	⇐center line
100	14/32	E F G H K	
100	13/32	E F G K	
100	12/3	E K	11 TPO
100	11/32	E	
100	10/32	E	
100	09/32	E	
100	08/32	E	

At this time traders can perform a "balancing" calculation. They ascertain that the widest price is 100 15/32 and infer that most of the day's volume was at that price (since they don't have any actual idea of volume, they are using price change activity to signal volume movements: the more price fluctuates, the greater the activity in the value area of a Market Profile chart). By counting the number of price changes and comparing the number of price changes above and below this center line, traders would be performing primitive Price/Time/Opportunity analysis. In this case, the number above the center line, 17, is compared with the number below the line, 11. The extreme tails are ignored in this count because of the assumption that tails have the thinnest volume activity. (This is where a *detailed* breakdown of volume activity would disclose whether or not volume was relatively large, and therefore not normal, or else it was small, and therefore was normal at the tails.) The strategy, based on this cursory count: sell any rallies. Traders sell because analysis shows that every time price reached to the high end of this profile, it met volume activity. Since it was at higher prices that volume came into play, traders can assume with high probability that the sellers were the more active participants.

Traders should wait for further information before committing themselves to a possible long position. A long position is warranted here because of the formation of the E tail which has to be balanced by a later period tail formation at the higher end. At this point, they have conflicting analysis: they could buy because the higher priced tail has not formed and must form if this is to be a normal day with a 70% probability of recurrence, or they could sell because their TPO count suggested lower prices. The further information is not long in coming, and it is a surprise! Instead of forming a tail on the upside, period L falls below any previous price level. At this point, it's still possible that the price is just embellishing the "tail" formed by E and will spend the rest of the day putting on that tail to the upside and filling out the distribution pattern that already exists. But now comes the bombshell, when period M plunges even more precipitously. The normal day pattern has failed! The day looks quite unpredictable, so traders do not yet call to tell their brokers to buy or sell. This is an erratic pattern, and it's still too early to call the shots.

Figure 10-12

100	20/32	I	J				
100	19/32	I	J	K			
100	18/32	I		J	K		
100	17/32	F	I	J	K		
100	16/32	F	G	H	I	K	
100	15/32	E	F	G	H	I	K
100	14/32	E	F	G	H	K	
100	13/32	E	F	G	K	L	
100	12/32	E	K	L			
100	11/32	E	L				
100	10/32	E	L				
100	09/32	E	L				
100	08/32	E	L	M			
100	07/32	L	M				
100	06/32	L	M				
100	05/32	L	M				
100	04/32	L	M				
100	03/32	M					
100	02/32	M					
100	01/32	M					
100		M					
99	31/32	M					
99	30/32	M					
99	29/32	M					
99	28/32	M					

At the day's close there is a pattern that might be called a "failure of a normal day pattern." In other words, one that looked like a normal day and then took off in another direction. Of course, since traders were not able to recognize the pattern as soon as in the first example, there is little possibility that they actually got off a trade to take advantage of the finally recognizable downtrend. However, this formation signals a weakness—the value area found around the 100-16/32 area offers much resistance to further upside moves and the inability for even a short tail to form on the high ends shows much selling—that will carry over into the next trading scenario…

Figure 10-13

100	20/32	I	J				
100	19/32	I	J	K			
100	18/32	I	J	K			
100	17/32	F	I	J	K		
100	16/32	F	G	H	I	K	
100	15/32	E	F	G	H	I	K
100	14/32	E	F	G	H	K	
100	13/32	E	F	G	K	L	
100	12/32	E	K	L			
100	11/32	E	L				
100	10/32	E	L				
100	09/32	E	L				
100	08/32	E	L	M			
100	07/32	L	M				
100	06/32	L	M				
100	05/32	L	M				
100	04/32	L	M				
100	03/32	M					
100	02/32	M					
100	01/32	M	N				
100		M	N				
99	31/32	M	N				
99	30/32	M	N				
99	29/32	M	N				
99	28/32	M	N	O			
99	27/32	N	O				
99	26/32	N	O				
99	25/32	N	O				
99	24/32	N	O				
99	23/32	N	O	P			
99	22/32	O	P	Q			
99	21/32	O		P	Q		
99	20/32	O	P				
99	19/32	O	P				
99	18/32	O	P				
99	17/32	O	P				
99	16/32	O					

Once again, traders can see the value of waiting to take a position unless one is absolutely certain of the day's pattern. If they had gone on first impressions after the first two hours, they might have diagnosed a normal day and gone long. Traders would have had time to cut their losses in period L, at a price of 100 6/32, but since the day was already shaping up in an erratic manner, they would not have had enough assurance about future price action in order to initiate a short position in time to recoup losses.

Trading March 1987 Treasury Bonds Using Market Profile

This example came from bond futures trading activity on January 13, 1987.

This day also begins looking like a possible trend day. It opens with two modest range periods in A and B and creeps slowly but steadily upward in C through E. F and G begin to fill out the distribution pattern, making it a little too wide for a trend day. This greater width would indicate that a normal day is going to emerge. Traders try to catch price at the top of the G range to go short in anticipation of a finish around the middle of the range.

Figure 10-14

100	25/32	G
100	24/32	E G
100	23/32	D E F G
100	22/32	D E F G
100	21/32	C D E F G
100	20/32	C D E F
100	19/32	C D E F
100	08/32	A B C DF
100	17/32	A B C D
100	16/32	A B C D
100	15/32	A B C D
100	14/32	A B
100	13/32	A B
100	12/32	A B
100	11/32	A
100	10/32	A
100	09/32	A

Statistically speaking, traders should now expect there to be no more action above G, and some activity to extend the bottom of the range coupled with a lot of activity to fill in and widen the distribution pattern.

Figure 10-15

100	25/32	G
100	24/32	E G
100	23/32	D E F G
100	22/32	D E F G H
100	21/32	C D E F G H
100	20/32	C D E F H J
100	19/32	C D E F H J
100	18/32	A B C D F H J
100	17/32	A B C D H I J
100	16/32	A B C D H I J
100	15/32	A B C D H I J
100	14/32	A B H I J
100	13/32	A B H I J
100	12/32	A B I J
100	11/32	A I J
100	10/32	A I J
100	09/32	A I
100	08/32	I

If they were lucky, traders got out on one of the higher price ranges for period K and watched L feint upwards, while M closed right in the middle. With hindsight, traders can say this was a non-trend day.

Figure 10-16

100	26/32	L
100	25/32	G K L
100	24/32	E G K L
100	23/32	D E F GK L
100	22/32	D E F GH K L
100	21/32	C D E F G H K L
100	20/32	C D E F H J K L
100	19/32	C D E F H J K L
100	18/32	A B C DF H J K L M
100	17/32	A B C DH I J K L M
100	16/32	A B C DH I J K L
100	15/32	A B C DH I J
100	14/32	A B HI J
100	13/32	A B HI J
100	12/32	A B I J
100	11/32	A I J
100	10/32	A I J
100	09/32	A I
100	08/32	I

Observations on Trading with Liquidity Data Bank®

As each of the three preceding examples shows, it is not a good idea for traders to use this method to trade until they have seen a good deal of data on how the day is shaping up. In other words, it is best not to initiate a trade based on Market Profile data indications until the day is almost half over: when the profile is evenly balanced in the middle. This is because the Market Profile method is based on the fact that statistical distributions of price activity tends to follow a number of well-defined patterns from day to day. Therefore, the more information one has on the day's pattern, the more likely one is to be able to predict the rest of the day's tendency.

Liquidity Data Bank® data offers traders more information on the breakdown of the Market Profile. The trading volume of each price segment is disclosed. Currently, the Chicago Board of Trade is the only exchange to offer such information on volume for its futures contracts. As an industry practice, futures exchanges have never disclosed volume data on each associated price transaction.

Figure 10-17 Liquidity Data Bank® for T-Bonds

Volume Summary Report for 08/19/86

Commodity—U.S. Bonds

Volume Breakdown per Price

*NOTE—Volume figures shown are actual number of contracts multiplied by 2.

Contract	Trade Price	Volume	% of Total	CTI 1%	CTI 2%	Half Hour Bracket Times at which prices occurred
Sept 86	101 25/32	482	0.1	35.3	2.1	A
	101 26/32	8502	2.5	30.9	8.3	A
	101 27/32	3934	1.2	49.5	6.5	A
	101 28/32	4214	1.2	35.7	8.3	A
	101 29/32	1270	0.4	56.2	9.1	ACD
	101 30/32	5950	1.7	58.1	13.0	ABCD
	101 31/32	14580	4.3	63.3	10.4	ABCD
	102	23108	6.8	61.3	10.1	ABCD
	102 01/32	22340	6.6	59.5	8.1	ABCDHI
	102 02/32	21052	6.2	54.8	12.5	ABCDHI
	102 03/32	24076	7.1	61.2	11.9	ABCDHIL
	102 04/32	23696	7.0	56.0	10.6	ABCDFHIL
	102 05/32	22740	6.7	54.1	13.7	ABCDEFHIKL
	102 06/32	23510	6.9	58.9	10.0	ADEFHIKL
	102 07/32	18002	5.3	54.9	12.	ADEFGHIJKLM
	102 08/32	34596	10.2	52.6	14.0	DEFGHIJKLM
	102 09/32	28862	8.5	57.3	11.8	DEFGHIJKLM
	102 10/32	20112	5.9	56.0	14.6	DEFGHIJKL
	102 11/32	18248	5.4	54.9	15.5	FGHIJKL
	102 12/32	11936	3.5	57.2	9.5	FGJKL
	102 13/32	6588	1.9	59.8	13.1	FJ
	102 14/32	2278	0.7	56.7	10.6	FJ
	102 15/32	68	0.0	50.0	2.9	J

↑ Hedger Volume   ↑ Local Volume

70% Range of Daily Volume	102 01/32 to 102 10/32	238986	70.3	56.4	12.0	ABCDEFGHIJKLM

			% of Total	
			CTI1	CTI2
Total Volume for Sept 86 U.S. Bonds	—	340,144	56.3	11.7
Total Volume for U.S. Bonds	—	363,500	55.5	11.3
Total Spread Volume for Sept 86 U.S. Bonds	—	8,019	16.8	12.6

Courtesy of CISCO

Stock exchanges do offer this type of information and good tape readers can track volume. Liquidity Data Bank® was created to offer comparable insight into futures trading activity. Volume of transactions are separated into locals trading or hedgers trading. The basic analysis of volume at associated price levels is to determine where volume activity is out of line. Since the normal Market Profile bulges in the middle, one would expect about 70% of the day's volume in that area. However, if there is volume at extreme tails, then one can tell that whoever is selling there is selling at levels that will never be seen again, or whoever is buying is buying at levels that will never be seen again. If price can gravitate towards these areas of volume activity where, statistically, there should be no activity, then one can forecast that a newer value area is developing with its corresponding tail yet to be formed at the other side of the value area.

When to Apply Market Profile

Market Profile can work well for the trader who plans to make a living in the pit from positions which last for a day or less. It is, in fact, the only fully-blown trading approach for that time frame. Also, knowing where the profiles are forming can help an off-floor trader to initiate trades correctly.

Market Profile also works well as a supplement to longer-term trading techniques. The knowledge of where volume is forming, with the use of Liquidity Data Bank® data, is beneficial.

Traders should not use Market Profile by itself if they plan to trade in a longer time frame than the daily market. Although Market Profile can give valuable signals for longer term trades, these signals should only be taken as confirmation of what other, more long-term techniques indicate.

Traders unfamiliar with a market, should watch the Market Profile information on that market for some time in order to get used to what its typical profiles look like and how they shape up during the course of a day.

The conventional Market Profile and Liquidity Data Bank® techniques are based on half-hour time segments. There are markets which will not show a continuous formation using such half-hour blocks. In such cases, the profiles can either be very narrow or very fat. The stock indices, because of their great daily trading ranges, do not show good profile or value area formations: every profile looks like a trend day. In such cases *hourly* ranges often form better profiles. Increasing the time per segment also creates greater risk. Half-hour ranges do work well for individual stocks which have high trading activity and are therefore likely to show a price at each level, even for the larger ranges (TDY is okay for this, IBM and GM give so-so patterns, and T offer nothing but continuing bulges).

The main caution for Market Profile, more so than for other techniques, is that traders should use it only if they have experience in the market they are trying to trade. Contrary to what is taught elsewhere, traders need to understand market activity well before they can implement this approach. It was designed to be useful to people with different trading strategies and it claims to make no in-depth assumptions about the nature of the market. This implies that the trader brings these things to the method rather than having the method dictate them—so it naturally assumes an experienced, seasoned trader.

Though the technique stands alone as a complete system for trading on the very short term, it can be used to supplement long-term trading techniques as well. Sometimes the indicators it gives about the type of trading day can be most useful as confirming indicators or warning flags to those who are trading on a somewhat longer time scale.

Trend days can give signals of breakouts or reversals, though usually this type of day is going to give just as strong a signal through the more traditional indicators of opening and closing price alone.

Non-trend days are perhaps the most valuable as far as giving signals about the longer term. Because they occur so infrequently (about one day out of every 20 is a non-trend day), they stand out as days when the market is confused, undergoing some kind of major re-structuring, and therefore could be signals of the current trend's weakness or of an imminent reversal point.

Normal days should neither be taken in themselves as confirmation nor negation of a trend or reversal points. Since they are what occur most frequently in the market, they provide a sort of backdrop against which to watch the relation of trend days and non-trend days.

Where to Find Out More About Market Profile

Books and Periodicals

The main printed source of information about Market Profile® and Liquidity Data Bank® philosophy and techniques is in the published works of Peter Steidlmayer, the originator of the method:

Steidlmayer, J. Peter, and Kevin, Koy. *Markets and Market Logic*. Chicago, Illinois: The Porcupine Press, 1986.

Steidlmayer, J. Peter, and Shera Buyer. *Analyzing the Long-Term Trends with CBOT Market Profile®*. Chicago, Illinois: Market Logic, 1986.
Postscript: As of this writing Peter Steidlmayer is no longer associated with Market Logic School as an instructor.

Consulting Services/Classes

J. F. Dalton Associates, Market Profile® and Liquidity Data Bank® instructions. Chicago, Illinois 60604.

Financial Options Consultants, electronic classes, live seminars, and personal trade recommendations. Chicago, Illinois 60605.

Market Logic School. Peter J. Steidlmayer's organization. Offers classes and manuals. Chicago, Illinois 60605.

Computer Software

CBOT Market Profile®, Chicago: Chicago Board of Trade. A service of the Board of Trade, conceived by Steidlmayer. LaSalle at Jackson, Chicago, IL 60604.

Market Profile®, CQG. Software for real-time analysis of all raw market data. Glenwood Springs, CO 81602.

P.C. Quote Market Profile® Service P.C. Quote, 1986. Real-time analysis software. Chicago, IL 60605.

11

Basic Charting Techniques
The Old Standby

Basic Charting Techniques at a Glance

Background and Philosophy of Basic Charting Techniques

Chart analysis is the study of various bar chart price and volume patterns in order to be able to make correct price forecasts. There is no attempt to make time and cyclical forecasts with basic charting techniques. Most of current charting analysis is a direct result of the pioneering work done by Robert Rhea.

Principles of Basic Charting Techniques

Bar chart price and volume patterns divide market action into major bull-bear cycles, which in turn are composed of intermediate-size actions, which are themselves composed of minor movements. Lines connect local highs and lows to form recognizable patterns, each of which has its own implications for future activity. All of these indicators must be confirmed by appropriate volume activity to be considered valid. There are three classes of indicators.

1) *Reversal patterns*—These show that a major top or bottom is near, and are usually accompanied by a lack of volume activity.

2) *Consolidation patterns*—Mean that the price activity stays stable for a while. Some of these indicators indicate which way the breakout may go, while others are ambivalent. The volume patterns are part of the key to which way these breakouts will occur.

3) *Trend continuation patterns*—Indicate that the present bull or bear trend will continue for the near future. Confirmed by steady volume.

How to Set Up and Maintain Basic Charts

Technicians keep bar-charts of each day's high, low and close prices with volume histograms.

How to Trade with Basic Charting Techniques

Traders buy bear market reversals on confirmation, sell bull market reversals and hold or initiate positions on trend continuation signals. They stay out of the market on ambivalent consolidation indicators and enter it on the appropriate side if the indicator is definitive.

When to Apply Basic Charting Techniques

Basic charting techniques can be applied in all markets traded. There are no times that charts may not be used since at the very least, the charts a trader creates might not indicate immediate entry or exit signals, but can indicate future developments. The strength of this type of analysis is such that traders can use this approach alone and have profitable results. However, to refine the accuracy of this technique traders can use Gann Analysis (Swing Charts) and Elliott Wave cycle counts to help place more accurate buy or sell limits orders. Traders should ascribe oversold/overbought indicators to heighten profits.

Glossary for Basic Charting

NOTE: Refer to the sample charts on the following pages in this chapter for further clarification of these terms.

Channels—Two parallel lines which contain price movements on a bar chart. These parallel lines can be straight or curved but they represent support and resistance lines extended into the future.

Diamond—A pattern which usually occurs at major tops. Prices trade in a range which widens out, then narrows into a diamond shape which can either signal a reversal or a consolidation.

Double Bottom/Top—Two extended lows/highs of equal strength signalling the reversal of a bull/bear market.

Fan—A series of three lines connecting a single high (in falling price action) or low (in rising price action) with three consecutively lower highs or higher lows. When price breaks the third fan-line contrary to the major trend, a reversal breakout is signalled.

Flag—Two parallel lines of highs and lows at right angles to the current trend. Indicates consolidation and further work prior to resumption of the current trend.

Gaps—Gaps are areas on the bar chart where no trades are made. There are four types of gaps and each have significance: breakaway, common, exhaustion, and runaway (measuring) gaps.

Head and Shoulders—A reversal pattern occuring at the end of a bull or bear market, which in a bull market consists of a left congestion area followed by a charge to new highs and then a second congestion area around the same price level as the first, but below the price high of the peak.

Intermediate Cycle/Action—Movements lasting several weeks or months and which make up major cycles.

Key Reversals—One day action in which the market opens violently in the direction of the major trend, then goes into new price levels not reached prior, and then reverses direction and closes in the opposite direction. High volume is a signature of this formation.

Major Cycle—A bull-bear swing of important dimension spread out over several years.

Minor action—A market movement lasting one or several days, occasionally useful in analyzing intermediate trends.

Neckline—In a bull market the line connecting the local lows just before and after a Head formation. When it is broken to the downside after the right shoulder has formed it confirms the reversal. Reverse is true in head and shoulders bottoms.

Pennant—A flag whose sides converge to the right. Another example of a consolidation pattern.

Rectangle—Either a reversal or continuation pattern which is bounded by parallel horizontal lines.

Right Triangle—A triangle with a horizontal side toward the current trend which usually breaks out in the same direction as the trend.

Rounded Bottom/Top—A long, curving pattern which signals the end of a bull/bear market. This pattern is more common in bottoming markets rather than topping out markets. Typified by very low volume except in upside breakouts from the pattern.

Symmetrical Triangle—A triangle whose sides both converge to an apex, but not determinate of a consolidation or reversal.

Trendline—An upward sloping or downward sloping line containing all sell-off lows or rally lows, respectively. A *parallel* trendline may be created to contain the respective selloff highs or rally highs.

Triangle (coil)—An area consisting of two converging lines bounded by one high and low price. Can be various types of triangles and most likely to be consolidation patterns.

Wedge—A narrowing triangle within which price stays as it moves up or down. A rising wedge usually signals a reversal in a previous bull trending market.

Background and Philosophy
of Basic Charting Techniques

This approach to categorizing market action as seen in bar charts is really just a modern version of the techniques and viewpoints which naturally evolved among the first technical traders using the Dow Theory. The basic assumption behind this method is that the market usually behaves in more or less the same way when it is going to do something. Those who learn to recognize its tell-tale price and volume activity patterns can therefore be forewarned and take appropriate anticipatory trading action. The method is preoccupied with turning points, or, more accurately, with predicting the significant reversal points in the market cycle. Thus, the method assumes an underlying cyclicity in market phenomena: a bull market is followed by a bear market, visa versa.

A good understanding of the basic patterns in charting is a necessity in order for the trader to learn other trading techniques. From these basic charts, one can derive second order charting and mathematical functioning analysis.

Principles of the Dow Theory

Overview of the Dow Theory

The Dow Theory was formulated by Robert Rhea, one of the founders of the *Wall Street Journal*. Rhea's basic premise was that the rise and fall of any economy can be predicted in advance with the use of comparative analysis of two technical indicators that he developed: economic health of industrial companies and the economic health of transport companies.

Rhea's basic concept implied that industrial activity is reflected in advance by the economic health of transportation companies since it is the transport companies which physically have to transport the raw materials from their sources to the industrial centers for further processing. Even before the industrial companies can reflect rising profitability, the transport companies will have increasing activities and hence increasing profitability first. Therefore, if one could observe increasing profitability in transportation companies, then one could eventually profit from industrial companies' healthy economics.

Rhea took the major industrial companies and the major transport companies of his time and created two indices: Dow Jones Industrial Averages and the Dow Jones Transportation Averages. The third component of the Dow Jones Indices trio is the Dow Jones Utilities Averages. The third component is currently used in modern Dow Theory Analysis, but it was not an original component of the analysis. The Utilities Averages functions more as an indicator of interest rate trends. Based on his premise, the Transportation Averages would reflect heightened activity before the Industrials in good economic conditions. He charted both averages and compared the two averages to each other to gauge each other's comparative strength or weakness, with one average always leading the other. In bad economic conditions which eventually developed, he would notice that the Industrials would go to new highs on bar charts while the Transportations would fail to follow the lead. This divergence of direction in the averages would signal main investment strategy changes. Out of this approach, Rhea developed the Dow Theory which revolved around confirmation or non-confirmation of each index's activities. Out of this Theory developed the school of bar chart analysis, which is the analysis of recurring pattern formations in the indices.

Over the years of technical analysis, many chartists have noticed particular recurring patterns in bar charts outside of the averages and have categorized such types of formations. This chapter provides a quick summary of important formation patterns.

Hierarchy of Cycles

The Dow Theory sees the market as following longer, irregular bull-bear cycles of several years' length, known as *major* movements. Major movements are composed of smaller series of movements called *intermediate* movements. Intermediate movements can last several weeks or months. Finally, minor movements, which may only last for a day, make up each intermediate movement. These *minor* movements are generally too erratic and unpredictable to be of any use to the Dow Theory.

Price Pattern Formation

A price pattern for Dow Theory analysis is usually formed by creating high-low bar charts. Just which highs or lows are significant is not totally clear-cut at the time of formation, so there can be several ways of extracting patterns for the same chart. However, as time goes on the real pattern should become clearer. Patterns are classified in three major groups: reversal, consolidation (reversals and continuations), and trending. Volume patterns are also a necessary adjunct of Dow analysis. In fact, without a volume *confirmation* for many of these patterns, the pattern is considered to be a false signal.

Reversal Patterns

These patterns indicate imminent or already-occurring "tops" in a bull market and "bottoms" in a bear market. Reversal patterns are important to forecast because they allow traders to reverse their positions and follow the correct trend. These patterns are almost always accompanied by some critical volume pattern, that is, with volume picking up toward the middle of the pattern and dropping off toward the end, or vice versa.

Consolidation Patterns

These patterns indicate some type of halt in the march of a price tendency, and represent an even contest between supply and demand while the market sorts itself out. Some of these patterns may indicate which way price will break after the pattern is completed, while others are not considered to be useful predictors of breakout direction. Volume usually diminishes during the period in which these patterns occur, and the longer a consolidation pattern lasts, the less significant the eventual breakout.

Trend Patterns

These patterns indicate the current direction of the market's price tendency. They are important for providing support or resistance areas which show when a breakout from the tendency has occurred. In general, volume can confirm or negate the current trend, signalling whether or not it is to continue.

Volume Patterns

From the discussion of the three price-trend patterns, the reader can see that volume plays a key role in deciding whether a pattern has actually occurred and what it may mean. Volume is generally considered to take on either upward- or downward-curving patterns. This chapter serves merely to offer the reader the quickest route to technical analysis with patterns on bar charts. It is beyond the scope of this chapter to offer enough technical analysis data for the complete analysis of charts. Hence discussion of volume analysis is greatly reduced. Volume-significant patterns will be pointed out where possible.

Underlying Dow Theory shares on-balance volume's (see chapter on On-Balance Volume) interpretation of high volume as being a sign of accumulation or distribution by "insiders" at the top or bottom of the market, and public interest during the running periods of market activity.

Following the Patterns Through Various Cycles

Three trading examples and their respective commentaries towards the end of this chapter illustrate the application of various bar-chart patterns. The pages following immediately display two samples of each pattern.

First Pattern Group: Reversals

A reversal occurs at the end of one half of a cycle and the beginning of another, (that is, at the end of a bear market and the beginning of a bull market, or vice versa). Most, but not all, of the classical bar chart reversal patterns are applicable to both bull and bear markets, though in relatively inverted form (special note must by given to volume activity differences).

The ability to discern in advance what patterns are reversal patterns benefits traders by allowing them to reverse trading strategies. If the market is bullish and they have been buying on every reaction, it would help them to know that a reversal pattern was forming at the end of this bull move and that they can now prepare to sell on every rally.

The following reversal patterns are examined:

1) Head and Shoulders top or bottom
2) Rounded bottom or top
3) Double bottom or top (multiple bottom or top)
4) Diamond as reversal
5) Wedge top

Head and Shoulders Top/Inverted Head and Shoulders

This pattern can mark both the top of a bull market and, in its inverted form, the bottom of a bear market. The price pattern first forms a local top (or bottom) known as the *left shoulder* (at the time of formation, it appears merely as another point of congestion or consolidation for same-direction thrust) on increasing volume, dropping off as it retracts from this top (bottom). A second top (bottom) called the *head* (at the time of formation, the head appears merely to be a move to new highs from a previous congestion area, the left shoulder) then forms on higher volume, and price moves significantly higher (lower), once again dropping off in volume as it retraces. The *right shoulder* (at the time this forms it is another congestion area but this time at about the same price level as the left shoulder) then forms, lower than the head, and often lower than the left shoulder. If this right shoulder top is not lower than the head or the left shoulder, but higher, then there is a strong possibility that this might not be a head and shoulder top but a consolidation pattern. A line drawn through the extreme points of the two shoulders constitutes what is called the *neckline*. This neckline is the support line and should be strong enough to contain all selloffs in Head and Shoulder top formations. Significantly, it shows decreasing volume on the third attempt to the upside and volume increases dramatically when price breaks through the neckline to the downside.

Figure 11-1   IBM Showing Head and Shoulder Bottom

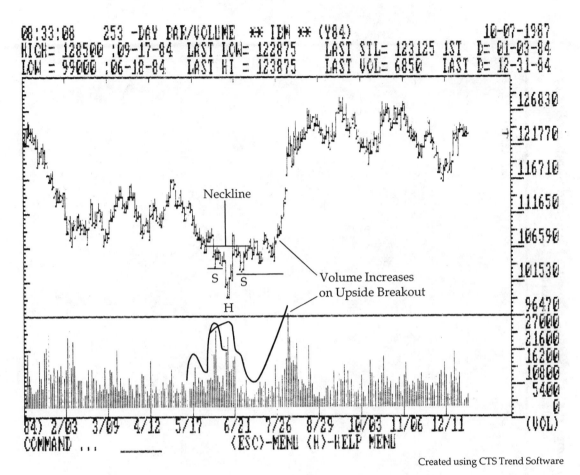

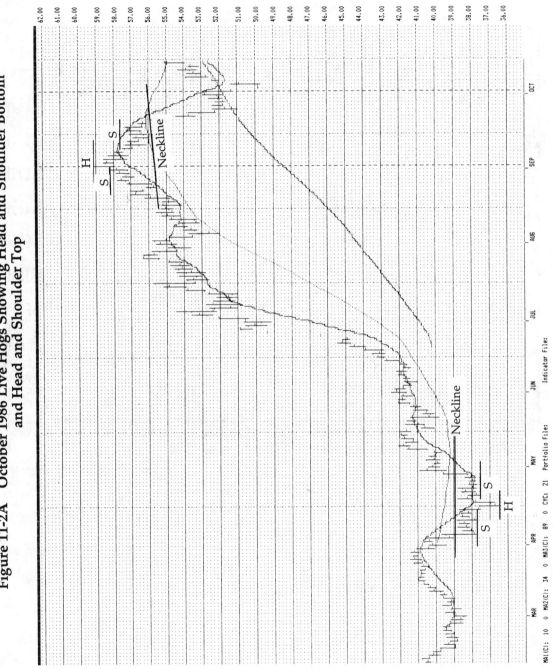

Figure 11-2A   October 1986 Live Hogs Showing Head and Shoulder Bottom
and Head and Shoulder Top

Created using Relevance III™ Software

Figure 11-2B

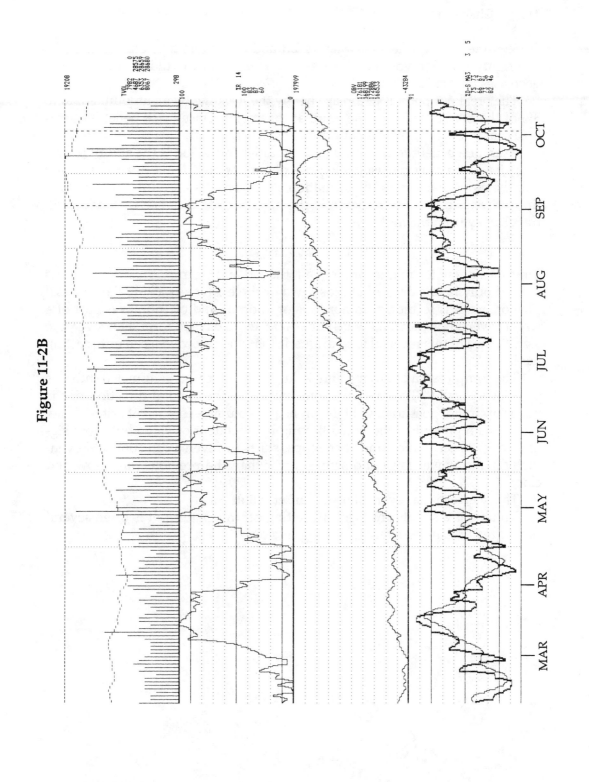

Volume action differs between Head and Shoulders tops and bottoms: at the right shoulder volume increases in Head and Shoulder bottoms and decreases in Head and Shoulder tops.

The breakout point is at a place below the neckline by an amount equal to 3% of the market value of the issue at that point. Once price penetrates this breakout point, the reversal pattern has been confirmed.

A unique benefit to the Head and Shoulder formation is the ability for the chart reader to project reasonable price objectives once the formation is made and the move away from the formation starts. The distance from the extreme tip of the head and the neckline is the approximate distance that price will travel away from the neckline.

One Day Reversals

This formation is unique among all the other patterns. This "pattern" is formed only in one day, or, at most, two or three days. As a singular reversal phenomena it is formed at minor tops or bottoms and oftentimes is part of a larger reversal phenomena which does take more days to form. However, the significance of this reversal is so dramatic that it is accorded a separate section here.

The compression of buying and selling fear and greed is funneled into this one day's activity. The market opens higher, in the general direction of the major up trend, goes to new highs on heavy volume—important criterion because this represents unheralded buying independent of value but more significant of sheer panic—and then stops, starts to reverse direction *and* eventually makes lower lows and settles lower than the previous day's low and close.

This scenario is a reversed bear market selloff.

Volume is a significant factor in setting off this pattern. It is often several times greater than the average trading session.

Figure 11-3   August Gold Showing One-Day Key Reversal

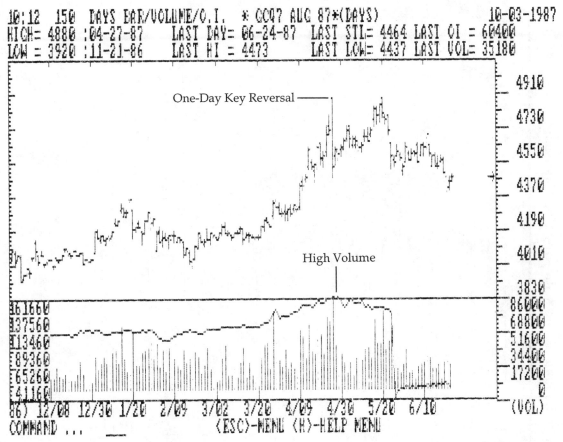

Figure 11-4A   September Swiss Franc Futures Showing One-Day Island Key Reversal

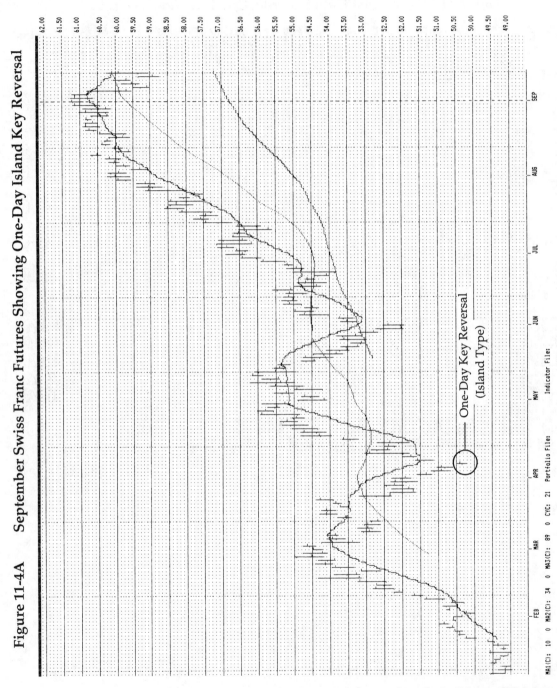

One-Day Key Reversal
(Island Type)

MA1(C): 10   0   MA2(C): 34   0   MA3(C): 89   0   CYC: 21   Portfolio File: Indicator File:

Figure 11-4B

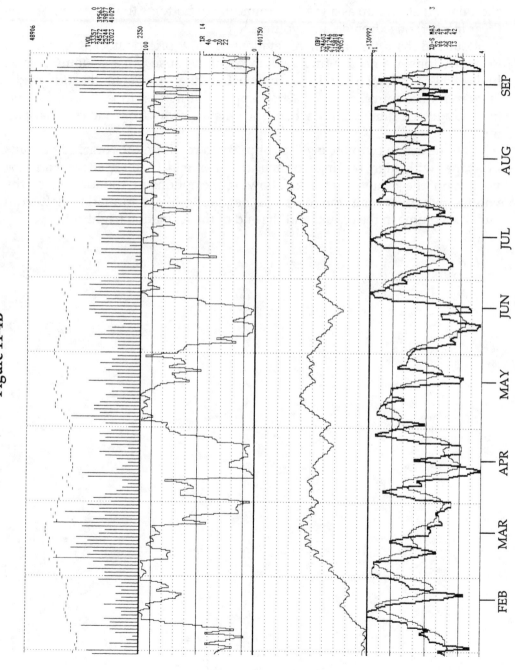

Rounded Top/Bottom

This is a smoother, less spectacular, but surer pattern than head-and-shoulders. It shows up as a gradual rounding of bottoms (bull market) or tops (bear market) on extremely low volume.

Rounded bottoms are more evident in low-priced stocks or futures. Rounded tops are rarities and seldom occur because price seldom stays at high levels for long periods of time before they move to the downside. However, once rounding price action appears at market tops, traders should be ready to sell immediately when price moves away from the reversal pattern.

Volume action of rounding tops appears to replicate the rounded bottoms in shape, with high trading volume at either end of the pattern and low volume in the center with the following exception: in rounded tops, the volume pattern is high volume at the beginning of the formation (left side) and low volume in the center, and the end of the formation (right side).

Figure 11-5   Pepsico Showing Rounded Top

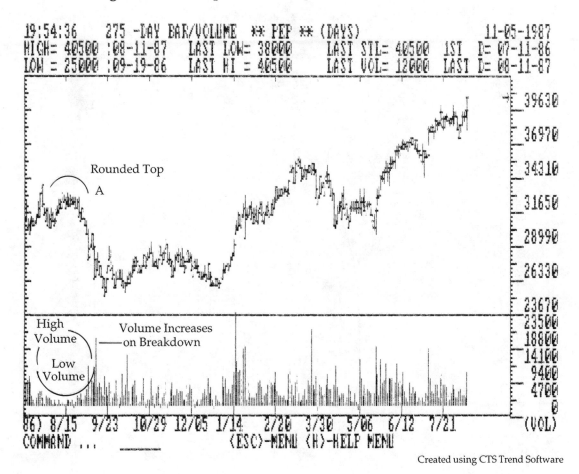

Figure 11-6   Firestone Tire & Rubber Showing Rounded Top

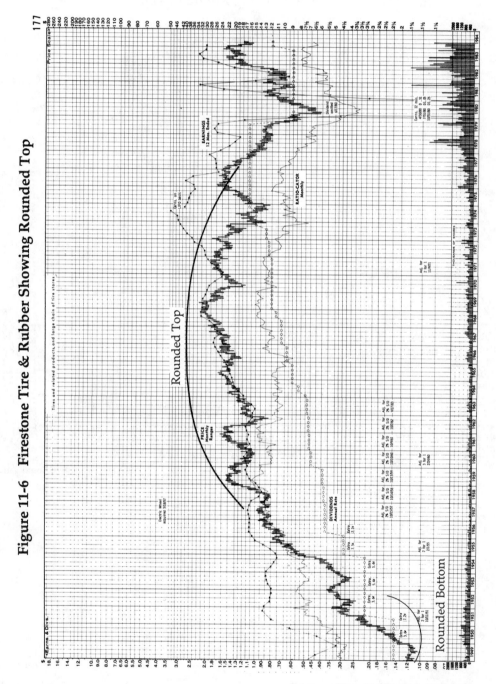

Courtesy of Securities Research Corporation

Double Top/Bottom

Less reliable than a head-and-shoulders or rounded top/bottom, this pattern is formed by market action which causes price to move close to a previous high, or a previous bottom, but fails to make new highs or lows. The price then retraces beyond the previous swing bottom, in a bull move, or the previous swing top, in a bear move.

Volume is low in the secondary test of the previous high or the previous low. With increasing market volatility, there can be new price territory moves made in the secondary test. In cases like these traders must observe whether or not these new highs can be held. If they cannot be held, then before the end of the day in the which the new highs are made traders can possibly find the formation of one day reversals if they are followed by high volume activity.

Multiple tops and bottoms may also occur. However, traders should use it with this caution in mind: the more times the price moves up to previous highs or down to previous lows, the greater the chance that eventually the price will trade through the multiple tops or bottoms. In the case of multiple top formations, the market has enough inherent strength to continually challenge sellers at the high prices, and eventually does break through the diminishing overhead supply created by sellers. Multiple bottoms are the same.

Figure 11-7   Hewlett Packard Showing Double Bottom

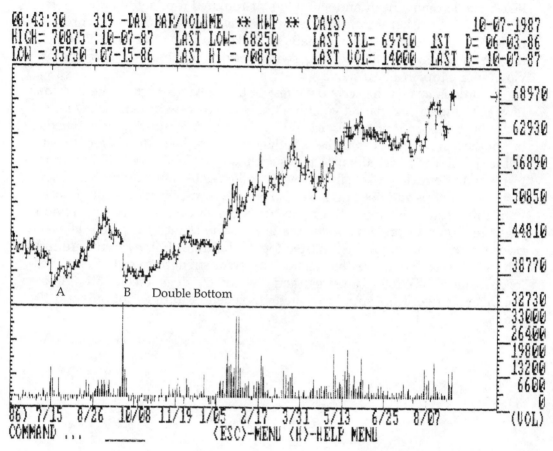

Figure 11-8A   December 1986 Live Cattle Showing Double Top

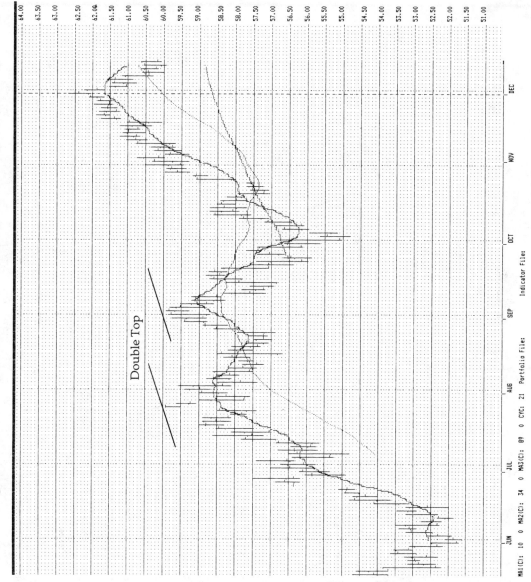

Created using Relevance III™ Software

Figure 11-8B

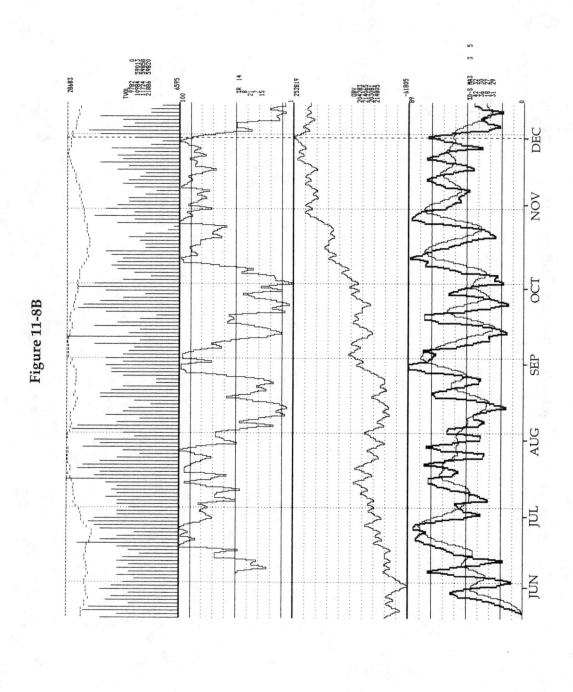

Diamond as Reversals

Unlike other formations in this category of reversal patterns, this one can also signal consolidation of buyers and sellers, only to continue after the completion of this pattern with the main direction from which prices came. This pattern can be viewed as a subset of a head and shoulders reversal formation. However, because of the wide ranging price travel of this pattern, it occurs at tops of markets. To form this pattern, price finds overhead resistance on heavy volume, fluctuates in a widening pattern on increasing volume, and then fluctuates in a decreasing pattern on decreasing volume, thus forming a rough diamond shape with its pattern of highs and lows. When the price breaks down, the formation is complete and traders can sell with good assurance that price had found overhead supply in a wide range, disclosing the fact that there was no basic agreement among sellers on a particular price, but rather agreement on a price range.

Figure 11-9A   December 1986 T-Bonds Showing Diamond Formation

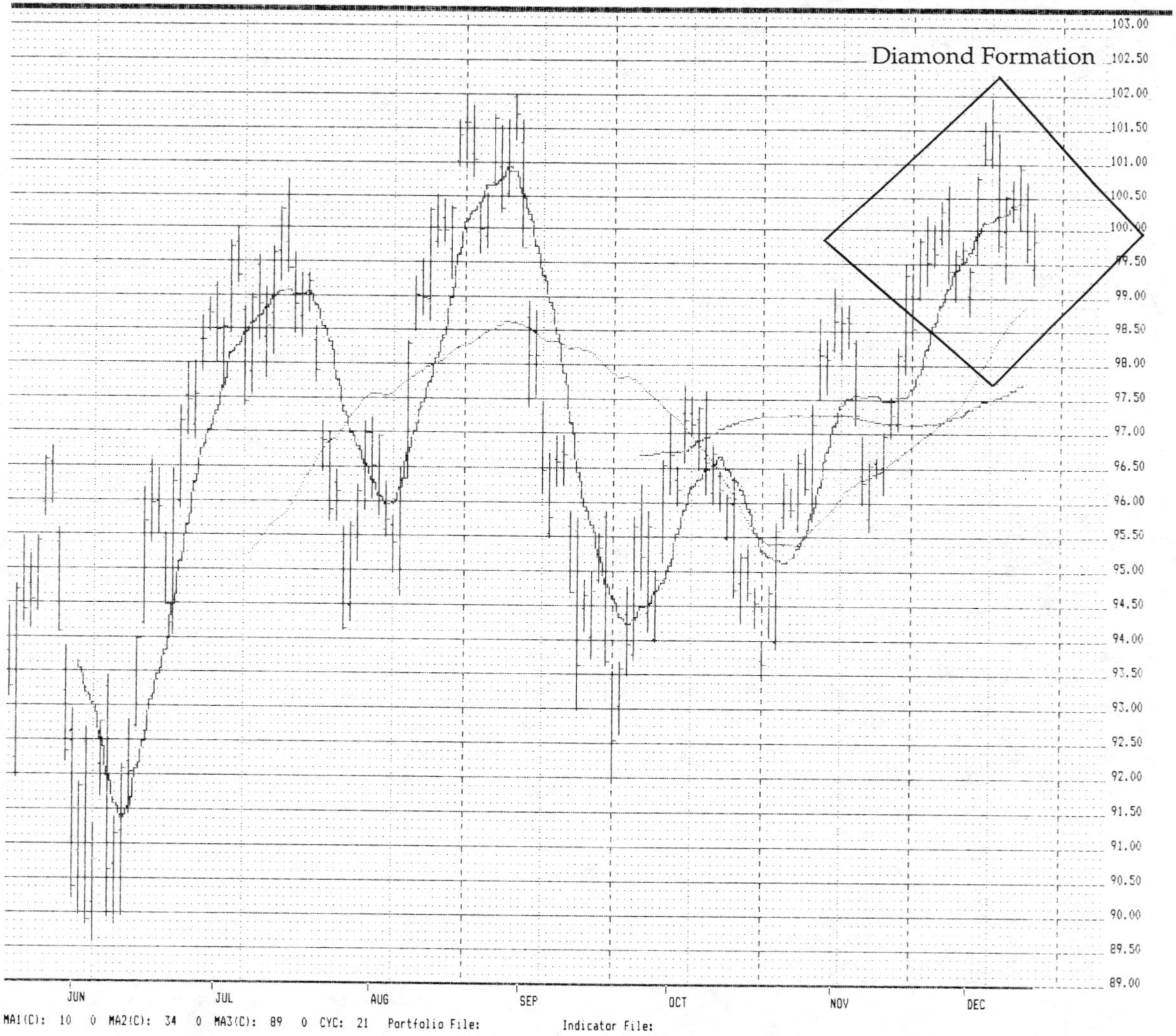

Diamond Formation

Figure 11-9B

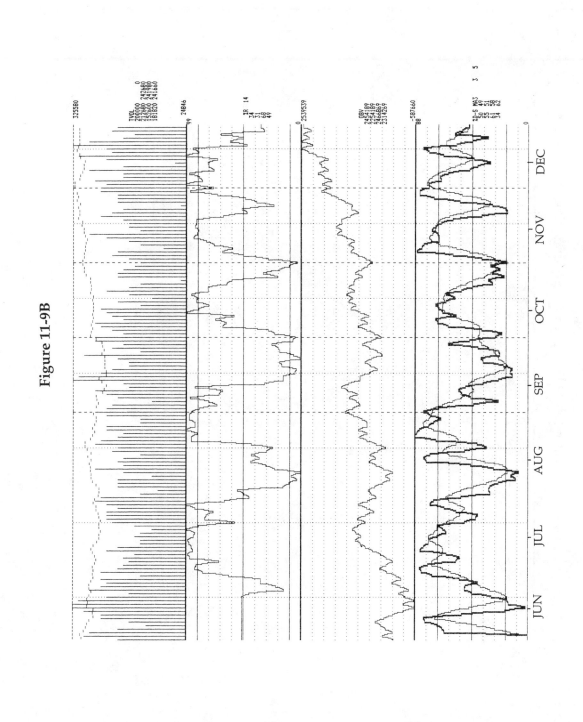

Figure 11-10A   November 1986 Soybeans Showing Diamond or Reversal

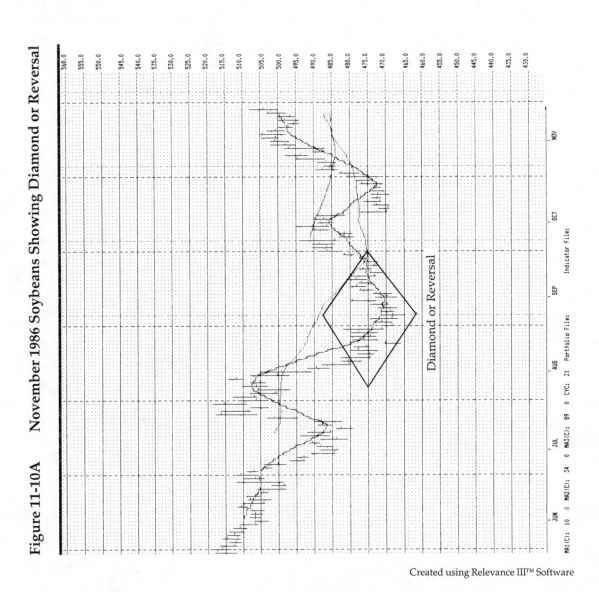

Diamond or Reversal

Created using Relevance III™ Software

Figure 11-10B

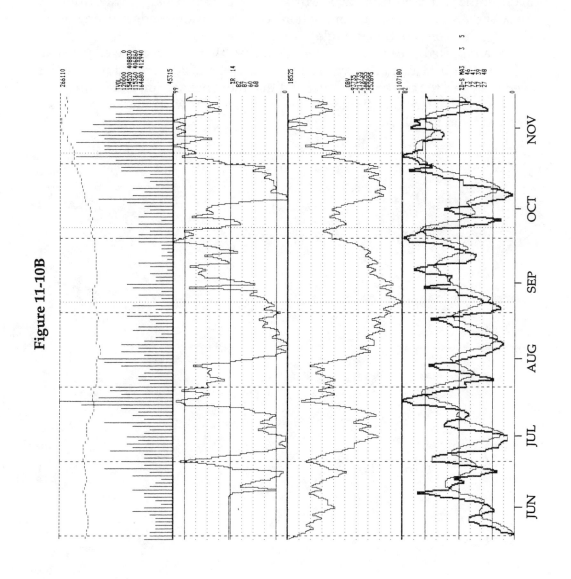

Wedge

A wedge is a pattern whose sides are not parallel but converge toward an intersection and whose volume steadily decreases until a breakout. The range of daily prices narrows as the price enters the wedge's intersection. Wedges slant in the direction from which they came, but eventually away from the apex of the wedge upon its completion. The slant of the wedge distinguishes it from other continuation triangle patterns.

A falling wedge can occur at various places, though a rising wedge usually occurs in a bear market correction, and a downside breakdown of this wedge signals the correction is over and that more bear action is imminent.

Volume decreases in the formation, but picks up when the market has a decided trend to follow.

Figure 11-11   IBM Showing Wedge

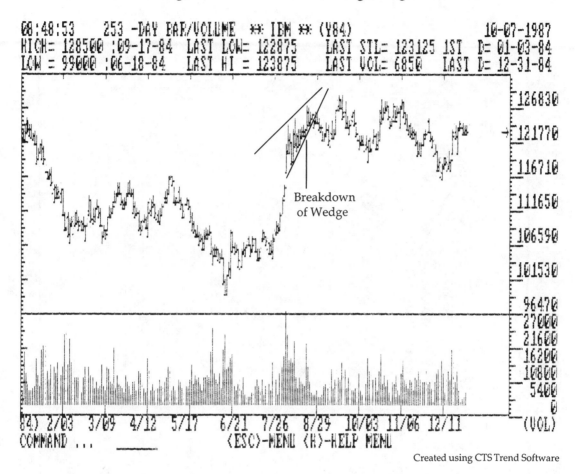

Breakdown
of Wedge

Created using CTS Trend Software

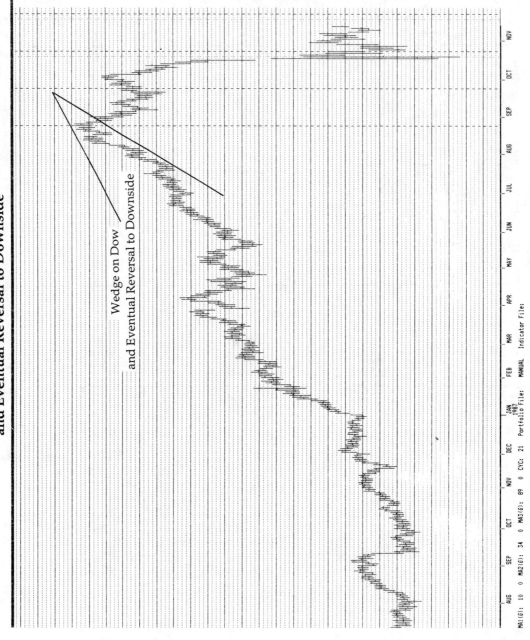

Figure 11-12   December 1988 Dow Jones Industrial Averages Showing Wedge
and Eventual Reversal to Downside

Wedge on Dow
and Eventual Reversal to Downside

Created using Relevance III™ Software

Second Pattern Group: Consolidations

Consolidation patterns occur in trending markets. No trending markets go straight up or straight down. After a sustained one-directional move, the market must stop, pause, and catch its breath, before resuming the move. These patterns of resting are consolidation patterns in which there are equal numbers of buyers and sellers at that point in time.

Traders should develop the ability to distinguish between consolidation patterns and reversal patterns for the patterns will dictate how they should trade. If traders recognize a consolidation pattern forming, they can prepare themselves for the breakout away from the pattern in the general direction from which it came. If traders categorize the patterns wrongly, they will find themselves buying when they should be selling, and vice versa.

The following are consolidation patterns:

1) Symmetrical Triangles
2) Right Triangles, ascending and descending
3) Rectangles
4) Flags
5) Pennants
6) Diamonds as consolidation

Symmetrical Triangle

This pattern is so called because the lines connecting highs and lows seem to converge on a point in the future. To qualify as a symmetrical triangle instead of a right triangle (see following section), both lines must slant from the horizontal.

Volume decreases during a symmetrical triangle formation, and the triangle seldom reaches its imaginary apex, generally breaking out before then. If price does not break out of the triangle before the apex is reached, then the chances are that it is not a triangle but rather some sort of reversal formation and that traders should not initiate positions in the direction of the trend prior to beginning the formation, but instead look for the reversal and set themselves up so that they can jump into action when the breakout occurs.

Figure 11-13   EFH Showing Symmetrical Triangle

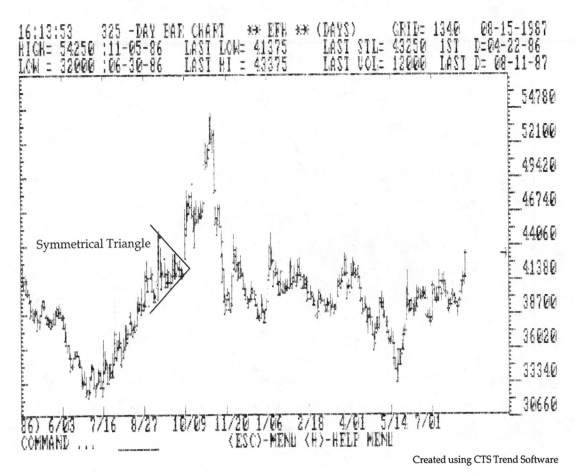

Figure 11-14A   March 1987 CBT Corn Showing Pennant Type

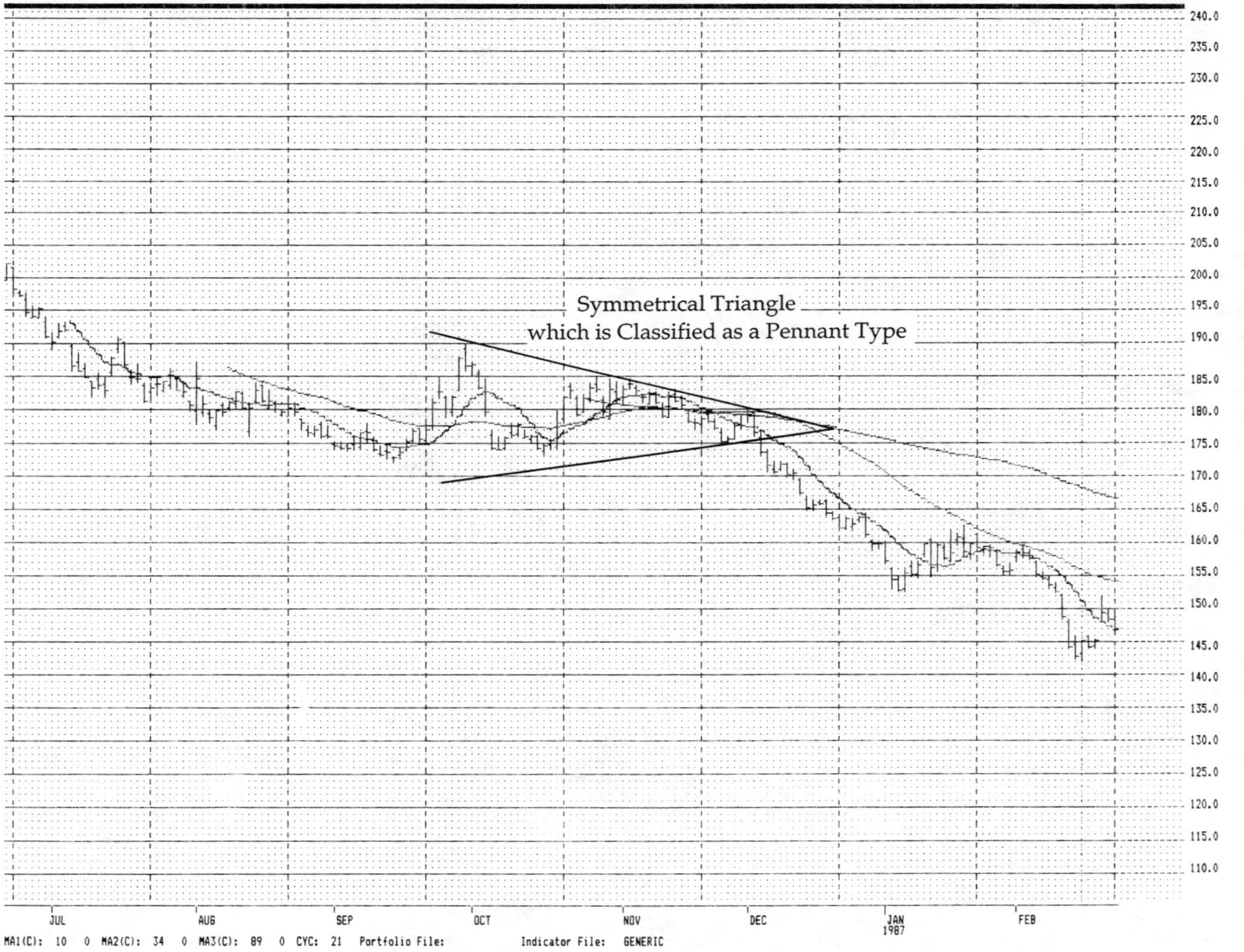

Symmetrical Triangle
which is Classified as a Pennant Type

Figure 11-14B

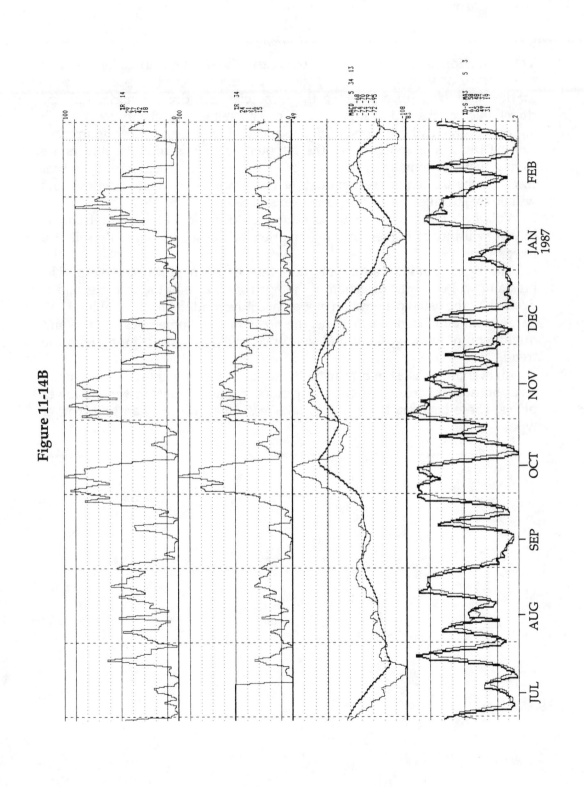

Right Triangle

This formation looks like a triangle, but one of the sides is horizontal, defining a resistance or support level. In right ascending triangles, supply comes to market at a fixed price level, so the technician can draw a horizontal line directly across the top of this formation. The selloffs, or absorption of such supply, is greeted by buyers at higher and higher prices, hence the upward sloping trend line which forms the hypotenuse of this triangle. Buyers are saying that not only will they buy but they will buy progressively higher prices. If the buying is great enough, it will absorb the sellers' offerings and will be able to take out the horizontal resistance.

Volume diminishes rapidly during the formation of a right triangle: buyers will buy at higher and higher prices while sellers will only sell at a fixed price.

The right triangle pattern predicts the direction of the breakout. The breakout will be in the direction of the horizontal side of the triangle, and is defined by the usual penetration of a point 3% beyond the horizontal line.

As with all triangle formations, the breakout can sometimes be false and might require more work around that price level before continuing with the trend.

Right triangles exist in bear markets, where support points are at one price level, but sellers become progressively more willing to sell at lower and lower prices. These bear market triangles take less time to form than bull market types.

Figure 11-15   Phillip Morris Showing Ascending Right Triangle

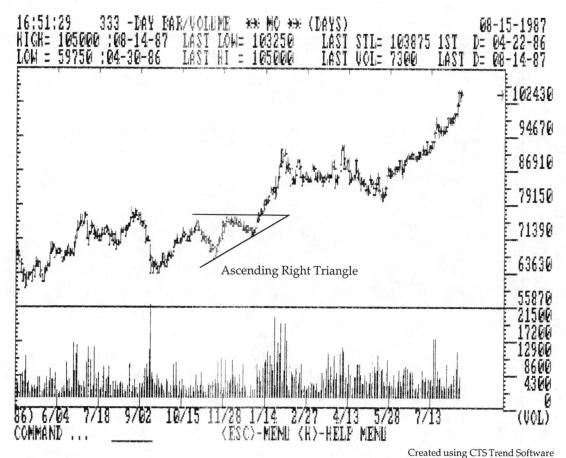

Ascending Right Triangle

Created using CTS Trend Software

Figure 11-16A   December 1986 Deutsche Mark
Showing Ascending Right Triangle

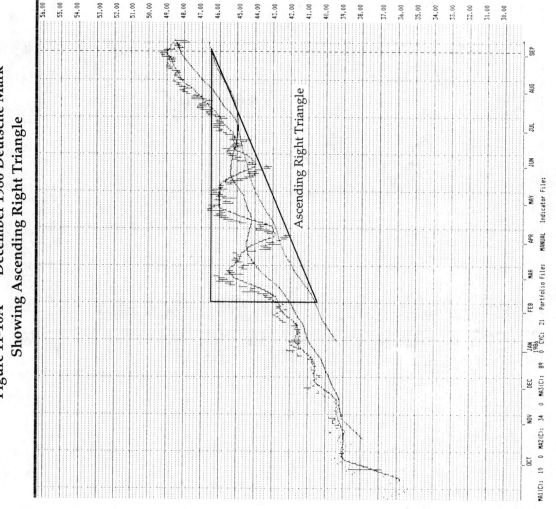

Figure 11-16B

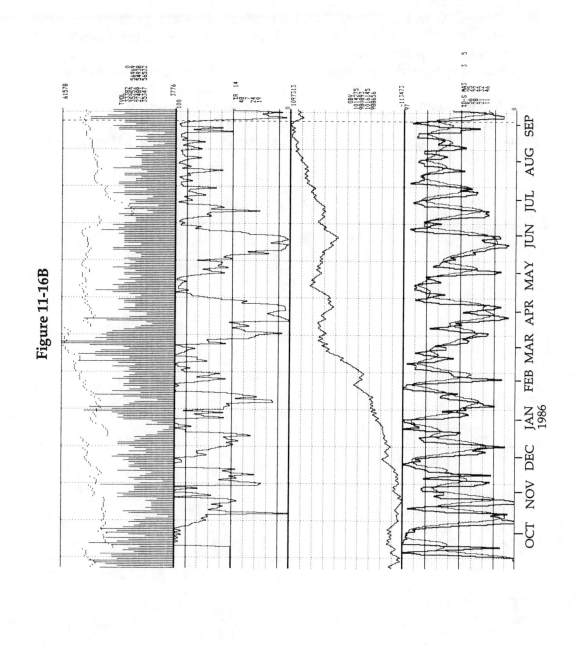

Rectangle

The rectangle is defined by a line connecting highs and one connecting lows, both of which are horizontal, thus indicating an even back-and-forth fluctuating of price. As in the case of the symmetrical triangle, a rectangle cannot predict the direction of the ultimate breakout. A rectangle's volume gradually diminishes as the pattern progresses.

Unlike a symmetrical triangle, the strength of the breakout is not affected by how long the rectangle lasts. A rectangle's breakout is usually more reliable than that signalled by a triangle. Bar chartists can measure the width of the rectangle and offer an eyeball price objective projection of the impending breakouts: the width of the pattern is the approximate distance that prices will travel on the breakout.

Figure 11-17   Digital Equipment Showing Rectangle with One Day Drop

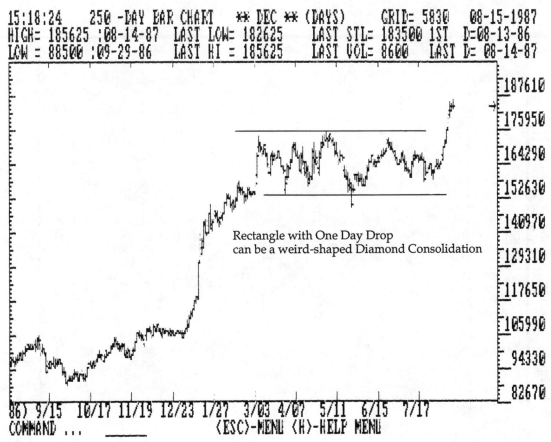

15:18:24   250 -DAY BAR CHART   ** DEC ** (DAYS)   GRID= 5830   08-15-1987
HIGH= 185625 ;08-14-87   LAST LOW= 182625   LAST STL= 183500 1ST D=08-13-86
LOW = 88500 :09-29-86   LAST HI = 185625   LAST VOL= 8600   LAST D= 08-14-87

Rectangle with One Day Drop
can be a weird-shaped Diamond Consolidation

187610
175950
164290
152630
140970
129310
117650
105990
94330
82670

86) 9/15   10/17 11/19 12/23 1/27   3/03 4/07   5/11   6/15   7/17
COMMAND ...   _____   (ESC)-MENU (H)-HELP MENU

Created using CTS Trend Software

Figure 11-18A   IBM Showing Rectangle which was Reversal

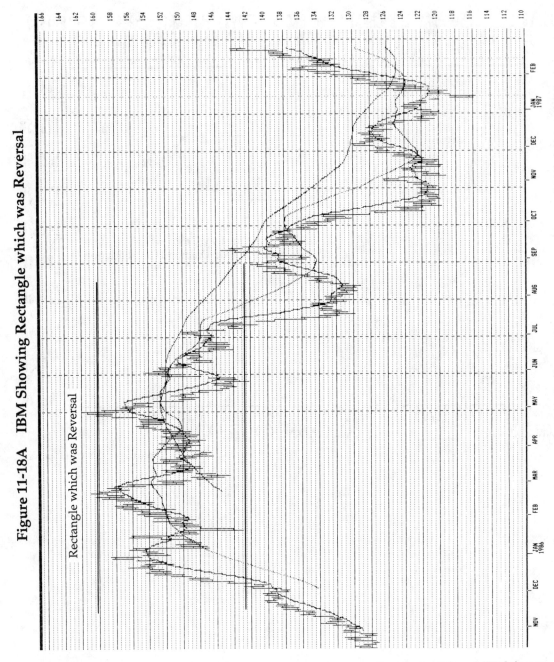

Rectangle which was Reversal

Created using Relevance III™ Software

Figure 11-18B

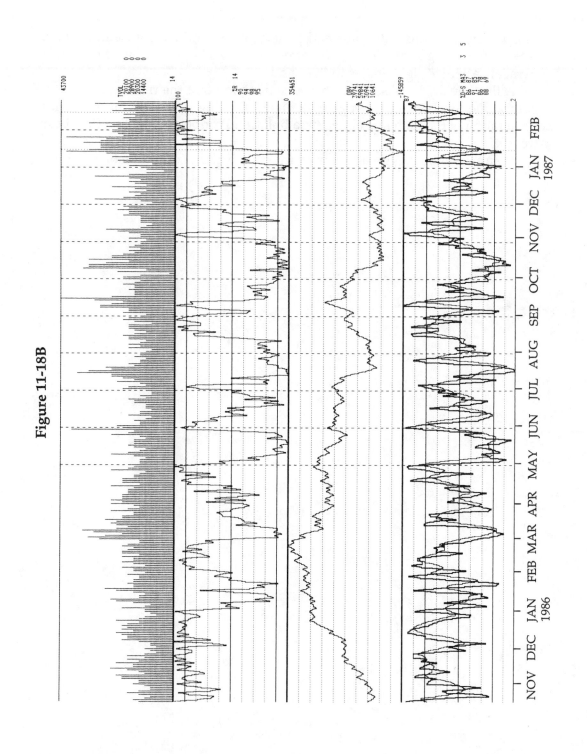

Flag

This is a hybrid consolidation-trend pattern. It forms during a trend channel (see the following section on trend patterns), and its high and low lines form a parallel pattern at right angles to the trend.

A flag usually breaks out in the same direction that the trend was already going, and its breakout is again defined as being a 3% of market price penetration of the high line above (in a bull trend) or below low line (in a bear trend).

Volume diminishes greatly during the course of the formation of a flag.

Figure 11-19   Pfizer Showing Flag

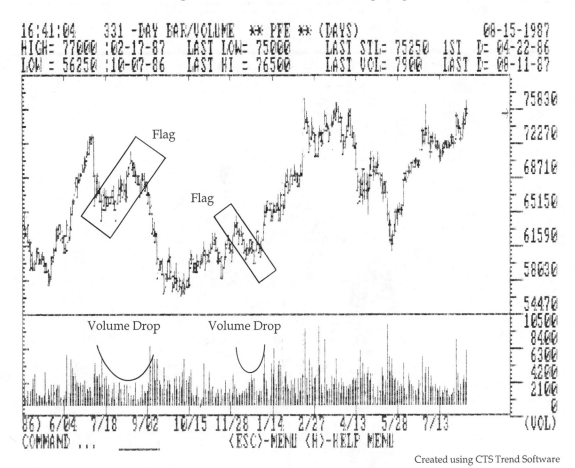

16:41:04   331 -DAY BAR/VOLUME ** PFE ** (DAYS)   08-15-1987
HIGH= 77000 :02-17-87   LAST LOW= 75000   LAST STL= 75250 1ST D= 04-22-86
LOW = 56250 :10-07-86   LAST HI = 76500   LAST VOL= 7900   LAST D= 08-11-87

Flag

Flag

75830
72270
68710
65150
61590
58630
54470

Volume Drop   Volume Drop

10500
8400
6300
4200
2100
0

86) 6/04   7/18   9/02   10/15 11/28 1/14   2/27   4/13   5/28   7/13   (VOL)
COMMAND ... ___   <ESC>-MENU <H>-HELP MENU

Created using CTS Trend Software

Figure 11-20   December 1987 Live Cattle Showing Flag

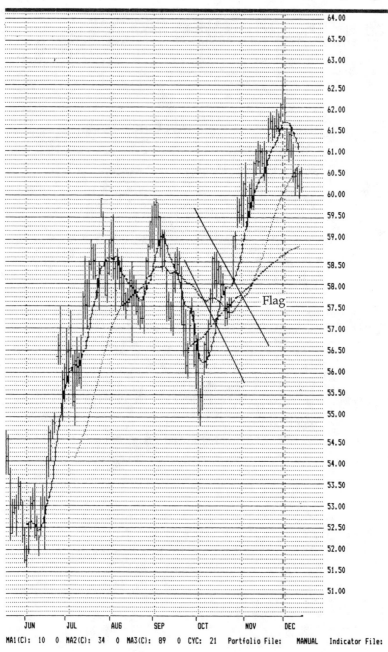

Flag

MA1(C): 10   0   MA2(C): 34   0   MA3(C):   89   0 CYC: 21   Portfolio File: MANUAL   Indicator File:

Created using Relevance III™ Software

Pennant

A pennant is a pointed flag formation with the two lines which form it converging toward an apex. The distinction between this pattern and any symmetrical triangles is the length of this formation: the width of the pennant is greater than the width of symmetrical triangles.

Volume dries up after the top is made and the formation begins.

Figure 11-21   US Steel Showing Pennant

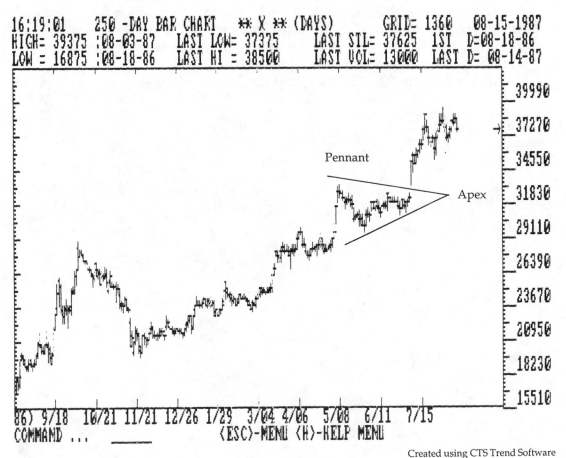

Created using CTS Trend Software

Figure 11-22 July 1987 CBT Corn Showing Pennant

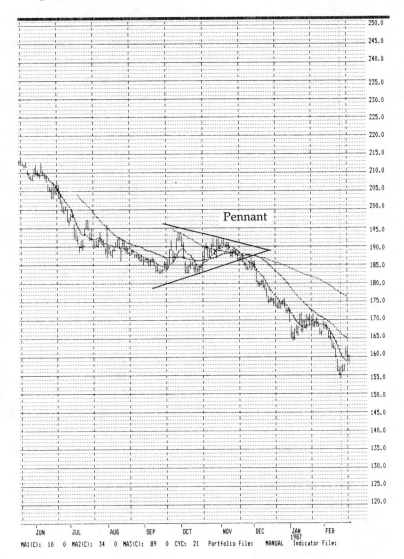

Created using Relevance III™ Software

Diamond as Consolidation

Diamonds indicate reversal patterns particularly in the case of "head and shoulder" type top formations. This pattern can be a consolidation pattern. To form this pattern, price fluctuates in a widening pattern on increasing volume, and then fluctuates in a decreasing pattern on decreasing volume, thus forming a rough diamond shape with its pattern of highs and lows. When the price moves out of the pattern in the same direction that it came from before the inception of the pattern, we see that it is a diamond formation. This is one of the most difficult patterns to recognize and for all practical purposes traders cannot rely on the development of this pattern for profit opportunities. The only way to capitalize on this pattern is to buy the breakout or sell the breakdown, thus minimizing the possibility that this a false move.

Figure 11-23   Digital Equipment Showing Diamond Consolidation

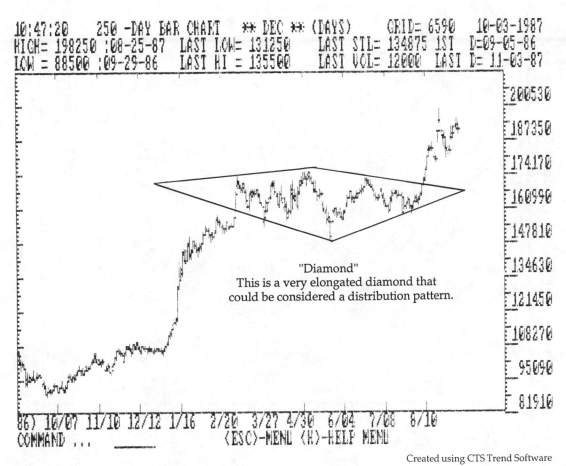

"Diamond"
This is a very elongated diamond that
could be considered a distribution pattern.

Created using CTS Trend Software

Figure 11-24   General Motors Showing Diamond as Consolidation

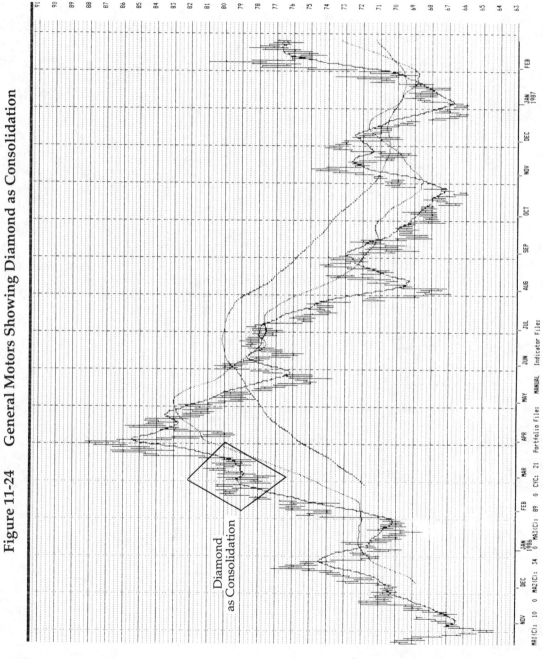

Pattern Group Three: Trending Patterns

The preceding pages identified reversal and consolidation patterns. Trend patterns connect and contain these two patterns in larger moves. They are:

1) Fan lines
2) Gaps
3) Trendlines and channels

Fan Lines

This formation is both a trend formation and a reversal predictor. It forms as a trend line, gradually losing more and more of its steepness. In a bull market, a low may break below the lower trendline, as in a bear market, a high may break above the upper trendline. The lower (bull) or upper (bear) trend line then gets redrawn, forming an angle with the first trendline. If this process happens a second time, then a third trend line is drawn.

Traders now see a fan-like pattern on the chart defined by the progressively opening angles of the three lines. When the third line is penetrated by 3% of market price on the upside (bear) or the downside (bull), a reversal is considered to have happened.

Fan lines generally are used to find when a correction has ended (when the third fan line is not broken) and where an accelerated move in the opposite direction will most likely occur. This, basically, is contrary to the purpose of fan lines application.

Figure 11-25 **General Motors Showing Fan Lines**

Fan Lines Showing Resistance Lines

Created using CTS Trend Software

Figure 11-26A   March 1987 Swiss Franc Showing Fan Lines

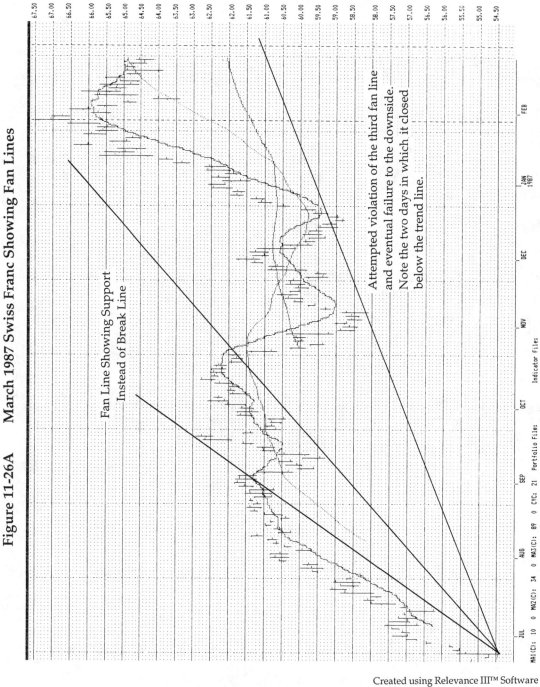

Fan Line Showing Support
Instead of Break Line

Attempted violation of the third fan line
and eventual failure to the downside.
Note the two days in which it closed
below the trend line.

Created using Relevance III™ Software

Figure 11-26B

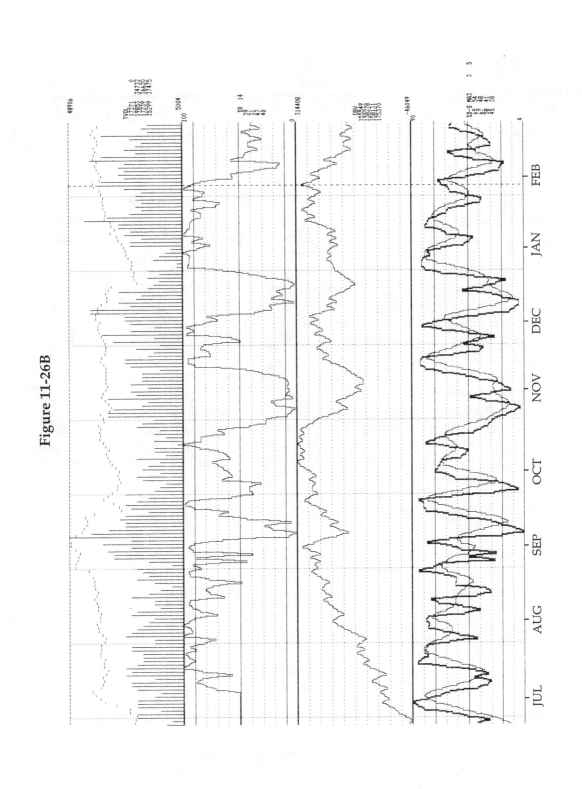

Gaps

Gaps are a lack of price and volume information on a bar chart where there should have been price and volume information; the activity in the market is so great that the price does not trade at that level but at higher or lower levels.

There are several types of gaps which can form in a bar chart: there are breakaway gaps, common gaps, exhaustion gaps, and run-away gaps (or measuring gaps).

Breakaway gaps are those formed immediately near the breakout of an important consolidation pattern. This gap is significant because it separates the price movement from the consolidation area: the stalemate represented by consolidation patterns has now been unbalanced to the direction of the breakaway gap. These occur when price moves away from a congestion area, such as triangles and rectangles. There are no possible projections based on the existence of such gaps except to say that the imminent move away from the congestion (either in the same or opposite direction from which it came) is a violent one. Upside breakaway gaps have large volume increases; downside breakaway gaps do not need heavy volume activity confirmation.

Common gaps are those formed in thinly traded markets and are relatively meaningless in gap analysis.

Exhaustion gaps represents the additional push that speculators representing uninformed trading activity execute. These gaps occur after an extended run or selloff. Reversals in price action often follow exhaustion gaps.

Runaway gaps are those formed in the middle of a runaway move and are particularly important because they oftentimes represent a halfway point in the whole move. When this gap forms in a runaway market, traders can be certain that the move is about half over.

Figure 11-27   Pepsico Showing Gaps

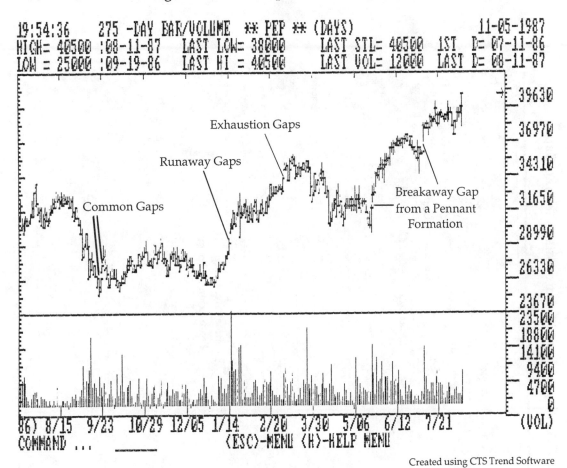

Created using CTS Trend Software

Figure 11-28A   September 1986 Eurodollar Showing Gaps

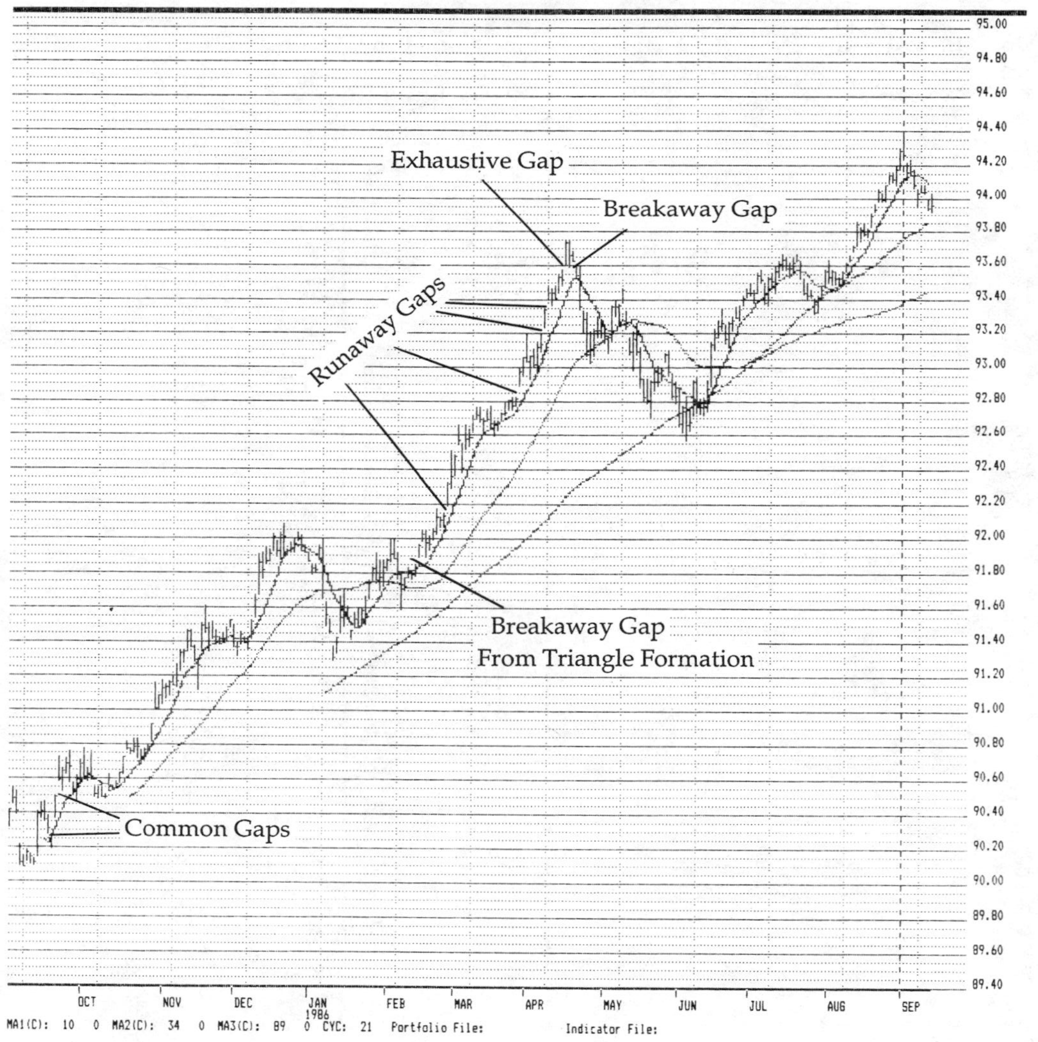

Created using Relevance III™ Software

Figure 11-28B

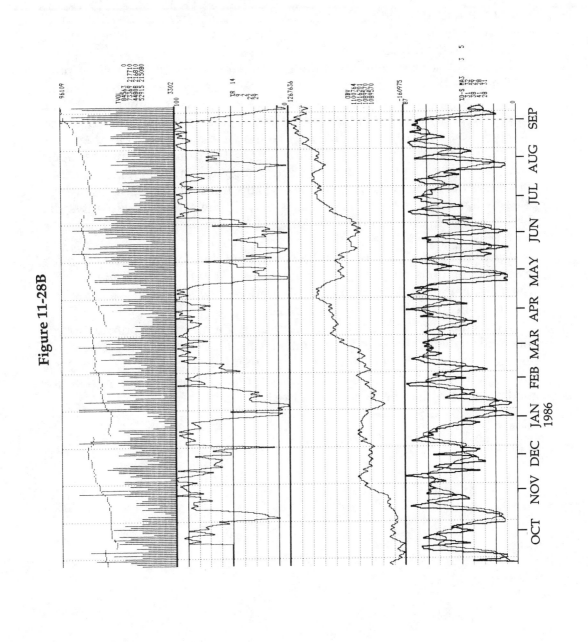

Trendline and Channel

This "formation," which is used in other techniques such as channeled moving averages, is formed by exact parallel lines defined by progressively higher highs (bull market trend) or lower lows (bear market trend). The significance of a trendline is due to the fact that it contains the support or resistance points extended into the future.

Upwardly sloping trendlines offer critical support points and traders must buy around these levels from selloff highs. Similar strategies must be employed for downwardly sloping trendlines which contain any rallies by not permitting price to trade above them. Selling at these resistance points is warranted. Traders can draw parallel lines on the other side of the bar charts, i.e. if they have already drawn an upward sloping trendline containing support levels, they may also draw a parallel line to this upwardly sloping trendline containing the highs of the bar chart. This is the uptrend resistance line where prices will encounter resistance. Traders may do the same with downwardly sloping trend lines offering price support by drawing parallel lines in a downward direction.

When the trend line is broken, however, (and this does happen with more frequency than one might think), then traders know that the previous trend was no longer intact. If formerly bullish, traders now lean to the sell side and if formerly bearish, they lean to the buy side.

Some clue as to where a trend might go is found in the confirmation or non-confirmation of the trend by volume levels. If price is able to get back to a trendline, volume should diminish if the trend is to resume. If, however, volume starts to increase when price nears a trendline, be aware that there is a good probability that the trendline will be broken.

Figure 11-29   Chevron Showing Trendline

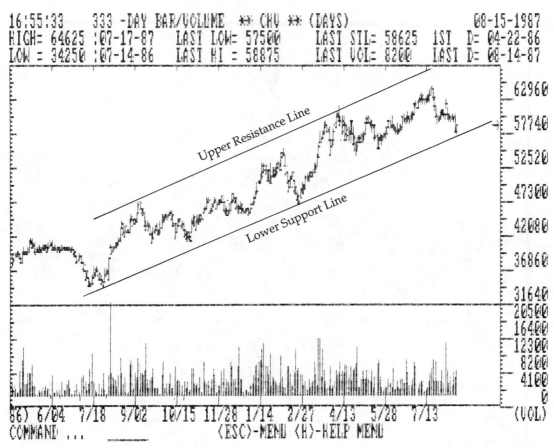

Created using CTS Trend Software

Figure 11-30A   December 1986 Comex Gold Showing Trendlines

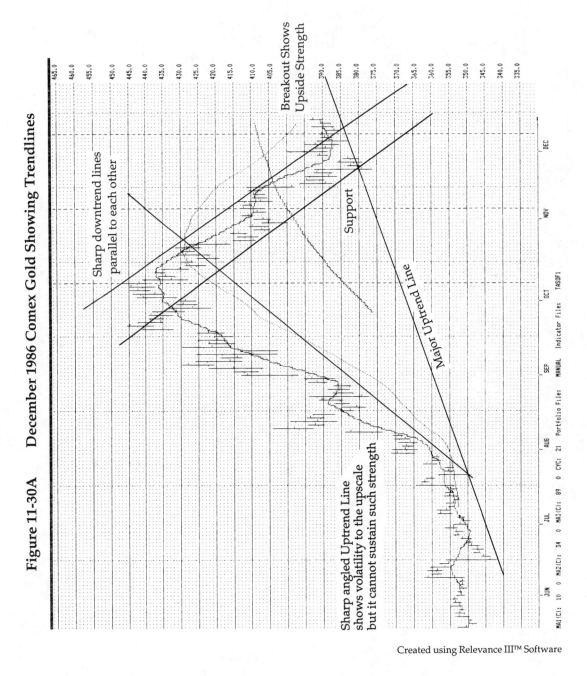

Created using Relevance III™ Software

Figure 11-30B

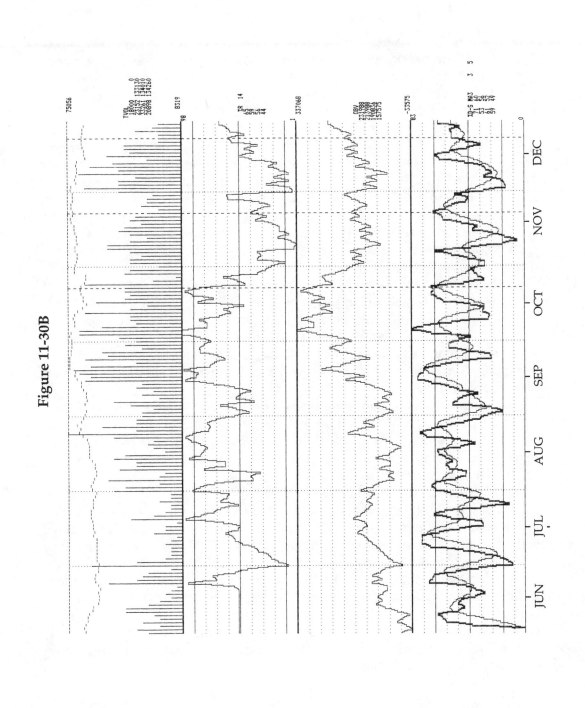

Trading General Motors Stock
Using Basic Charting Techniques

This example shows General Motors, bar chart from October 1985 to February 24, 1987, a time period which encompasses 18 months and sees the price of General Motors stock move from about $64.00 per share to over $88.00 share.

At the start of the move upwards, the development of the pennant first appears on the chart. Pennants are consolidation patterns and indicate a continuation after the breakout from the pattern. When the price narrows further into early December, a sharp breakout to the upside occurs. The price trades above $71.00 a share in the early week of December and traders immediately go long at around the $72.00 level. Staying long, they see the stock go to a high slightly above $77.00 in the third week of December, or a gain of about $5.00 in less than a month. Remembering that the move started at around the $64.00 level, traders could determine that the pennant formed is about halfway of the full move, and therefore they could sell their long positions for a profit at the $77.00 to $78.00 level.

If the traders have not sold, they could wait to buy more on a retracement back to the $70.00 level, and even lower to the $68.50 level. The rounding bottom at the $70.00 level could possibly be interpreted as a head and shoulder Bottom, with a one day spike down to form the "head" and several weeks on either side of the head that forms the "left shoulder" and the "right shoulder" in January 1986: the counted projection from the head-to-shoulder surpasses any upside projections.

The breakout of the rounding bottom into an accelerated upmove comes when the price trades above $71.00 again. Buying at this level would show additional profits. The price moves up to the $76.75 level and encounters resistance—this second time up to the previous $77.00 level now forms a double top which as to be broken to the upside.

The market chews around slightly below the $77.00 level for several days and finally gaps up one day, in early February, above the $77.00 level. The gap is considered a measuring gap—halfway between the move. If the move started at $64.00 and creates a halfway gap at $77.00, traders can conclude that the top of this move should be around $90.00. This begins the formation of the diamond pattern. The diamond pattern is a consolidation pattern and indicates a future continuation to the direction from which it came—in this case, to the upside. For about four weeks the diamond pattern is forming—above the double top at $77.00, a further indication of strength. Finally, General Motors breaks above $81.00 in mid March and the price is now moving onwards to new highs.

298

Figure 11-31A   Trading General Motors Using Basic Charting

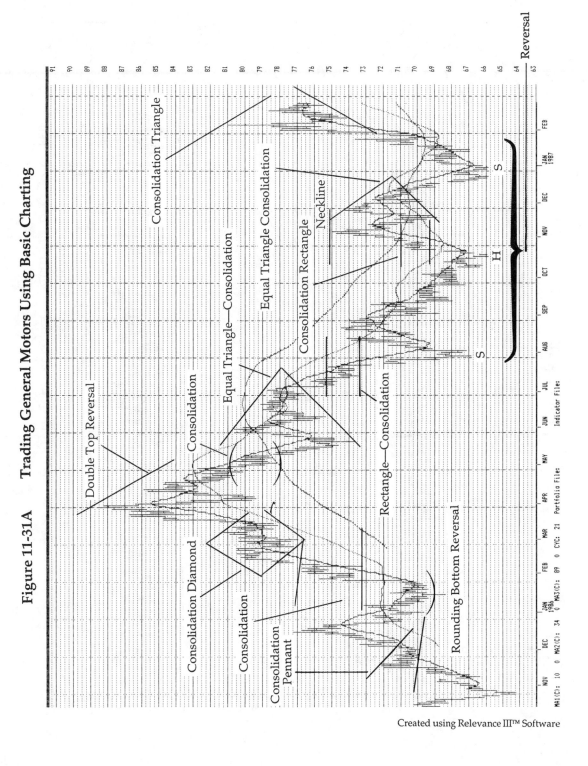

Created using Relevance III™ Software

Figure 11-31B

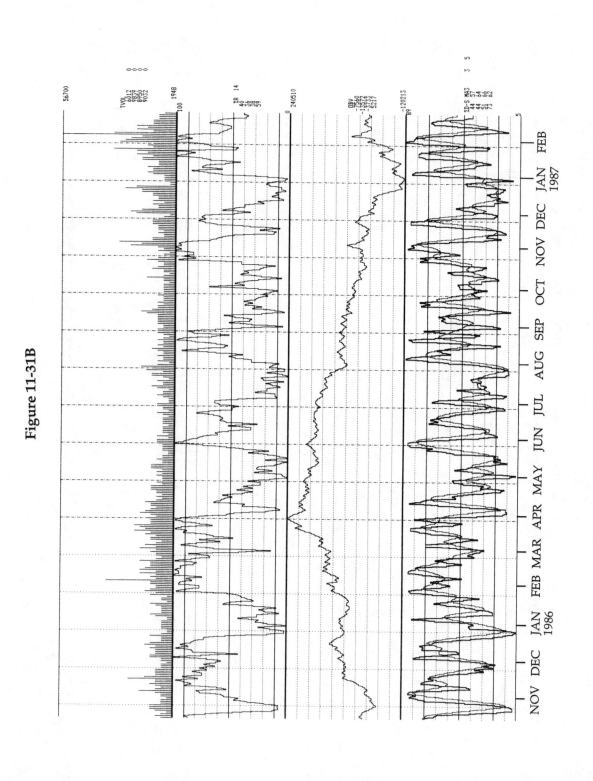

The price tops out at $87.75 and backs off within five trading days to the $79.50 level. This selloff is severe, in light of the fact that this is General Motors Stock, a relatively less volatile stock. A drop of $8.25 in five days is great—perhaps a sign of weakness? The traders had projected an imminent top of close to $90.00 within their halfway gap analysis and the top of $87.75 is only $2.25 away from this projected top. This is another reason to consider selling longs.

Instead they wait to see the upmove to new highs again. From the local bottom, the traders see the stock recover only up to $85.75 in five days before starting to back off. It takes 5 days to lose $8.25 and 5 days to recover $6.25 of that loss—an additional sign of weakness. Perhaps also a tremendously weakened second top of a double top formation?

The next few days show that the stock stays around the $84.00 level for only several days before it sells off again. The traders now have their weakness confirmation. They unload all their longs between $82.00-$84.00, thereby netting us profits of about $10.00-$12.00 per share. They weren't able to buy the lows nor sell the highs but they did make profits of $10.00 on a $23.00 move.

The double top is a very weak double top. The price continues to drop to a congestion area bounded by $78.12 and $80.75. This formation, whatever it is, is critical because it balances the diamond pattern at the $80.00 level. If the price holds here, it should go back up and test the highs. Instead, it drops to the $74.00 level—a sign of weakness.

The traders now give themselves a bit of leeway and watch for a larger formation of possible reversal patterns indicating that the upmove might be over. Using their imaginations they assume that the diamond formation to the left of the all-time high is a possible left shoulder of a head-and-shoulders formation. They anticipate the price to rally back to somewhere into the $80.00 range and observe the price behavior. The price does move back up, from the $74.00 level to $81.00 on one big swing of five days! However, it can't muster enough strength to continue, and instead backs off. The traders sell into the weakness at around the $79.00 level, expecting this to be a right shoulder.

The price now backs off to around the $75.25 level and rallies, weakly, back to the $79.00 level. Traders now see the development of a congestion or consolidation pattern—some sort of triangle is forming. The lines bounding the triangle narrow into some peak and traders expect a selloff beyond this line of support or rally above the downward sloping line of resistance. In early July, the price plunges below $77.00, thereby offering an indication that the price will continue to sell off until it finally reaches their objective determined from the head and shoulders count of $66.00 ($88.00-$75.00, or $13.00 lower from the right should selloff point of $79.00). If it gets anywhere near

$66.00, the traders cover their shorts, and in fact they should probably sell more on the way down!

The first bottom is at the end of July at $67.00, close enough to the traders' objective of $66.00. In fact, the price rallies substantially to above $74.00. They can cover their shorts and stand aside. Instead, they do what all conservative traders do—cover only half their positions and allow the other half to show profits, if there are any. The strength of this rally from a selloff bottom gives pretty good indications that this is a sharp bear market rally and traders should see a test of the $67.00 low.

The price now sells off again, this time to a bottom of $65.75 in mid-October 1986. The traders have now reached their objective and cover all shorts. They have profits derived from shorting at $80.00 and covering at $66.00, or $14.00.

The move from the head and shoulder bottom made in October, forms a small interim Rectangle formation. Of course, this was subject to artistic interpretations—who does really know that this is a rectangle in formation or whatever else it might be? But, this formation is critical because it marks the halfway point between the low of $65.75 and the rally top of $75.00 before it backs off again to the late December secondary bottom, which so happens to be the lower right shoulder of a massive head and shoulders formation.

On the way down from the $75.00 high to the $65.75 double bottom, an equal sided triangle formed and developed. The gap formed in the middle October 1986, period and the gap formed at the late December 1986 period, set off a formation above it—one could call it a mini-double top!

Once the right shoulder formed and the head and shoulder bottom reversal was seen in a broader perspective, traders could start to make upside projections about price objectives. The final triangle formed in February-March 1987, marked a possible halfway point of the final move from $65.75: $77.00-$65.75=$11.25, or a final objective of $77.00+$11.25=$88.25. The stock eventually topped out at $94.75.

Figure 11-32A   Trading December 1987 T-Bond Futures Using Basic Charting

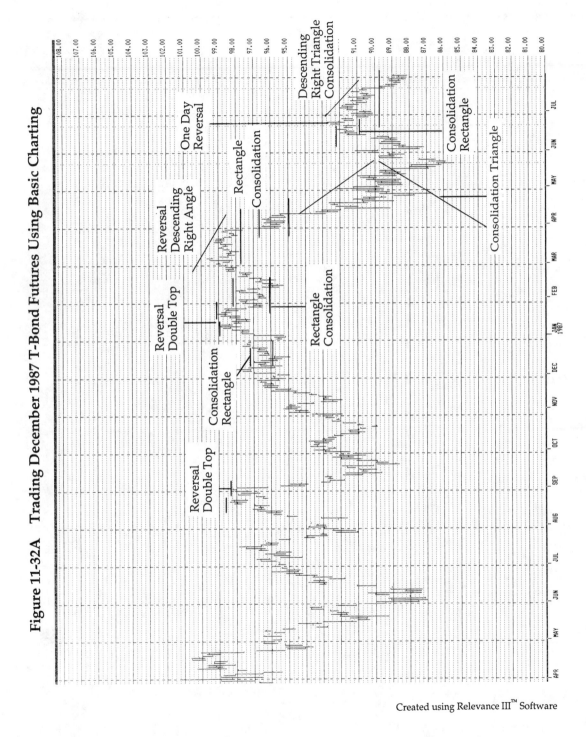

Figure 11-32B

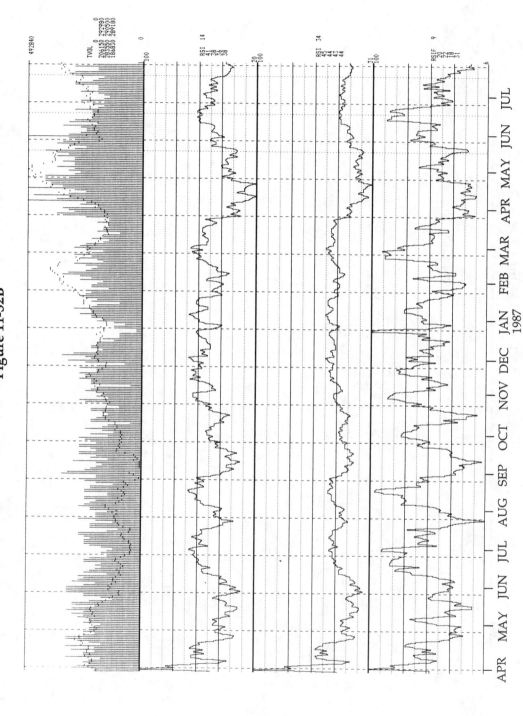

Trading December 1987 Treasury Bond Futures
Using Basic Charting Techniques

This example follows the December 1987 Treasury Bond Futures contract traded at the Chicago Board of Trade from April 1986 to August 1987, a time period which encompasses 18 months and sees the price of the futures trade between $85.00 and $100.00.

This futures contract was a difficult one to trade with strict charting pattern approaches. There were smaller patterns within bigger patterns and even smaller ones within the smaller ones that traders could have used to *signal* buy and sell signals. This 18 month period itself was a trading range, perhaps a larger rectangle formation within the whole price pattern.

The first valid signal, that of a double top formation separated by merely days, instead of weeks or months, indicates a sell signal. The first top is a three-day island formation separated by gaps going into the three days and by a gap after the formation. It is as if the market left the longs stranded up there at the top. The price of $98.00 eventually gives way to a low of $89.00 in September 1986.

Very weak patterns are seen throughout this time period. Hardly any money could have been made using the conventional charting pattern recognition techniques. True, rectangles formed all the way through, but their formation was hard to discern. The only triangle that could have been observed to be forming at the time was the one created in March 1987, with a price high of $99.00+ and a low of $98.00. This descending right triangle eventually showed the way down. The rectangle immediately created around the $96.00 level in early April demonstrated more weakness.

The formation of the large Triangle formation did not foretell the price objective of $78.00 ($100.00-$90.00=$10.00, $90.00-$10.00=$80.00 or so) and instead showed strength. The price could not sell below $85.16, despite facts to the contrary. As a mid point, this large triangle failed, but the market did show underlying strength.

Trading IBM Stock Using Basic Charting Techniques

This is the chart of IBM for the period from October 1985 to February 1986, which encompasses 18 months in which the price moved from a high of $159.00 to a low of $116.00.

Because of the wide price range and large one-directional moves, traders can apply conventional bar chart analysis to this chart and have valid entry and exit signals.

Triangles that form for IBM hold true to form in their ability to measure at least half-way moves. Channels hold very well for this stock. There are also rare formations—the one day and two day reversals—that do not appear in the other trading examples.

One day reversals are signals that should not be ignored. They can signal major reversal points, or at least intermediate reversal points. The market charges onto new highs and the buying public gets so bullish that they are buyers on the opening price. The opening buy orders cause the price to gap open above the previous day's highs. The buyers panic and push the price above previous highs into new territory. Once the buyers have exhausted the upside, they sit back and watch what will happen next. They see that the price action cannot sustain such a high price level and as the trading draws to a close, they start to sell their positions out and in the process take out yesterday's lows, thereby bracketing the previous day's high and low within the current day's high and low prices. There is tremendous volume which goes along with this formation.

The one-day reversal can extend into two days, in which an island is formed. This is what happened to the price of IBM in January 1987, between $116.00 and $119.00. Price broke to new lows and settled lower. The next day the price opened lower, took out recent lows and started a powerful move to the upside. The longs that went into that day long got out at the bottom and others sold some more to get short. The fact that the prices did not drop lower after the shorts sold caused panic and they started to cover the shorts at rapidly escalating prices.

The bar signal adequately signalled a reversal.

The overall chart of IBM shows regular rectangle, triangle, and rounding bottom formations, each offering very good price movement projections.

306

Figure 11-33A   IBM Showing Conventional Charting

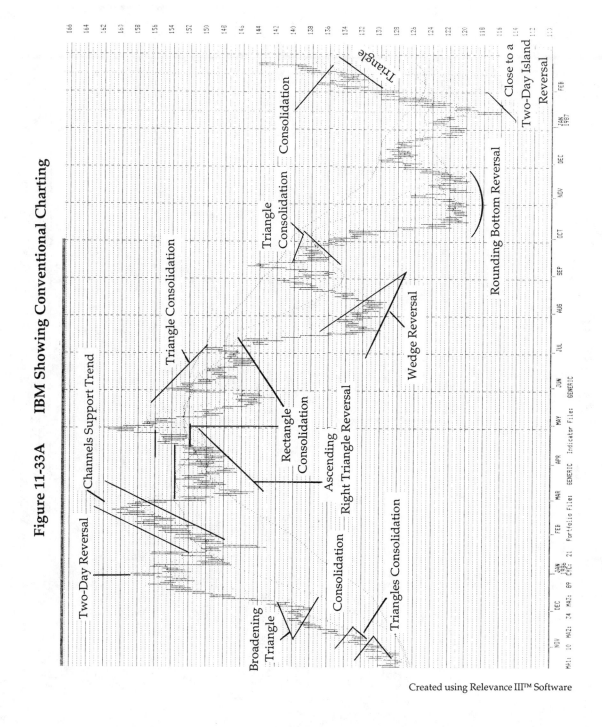

Created using Relevance III™ Software

Figure 11-33B

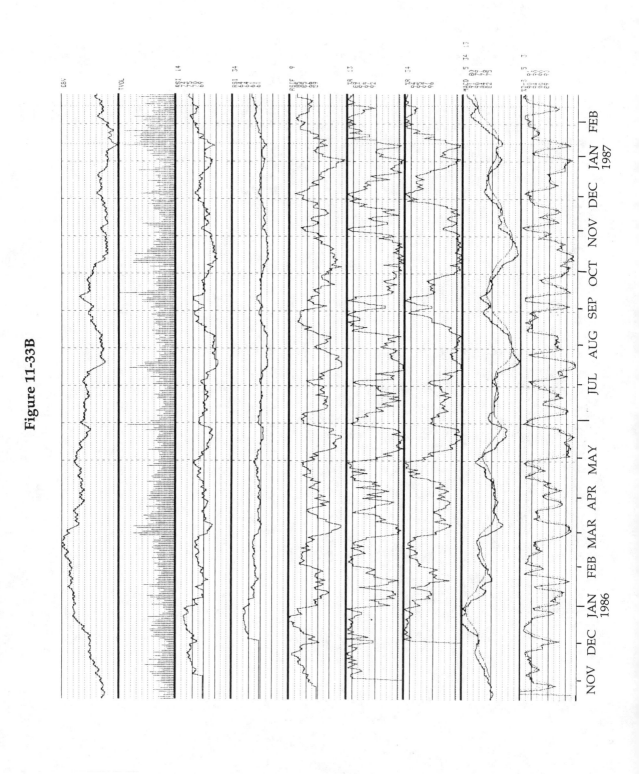

When to Apply Basic Charting Techniques

This approach is an attempt to categorize price action, as defined by bar charts, into predictable patterns which can be recognized, and therefore, forecasted. It is best used for trades which are of the same order of magnitude of an Intermediate movement for that particular market's activity cycle.

Since the Dow method is primarily concerned with cyclic movements, it obviously does not work well with time frames which are considerably smaller than major or intermediate cycles. Therefore, the method is not very suitable for day trading or scalping. Day traders and scalpers, however, have modified pattern recognition approaches such as this one by looking at more discrete time intervals. Instead of viewing the markets in daily fashion, these professionals break down price action into fractions of days and fractions of hours, thereby setting up situations where patterns like the ones in the daily chart examples in this chapter, can also be seen on these shorter time charts.

As a pattern-recognition technique, the approach can be supplemented by methods which help to sharpen its more global perceptions.

Volume-tracking techniques are a natural adjunct to this method, which depends so much on volume for *confirmation* of many of its signals.

Although not suitable itself for very short-term trading, this technique is useful for giving the context within which day trades can be executed, indicating for instance, whether or not a day is likely to close lower or higher than it opened.

Where to Find Out More About Basic Charting

Edwards, Robert D., and John Magee. *Technical Analysis of Stock Trends*, 5th Ed. Springfield, Massachusetts: John Magee, 1973. This is the classic work on conventional bar charting. The book, which first appeared in 1948, is still the best, most comprehensive single source of information on the subject.

Kaufman, Perry J. *Commodity Trading Systems and Methods*. New York: John Wiley & Sons, 1978. Chapter 10 covers basic chart reading techniques.

Murphy, John J. *Technical Analysis of the Futures Markets: A Comprehensive Guide to Trading Methods and Applications*. New York: New York Institute of Finance/Prentice-Hall. Chapters 2-6 passim.

Rhea, Robert. *The Dow Theory: an Explanation of Its Development and an Attempt to Define its Usefulness as an Aid to Speculation*. New York: Barron's, 1932.

Software to Run on the IBM Personal Computer

Chart Trader Plus—Interday charting package with the following: median lines, Fibonacci lines and spheres, recursion lines, percentage retracements, simple moving averages with bands, oscillators, relative strength index, on-balance volume, %R, cycle intervals, and parallel channels. Investor's Toolkit Ltd., Summit, IL 60501.

Computrac—Interday charting package has the following studies: moving average, rates of change, oscillators, ratios and spread RSI, stochastics, on-balance volume, moving average convergence divergence, point-and-figure, etc. Chart zooming, trend lines and parallel channels, cycle analysis with Fourier analysis. Computrac, Inc., New Orleans, LA 70175.

CTS Trend—A software package which is a basic miniversion of Tradecenter. It creates many different types of studies, including realtime studies. CTS Trend, Newark, NJ 07974.

Dow Jones Market Analyzer Plus—Interday charting with the following: moving averages, trading bands, volume oscillators, support/resistance lines, RSI, trend and parallel lines, speed lines, point-and-figure charts, split screen. Dow Jones Software, Princeton, NJ 08540.

Ganntrader I—Interday charting package for the technician with trading knowledge of William D. Gann's approach. No screen displays but excellent hardcopy charts. Gannsoft Publishing Company, Leavenworth, WA 98826.

MetaStock—Interday charting package has graphics, but primitive hardcopy features. Many moving averages, trading bands, parallel channels, linear-regression lines, cycle-interval lines, on-balance volume, RSI, positive/negative volume and relative-performance ratios. Computer Assist Management, Salt Lake City, UT 84126.

Quickplot—Interday charting package creates daily, weekly, or monthly charts, with moving averages of all types, trend lines and parallel channels, oscillators and RSI. This is a basic program without advanced studies. Commodity Systems, Inc., Boca Raton, FL 33432.

Relevance III™—Interday charting package which creates above-average screen graphics and the finest hardcopy chart available using regular computer equipment. Performs many advanced type studies and has the only available Elliott Wave ratio analysis program. Holt Investments, Nashville, TN 37238.

Telescan Analyzer—A front-end interday charting package which accesses only their own database of 7000 stocks and 150 market indices. Data retrieval cost: 50 cents peak hours, and 25 cents off peak access. Telescan, Inc., Houston, TX 77042.

12

Swing Charting
A Useful Risk Management Technique

Swing Charting at a Glance

Background and Philosophy of Swing Charting

Swing charting is based on a study of Gann methods. Over years of floor trading, this technique has proven effective. This method does not try to predict anything about the market—rather, it tells traders how to manage their position especially the positions that are current losers.

Principles of Swing Charts

A swing chart shows daily price bars with lines connecting local high and low breakout points. Local bottoming-out points give stop-sell levels, and topping-out points give stop-buy levels. This is basically a system for limiting losses, and it should be adhered to mechanically for best results.

How to Set Up and Maintain Swing Charts

1) Determine the number of trading periods for a reversal
2) Begin plotting daily bars, connecting their bottoms, if downtrending
3) Swing line to top of bars with first upside reversal
4) The first stop-sell point is slightly below the last bottom
5) Swing line to bottom of bars with first downside reversal
6) Last top is your first stop-buy point
7) Wait for next upside reversal, repeating the process
8) Wait till the swing line has broken previous buy-order point to enter long position
9) Get out of market if stop-sell point is penetrated
10) Repeat process in converse manner for bull markets

How to Trade with Swing Charts

Remember the following general rules:

1) Always determine a stop-loss point before entering a position.
2) Obey stop-loss orders immediately.
3) Adjust the stop-loss order to follow the movements of prices.
4) Don't pyramid unless the trader is experienced.
5) Take profits cautiously, using other techniques to generate signals to exit trades if desired.

When to Apply Swing Charts

Always use swing charts to determine when to get out of a trade, profitable or not. Don't use them as primary position entry indicators. Swing charts work well as supplements to trend-following and overbought/oversold methods.

Glossary for Swing Charting

Reversal—The point at which the swing chart's trend line swings from following price bottoms to following price tops. This reversal point is determined only after there have been two subsequent days of higher highs with no lower lows (in the case of a bottom reversal) or lower lows with no higher highs (in the case of a top reversal).

Stop-Buy Point—A price entry point put on a price chart by a technician at the previous local top reversal's price level. If price exceeds the current stop-buy point, then the technician should consider buying if short or going long.

Stop-Sell Point—A price entry point put on a price chart by a technician at the previous local bottom reversal's price level. If price goes below the current stop-sell point, then the technician should consider selling if long or going short if not already short.

Swing Chart—The swing chart operates with a trend line swinging between the bottoms and tops of daily prices and with stop-sell and buy-order points.

Trend Line—A line on a swing chart which follows the bottoms or tops of daily price bars, switching between the tops and bottoms at reversal points.

Background and Philosophy of Swing Charting

Although swing charting originally developed from Gann's trading techniques, swing charting does not make any up-front assumptions about the nature or future behavior of the market. It does not try to predict where the market might be at some time in the future, and it does not try to discern the trend, the accumulation, the strength, the wave phase, or any other factor that could be called a "technical indicator" for market prediction. Instead, swing charting works on what might be called the reverse type of strategy: it prepares traders for any eventuality and at any point it lets them know just what their maximum risk or assured profit is going to be. This is in contrast to those other methods which prepare traders for the market to do something more or less specific but cannot assure them what will happen to their position.

Swing charting also gives completely unequivocal signals for buying and selling. Thus, unlike most of the other methods discussed in this book, swing charting will tell traders little about what is going to happen, but everything about what to do at any given moment. The other methods purport to tell traders everything about what is going to happen and why, but do not tell how to use the information they provide.

In a sense, then, swing charting is not really a technical market analysis method, since it analyzes nothing and makes no promises. It is, rather, a position management technique. As such, this makes swing charting a method for separating the sheep from the goats among traders: those who really have the discipline to be good traders will find swing charting extremely useful, even indispensable; on the other hand, to those who don't have that discipline, swing charting will seem like a bothersome shackle to their creativity and they will constantly be trying to outplay the market, ignoring the signals that the swing chart gives.

Although swing charting does not make any assumptions about the market, obviously, any method that gives unequivocal buy and sell signals has to operate on some sort of assumption about the nature of the market. Remember, though, that swing charting makes no *up-front* assumptions about the market's nature. What the method does assume implicitly are certain things about how a trader's position will fare in a relatively stable market situation.

These assumptions are quite simple and are, in fact, a systematization of the very important rules of thumb which state:

- Know when to take losses. Don't let them run.
- Don't sell a stock just because it is up.
- Don't buy a stock just because it is down.
- Use buy and sell stop points and stick to them.

318

Principles of Swing Charting

A bar swing chart uses a swing-line which looks like a line drawn through the various bars on a price chart. This line connects highs and lows, and if traders look at a bar swing chart which someone has set up, they will see that the line follows each period's highs for some time, then abruptly shifts to the lows, following them for a while, until, once again, there is a shift and the line goes back to following the highs.

Upside and Downside Reversal Points

Basically, the line breaks from low to high or from high to low when the technician who is maintaining the chart sees that there has been a significant break to the upside or the downside.

- *A significant break to the upside* is defined as happening after the line has been following the lows. Then, for a predetermined number of periods (usually two price bars), the price shows higher highs without showing lower lows. When this happens, the line swings up to begin following the highs until a significant break to the downside happens.
- *A significant break to the downside* happens after the line has been following the price's highs. When the price shows lower lows without showing higher highs for one's predetermined number of periods, one should swing the line downward to start following the lows.

The technician may, and in fact should, keep several charts for the same market at different time frames, for example, a daily chart, an hourly chart and a fifteen-minute chart.

Buy and Sell Points

The technician will then use these charts of the same market for different time frames to find points at which to place stop sell and buy orders.

A reversal on the bottom toward the top gives a stop-sell order point. The idea is that this reversal point has established a point of strength for the current market below which it will fall only with difficulty. If price does, however, fall below this point, it is probably a shakeout in the price structure and it will be difficult to tell how far it will descend. Thus, going short at this point is the most prudent course. If traders fail to do this, they run the very probable risk of letting their losses run to alarming proportions. Actually, the best placement of a stop-loss order should be somewhere just below this point, since, if it really is an indicator of rock-bottom strength, the market might dip down just to that point momentarily without initiating a precipitous plunge.

A reversal at the top toward the bottom gives a buy order point for the next uptrend. Note here that it is best for traders only to use these buy order points to get into the market if they have not yet initiated a position in the current market—it is not wise to pyramid on top of an existing position in the same market. This only increases their risk exposure while giving them a smaller potential return on their investment. It is better to invest that same money in a new position elsewhere.

The reason that traders should use this point as a buy order is the inverse of the reason for using a lower reversal as a stop-loss order: the market has reversed toward the bottom here because there is a basic resistance to any higher moves at this point. However, if the price should rise above this level at some later time, it is most probably a signal that the market is being redefined to accommodate a new, higher price range. Therefore, going long at this point gives the very real possibility of riding the new trend upward for some appreciable distance.

The Cautious Nature of This System

Please note the following observations:

- The system is as cautious on the sell side as it is on the buy side. In other words, a sell or a buy signal is only used after stop-loss points have been clearly defined, and then only if it is to enter a market. A buy signal should never be used before the stop-loss point has been established nor should traders initiate a second position after already having established a previous position in the same market.

- A sell signal, on the other hand, should always be taken seriously and obeyed post-haste. This is attributable to the fact that markets collapse faster than they go up.

Thus, once traders have gone long on a buy signal, their trading stop-sell order may move upward as the market fluctuates up and down above the original reversal point which determined their first sell signal. This means that the longer traders hold a position without falling below any stop-loss point, the higher their sell-stop signal will move. If traders stick to the rule about not pyramiding on top of their original purchase, their risk will diminish as the market oscillates upward, since their stop-sell order will approach their purchase price.

In effect, traders can always measure how much they are at risk by finding the difference between their purchase price and their initial stop-sell order. If the market runs on long enough, traders' stop-sell order points will actually begin to move above their original purchase price. Thus, their risk as defined in the previous paragraph will show a reduction.

Using the System to Take Profits

Up to this point it may appear that the whole swing chart technique has a rather negative objective, that is, to limit losses. In essence, this is true. The system tells traders when to get out of a trade to cut short their losses and when it is safe to get into a position which has a good chance of not losing. It does not, however, tell traders as unequivocally when to take a profit.

If they keep several charts on different time-frames, as suggested above, traders can get a better idea of how to take profits with this system.

The basic way to do this is to keep track of the interaction between reversal points on the different time-frame charts. While they are long in the market, traders should watch the three different levels of charts. If their daily chart gives a reversal point, then they should check their hourly and fifteen-minute charts for that day. If these are also showing downward reversals for the day, traders might decide that they have a major upward limit defined at that point and that the market will only come back up this way again after a major downturn. This could then be a signal that their profit is ready to be taken, because they may be at or near the high point of the trend.

How to Set Up and Maintain Swing Charts

Determining the Number of Periods for a Significant Reversal

The number of periods for a significant reversal is the number of days in which higher highs without lower lows would mean a reversal to the upside, or in which lower lows without higher highs would mean a reversal to the downside. This will almost always be two days, never less. If the market is extremely erratic, traders might want to experiment with a three- or even a four-day period, but on the whole they will find that two days is the best choice. Otherwise, traders may find themselves missing out on some plays.

With these shorter periods, there is always the danger of whipsaws, but because of the nature of the system, losses are limited by the stop-sell orders.

Initiating the Chart

Traders begin by plotting the bars on a price chart. When they have found their selected number of days with lower lows and no higher highs, they can begin plotting along the bottom of the bars. They reverse the scenario in upwardly trending bar charts.

The First Market Bottom

When traders get their reversal to the upside (the requisite number of days of higher highs without lower lows), they should swing the line up to the tops of the bars. A point somewhat below the low point from which they began their upswing (usually a tic or two below it) now defines their first bottom point and the consequential stop-sell order point for all long postions.

Notice, however, that they still have not initiated a position.

The First Market Top

Now traders wait for their first reversal to the downside to help define their first stop-buy point. They note this point on the chart. Traders will place an order to enter the market once this level is broken on the next upswing.

The Market Top is Broken to the Upside

Traders must now let the price go all the way down and reverse again, retracing itself all the way back to their previously marked stop-buy point. They need to wait for the line to penetrate, not just approach, the old high.

Initiating a Position

Once the line has broken through the old high barrier, traders can be fairly confident that they can be buyers on strength, and then can enter an order to go long.

How to Trade with Swing Charting

The bar-swing chart technique is basically a system that dictates moves to the trader, and therefore the trader has very little discretion about how to interpret the system's signals. Therefore, most of what traders need to know about how to trade with this system was contained in the general discussion of principles and in the section on how to set up the system.

However, here are some brief rules for buying and selling with this system which summarize what was discussed in the above sections:

1) Never initiate a trade without first having the stop-loss point determined. Other signals will probably be useful to determine other types of indicators for position entry signals, but before going into positions always make sure that the bar-swing chart has a clearly defined stop-loss point marked at the first marked reversal point.

2) Sell promptly when the stop-loss point has been broken to the downside. Again, other criteria from other market techniques may

give a signal to sell before this point is reached. That is fine, but do not stay long below the bar-swing chart's sell signal because of these other techniques.

3) Move the stop-loss point upward while the position lasts.

4) Don't pay attention to new buy signals after establishing a position, i.e., don't pyramid. This increases risk and reduces profit ratio.

5) Take profits cautiously, using daily, hourly and quarter-hourly charts to confirm possible over-extension on the upside, which could indicate that it is time to sell, or possible over-sold conditions to the downside, which could indicate that it is time to buy. This is also the point at which other techniques can give more accurate position exit orders.

Three Trading Examples and a Fourth
Showing How to Do It Right

The first three examples of swing charting which use daily charts show very discouraging results. However, a refinement of this technique has given great success for many years, and that is what is used in the fourth example. This example includes the use of daily, hourly and quarter-hourly price charts. This technique, if used with the refinements, will not let traders down and will be a consistent profit-maker.

Swing charts work best when traders use a continuous position (flipping between long and short, never closing out their positions entirely) and add to that position when they get a string of the same signals. That is the assumption common to each of the examples which follow.

Trading Example for August 1987 Gold Futures
Using Swing Charting

This chart gives the 87-day bar chart from March 1 through June 24, 1987. The price of gold goes from a low of $406.00 to a high of $486.00. The price scale is in ten-cent increments of the American dollar, so, for example, 4960 means $496.00.

The third day forms a high and is immediately followed by two days of lower lows without higher highs, so this day will give traders a swing chart top.

Two days of higher highs without lower lows follow immediately, so this is the first bottom and traders can draw a line from the first top to this point.

Another reversal defines a second top and also breaks below the previous bottom (point A), giving traders their first sell signal. They go short at this point, on a price of $413.50.

Three days after the 12th two higher highs without lower lows signal another reversal. The trend is now upward. It is not enough, however, to make traders cover their short, since it has not gone beyond the previous high. The two following days tell them that they were at a top below the previous high, so their short position holds steady.

However, another two days tell traders that a bottom has happened again, and when price reaches point B, it takes out the previous top. This is a buy signal and a warning to cover the short.

They close their short at $417.00, for a loss on this trade of $3.50. Traders open a long position at $417.00 at the same time.

324

Figure 12-1   Trading August 1987 Gold Futures Using Swing Charting

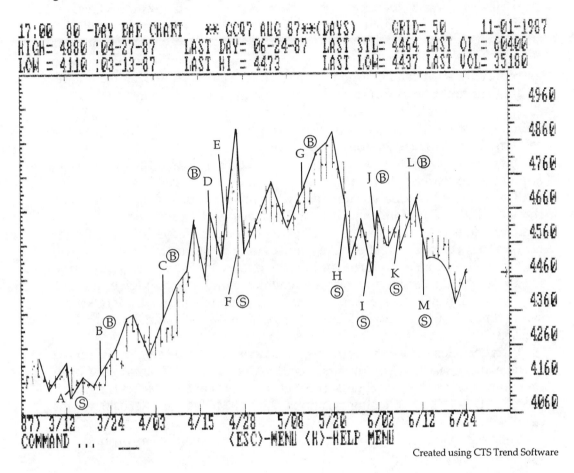

Created using CTS Trend Software

The rising trend runs the last few trading days in March, when two falling days allow traders to identify a top. The trend falls for three more days, and then two rising days signal a bottom. The incipient rise seems to stall, then shoots up, exceeding the previous top and giving traders another buy signal (point C) at a price of $434.80, so the traders add a second long position. For exemplifying what can be done with judicious use of pyramiding techniques, traders can continue to add to positions in the direction of the main trend.

Price goes rapidly upward for three more days, then two falling days define a reversal. Price would have to go much lower, however, to define a sell signal, since the last bottom is far below this range.

Two up days define this small bottom and break beyond the previous top at point D. So traders add on a third long position at a price of $464.80.

Two down days follow immediately, defining a top. Two up days follow these, and give a bottom, which is still not below the previous bottom and therefore does not yet signal a sell. The second of these days (E) takes traders beyond the previous top. They take a fourth long position at $466.00.

On the trading day before April 28 the one exception to the simple rules for swing-chart reversals appears: a day which simultaneously gives a higher high and a lower low. This signals an instant reversal, and traders see the swing line plunge below the previous bottom—a sell signal (point F) at $453.50.

If traders close out their long positions now, they will see a profit on two of them and losses on two. The first position opened at $417.00, so their profit on that position is $36.50. Their second position was at $436.00, so their profit there is $17.50. The two losing positions were at $464.80 and $466.00, for losses of $11.30 and $12.50, respectively.

Subtracting the earlier loss of $3.50, traders received a net profit at this point (F) of 267, or $26.70.

They also initiate a short position at $453.50.

After this point, a series of up days definitely tells traders that F was a bottom. This tendency continues until May 9, when two down days signal that a top has happened on the 7th. The previous high was in the stratosphere, so this top did not exceed it and therefore no buy signal happened.

A series of up days now tells traders that May 10th is a bottom, and at point G they exceed the previous top.

The buy signal at G makes traders cover their short at $476.00, for a loss on this trade of $22.50. They also go long at this point. Another top and then a breakdown past the previous bottom cause them to sell at about $460.00 (point H), for a loss of or $16.00.

Traders also initiate a short at $460.00. The ensuing bottom and top break no new ground, but the bottom immediately after that at point I breaks below the previous bottom, and so signals to add a second short position at $451.00.

Another bottom and the upward swing takes out the previous high at $461.00 (point J). Traders, therefore, cover their two shorts for respective losses of $1.00 and $10.00, giving a total loss for these two positions of $11.00.

Traders also go long at this point at a price of $461.00.

An immediate top and then a bottom two days later break no new ground. At K traders see another anomalistic day similar to the day at F, and so another high-to-low reversal is signalled. At point K they take out the previous bottom at around $456.00. Traders close out their long for a loss of $5.00 and initiate a short position.

Two more days of high give another bottom and a buy signal at about $465.00 (point L). Traders close out the short for a loss of $9.00 and go long.

Another reversal, and a bottomside breakthrough, generate a sell signal at about $444.50 for a loss on their previous long position of $20.50.

Traders go short at this point and watch the chart make new lows, bottoming just before June 24.

In summary, the method was a money-maker for the first half of the time period under consideration, making traders $26.70. During the second half, however, they lost a total of $52.50, or almost exactly double the previous earnings.

Notice that the first half was a fairly clear upward-trending market while in the second half price showed a great deal of hesitation about where it was going. This "choppy" motion which took place while the trend was sorting itself out was responsible for the whipsaw signals. Additionally, the use of the basic pyramiding technique was profitable in decidedly trending markets. Once the market turned to less one-directional movements, the losses on pyramiding mounted. This is not to say that pyramiding techniques should not be used, but rather that the times during which profitable pyramiding works are limited. For the safety of the trader's capital it is best not to pyramid unless all signals point to a runaway market.

Figure 12-2   Trading Coastal Gas Stock Using Swing Charting

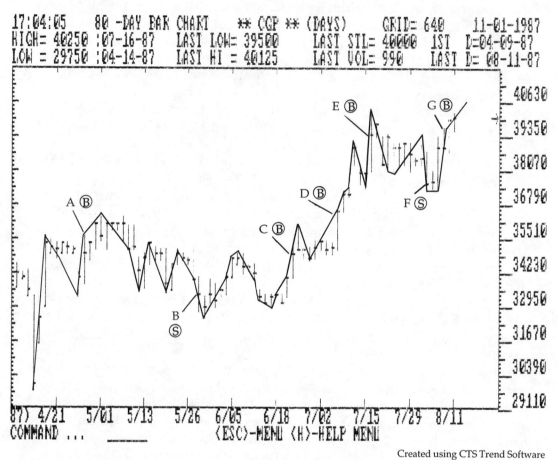

17:04:05   80 -DAY BAR CHART   ** CGP ** (DAYS)   GRID= 640   11-01-1987
HIGH= 40250 :07-16-87   LAST LOW= 39500   LAST STL= 40000   1ST D=04-09-87
LOW = 29750 :04-14-87   LAST HI = 40125   LAST VOL= 990   LAST D= 08-11-87

COMMAND ... ___   〈ESC〉-MENU 〈H〉-HELP MENU

Created using CTS Trend Software

Trading CGP Stock Using Swing Charting

This Coastal Gas chart is for 80 days from April 1987 to August 1987. The stock moves from a low of $29.00 to a high of $40.00 per share. The scale is in tenths of a cent, so 35510 is equivalent to $35.51. The analysis of this example simply points out the trade signals, which are fewer than in the last example.

Six days into the chart, two up days define the first price bottom and then some chewing around takes place until a definite downtrend is defined, giving a top.

The bottom (half-way between April 21 and May 10) is nowhere near low enough to break the previous bottom, but a few days later traders get their first buy signal at $35.670 (point A).

Tops and bottoms refuse to break above each other for a few weeks, until the trend finally goes low enough to break a previous low (point B) and therefore signal a sell at $33.430, for a loss of 2240, or $2.24.

Traders also initiate a short position at $33.430.

The next top and bottom fail to break above the previous top and bottom, but the ensuing upswing (after June 18) breaks the previous high at point C, gives traders a signal to cover their short and go long at $35.190. Covering their short brings a loss of $1.76.

Another top/bottom pair in late June, and then a massive upswing takes price beyond that top, signalling a second long position at $36.150 (point B).

The top/bottom pair in the second week of July is followed by another upswing which takes out the previous high at point B, signalling a third long position at $39.190.

A top, a bottom and a top carry traders into the beginning of August without breaking any new ground. The downtrend finally (point F) goes beyond the previous bottom at $38.070 for a sell signal. Traders have three long positions open at this point. The first two bring profits of $2.880 and $1.920, respectively, while the last position hands them a loss of 1120, netting them a profit of $3.68.

They initiate a short position at $38.070.

A reversal finds the trendline soon exceeding the previous top (point G) and traders cover their short at $39.350, for a loss of $1.28.

There is a net loss for this trading period of $1.60.

Figure 12-3 Trading the New York Averages Using Swing Charting

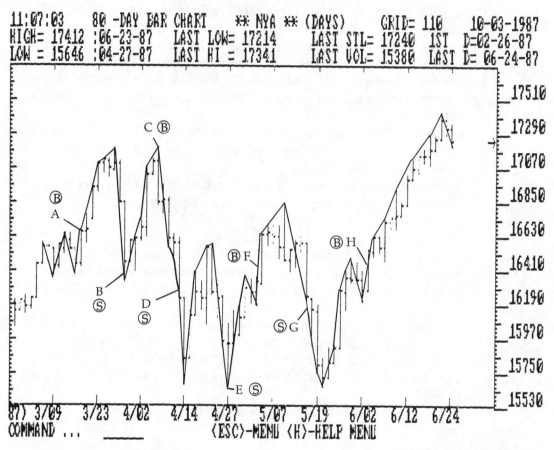

Trading the New York Averages Using Swing Charting

The New York Averages is portrayed here for a period from March 1987 to about the end of June 1987. The index moves in a range from $115.00 to a high of $173.00.

It is not necessary to comment on the individual trades on this chart. Please note, however, that the signals are uniformly bad.

These swing chart signals tell traders to consistently buy high and sell low. The final buy signal looks like it might be on the right side of the market, though a precipitous plunge all at once could again have them selling at a lower price.

Note the "chopping" effect brought on by the fact that, as in the second half of the first trading example, the trend is not well defined during this trading period. In this chart, the situation is aggravated by the fact that each "chop" is fairly violent, covering a wide price range in little time, and so giving traders little chance to salvage any of their position before the next wrong signal.

The next example will illustrate how to dampen this choppiness which may be evident in more volatile markets.

A Way to Improve on These Swing Chart Signals

More detailed charts would have helped in all three cases. In addition to daily charts, hourly or even half-hourly charts would give a wealth of refined signals which would keep traders from always being short at the bottom and long at the top. Let's see how that would work in the following example, which is a record of trades actually made during the first part of 1986.

Figure 12-4 is a daily bar chart of the March 1986 Treasury Bond Contract from January 17, 1986 to February 19, 1986. Look at how a two-day swing chart is created from this daily bar chart. On the start date of this two-day swing chart, January 18 (point A), a line is drawn from the bottom connecting with the high of January 22 (point B). This is done because the two days following the start of the swing chart have two consecutive higher highs. Granted, the January 18 low is lower than the previous day's low, the swing chart line is drawn upwards because the trader is looking for a potential reversal point.

On January 23 and 24 bonds traded lower. January 24 and 25 did not give two lower lows so they are ignored. On January 27 (point C), the high exceeded the previous swing high (B). Therefore, the swing chart line from the high of January 22 is drawn to connect this high (C). The swing chart line is drawn to connect the next higher highs until there are two days of consecutive lower bottoms.

The upside swing line top reached on February 4 (D) is reversed and drawn down because the next two days' bottoms are consecutively lower. The swing line is now drawn to connect the lower bottoms.

On February 7, the final low (E) is made and the two following days show higher highs (F) and higher bottoms (G). The swing line low is now drawn to connect the tops of February 11 and 12 and any high of any single day following.

On February 13, traders receive their first buy signal based on the two-day swing chart (H). Breaking above 86.24, which was the previous swing top high made on February 4, this trade looks to be a buy on weakness as opposed to being a sale on strength.

Look at what the hourly swing chart (Figure 12-5) indicates. Having followed the swings on this chart, traders can see that on the last hour of February 11 the bonds (K) took out the previous two-hour swing top made on the same day in the second hour of trading (J). The hourly swing chart confirms that traders must also buy.

Finally, look at the 15-minute chart (Figure 12-6) which indicates at what price the bond should be bought. The previous two chart types, the daily and

Figure 12-4 T-Bonds Daily Swing Chart

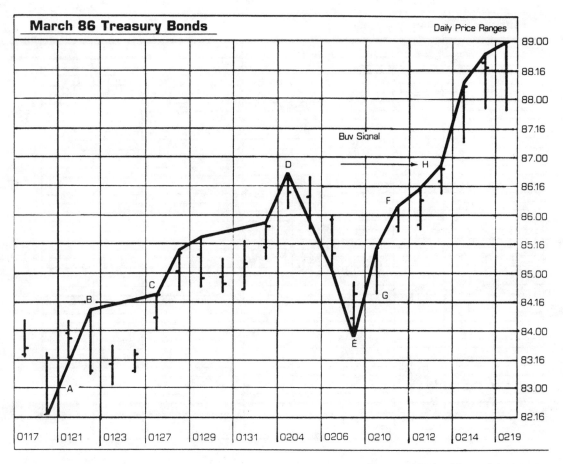

Courtesy of *Stock and Commodities Magazine*

Figure 12-5   T-Bonds Hourly Swing Chart

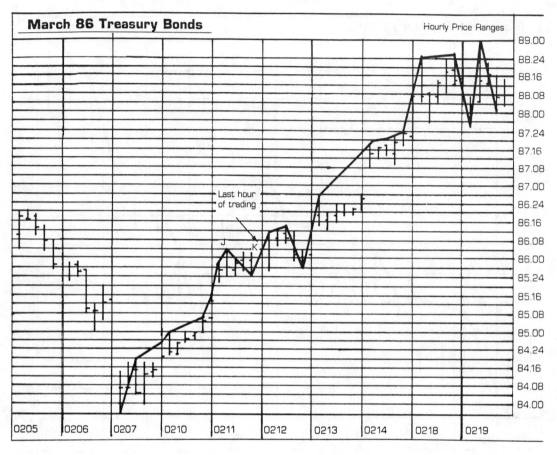

Courtesy of *Stock and Commodities Magazine*

Figure 12-6   T-Bonds 15-Minute Swing Chart

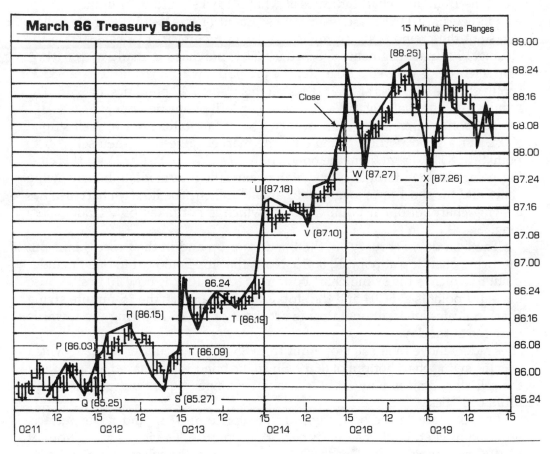

Courtesy of *Stock and Commodities Magazine*

the hourly, indicated whether or not the bond should be bought or sold. Now, the 15-minute chart indicates at what price it should be bought.

On February 11 the last 15-minute segment of the 15-minute swing chart takes out the previous swing highs by reaching point P at price 86.03. In the closing 15-minute segment of February 11 a purchase is made at $86.04. A stop sell order is entered a tic under the previous swing chart bottom at $85.25 (point Q). The stop was at 85.24. Risk on this trade is 12 bond tics, or $375. The bonds closed on that day at 86.05, a closing profit of one tic.

The bonds open lower on February 12, but fail to take out the sell stop at 85.24. For a good portion of the day, the market rallies and then sells off to point S, at 85.27. From there the bonds rally to a close of 86.09 (T). At this closing point, the long-term two-day swing chart, the intermediate hourly swing chart, and the short-term swing chart are all bullish. The hourly chart also has a swing chart bottom at point Q, 85.25, which is not taken out. Traders stay long.

The next day, February 13, the bonds gap up and in the process take out the swing chart top at point R, 86.15. Now, the stop is moved to one tic under point S, which is the swing chart bottom of 85.27. Risk is now 10 tics because the entry point is at 86.04 and the stop is at 85.26. In fact, the 15-minute swing chart indicates an additional upside breakout of the 86.24 swing top towards the close of the day.

Traders move their sell stop limit from 85.24 to a tic under point T, which was the swing chart bottom of 86.19. Since the bond is purchased at 86.04, and the sell stop limit is now 86.19, there is no longer a risk, but a guaranteed profit of 15 tics.

On February 14 the bonds gap up at a price of 87.16 and never retrace. From point U at 87.18, the bonds sell off to point V, a swing chart bottom of 87.10. Once the reversal exceeds 87.18, traders move the sell stop to 87.09, a tic under the swing chart bottom of point V. The guaranteed profit is now 37 tics since the bond was bought at 86.04 and can be stopped at 87.09.

Looking over the daily and hourly swing charts, traders will have discovered that there were no swing chart reversals generated in the long-term chart, intermediate chart or short-term chart. Therefore, they can continue to be bullish. The bonds keep moving up and close at 88.07 on February 14. Still no sell signal is given. At this point, since the open one lot trade has shown a profit of over 60 tics in three days, traders start to look for more short-term sell signals to take a profit.

On February 18 the bonds open higher but sell off. Strict adherence to the swing charts would not get traders out since the stop at 87.09 was not caught. However, they start to look for reasons to move their stop higher. At point W, 87.27, the bonds stop selling off and rally. Once the reversal takes place, traders move the stop from 87.09 to 87.26, a tic under point W, and a guaranteed a profit of 54 tics if the stop were caught. Otherwise, the profits are allowed to run. The bonds rally into new highs by a tic to 88.26 and closed at 88.18.

On February 19, the bonds gap down and sell off to a low of 87.26 (X) and reverse. This is still not a *penetration* of the sell stop order, so traders remain long into the future with a guaranteed profit of at least 54 tics or $1687.50.

When to Apply Swing Charts

This method is the watchdog for any other trading technique traders might choose to use. A method will never be right 100% of the time, and traders won't be, either. Admitting this is another thing, and determining when losses have come to the point where they must be cut short can be both emotionally and conceptually difficult. If traders let a bar-swing chart take the driver's seat when it comes to this difficult decision, they will reduce their worry and also will never take undue losses. Therefore, they should have something like this system in place for all their trades, no matter what market condition they are experiencing or what other method they may be using. If the market seems quite volatile, traders might want to go to more than two periods for the number of significant higher highs without lower lows to use in determining a lower reversal point and lower lows without higher highs for determining an upper reversal point.

An extremely mercurial market might also mean that traders would need to ignore the shorter-period charts.

In general, it is best for traders not to use this technique as their only indicator for getting into a market. Bar-swing charting is not primarily an initial position entry indicator, but rather an indicator which enables its disciplined users to cut their losses on their positions. The method does, however, work well as a supplement to trend-following and volume-determining methods which try to monitor overbought and oversold conditions.

Where to Find Out More About Swing Charts

For theoretical background on this method, traders might wish to study the section in this book on Gann's methods, particularly the one on Gann angles.

This chapter is based entirely on the article that was written for *Technical Analysis of Stocks and Commodities Magazine*, July 1986.

Readers may obtain technical advice on the use of this method from:

Financial Options Consultants
780 South Federal, #314
Chicago, Illinois
USA
312/663-9339 (voice)
312/922-3626 (computer)

13

Astronomical Cycles

Time Can Be Forecasted

Astronomical Cyles at a Glance

Background and Philosophy of Astronomical Cycles

A surprising number of prominent traders and market theoreticians use astronomical indicators in their personal trading. They have found that astrology provides a way for studying complex cyclic phenomena such as the markets.

Principles of Astronomical Cycles

This chapter discusses three types of astronomical indicators: 1) moon phase indicators 2) astrological charts and 3) the composite aspectivity indicator of planetary positions. Astrological charting can be further broken down into three sub-types: 1) the birth chart, or "snapshot" of the heavens at birth; 2) the transit chart, or picture of the heavens at the present and 3) the progressed chart, which is a combination of birth chart and transit chart.

How to Set Up and Maintain Astronomical Cyles

- With the moon, one need simply plot phase fluctuations on a chart below price. Of course, astronomical indicators may be plotted far into the future of price since they are known for the future.
- For astrological charts, it is best to obtain an astrological software package and follow some astrological market consultant's newsletter.
- For aspectivity, the table provided in the body of this chapter and the rules for the relation between each planet must be observed to obtain both individual and composite values. These may also be plotted in advance on a price chart.

How to Trade with Astronomical Cycles

Lunar phases will work to signal reversals in such monthly commodities markets as sugar, cocoa, silver, soybean oil, corn, and wheat. Astrological charts can tell traders about the advisability or present weakness or strength of a position. Aspectivity can tip off traders to possible future reversal points in the market.

When to Apply Astronomical Indicators

Astronomical indicators work best when mass investment psychology is crucial to a given market situation, in cyclical markets and for long-range trading.

Ignore astronomical cycles when trading in short-term situations, in irregular and non-cyclic markets with fairly mechanical restraints on price and do not use them by themselves. Traders can use astronomical indicators to confirm signals from relative strength and volume-based overbought/oversold indicator techniques.

Glossary for Astronomical Indicators

Aspect—Angular relationship between the Right Ascensions of any two planetary bodies (Moon and Sun are considered planetary bodies for this purpose) as seen from the Earth. These angles have special names, the most important being conjunction, declination, opposition, sextile, square and trine.

Aspectivity—A special composite indicator in Donald Bradley's method derived from all the heavenly bodies' respective nearness to any aspect points. It is found by adding the Long Term to the Declination Factor, multiplying by a pre-determined normalizing factor, and then adding the Short Term.

Birth Chart—A "snapshot" of the planetary positions taken when a person is born or when a trade or corporation is initiated.

Conjunction—An aspect of two heavenly bodies occurring when there is 0 degrees' angle between their respective Right Ascensions.

Declination—The celestial latitude, or degrees north or south of the equator, of a heavenly body's position. North declination is positive and south declination is negative.

Declination Factor—The sum of the declinations of Venus and Mars.

Ephemeris—An almanac of planetary, lunar and solar positions.

Full Moon—When the Moon is opposite the Sun in the sky and is fully illuminated.

Long Term—In Bradley's method, the sum of the relative aspectivity of the outer planets Jupiter, Saturn, Uranus, Neptune and Pluto. Some aspects are given a negative sign, others a positive sign, by Bradley.

Middle Term—In Bradley's method, the sum of the relative aspectivity of the inner planets: Mercury, Venus and Mars. Some aspects are given a negative sign, others a positive sign, by Bradley. Not used in Bradley's short method.

Natal Chart—Same as **Birth Chart.**

New Moon—When the Moon is at the same Right Ascension as the Sun and sets with it, so that the side facing us is completely unilluminated and therefore invisible.

Normalizing Factor—In Bradley's method, an arbitrarily chosen number which one uses to multiply by the Long Term + Declination in order to obtain an indicator which is on the same scale as price.

Opposition—An aspect which occurs when two heavenly bodies are on opposite sides of the sky (that is, when they are 180 degrees apart).

Progressed Chart—An astrological chart showing the relations among the entity's birth chart with a chart of planets adjusted by a time progression factor imposed on it.

Right Ascension—Celestial longitude, or east-west position in the sky, of a heavenly body. Measured in hours, minutes and seconds.

Sextile—An aspect which occurs when two heavenly bodies are one-sixth of a full circle apart in the sky (that is, when they are 60 degrees apart).

Square—An aspect which occurs when two heavenly bodies are one quarter of a full circle apart in the sky (that is, when they are 90 degrees apart).

Transit Chart—An astrological chart composed of an entity's birth chart (see above) with a chart of current planetary positions imposed on it.

Trine—An aspect which occurs when two heavenly bodies are one-third of a full circle apart in the sky (that is, when they are 120 degrees apart).

Background and Philosophy of Astronomical Cycles

What Place Does Astrology Have in a Scientific Trading System?

Readers may be surprised to read a book written in the 1980's which is going to seriously discuss the use of astronomical cycles for trading the markets. They will also be surprised, then, to know that there are a number of individuals who make their living primarily by giving the market community astrological advice and that many successful traders who are the founders or main exponents of more "scientifically" based methods have used astronomical cycles and astrology, as well, in their work. Some examples are William Gann, originator of the Gann trading system; Larry Williams, the originator of the Percentage R indicator; Arch Crawford, the publisher of *Crawford Perspectives*; Mason Sexton, publisher of *Harmonic Newsletter* and Joe Granville, the foremost modern practitioner of on-balance volume techniques.

Why have so many sensible, successful traders turned to astronomical cycles and astrology? They have found that if one removes all the hocus pocus and obscure jargon associated with the astrological art one can utilize astrology for what it really is—a study of time and cyclicity. Thus, when traders remove planetary meanings and house influences, they find that astrology can give them a shorthand method of tracking the unfolding of complex events through time.

Without time there is no price and volume in a market. Without price and volume there is still time.

Complex Time Cycles and How We Measure Them

The most common measuring devices for tracking time cycles are the calendar and the clock. The traditional clockface contains three hands, each of them measuring a different time cycle: the minute (measured by the second hand), the hour (measured by the minute hand) and the half-day (measured by the hour hand).

Now think of a clock face which has four more hands representing the units of calendrical time: the day, the week, month and year. The clock hands representing these time units are not completely synchronized with each other: the year is 365 days plus a fraction; the months and days gradually get out of step with the year, so that the year needs periodic adjustment with leap years and the weeks do not divide evenly into the year or the months. We thus have a clock face which shows relations of great complexity. Please note that these are astrological indicators: conventional time cycles are determined by the motions of the Earth, Sun and Moon.

Astrology as an Extension of Everyday Time Measurements

To talk about astrology, as such, picture more hands on the imaginary clock—one for each of the eight planets besides the Earth and Moon (in astrological terminology the Sun and Moon are called "planets," contrary to the usage by astronomers).

The other "hands" on the astrological clock, then, are represented by the planets, which make one revolution about the "clock face" in the following times:

Table 13-1 Days to Travel Around the Sun

Mercury	83	days
Venus	224.5	days
Mars	1	year and 322 days
Jupiter	12	years
Saturn	29.5	years
Uranus	84	years
Neptune	165	years
Pluto	248	years

Observe that, from this viewpoint, the Sun is at the center of the clock and that the "hands" are moving counter-clockwise..

Figure 13-1

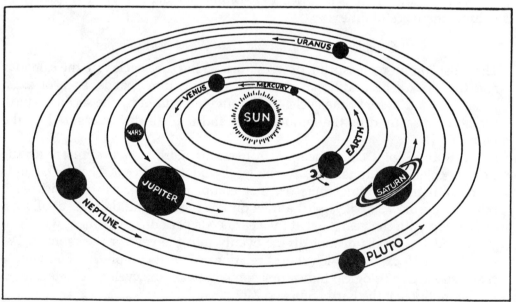

Our Solar System

Courtesy of Llewellyn Publications

Since these motions are observed from the earth, while their center is the Sun, they are somewhat off-center. They sometimes seem to speed up, slow down, or even reverse direction for a while (a phenomenon called "retrograde motion"). Astrology takes all these phenomena into account in its study of cyclic behavior.

This chapter discusses three types of astronomically-based trading systems:

1) The moon-phase system for certain commodities as discussed by Pugh;

2) The use of astrological charts or "horoscopes;"

3) An indicator called "aspectivity" based on the composite positions of the planets, which was developed by Bradley four decades ago.

Principles of Astronomical Cycles

Trading with the Moon

As a number of traders have noted, the Moon's correlation to monthly commodity prices is well documented:

Full moon—higher price.
New moon—lower price.

Trading with Astrological Charts

There are three ways to use astrological charts to observe the effects of planetary motion on an event:

1) A static snapshot of planetary positions at the time of the event, known as a "birth chart;"

2) A view of the continuing movement of planets and how they relate to any one static snapshot, or a "progressed chart;"

3) A combination of the static and the continuing movement charts, known as a "transit chart."

The Birth Chart

Astrologers make a "snapshot," or chart, of the heavens at birth and identify the person or other entity born at that time as a certain type of entity or person with such and such heavenly identifiers. In short, it is possible to make a birth chart of the planetary motions of any event, be it the birth of a baby, the founding of a corporation or the beginning of a trade in the market, and find valid correlations with previous observations.

The Progressed Chart

The second method of using planetary motion is to observe the dynamic motion of the planets and track how the planets interact among themselves. At any point in time there are relations of one sort or another among the planets in the heavens, just as in the clock face example there are hour-to-minute, minute-to second, hour-to-second relationships at any point in time. In the case of the planetary "clock face" there are ten planets (Moon and Sun are considered planets) which interact with each other. The number of possible relationships increase tremendously. Astrologers correlate events with current planetary position and pull out previously observed data for similar planetary positions.

The Transit Chart

This type of chart is composed of one birthchart inside and one type of progressed chart outside. The internal wheel is shorthand to see how each of the planets are related to all the others: trines, oppositions, squares and sextiles. The trines, oppositions, squares and sextiles are angular relationships (Ptolemaic angles) that have been observed by the ancients to have definite relationships. Recent scientific studies have shown that when planets are related to other planets in certain angular fashion, there is an increase in radio wave transmissions from both planets.

   An example of each of these types of charts is illustrated and interpreted in the Trading Examples section in this chapter. It would take many pages to explain just exactly how one arrives at a chart interpretation. Several of the books in the last portion of this chapter are excellent primers on how to get started using astrological charts to track the market.

Trading with Aspects

The planetary system discussed here was worked out by Donald A. Bradley in 1948 after much empirical observation and trial and error. It is, therefore, not based on mere folklore about what the planets should do to life here on earth, but rather on observed correlations between planetary positions and market behavior.

The Significant Aspects

Bradley based his system on what he called *aspectivity*, that is, the degree to which the planets as a whole are in certain relationships with each other at any given point in time. Two heavenly bodies are said to be in a certain *aspect* with regard to each other when the angle between their two positions as seen from earth takes on a certain value. For the planets, there are five major aspects discussed here. They are determined by how far apart two heavenly bodies are on the star sphere as seen from Earth:

Conjunction—when the two bodies are at the same position, but not on the same plane

Sextile—when they are 1/6 of a circle, or 60° apart

Square—1/4 of a circle, or 90° apart

Trine—1/3 of a circle, or 120° apart

Opposition—on opposite sides of the circle, or 180° apart

Bradley found that the approach of any two heavenly bodies to some aspect position would have an influence on stock market investor psychology proportional to the proximity in degrees to the aspect. He further found that this influence diminished to zero if the two bodies were more than about 15 degrees of arc from being in an aspect position.

Bradley, therefore, assigned an arbitrary value of ten to two planets' relative position when they were exactly at an aspect point and a value of zero when they were 15 degrees or more away from being in some aspect relationship, with intermediate values for distances between 0° and 15°.

Furthermore, a specific algebraic sign was assigned to each combination. All sextiles and trines are positive, while squares and oppositions are negative. Conjunctions may be considered positive or negative depending on the two bodies involved. The sign of a conjunction is assigned according to the following chart:

Figure 13-2

Algebraic Sign of Conjunctions*

	Sun	Merc	Ven	Mars	Jup	Sat	Ur	Nep
Sun								
Mercury	+							
Venus	+	+						
Mars	-	-	-					
Jupiter	+	+	+	-				
Saturn	-	-	-	-	-*			
Uranus	+	+	+	-	-*	-*		
Neptune	-	+	+	-	+*	-*	-*	
Pluto	-	-	+	-	-*	-*	-*	-*

*Long terms

The planets fall into two classes as far as aspect relations are concerned: the planets Jupiter through Pluto, on the one hand, and the remaining planets and the Sun, on the other. The first group of planets are given higher weight when the relations among them are taken into account. The sum of their aspects is known as the long term, and the sum of the other planets' aspects, including their aspects with planets of the first group, is known as the middle term.

There was one other planetary relation which Bradley found to be highly significant, and so he included it in his system: the sum of Mars' and Venus' declinations. Declination, in astronomical terms, is the latitude north or south of the equator of a celestial body, as seen from the Earth. Declination north of the equator has a positive value and south of the equator it is negative. Thus, if at a given point Mars were at 15° north and Venus at 5° south, the declination sum value would be 10°.

The bottom line number for Bradley's system is a value derived from all these relations which he called the system's total *aspectivity* at any one given moment.

Aspectivity is determined in the following way:

1) Determine the value of each individual outer planetary relationship, or long term, for the moment in question. There will be ten in all. This is done by determining whether each possible combination of two outer planets (i.e., Jupiter-Saturn, Uranus-Pluto, etc.) is within 15 degrees of arc of one of the five aspects. If it is, then determine just how close it is in degrees, subtract this distance from 15, divide the result by 15, and multiply by 10 (remember, a relationship gets a 10 if the two planets are exactly at the aspect point, and a 0 if they are 15 degrees or further away—so all this procedure does is assign proportional weight to intermediate distances).

2) Give a sign to each value according to the rule: sextiles and trines are positive, squares and oppositions are negative, and all conjunctions are negative except for Neptune-Jupiter (see chart on previous page).

3) Add all these values together. The resulting sum is known as the *long term*, so called because it represents the longer planetary cycles as opposed to the shorter ones.

4) Add to this the sum of the declinations of Mars and Venus.

5) Multiply this overall result by a pre-determined normalizing factor. This factor will be employed simply to make the curve which will result from all these calculations more pronounced when it is compared to the price curve.

6) Determine the middle terms in the same way that the long terms were determined above.

7) Finally, add the sum of the middle terms to the result obtained in step 5. This value will be the aspectivity index.

This aspectivity index should be entered on the same graph where traders keep track of price information.

Unlike other indicators, which depend to some degree on what the market is doing and therefore cannot anticipate the market very much, there is no limit to how far ahead traders can chart aspectivity, since the positions of the planets are known for thousands of years into the future.

Since graphing aspectivity requires repetition of the same sorts of calculations, a computer is definitely necessary for traders to avoid having nightmares about columns of numbers. Perhaps the main reason that not many people have ever used Bradley's method is the tedium of computation to obtain each periodic figure. In the 1940's, when Bradley came out with his system, there were no personal computers in offices, and even interested traders must have soon despaired. However, with the advent of electronic computing it is time to re-examine Bradley's method to see if traders armed with an ephemeris and their favorite spreadsheet software might not be able to use it.

How to Set Up and Maintain Astronomical Cycles

To Trade with the Moon

Traders need a calendar with moon phases to chart new and full moons on a price chart which shows at least several months in advance of the present. They might pencil in buy signals at the new moon dates and sell signals at the full moon dates and watch particularly on those dates to see if other entry-type techniques might not be employed.

To Trade with Charts

Unless traders employ a full-time astrologer, they will definitely need some computer software package for generating the three kinds of charts. They will probably also need to follow some astrological market consulting service for a period until they understand the concept of this admittedly subjective technique.

To Trade with Aspects

This entire setup is best done on some automatic calculating medium, such as an electronic spreadsheet. Although it is a cut-and-dried indicator which requires no analysis of any market phenomena to chart, and although it only requires some simple algebra, each indicator is composed of a long, tedious series of subtractions and summations. If this were set up on a spreadsheet, traders would only need to enter the actual positions for every five or ten day period, and then let the spreadsheet take care of generating the actual indicators and trend lines.

The first step in order to get started with aspectivity would be to obtain an ephemeris, which is a book with tables of the positions of heavenly bodies for each day. The *American Ephemeris and Nautical Almanac* for the current year is available from the Superintendent of Documents in Washington, D.C.

When they set up this system, traders will probably want to do all the calculating for a whole year or other long period at once. For this, a spreadsheet should be set up appropriately. In general, the planets do not change position rapidly enough for traders to worry about charting their aspectivity every day. Charting them once every two to five days is sufficient for the middle terms and once every seven to ten days is fine for the long terms.

Once traders have computed the aspectivity over the desired period, they can superimpose the chart of aspectivity on a price chart. It is good to have aspectivity calculated for some past time as well, because this way traders can compare aspectivity with actual price behavior. Traders are also going to want to adjust their normalizing factor (discussed in the previous section under step 5)—this should be no problem if they are using spreadsheet software. The adjustment should bring the amplitude of the aspectivity wave into line with one's price variance, thus allowing for easier comparison.

Due to the complexity of this technique a future volume will be published concerning it and no examples are given here to illustrate how to use aspects.

How to Trade with Astronomical Cycles

Trading with the Moon

To trade with the moon traders simply follow the new/full cycle, preparing to find buy signals at the new moon and sell signals at the full moon. Actually, a responsible use of this would be to use the upcoming new or full phase to begin checking other indicators for signs of an imminent break. While the moon's phase can alert traders that the market might be open to a change, pegging the exact turning point is best left to other indicators.

Certain markets are more susceptible to lunar cycles than others. These include mostly a number of commodities which are subject to cyclic price variations:

- Sugar
- Cocoa
- Silver
- Soybean Oil
- Corn
- Wheat

Though traders should not use lunar phases as their only signal, the fact that they can chart the moon's phases as far ahead into the future as they wish will mean that they can look down the road a week or two to the next full or new moon and decide on how to set their house in order to be ready for the possible rally or plunge that the market will take at that time.

Trading with Charts

The examples in the following section of this chapter will give traders an idea of how one might interpret charts. There is a lot to learn before traders can actually make their own decisions based on these charts. In the long interim, traders might want to find an astrological market consultant who will guide them and explain the trading consequences of various charts.

Trading with Aspects

It is wise to recall that astrological indications say nothing about where the market is going to go, but they do purport to indicate something about the mood swings of the investment community. Therefore, astrological aspects are a good check on certain time-honored fundamental indicators, such as the news or the economy. They may help traders to remember that they should not buy or sell the news, because what they are really interested in is market psychology. The news may or may not have anything to do with this psychology and astrological indicators may tell traders whether or not it does.

This trading system works best with a whole portfolio of stocks, futures or options, rather than just one (it is a measure of mass psychology and therefore the more widespread the phenomenon it measures, the more accurate it will be). Since these indicators can be plotted far in advance of the present moment, as with the phases of the moon, traders can use them to position themselves for basic trend reversals. Though this system may tell traders the exact time to the hour and minute when some event might possibly happen in the market, it will allow them plenty of time to prepare for it.

Trading Examples with Astrological Charts

Trading Examples with the Moon

Moon Cycle Trading with August 1986 Live Cattle

This trading example is for the Live Cattle contract from April 1, 1986 to August 18, 1986, a span of four months in which the price of cattle ranged from a low of about 49.8 cents to a high of 61.5 cents. The chart is delineated to include weekends and holidays. It is the author's experience to always include weekends and holidays in cycle work since cycles do not stop to take holidays.

On April 10, 1986 the Moon turned Full and the trader used this as an indication to sell (point A). This was around the 54.35 cent level. The price moved up slightly beyond the sell point the next two days and sold down to the next cycle low immediately: Point B, the New Moon on April 26, 1986, at about the 51.60 cent level. This trade showed a profit in excess of 2.70 cents.

From Point B, about the 51.60 cent level, a cycle buy point was indicated the trader went long till the next Full Moon arrived at Point C, on May 9, 1986, at the 55.30 cent level. This trade showed a profit in excess of 3.70 cent.

At Point C, the trader sold again and the price dropped to the Full Moon (Point D) which occurred on May 24, 1986, at the 51.30 cent level. This trade showed a profit of about 4.00 cents.

Point D offered a buy point at the 51.30 level. The trader bought and the price dipped lower to the 49.80 cents level, an unrealized loss of 1.30 cents. Had the trader closed out his position at this point he would have taken his first loss since the inception of this timing approach. Instead, he sat this position out because he did not get a cycle high to sell into.

At Point E (June 8, 1986), the first New Moon after Point D, the price traded up to about the 51.40 level, and was the trader's sell signal. He sold out at a 0.10 cents profit, or a basic scratch.

At Point E, the trader sold again, waiting for a cycle low to cover his position. The market went higher—much higher, and he eventually covered this position at 54.60 cents at Point F (Full Moon on June 23, 1986) for a loss of 3.20 cents. This was his first loss and it was a substantial loss.

Covering his position at Point F (Full Moon) the trader bought again for the next cycle sell point—the New Moon on July 7, 1986 (Point G). Point G occurred about the 57.00 cents level. This trade netted a large profit of 2.40 cents. From Point G, the trader sold again based on the New Moon cycle high and waited for a cycle low to cover again.

This final cycle low occurred at Point H (Full Moon) and was about the 57.80 cents level. This final trade netted a small loss of 0.80 cents.

Figure 13-3   Trading Daily Live Cattle with the Moon

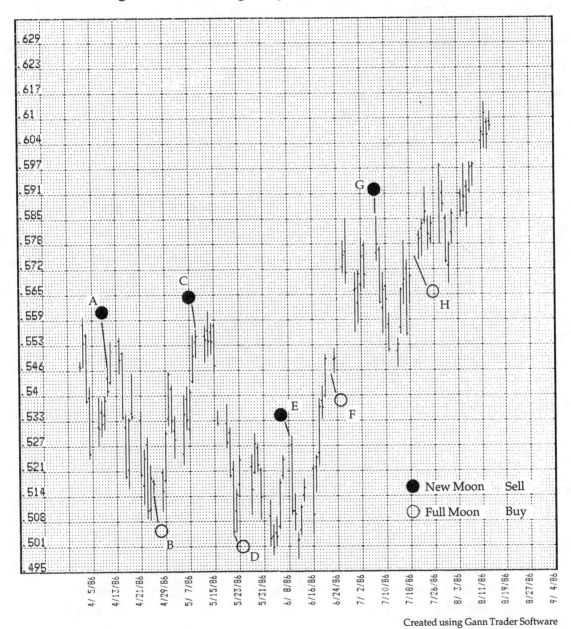

Created using Gann Trader Software

The cycle high and low signals generated by the Moon's 28-29 day periods were profitable enough to trade. The loss created by the sale at Point E and the eventual cycle covering at Point F was large. However, examining the price travelled in this period shows that even after the sale was made at Point E (price of 51.30 cents) the price did drop to a low point, around the 50.00 cents level four days later. Strict adherence to the cycles peak and troughs as respective sell and buy points caused the loss. If the trader had used additional filtering techniques and proper money management, he would have used the drop into new lows as a profit-taking opportunity. But this particular "modification" of the example is not warranted here since it deals only with the New Moon/Full Moon approach.

A Major Upheaval for the New York Stock Exchange in October 1987 Interpreted Using Astrological Charts

The planet of constriction and want, Saturn (A) is in the tenth house (B), the house of fame and reputation. For the whole month of October 1987, the planet of good fortune, Jupiter (C), is transiting the tenth house, first forward, then backward, finally continuing forward again in November.

The planet of expansion and good fortune was being confronted by the planet of constriction and contraction. The interpretation of these planetary motions is that there would be continual bouts of fame and fortunes being made for the New York Stock Exchange. Volume was increasing and new highs were being made for the Dow Jones Industrials. The groundwork was being laid for constriction and contraction. All that was needed was a trigger to set off the chain reaction of ultimate contraction.

There were other observations which indicated this as well: Transiting Moon (N) was conjunct natal Mars (E)—violent emotions and flareups associated with the natal moon—a warning of danger. The New York Stock Exchange ascendant is Cancer (F), a sign ruled by the planet Moon: danger warnings to the exchange's physical well-being. Transiting Sun (G) in Libra (H) is in direct opposition to natal Saturn (A)—an all or nothing situation.

Midheaven for New York Stock Exchange (J) is in grand trine with natal Uranus (K) and transiting Saturn (L)—which could either be good or bad. Uranus is the planet of suddenness, so all that was needed was a trigger to set everything off for either a massive sell-off or a volatile rally (much less probable).

Figure 13-4A   New York Stock Exchange Astrological Chart for May 17, 1792

FinOpCo
Financial Consulting
780 S. Federal St.,314
Chicago, IL 60605 USA
Voice 312-663-9339
Computer 312-922-3626
GEOCENTRIC   TROPICAL

KOCH HOUSES
ST: 0h39m58s
RAMC: 10° 00'

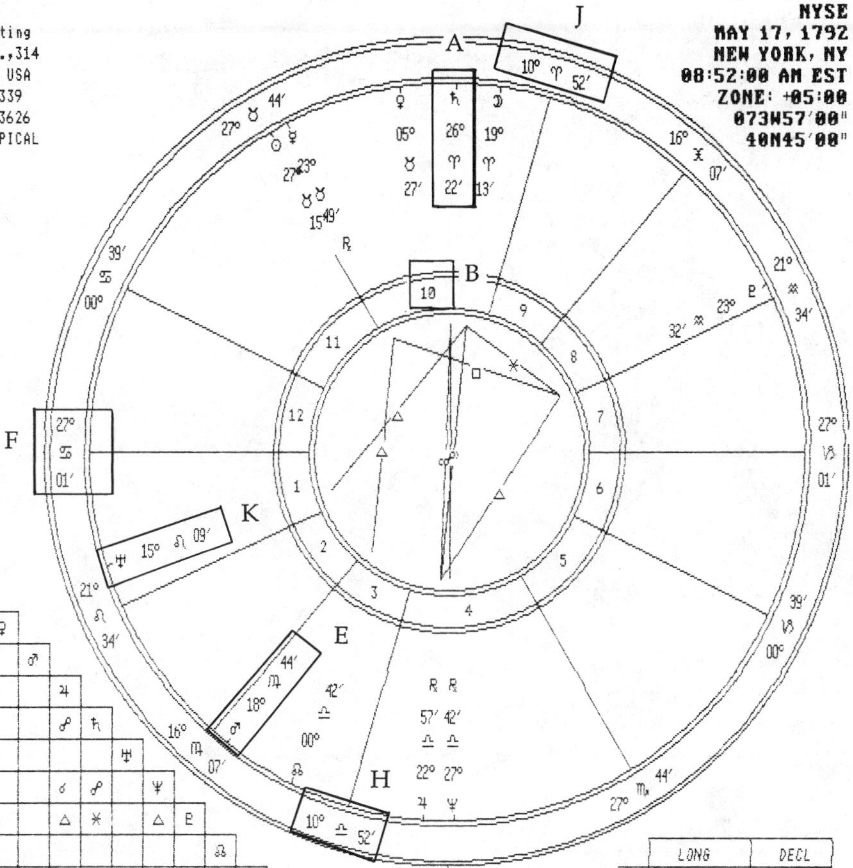

NYSE
MAY 17, 1792
NEW YORK, NY
08:52:00 AM EST
ZONE: +05:00
073W57'00"
40N45'00"

	CARD	FIXED	MUT
FIRE	2	1	0
EARTH	0	3	1
AIR	2	1	0
WATER	0	0	0

PLANETS		ELEM	+/-	TRIP	HOUSE	DIGNI	ZODIAC SIGNS		HOUSES		ASPECTS	
☽	MOON	FIRE	POS	CARD	ANG 10		♈	ARIES	1	27° ♋ 01'	☌	CONJUNCT 0°
☉	SUN	EARTH	NEG	FIX	ANG 10		♉	TAURUS	2	21° ♌ 34'	☍	OPPOSITION 180°
☿	MERCURY	EARTH	NEG	FIX	ANG 10		♊	GEMINI	3	16° ♍ 07'	△	TRINE 120°
♀	VENUS	EARTH	NEG	FIX	ANG 10	RULER	♋	CANCER	4	10° ♎ 52'	□	SQUARE 90°
♂	MARS	EARTH	NEG	MUT	CAD 3		♌	LEO	5	27° ♏ 44'	✳	SEXTILE 60°
♃	JUPITER	AIR	POS	CARD	ANG 4		♍	VIRGO	6	00° ♑ 39'		
♄	SATURN	FIRE	POS	CARD	ANG 10	FALL	♎	LIBRA	7	27° ♑ 01'		
♅	URANUS	FIRE	POS	FIX	ANG 4	DETRI	♏	SCORPIO	8	21° ♒ 34'		
♆	NEPTUNE	AIR	POS	CARD	ANG 1		♐	SAGITTARIUS	9	16° ♓ 07'		
♇	PLUTO	AIR	POS	FIX	SUC 4		♑	CAPRICORN	10	10° ♒ 52'		
☊	NODE	AIR	POS	CARD	CAD 3		♒	AQUARIUS	11	27° ♉ 44'		
Mc	MIDHEAVEN	FIRE	POS	CARD	3		♓	PISCES	12	00° ♋ 39'		
As	ASCENDANT	WATER	NEG	CARD	3							

	LONG	DECL
☽	19° ♈ 12'43"	+ 6° 03'
☉	27° ♉ 14'42"	+19° 34'
☿	23° ♉ 48'38"R	+17° 13'
♀	05° ♉ 26'44"	+11° 57'
♂	18° ♏ 44'04"	+ 5° 37'
♃	22° ♎ 57'16"R	- 7° 34'
♄	26° ♈ 22'25"	+ 8° 03'
♅	15° ♌ 09'09"	+16° 58'
♆	27° ♎ 42'12"R	- 3° 59'
♇	23° ♏ 31'58"	-23° 03'
☊	00° ♉ 41'40"	- 0° 17'
Mc	10° ♈ 52'21"	+ 4° 18'
As	27° ♋ 01'16"	+20° 47'
Vx	12° ♌ 54'09"	-22° 22'
Ep	09° ♋ 10'51"	+23° 09'
⊕	18° ♊ 59'17"	+23° 00'

Figure 13-4B   New York Stock Exchange Astrological Chart for October 19, 1987

FinOpCo
Financial Consulting
780 S. Federal St.,314
Chicago, IL 60605 USA
Voice 312-663-9339
Computer 312-922-3626
GEOCENTRIC   TROPICAL

KOCH HOUSES
ST: 11h24m20s
RAMC: 171° 05'

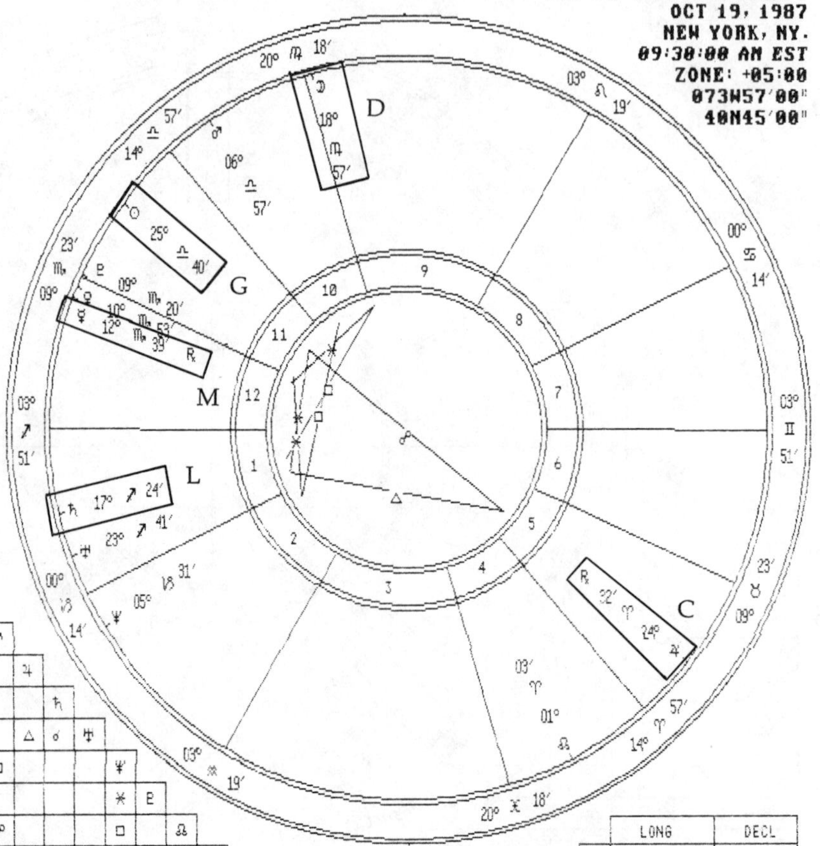

OCT 19 9:30 AM TRANSIT
OCT 19, 1987
NEW YORK, NY.
09:30:00 AM EST
ZONE: +05:00
073W57'00"
40N45'00"

PLANETS		ELEM	+/-	TRIP	HOUSE	DIGNI	ZODIAC SIGNS		HOUSES			LONG	DECL
☽	MOON	EARTH	NEG	MUT	CAD	9	♈	ARIES	1	03° ♐ 51'		☽ 18° ♏ 56'33"	+ 5° 30'
☉	SUN	AIR	POS	CARD	SUC	11 FALL	♉	TAURUS	2	00° ♑ 14'		☉ 25° ♎ 39'59"	- 9° 55'
☿	MERCURY	WATER	NEG	FIX	CAD	12	♊	GEMINI	3	03° ♒ 19'		☿ 12° ♏ 52'39"R	-18° 29'
♀	VENUS	WATER	NEG	FIX	CAD	12 DETRI	♋	CANCER	4	20° ♓ 18'		♀ 10° ♏ 52'39"	-14° 44'
♂	MARS	AIR	POS	CARD	ANG	10 DETRI	♌	LEO	5	14° ♉ 57'		♂ 06° ♏ 56'37"	- 1° 52'
♃	JUPITER	FIRE	POS	CARD	SUC	5	♍	VIRGO	6	03° ♊ 51'		♃ 24° ♐ 32'23"R	+ 8° 02'
♄	SATURN	FIRE	POS	MUT	ANG	1	♎	LIBRA	7	03° ♊ 51'		♄ 17° ♐ 23'36"	-21° 37'
♅	URANUS	FIRE	POS	MUT	ANG	1	♏	SCORPIO	8	00° ♋ 14'		♅ 23° ♐ 40'31"	-23° 27'
♆	NEPTUNE	EARTH	NEG	CARD	SUC	2 FALL	♐	SAGITTARIUS	9	03° ♌ 19'		♆ 05° ♑ 31'02"	-22° 20'
♇	PLUTO	WATER	NEG	FIX	SUC	11 RULER	♑	CAPRICORN	10	00° ♐ 18'		♇ 09° ♏ 20'10"	+ 0° 18'
☊	NODE	FIRE	POS	CARD	SUC	11	♒	AQUARIUS	11	14° ♎ 57'		☊ 01° ♈ 03'11"	+ 0° 25'
Mc	MIDHEAVEN	EARTH	NEG	MUT		11	♓	PISCES	12	09° ♏ 23'		Mc 20° ♏ 17'41"	+ 3° 57'
As	ASCENDANT	FIRE	POS	MUT		11						As 03° ♐ 51'03"	-20° 55'
												Vx 17° ♋ 55'19"	+22° 15'
												Ep 21° ♐ 48'29"	-23° 11'
												⊕ 27° ♎ 07'38"	-10° 27'

	CARD	FIXED	MUT
FIRE	1	0	2
EARTH	1	0	1
AIR	2	0	0
WATER	0	3	0

	ASPECTS	
☌	CONJUNCT	0°
☍	OPPOSITION	180°
△	TRINE	120°
□	SQUARE	90°
✶	SEXTILE	60°

(c) 1986 Matrix Software Big Rapids Mi. 49307

Figure 13-4C   New York Stock Exchange Astrological Chart Showing May 17, 1792 and October 19, 1987

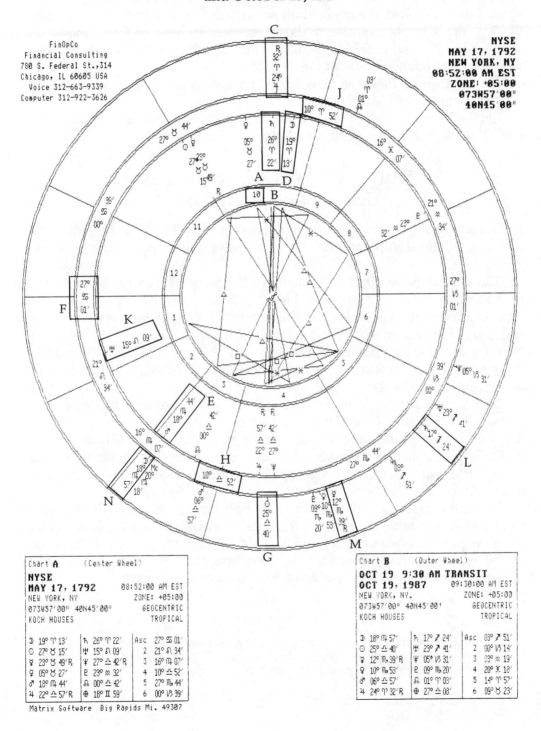

FinOpCo
Financial Consulting
780 S. Federal St.,314
Chicago, IL 60605 USA
Voice 312-663-9339
Computer 312-922-3626

NYSE
MAY 17, 1792
NEW YORK, NY
08:52:00 AM EST
ZONE: +05:00
073W57'00"
40N45'00"

Matrix Software Big Rapids Mi. 49307

Chart **A**	(Center Wheel)	
NYSE		
MAY 17, 1792	08:52:00 AM EST	
NEW YORK, NY	ZONE: +05:00	
073W57'00" 40N45'00"	GEOCENTRIC	
KOCH HOUSES	TROPICAL	
☽ 19° ♈ 13'	♄ 26° ♈ 22'	Asc 27° ♋ 01'
☉ 27° ♉ 15'	♅ 15° ♌ 09'	2 21° ♌ 34'
☿ 23° ♉ 49'R	♆ 27° ♎ 42'R	3 16° ♍ 07'
♀ 05° ♉ 27'	♇ 23° ♒ 32'	4 10° ♎ 52'
♂ 18° ♍ 44'	☊ 00° ♎ 42'	5 27° ♏ 44'
♃ 22° ♊ 57'R	⊕ 18° ♊ 59'	6 00° ♑ 39'

Chart **B**	(Outer Wheel)	
OCT 19 9:30 AM TRANSIT		
OCT 19, 1987	09:30:00 AM EST	
NEW YORK, NY.	ZONE: +05:00	
073W57'00" 40N45'00"	GEOCENTRIC	
KOCH HOUSES	TROPICAL	
☽ 18° ♍ 57'	♄ 17° ♐ 24'	Asc 03° ♐ 51'
☉ 25° ♎ 40'	♅ 23° ♐ 41'	2 00° ♑ 14'
☿ 12° ♏ 39'R	♆ 05° ♑ 31'	3 03° ♒ 19'
♀ 10° ♏ 53'	♇ 09° ♏ 20'	4 20° ♓ 18'
♂ 06° ♏ 57'	☊ 01° ♈ 03'	5 14° ♈ 57'
♃ 24° ♈ 32'R	⊕ 27° ♎ 08'	6 09° ♉ 23'

The trigger turned out to be the retrograde Mercury (M). On October 16, 1987, Mercury went retrograde at 11:52 A.M. Chicago time. Going into the week, the market had already sold off as early as October 6, 1987—it dropped 91.55 points—thereby pointing in the direction of the next probable move. On October 16, the market sold off 108.35 points, a precursor to the violence that would be a watershed mark for the Dow Jones Industrials.*

On October 19, 1987, the Dow Jones Industrials Averages sold off 508.00 points on volume of 604,330,000 shares.

On October 20, 1987, the Dow Jones Industrials Averages traded over 608,000,000 shares on dramatic volatility.

Analyzing IBM as an Industry Leader Using Astrological Charts

Analyzing the IBM chart as an event created on June 16, 1911, the incorporation date of the company, one discovers several important strengths and weaknesses.

The ascendant is Virgo (A), ruled by the planet Mercury (B), which is found in a very elevated position. Mercury is tied into communications and short distance travels. Virgo is also the sign which represents precise thinking and logic, with strong emphasis on details. The Sun (C), representing entity's energies, is in the sign of Gemini (D), ruled by the planet Mercury. Gemini is the sign of communications and verbosity. The Sun is conjunct Pluto (E), the planet of death and regeneration.

The planet Uranus (F) rules electronics and sudden events. It is in the 5th house (G), the house of creativity and pleasures. This is where IBM as an entity will find pleasure—electronics. Uranus rules the sign of Aquarius (H), which is placed in the sixth house (I) of work, where the entity makes its living. IBM exists because it works with electronics combined with communications.

A grand cross among the natal planets of Jupiter (I), Uranus (F), Neptune (J) and the north node (K) brings the issues of wealth, creativity, friends and other people's resources continually into play. When any of these planets are set off with transits, all these issues come into play. When any transitting planet touches any of these four areas, all the other three areas will come into play.

*On October 12, 1987, the author called his clients and suggested to them that they unload all stocks and go short saying, "We are heading into a severe break. This break will make 100 point down days look like parties. This will happen in the next two weeks."

Figure 13-5A   IBM Astrological Chart for June 16, 1911

FinOpCo
Financial Consulting
780 S. Federal St.,314
Chicago, IL 60605 USA
Voice 312-663-9339
Computer 312-922-3626
GEOCENTRIC   TROPICAL

KOCH HOUSES
ST: 4h39m24s
RAMC: 69° 51'

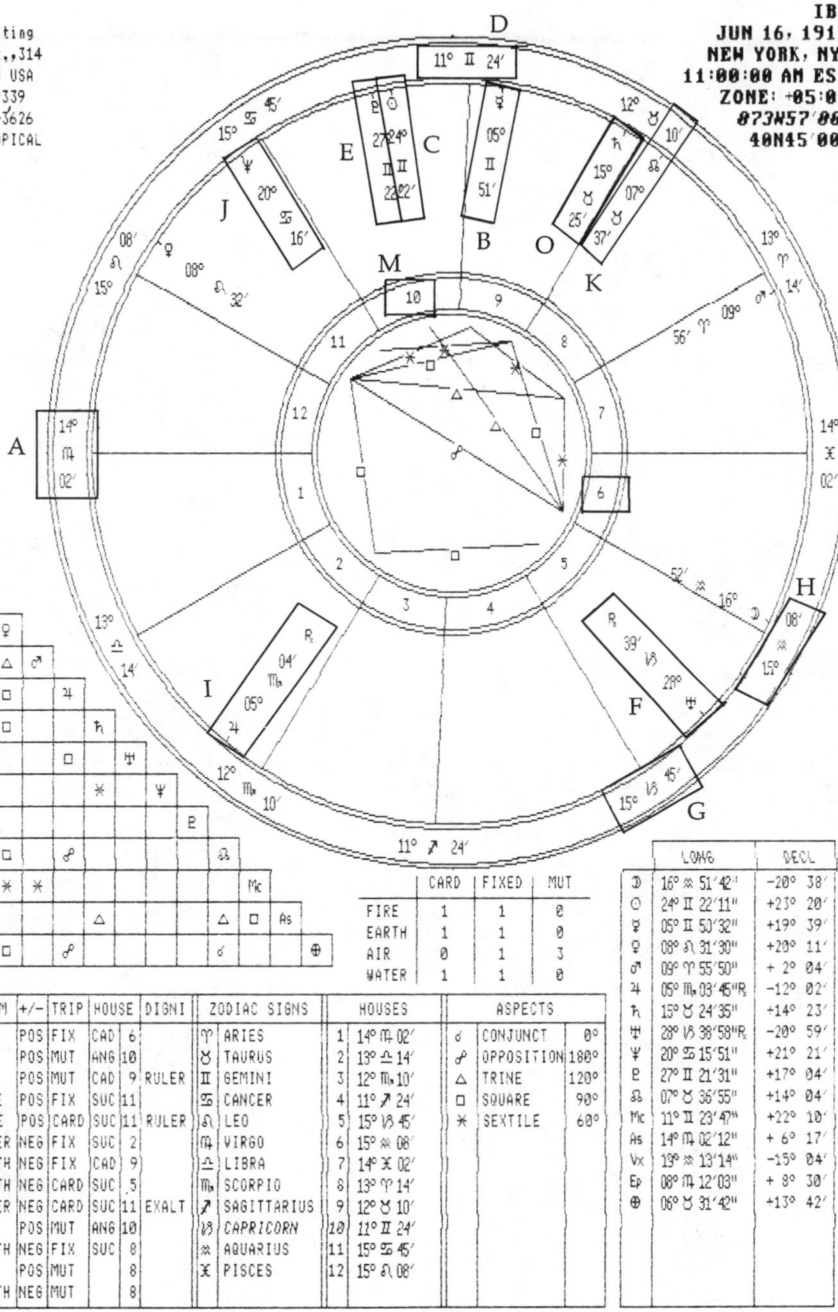

IBM
JUN 16, 1911
NEW YORK, NY.
11:00:00 AM EST
ZONE: +05:00
87W57'00"
40N45'00"

	CARD	FIXED	MUT
FIRE	1	1	0
EARTH	1	1	0
AIR	0	1	3
WATER	1	1	0

	LONG	DECL
☽	16° ♒ 51'42"	-20° 38'
☉	24° ♊ 22'11"	+23° 20'
☿	05° ♊ 50'32"	+19° 39'
♀	08° ♌ 31'30"	+20° 11'
♂	09° ♈ 55'50"	+ 2° 04'
♃	05° ♍ 03'45"R	-12° 02'
♄	15° ♉ 24'35"	+14° 23'
♅	28° ♑ 38'58"R	-20° 59'
♆	20° ♋ 15'51"	+21° 21'
♇	27° ♊ 21'31"	+17° 04'
☊	07° ♉ 36'55"	+14° 04'
Mc	11° ♊ 23'47"	+22° 10'
As	14° ♏ 02'12"	+ 6° 17'
Vx	19° ♒ 13'14"	-15° 04'
Ep	08° ♏ 12'03"	+ 8° 30'
⊕	06° ♐ 31'42"	+13° 42'

PLANETS	ELEM	+/-	TRIP	HOUSE	DIGNI	ZODIAC SIGNS	HOUSES	ASPECTS	
☽ MOON	AIR	POS	FIX	CAD	6	♈ ARIES	1 14° ♏ 02'	☌ CONJUNCT	0°
☉ SUN	AIR	POS	MUT	ANG	10	♉ TAURUS	2 13° ♎ 14'	☍ OPPOSITION	180°
☿ MERCURY	AIR	POS	MUT	CAD	9 RULER	♊ GEMINI	3 12° ♏ 10'	△ TRINE	120°
♀ VENUS	FIRE	POS	FIX	SUC	11	♋ CANCER	4 11° ♐ 24'	□ SQUARE	90°
♂ MARS	FIRE	POS	CARD	SUC	11 RULER	♌ LEO	5 15° ♑ 45'	✳ SEXTILE	60°
♃ JUPITER	WATER	NEG	FIX	SUC	9	♍ VIRGO	6 15° ♒ 08'		
♄ SATURN	EARTH	NEG	FIX	CAD	9	♎ LIBRA	7 14° ♓ 02'		
♅ URANUS	EARTH	NEG	CARD	SUC	5	♏ SCORPIO	8 13° ♈ 14'		
♆ NEPTUNE	WATER	NEG	CARD	SUC	11 EXALT	♐ SAGITTARIUS	9 12° ♉ 10'		
♇ PLUTO	AIR	POS	MUT	ANG	10	♑ CAPRICORN	10 11° ♊ 24'		
☊ NODE	EARTH	NEG	FIX	SUC	8	♒ AQUARIUS	11 15° ♋ 45'		
Mc MIDHEAVEN	AIR	POS	MUT		8	♓ PISCES	12 15° ♌ 08'		
As ASCENDANT	EARTH	NEG	MUT		8				

Figure 13-5B   IBM Astrological Chart for May 15, 1988

FinOpCo
Financial Consulting
780 S. Federal St.,314
Chicago, IL 60605 USA
Voice 312-663-9339
Computer 312-922-3626
GEOCENTRIC   TROPICAL

KOCH HOUSES
ST: 4h14m07s
RAMC: 63° 32'

☽⚼♄
☽⚼♅
☽⚼♆
♂⚼♃
♄∥♆

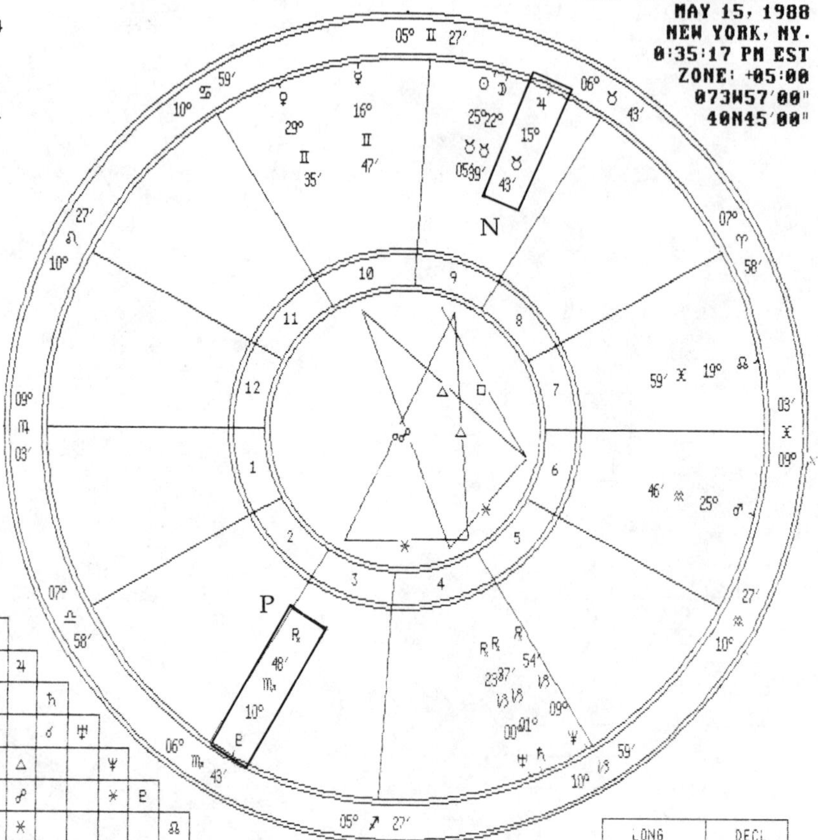

MAY 15,1988 TRANSIT
MAY 15, 1988
NEW YORK, NY.
0:35:17 PM EST
ZONE: +05:00
073W57'00"
40N45'00"

	CARD	FIXED	MUT
FIRE	0	0	0
EARTH	3	3	0
AIR	0	1	2
WATER	0	1	0

PLANETS		ELEM	+/-	TRIP	HOUSE	DIGNI	ZODIAC SIGNS		HOUSES		ASPECTS	
☽	MOON	EARTH	NEG	FIX	CAD	9 EXALT	♈	ARIES	1	09° M 03'	☌ CONJUNCT	0°
☉	SUN	EARTH	NEG	FIX		9	♉	TAURUS	2	07° ≏ 58'	☍ OPPOSITION	180°
☿	MERCURY	AIR	POS	MUT	ANG	10 RULER	♊	GEMINI	3	06° M 45'	△ TRINE	120°
♀	VENUS	AIR	POS	MUT	ANG	10	♋	CANCER	4	05° ♐ 27'	□ SQUARE	90°
♂	MARS	AIR	POS	FIX	CAD	6	♌	LEO	5	10° ♑ 59'	✶ SEXTILE	60°
♃	JUPITER	EARTH	NEG	FIX	CAD	9	♍	VIRGO	6	10° ≈ 27'		
♄	SATURN	EARTH	NEG	CARD	ANG	4 RULER	♎	LIBRA	7	09° ♓ 03'		
♅	URANUS	EARTH	NEG	CARD	ANG	4	♏	SCORPIO	8	07° ♈ 58'		
♆	NEPTUNE	EARTH	NEG	CARD	ANG	4 FALL	♐	SAGITTARIUS	9	06° ♉ 43'		
♇	PLUTO	WATER	NEG	FIX	CAD	3 RULER	♑	CAPRICORN	10	05° II 27'		
☊	NODE	WATER	NEG	MUT	CAD	3	≈	AQUARIUS	11	10° ♋ 59'		
Mc	MIDHEAVEN	AIR	POS	MUT		3	♓	PISCES	12	10° ♌ 27'		
As	ASCENDANT	EARTH	NEG	MUT		3						

	LONG	DECL
☽	22° ♉ 39'14"	+22° 44'
☉	25° ♉ 05'17"	+19° 02'
☿	16° II 47'07"	+25° 12'
♀	29° II 34'39"	+27° 24'
♂	25° ♌ 45'33"	-14° 50'
♃	15° ♉ 43'04"	+15° 41'
♄	01° ♑ 36'56"R	-22° 16'
♅	00° ♑ 22'39"R	-23° 39'
♆	09° ♑ 53'34"R	-22° 05'
♇	10° M 48'08"R	+ 0° 44'
☊	19° ♓ 58'44"	- 3° 53'
Mc	05° II 26'56"	+21° 13'
As	08° M 02'56"	+ 3° 11'
Vx	08° ≈ 53'38"	-18° 02'
Ep	01° M 30'40"	+10° 56'
⊕	06° M 36'53"	+ 9° 05'

Figure 13-5C   IBM Astrological Chart Showing June 16, 1911 and May 15, 1988

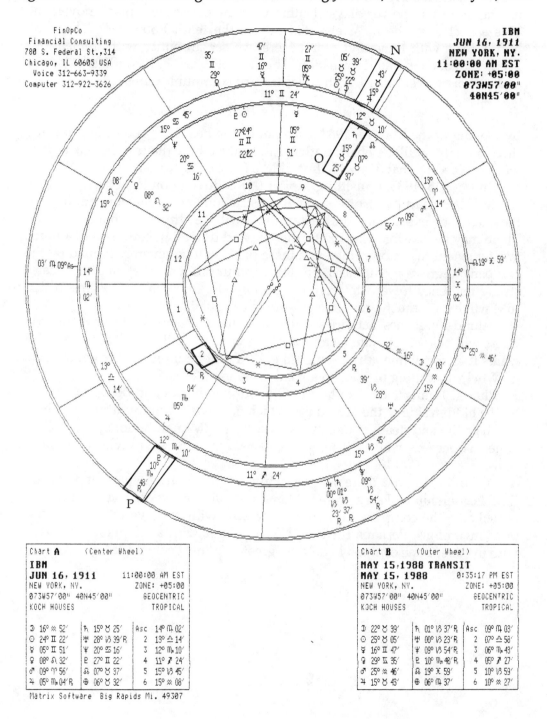

FinOpCo
Financial Consulting
780 S. Federal St.,314
Chicago, IL 60605 USA
Voice 312-663-9339
Computer 312-922-3626

IBM
JUN 16, 1911
NEW YORK, NY.
11:00:00 AM EST
ZONE: +05:00
073W57'00"
40N45'00"

Chart **A**   (Center Wheel)

IBM
JUN 16, 1911   11:00:00 AM EST
NEW YORK, NY.   ZONE: +05:00
073W57'00" 40N45'00"   GEOCENTRIC
KOCH HOUSES   TROPICAL

☽ 16° ♒ 52'	♄ 15° ♉ 25'	Asc 14° ♏ 02'
☉ 24° ♊ 22'	♅ 28° ♑ 39'R	2 13° ♎ 14'
☿ 05° ♊ 51'	♆ 20° ♋ 16'	3 12° ♏ 10'
♀ 08° ♌ 32'	♇ 27° ♊ 22'	4 11° ♐ 24'
♂ 09° ♈ 56'	☊ 07° ♉ 37'	5 15° ♑ 45'
♃ 05° ♏ 04'R	⊕ 06° ♉ 32'	6 15° ♒ 08'

Chart **B**   (Outer Wheel)

MAY 15,1988 TRANSIT
MAY 15, 1988   0:35:17 PM EST
NEW YORK, NY.   ZONE: +05:00
073W57'00" 40N45'00"   GEOCENTRIC
KOCH HOUSES   TROPICAL

☽ 22° ♉ 39'	♄ 01° ♑ 37'R	Asc 09° ♏ 03'
☉ 25° ♉ 05'	♅ 00° ♑ 23'R	2 07° ♎ 58'
☿ 16° ♊ 47'	♆ 09° ♑ 54'R	3 06° ♏ 43'
♀ 10° ♏ 48'R	♇ 10° ♏ 48'R	4 05° ♐ 27'
♂ 25° ♒ 46'	☊ 19° ♓ 59'	5 10° ♑ 59'
♃ 15° ♉ 43'	⊕ 06° ♏ 37'	6 10° ♒ 27'

Matrix Software Big Rapids Mi. 49307

Another natal aspect, is the natal Pluto (E) conjunct natal Sun (C). The ego is wrapped up in power plays, dealing with the masses and mass movement. This aspect is in the most elevated house, the tenth house (M). The tenth house deals with fame and glory. Here, we see an entity with tremendous needs for coercion and domination. This aspect deals with conflicts of power and authority over others, with a bias toward communications.

New Fields, New Problems for IBM in April-May 1988

By looking at the May 15, 1988 snapshot of the heavenly bodies and placing them directly on IBM's chart, traders can analyze how the transits one to four weeks preceding that day will affect IBM's fame or fortunes.

On May 15, 1988, transitting Jupiter (N) is directly on top of natal Saturn (O) in IBM's chart. Saturn represents constriction and diminishment. Jupiter, the planet of expansions and extensions, will be directly limited by IBM. There may be possible plans to further expand in foreign countries to a much greater extent than now. However, these plans will be severely limited by the company's greater emphasis on telecommuncations. The chart indicates strong tendency toward telecommunications. In any form, it will mean that IBM will have a much broader exposure to the public eye.

Behind-the-scenes activities will limit the company's physical growth. There will be two separate factors working here: the public will see what IBM wants it to see, while at the same time, IBM will be limiting its own internal growth by curtailing physical plant expansions.

Pluto (P) transits the 2nd house (Q), house of wealth and possessions, also on the hidden side of the 3rd house, which deals with communications. There will be a life and death situation with the way IBM makes money for itself—either it succeeds well or it fails. It will be, again, tied into telecommunications.

Around this time there will be a tremendous market share at stake for IBM. Leadership will arise from IBM and it would not be suprising if it tries to consolidate the company and launch forward with massive telecommunications inventions. Perhaps there will be a merger with a telephone company with the telephone company wielding greater influence over IBM.

Great Opportunities, High Risk for Treasury Bonds Futures

Treasury bonds futures with an event date of August 22, 1977, in Chicago, Illinois, show a multi-faceted influence on things and events around them. Pluto (A), the planet of death and regeneration, is on the hidden side of the ascendant, indicating a massive, powerful influence on the bond issue's partners, institutions and corporations represented by the twelfth house, Virgo (B) (grain houses).

The bond contract is the world's most actively traded contract, dwarfing the S&P futures contracts and the Comex gold contract in their heydays.

The north node (C) in the first house (D) represents good fortune for the well-being of the contract and lesser benefits to its partners, or in this case, people who trade or own the futures contract.

Jupiter (Z) in the 9th house (E) shows that foreign owners or participants in the U.S. bond market will be very favorable for it.

The mere placement of the Cancer midheaven (F), in opposition to the Capricorn nadir (G), foretells tremendous volatility in the next several years when the heavy outer planets move into the sign of Capricorn, in direct opposition to the midheaven.

Participants will either make a killing or be killed. No prisoners will be taken in the bond contract if one is wrong. To the victor belong spoils of tremendous magnitude.

Danger to the Bond Contract in August 1989

On August 2, 1989, the U.S. Bond contract will undergo its first Jupiter return. Jupiter returns, as a general rule, are very favorable since the benefactor planet at the time of the natal event will again have the powers of Jupiter, reinforcing its beneficent natal powers. In this case, the transit of Jupiter (H) will be in direct opposition to the heavier outer planet transits, Uranus (I), Saturn (J), and Neptune (K), all in retrograde motion. Their power and impact will be magnified. Uranus is suddenness; Saturn is constriction and contraction; and Neptune is dispersion and inflation.

About this time period traders can expect a great amount of communications to deal with the bonds—perhaps great volatililty to the downside, followed by an easing, followed by greater downside volatility. The bonds will be very prominent in the public eye. Great speculations will be made in the bond contract—it will be on display for the world to see. Many players will trade the contract.

Gold, ruled by the sign Leo (L), will come into strong play in this time period. Bonds will have greater influence over gold about this time due to the transitting planets (M) in Leo going over the Bond's Saturn (N) while the sign Leo is trine the natal south node (O) of Bond. There is a chance that the bond contract could be very easily affected by the value of gold.

Figure 13-6A Treasury Bonds Futures Astrological Chart for August 22, 1977

FinOpCo
Financial Consulting
780 S. Federal St.,314
Chicago, IL 60605 USA
Voice 312-663-9339
Computer 312-922-3626
GEOCENTRIC TROPICAL

KOCH HOUSES
ST: 7h12m37s
RAMC: 108° 09′

♀#♆
♂||♃

TREASURY BONDS
AUG 22, 1977
CHICAGO, IL
10:00:00 AM CDT
ZONE: +05:00
087W39′00″
41N52′00″

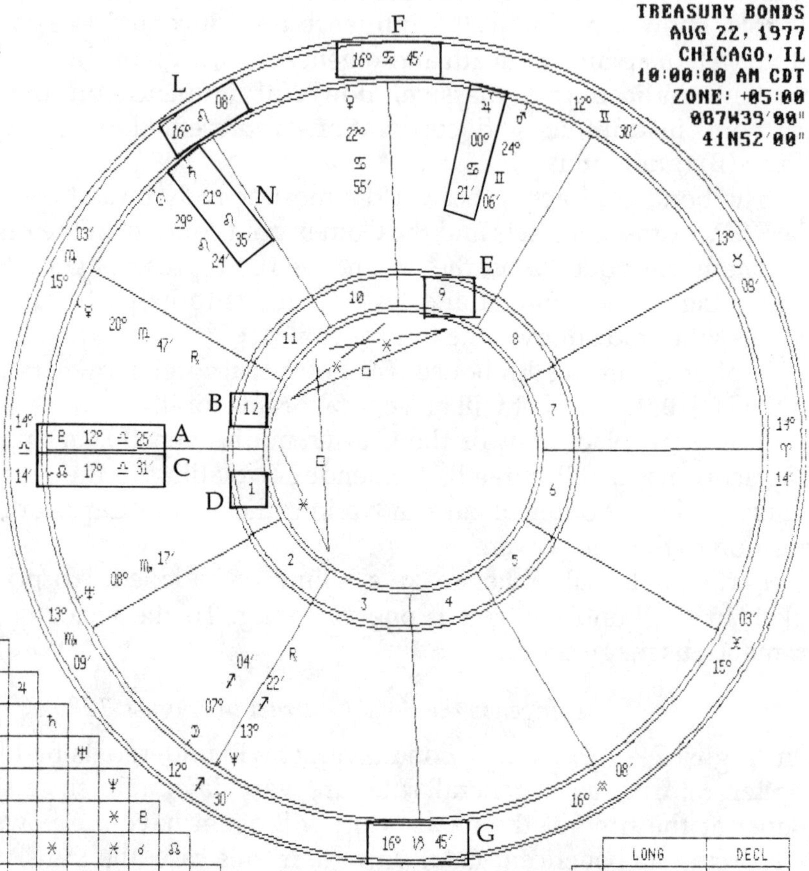

	☽													
☉	□	☉												
☿			☿											
♀			⚹	♀										
♂		⚹	□		♂									
♃		⚹			☌	♃								
♄		☌			⚹		♄							
♅								♅						
♆	☌								♆					
♇	⚹								⚹	♇				
☊				□	△		⚹		⚹	☌	☊			
Mc			⚹	☌						□	□	Mc		
As									⚹	☌	☌	□	As	
⊕			△	☍							□	☍		⊕

	CARD	FIXED	MUT
FIRE	0	2	2
EARTH	0	0	1
AIR	1	0	1
WATER	2	1	0

	LONG	DECL
☽	07° ♐ 03′39″	−17° 33′
☉	29° ♌ 23′48″	+11° 41′
☿	20° ♍ 46′37″℞	− 0° 04′
♀	22° ♋ 55′20″	+20° 49′
♂	24° ♊ 05′48″	+23° 11′
♃	00° ♋ 21′10″	+23° 02′
♄	21° ♌ 35′29″	+15° 17′
♅	08° ♏ 16′57″	−13° 53′
♆	13° ♐ 22′30″℞	−20° 56′
♇	12° ♎ 25′01″	+10° 26′
☊	17° ♎ 30′38″	− 6° 52′
Mc	16° ♋ 44′32″	+22° 23′
As	14° ♎ 13′58″	− 5° 37′
Vx	06° ♉ 03′19″	+13° 32′
Ep	19° ♎ 39′55″	− 7° 42′
⊕	21° ♑ 53′49″	−21° 40′

	PLANETS	ELEM	+/−	TRIP	HOUSE		DIGNI		ZODIAC SIGNS		HOUSES		ASPECTS	
☽	MOON	FIRE	POS	MUT	SUC	2		♈	ARIES	1	14° ♎ 14′	☌	CONJUNCT	0°
☉	SUN	FIRE	POS	FIX	SUC	11	RULER	♉	TAURUS	2	13° ♏ 09′	☍	OPPOSITION	180°
☿	MERCURY	EARTH	NEG	MUT	CAD	12	RULER	♊	GEMINI	3	12° ♐ 30′	△	TRINE	120°
♀	VENUS	WATER	NEG	CARD	ANG	10		♋	CANCER	4	16° ♑ 45′	□	SQUARE	90°
♂	MARS	AIR	POS	MUT	CAD	9		♌	LEO	5	16° ♒ 08′	⚹	SEXTILE	60°
♃	JUPITER	WATER	NEG	CARD	CAD	9	EXALT	♍	VIRGO	6	15° ♓ 03′			
♄	SATURN	FIRE	POS	FIX	SUC	11	DETRI	♎	LIBRA	7	14° ♈ 14′			
♅	URANUS	WATER	NEG	FIX	ANG	1	EXALT	♏	SCORPIO	8	13° ♉ 09′			
♆	NEPTUNE	FIRE	POS	MUT	CAD	3		♐	SAGITTARIUS	9	12° ♊ 30′			
♇	PLUTO	AIR	POS	CARD	CAD	12	FALL	♑	CAPRICORN	10	16° ♋ 45′			
☊	NODE	AIR	POS	CARD	ANG	1		♒	AQUARIUS	11	16° ♌ 08′			
Mc	MIDHEAVEN	WATER	NEG	CARD		1		♓	PISCES	12	15° ♍ 03′			
As	ASCENDANT	AIR	POS	CARD		1								

Figure 13-6B   Treasury Bonds Futures Astrological Chart for August 2, 1989

FinOpCo
Financial Consulting
700 S. Federal St.,314
Chicago, IL 60605 USA
Voice 312-663-9339
Computer 312-922-3626
GEOCENTRIC ·TROPICAL

KOCH HOUSES
ST: 8h55m38s
RAMC: 133° 54'

AUG 02, 1989 Transit
AUG 02, 1989
CHICAGO, IL
00:01:00 PM CST
ZONE: +06:00
087W39'00"
41N52'00"

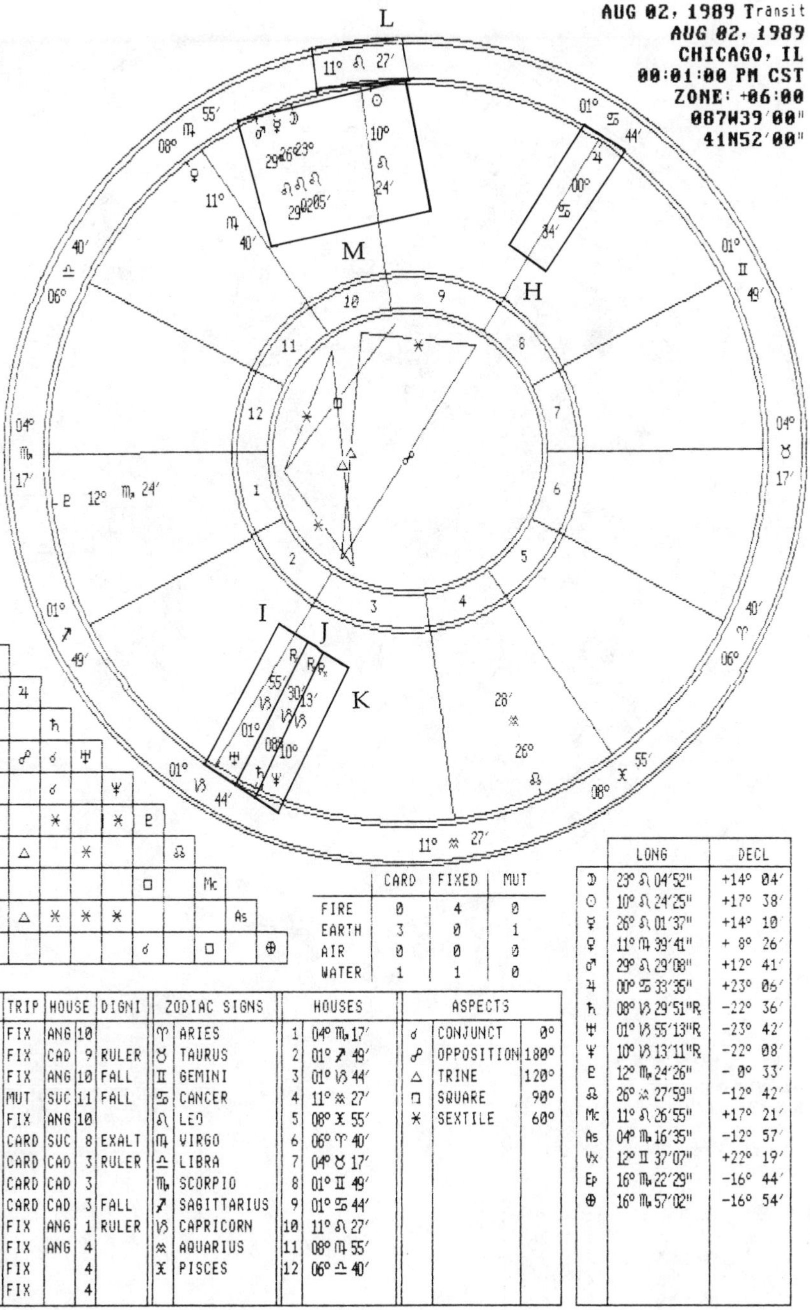

	LONG	DECL
☽	23° ♌ 04'52"	+14° 04'
☉	10° ♌ 24'25"	+17° 38'
☿	26° ♌ 01'37"	+14° 10
♀	11° ♍ 39'41"	+ 8° 26'
♂	29° ♌ 29'08"	+12° 41'
♃	00° ♋ 33'35"	+23° 06'
♄	08° ♑ 29'51"R	-22° 36'
♅	01° ♑ 55'13"R	-23° 42'
♆	10° ♑ 13'11"R	-22° 08'
♇	12° ♏ 24'26"	- 0° 33'
Ⓔ	26° ♒ 27'59"	-12° 42'
Mc	11° ♌ 26'55"	+17° 21'
As	04° ♏ 16'35"	-12° 57'
Vx	12° ♊ 37'07"	+22° 19'
Ep	16° ♏ 22'29"	-16° 44'
⊕	16° ♏ 57'02"	-16° 54'

	CARD	FIXED	MUT
FIRE	0	4	0
EARTH	3	0	1
AIR	0	0	1
WATER	1	1	0

PLANETS	ELEM	+/-	TRIP	HOUSE	DIGNI	ZODIAC SIGNS	HOUSES	ASPECTS
☽ MOON	FIRE	POS	FIX	ANG 10		♈ ARIES	1 04° ♏ 17'	☌ CONJUNCT 0°
☉ SUN	FIRE	POS	FIX	CAD 9	RULER	♉ TAURUS	2 01° ♐ 49'	☍ OPPOSITION 180°
☿ MERCURY	FIRE	POS	FIX	ANG 10	FALL	♊ GEMINI	3 01° ♑ 44'	△ TRINE 120°
♀ VENUS	EARTH	NEG	MUT	SUC 11	FALL	♋ CANCER	4 11° ♒ 27'	□ SQUARE 90°
♂ MARS	FIRE	POS	FIX	ANG 10		♌ LEO	5 08° ♓ 55'	✶ SEXTILE 60°
♃ JUPITER	WATER	NEG	CARD	SUC 8	EXALT	♍ VIRGO	6 06° ♈ 40'	
♄ SATURN	EARTH	NEG	CARD	CAD 3	RULER	♎ LIBRA	7 04° ♉ 17'	
♅ URANUS	EARTH	NEG	CARD	CAD 3		♏ SCORPIO	8 01° ♊ 49'	
♆ NEPTUNE	EARTH	NEG	CARD	CAD 3	FALL	♐ SAGITTARIUS	9 01° ♋ 44'	
♇ PLUTO	WATER	NEG	FIX	ANG 1	RULER	♑ CAPRICORN	10 11° ♌ 27'	
☊ NODE	AIR	POS	FIX	ANG 4		♒ AQUARIUS	11 08° ♍ 55'	
Mc MIDHEAVEN	FIRE	POS	FIX	4		♓ PISCES	12 06° ♎ 40'	
As ASCENDANT	WATER	NEG	FIX	4				

(c) 1986 Matrix Software Big Rapids Mi. 49307

Figure 13-6C   Treasury Bonds Futures Astrological Chart Showing August 22, 1977 and August 2, 1989

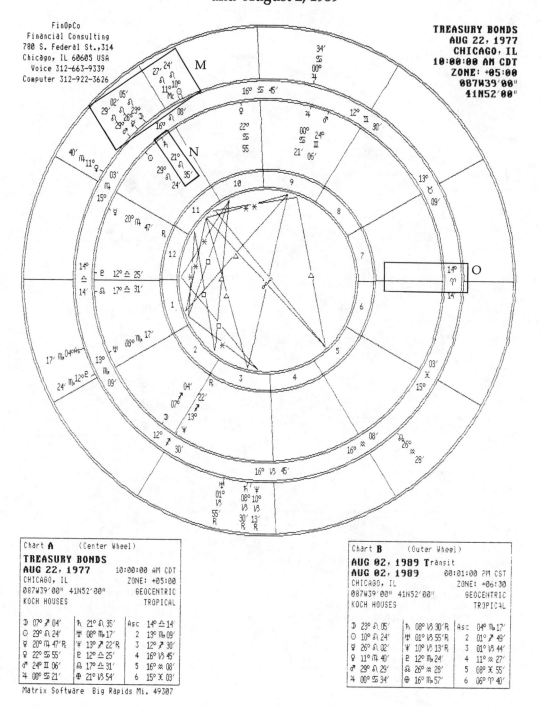

Matrix Software Big Rapids Mi. 49307

Chart **A**   (Center Wheel)

TREASURY BONDS
AUG 22, 1977   10:00:00 AM CDT
CHICAGO, IL   ZONE: +05:00
087W39'00" 41N52'00"   GEOCENTRIC
KOCH HOUSES   TROPICAL

☽ 07° ♐ 04'	♄ 21° ♌ 35'	Asc 14° ♎ 14'
☉ 29° ♌ 24'	♅ 08° ♏ 17'	2 13° ♏ 09'
☿ 20° ♍ 47' ℞	♆ 13° ♐ 22' ℞	3 12° ♐ 30'
♀ 22° ♋ 55'	♇ 12° ♎ 25'	4 16° ♑ 45'
♂ 24° ♊ 06'	☊ 17° ♎ 31'	5 16° ♒ 08'
♃ 00° ♋ 21'	⊕ 21° ♑ 54'	6 15° ♓ 03'

Chart **B**   (Outer Wheel)

AUG 02, 1989 Transit
AUG 02, 1989   00:01:00 PM CST
CHICAGO, IL   ZONE: +06:30
087W39'00" 41N52'00"   GEOCENTRIC
KOCH HOUSES   TROPICAL

☽ 23° ♌ 05'	♄ 08° ♑ 30' ℞	Asc 04° ♏ 17'
☉ 10° ♌ 24'	♅ 01° ♑ 55' ℞	2 01° ♐ 49'
☿ 26° ♌ 02'	♆ 10° ♑ 13' ℞	3 01° ♑ 44'
♀ 11° ♍ 40'	♇ 12° ♏ 24'	4 11° ♒ 27'
♂ 29° ♌ 29'	☊ 26° ♒ 28'	5 08° ♓ 55'
♃ 00° ♋ 34'	⊕ 16° ♏ 57'	6 06° ♈ 40'

FinOpCo
Financial Consulting
780 S. Federal St.,314
Chicago, IL 60605 USA
Voice 312-663-9339
Computer 312-922-3626

TREASURY BONDS
AUG 22, 1977
CHICAGO, IL
10:00:00 AM CDT
ZONE: +05:00
087W39'00"
41N52'00"

When to Apply Astronomical Cycles Analysis

Astronomical cycles analysis works best for traders when they need information on mass investor psychology. Astronomical cycles analysis also applies in cyclical markets. The shortest term traders should ever use with such indicators is the monthly one provided by lunar indicators. Otherwise, terms which are on the order of several months are most recommended, since aspectivity covers yearly time frames best.

Traders should never use Astronomical Cycle timing over the short term. As this chapter has tried to emphasize repeatedly, *astronomical* techniques will not allow traders to draw an exact bead on the moment of some market event's occurrence, since they do not measure the market itself, but rather the market's chief determinant, investor psychology. Therefore, it is logical to conclude from this that traders cannot be very specific about short time frames with such a technique, since a short run indicator must have quite a bit of accuracy with regard to time—otherwise, it is not a short-run indicator.

Since astrological indicators themselves are cyclic phenomena, it is also obvious that they are not suited to market phenomena which show highly irregular, non-cyclic fluctuations.

Astrological phenomena do not measure or attempt to predict the market itself, but rather human mood swings. These mood swings can mean different things at different times for the market—and therefore, traders need other indicators to help them interpret the market itself. Because astrological indicators cannot tell traders exactly when the consequences of certain mood changes will show up in the market, it is wise to have other indicators for this reason as well. Astrological indicators will help traders anticipate the most likely reversal points in the market, but they will not help traders predict it in the strict sense of the word.

These market monitoring techniques and astrological indicators complement each other nicely, since at their core lies the same assumption about the market: there must be gradual but inevitable changes between extremes of high and low prices in the market, and the imminence of these extremes can be heralded by certain changes in investor behavior. Astrological techniques, then, indicate when the underlying motivations for this behavior might change.

Strength indicators and overbought/oversold indicators actually herald when these motivations are beginning to *change* that behavior. Therefore, if, by using astrological indicators traders forecast far enough in advance at approximately what time period the mood is going to change, they should then be particularly heedful of the technical indicators' signals at these points. At times it is difficult to know just what to make of certain evidence that accumulation is happening or that the support for a price is weakening. Awareness of where they are in the astrological cycle should give traders more confidence in interpreting these signals.

Where to Find Out More About Astronomical Cycles

Books and Periodicals

Boyd, Mary Witty. *Financial Astrology Techniques and Horoscopes of Gold Stocks.* Mary Boyd, 1979.

Bradley, Donald. *Picking Winners.* Saint Paul, Minnesota: Llewellyn Publications, 1954.

Foster, William G. *Commodology Secret of Soybeans: a Study of Astrology and the Commodity Market.* Loveland, CO: William G. Foster, 1980.

Futia, Carl. *Predicting Market Trends with Periodic Number Cycles.* Morris Plains, NJ: Cyclic Forecast, 1982.

Gillen, Jack. *The Key to Speculation on the New York Stock Exchange.* San Antonio, TX: The Bear Publishers, Inc.,1979

Jensen, L. J. *Astro-cycles and Speculative Markets.* Lambert-Gann Publishing Company, Inc., 1978.

Langham, James Mars. *Cyclical Market Forecasting Stocks and Grain.* Los Angeles, CA: Maghnal Publishing Co., 1938.

Langham, James Mars. *Planetary Effects on Stock Market Prices with Indications for 1933-1934-1935.* Los Angeles: Maghnal Publishing Co., 1932.

Lynes, Barry. *Astroeconomics: the Union of Astrology and Economics.* Springfield, MA: Astroscience, P.O. Box 15247, 1984.

McWhirter, Louise. *Astrology and Stock Market Forecasting.* New York: ASI Publishers, 1938.

Merriman, Raymond A. *The Gold Book: Geocosmic Correlations to Gold Price Cycles.* Birmingham, MI: M.M.A. Publishing Co., 1982. Raymond Merriman publishes a yearly forecast of markets with a cyclic emphasis.

Tyler, J. Ross. *Financial Astrology.* Chicago, Illinois: D. G. Nelson, 1947.

Williams, Lcdr. David. *Financial Astrology: How to Forecast Business and the Stock Market.* Tempe, AZ: American Federation of Astrologers, 1982.

Software to Run on the IBM Computer

Computrac—Interday charting package has the following studies: moving averages, rates of change, oscillators, ratios and spread, RSI, stochastics, on-balance volume, moving average convergence divergence, point-and-

371

figure, etc. Chart zooming, trend lines and parallel channels, cycle analysis with Fourier analysis. Computrac Inc., New Orleans, LA 70175.

Ganntrader I—Interday charting package for the technician with trading knowledge of William D. Gann's approach. No screen displays but excellent hardcopy charts. Gannsoft Publishing Company, Leavenworth, WA 98826.

Matrix—Has an astrology calculation program, Blue Star 521, which creates horoscope chart for any time event, performs geocentric and heliocentric charts, and has secondary progressed charts. Matrix Software, Big Rapids, MI 49307.

Nova—An astrology calculation program which creates horoscope charts for any time event, includes fixed strars, Arabic parts, solstice points and antiscia, planetary pictures, astro-mapping, etc. Available for Apple computers also. Astrolabe, Orleans, MA 02653.

14

Elliott Wave Theory
Corrections Are the Problems

Elliott Wave Theory at a Glance

Background and Philosophy of Elliott Wave Theory

Elliott Wave Theory is based on the idea that any type of market must behave in some kind of irregular cyclic fashion, and that this cyclic behavior is classifiable and predictable.

Principles of Elliott Wave Theory

The market is seen to move through time in alternately uptrending and downtrending waves. The upside of a bull market constitutes an uptrending wave divided into five smaller waves (three up and two intervening down waves), while the correction to the downside is composed of three smaller waves (two down and one intervening wave up). A bear cycle is formed with three waves to the downside (two down and one intermediate up, each of the two waves down is composed of smaller waves of either three or five waves). In turn, each bear or bull cycle can, itself, make up smaller waves in a longer-term cycle. Thus, cycles can be nested in cycles, so that some have a scope lasting for decades or centuries, while others are on the scale of days or hours. A large body of rules exists for determining at what point a given market is in the Elliott Wave pattern (see tables in the body of this chapter.)

How to Set Up and Maintain Elliott Wave Theory

Traders must begin to track price on a bar chart after first deciding what timeframe they are interested in. Once they have observed a definite reversal point, traders must go back in the recent history of that market to determine where the reversal fits in the overall wave pattern for the timeframe they have chosen. The rules given in the body of this chapter should help them to do this. After that, it is then a matter of using the daily price information and wave-following rules to keep track of the developing wave cycle.

How to Trade with Elliott Wave Theory

Traders can enter buy and sell orders in advance of tops and bottoms as predicted by the Theory. The more cautious traders can simply ride a bull market all the way through the five-part impulse wave, liquidating their positions and staying out of the correction phase. Speculation can trade corrections continuously for quicker profits.

When to Apply the Elliott Wave Theory

An experienced chart reader will find Elliott Wave Theory flexible enough to cover all trading situations. Beginning chart readers should not use Elliott Wave Theory as a primary method. It is better to use it as a confirming tool until one's chart-reading skills have grown in the application of the Theory. The beginning trader should use this as a backup to more mechanical, short-range systems. Experienced traders can use it as a primary technique with other techniques as confirming indicators.

Glossary for Elliott Wave Theory

Correction Wave—A wave or cycle of waves moving against the current impulsive trend's direction.

Fibonacci Ratio—Any ratio between two successive numbers in the series 1, 1, 2, 3, 5, 8 . . . . This ratio approaches 1.618. See the chapter on Fibonacci series for further information. This ratio is sometimes useful for determining the length of successive waves.

Impulse Wave—A wave or cycle of waves which carries the current trend further in the same direction.

Running Mode—Said of a market whose prices are rapidly increasing or decreasing.

Trading Mode—Said of a market whose prices are relatively static.

Wave—In Elliott Wave Theory, a sustained move by a market's price in one direction as determined by the reversal points which initiated and terminated it.

Wave Cycle—An impulse wave followed by a correction wave, the impulse wave being made up of five smaller, numbered waves of alternating direction designated 1, 2, 3, 4 and 5, and the correction wave being composed of three smaller alternating waves designated a, b and c.

Background and Philosophy
of Elliott Wave Theory

The Elliott Wave Theory is based on the perception that market activity follows repeatable cycles. Every other technique, except for Gann's, bases its projections and signals on price's performance in the immediate past with set rules for interpreting this behavior. Elliott Wave Theory, on the other hand, draws a working relation between current price behavior and historical patterns. Moreover, it connects observed patterns with universal cyclic models.

In 1934, Ralph N. Elliott formulated the set of tenets which would become his Theory. In 1935, at the age of 64, he started a career as a market analyst and newsletter author. After his death in 1948, others came to the forefront in applying Elliott's Theory to markets, most notably Richard Martin, a former student of Collins; Hamilton Bolton, publisher of *The Bank Credit Analyst* and A.J. Frost, Bolton's business associate.

The Elliott Wave Theory has gained an increasing number of followers among stock, bond and commodities analysts over the last five years. This is not surprising, since the accuracy of market reversal points projected by the Elliott Wave Theory has been very precise. Robert Prechter, author of the *Elliott Wave Theorist*, has made some remarkable calls in the past. In several instances he has been able to call market reversal points to within the hour several days in advance.

Prechter has established himself not only as a notable newsletter writer but also as a capable practitioner of what he teaches by trading stock index options using the Elliott Wave Theory in real time. His finesse was highlighted in the final rankings of the February 1, 1984 to June 1, 1984, *United States Stock, Options & Commodity Trading Championship.* In the Options Division, Prechter ranked first with a 444.4% return on invested capital for the four months of trading activity. The next best contestant in this division showed a mere 84.2% return. He was no slouch either in trading activity: he traded approximately 200 times.

Traders are always in need of guidelines for gauging and measuring market movements, and so the Elliott Wave Theory will continue to gain followers as the markets' movements approximate the Theory's predictions ever more closely. With more practitioners, the theory's projections will start to become self-fulfilling prophecies.

Principles of Elliott Wave Theory

Elliott's Theory can analyze any type of market behavior with irregular upswings and downtrends.

A *wave*, as defined by the theory, is the *price change* over a given *time* between a major high price and a major low price. Although Elliott considered both price and time in his original theory, he was much less interested in the time factor, concentrating on price as the definitive element. Prechter, however, has placed more emphasis on cycle lengths and has made time-based analysis an important adjunct to price analysis in his application of Elliott's theory. This may partly explain why Prechter has been able to outperform Elliott himself in his application of the theory.

The theory has its own wave-based terminology for running and trading markets:

- *Impulse* waves are the equivalent of running or trending markets. All the examples here will talk about bull-market impulses—but traders should keep in mind that bear markets also have their downward impulse waves.

- *Corrective* waves correspond to trading markets.

Since there are only two kinds of waves, an impulse wave can only be followed by a corrective wave, and a corrective wave can only be followed by an impulse wave. That is, the market has a continual impulse-correction-impulse-correction pattern. Nothing else is possible. Therefore, an upward impulse wave has ended when traders begin to see a downtrend, signalling the beginning of a corrective wave. Likewise, a corrective wave in a bull market ends when the next upswing starts a new impulse.

The theory's most basic concept, the *wave cycle*, is simply an impulse wave followed by a correction. However, such simplicity does not give the analyst any advantage in the market.

Elliott precisely specified the more detailed form of an impulse wave: such a wave has five smaller waves which undulate upwards in uptrending markets in an impulse-correction pattern. These waves are so predictable that Elliott Wave technicians refer to them by number (Figure 14-1). Numbers 1, 3, and 5 are the smaller impulse waves contributing to the larger wave's upward trend. Numbers 2 and 4 are corrective waves serving to break the sustained upward movement.

Figure 14-1 Impulse Wave

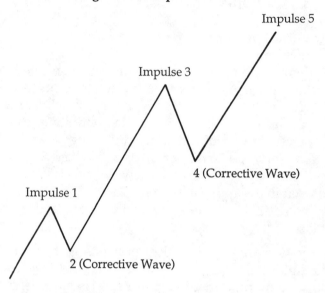

The larger corrective wave which follows this five-fold composite impulse wave can also be broken down in a completely predictable fashion. It contains three smaller waves in a down-up-down pattern. In order to better distinguish them from the five waves making up the impulse, these three waves are given the letter a,b,c. Waves a and c are downtrending waves, while the connecting wave, b, trends upward (Figure 14-2).

Figure 14-2 Correction Wave

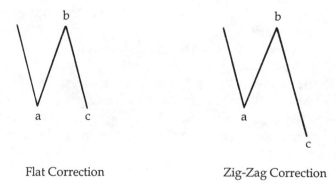

Flat Correction   Zig-Zag Correction

Thus, while the wave cycle might be represented as simply a bull-wave impulse followed by a bear-wave correction, it is much more useful to portray it as an impulse wave composed of five smaller waves and a corrective wave made up of three smaller waves, as in Figure 14-3. The most powerful idea behind the Elliott Wave Theory is that any wave can be dissected into smaller subwaves.

The smaller subwaves can be broken down in turn. In fact, any impulse-correction cycle can be broken down further into the five-and-three pattern, even when it forms part of a larger cycle. Thus, wave cycles can last years, months, days or hours.

Figure 14-3 Five-and-Three Pattern

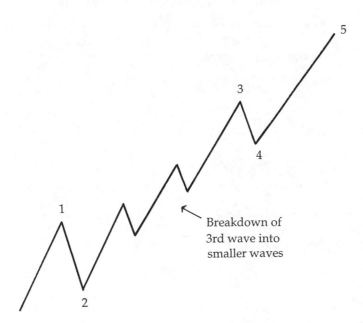

Breakdown of
3rd wave into
smaller waves

The problem for the Elliott Wave trader is to know what the current trend represents. In other words, the trader must be able to tell at what point in the eight-part cycle the market is. After all, an up-trending wave might represent any one of waves 1, 3, 5 or b. The trader must also decide what size cycle he or she is working with: one where positions are measured in terms of minutes and hours or one which measures the market in terms of several-month or even century-long cycles.

Elliott provided traders with tools for analyzing individual waves' behavior and so determining exactly where in a wave cycle the market is and how long the current trend might reasonably last. It is this last contribution that gives the Theory its unique power to go beyond analysis and actually become a tool for decision-making. This is a brief, non-exhaustive list of some of the handier rules for wave behavior as laid down by Elliott:

- *Correction Waves* are of two types: zig zag and flat. These types alternate in any given cycle. For example, if wave 2 is zig zag, then wave 4 will be flat.

- *Wave 1* impulse wave can be confused as being the "a" portion of an a-b-c correction. *Wave 1* forms immediately after the end of a corrective wave, hence the confusion is very likely at this point.

- *Wave 2* corrective wave can correct all the way back to the beginning of *Wave 1* and often it does. To further add to confusion, it is often an a-b-c correction of the zig-zag type.

Figure 14-4 Wave 2 Corrections

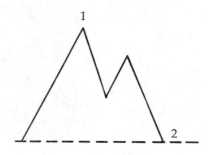

Wave Corrections

- *Wave 3* will be longer in price, but not in time, than Waves 1 and 5. Under certain exceptional conditions covered by Elliott, Wave 5 might exceed Wave 3 in length. These conditions cause *Wave 5* to have more *extensions* than wave 3 (a series of impulse and corrective waves of lesser degree). They can be detected by observing the 15-minute and half-hour charts in order to detect the smaller waves which make up the extensions. *Wave 3* moves strongly and violently as compared to the other uptrending waves. *Wave 3* often contains the greatest one-day volume activity of all three uptrending impulse waves.

- *Wave 4* will never descend lower than the end of *Wave 2*.

Figure 14-5 Wave 4 Support at Wave 2 End

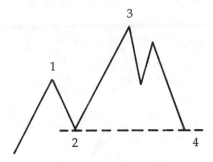

Wave 4 Support at Wave 2 end

- *Wave 5* will end considerably higher than the beginning of *Wave 1* and will have relatively lighter volume of all the impulse waves.

Figure 14- 6 Wave 5 Ends Higher than Wave 1

Wave 5 higher than Wave 1

- *The a-b-c corrective sequence* will not end at a lower price than the end of *Wave 4*. Wave a will be similar to Wave c with the following caveats. Wave a can either be composed of an a-b-c, three wave sequence, or a 1-2-3-4-5 wave sequence; Wave b is always made up of a three wave a-b-c, never a five wave; and Wave c is always made up of a five wave sequence, 1-2-3-4-5. If certain conditions are met then Wave c will approximate the shape and length of Wave a.

Figure 14-7 Wave Types a-b-c

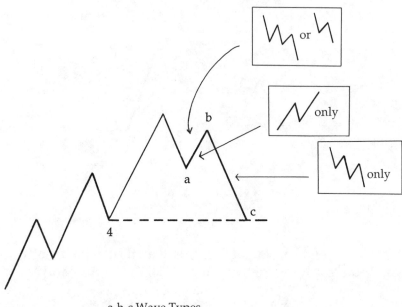

a-b-c Wave Types

How to Set Up And Maintain an Elliott Wave Trading System

Deciding on Timeframe

Timeframe will depend on traders' investment objectives. If one is a day-trader, he or she will be looking at daily and hourly charts for buy and sell signals, but must still take the long term into account because this will be affecting daily price behavior. The conventional approach is to chart half hourly closes on the Dow Jones Industrial averages.

Longer-term traders' buy and sell signals will come from the yearly and monthly charts—but it is still a good idea for them to keep an eye on daily charts, because traders can often pinpoint turning points for the different waves by watching these charts.

Keeping a Bar Chart

It is best for traders to get charts for as far into the past as possible, which should not be a problem if they contact such charting services as CSI in Boca

Raton, Florida and use computer charting software to download the information onto a chart.

Once traders have the past price chart, they add daily to their price chart.

Determining Where Market is in the Cycle with a Systematic Breakdown of the Chart

This is a much more subjective operation than the sorts of things required by other techniques. For this reason, the Elliott Wave technique is best practiced by a person who has a fair amount of experience in observing the market. The professional Elliott Wave tracking services listed in the final section of this chapter can also be of great help here. However, to really be able to trade with Elliott Wave, traders must form their own ideas of what the Elliott Wave Cycle is doing, which means they really have to do their own work with market prices. There are several things traders can do to analyze the master chart for the proper Elliott Wave signals.

The first thing for traders to do, however, is to look at the yearly charts, then break them down into monthly, daily and quarter hourly charts at crucial points. Traders must break price action down into as much detail as they need until they are satisfied that they have identified the wave cycle most useful to them.

While it is beyond the scope of this introductory chapter to tell traders exactly how this works, the following general techniques apply for determining just where the market is in the current Elliott Wave cycle.

Looking for the Five-Wave Impulse Pattern...

Traders should examine a period which interests them for a recognizable five-wave impulse pattern. If traders feel they have found such a pattern, then they need to track beyond it through the A-B-C correction. If traders can then identify another five-wave impulse after that, they are on the right track.

Wave 3 is the key to identifying the impulse pattern because of its characteristically violent and therefore distinctive behavior. "Just how violent is violent?" Traders need only try using some sort of volatility indicator, such as a short moving average. Short-term moving average indicators give many quick, false breakout signals in even moderately static markets. If traders are in a wave 3 upswing, such an indicator should give few signals, if any. Additionally, if price gaps are to form anywhere in the Elliott Wave Cycle, it is here that they will be found in abundance. Volume will be extremely high in Wave 3s.

...or Looking for a Strict A-B-C Correction

If traders seem to have identified the classic down-up-down of an A-B-C correction, they should check to see if they can identify the five-wave impulse wave later.

Try to Fit the Pattern into Larger and Smaller Cycles

A final confirmation that traders have correctly identified the pattern is to extend it backwards and forwards in time until they have enough impulse-correction cycles to try to identify a larger-scale, five-wave cycle. For instance, if traders are able to identify an a-b-c correction, check to see if they can identify it as Waves 2 or 4 of a larger-scale impulse wave, or the A or C wave of a much, much larger correction.

Once traders are sure of their analysis, then they should try to fit their wave into its component eight-wave impulse-correction cycle.

The Analysis is always Subject to Correction

Traders should keep a firm grip on the wave patterns and be constantly on the lookout for anomalistic patterns which may tell them that they need to rethink the way they have identified and sequenced the waves.

If a trader's initial analysis is incorrect, then he must go back over his chart and reconstruct it with a different count. What he needs to do, for all practical purposes, is to determine where the next closest corrections are since his objective is only to be able to predict the next impulse wave formation.

How to Trade with The Elliott Wave Theory

The driving motive behind Elliott Wave Theory is not mere *profit*—rather, it is the *maximum possible profit*. Those who practice the Theory are consistently able to buy the bottom and sell the top, often with uncanny accuracy.

In the next section, are examples of how a beginning trader might use the Elliott Wave Theory during one complete impulse-correction cycle in a bull market. Before moving on to these examples, let us examine the strategy behind this approach by looking closely at what we know about the five-wave cycle. This strategy is summarized in the table on the following page, which will serve as a general outline of the theory.

The theory's elegant simplicity has the unfortunate effect of lulling many practitioners into a certain laxity toward some of its more detailed tenets. For example, many practitioners might ignore the rule that Wave 3 is the longest of the impulse waves, and so they would sell themselves short on many occasions.

Market Strategy Through One Elliott Wave Cycle

Wave Movement	Trader Action	Comments and Rationale Based on Elliott Wave Theory*
Wave 1 Begins	Sit tight	Not yet clear that a new cycle has begun. More
Wave 1 Ends		to wait until Wave 3 takes out Wave 1 high
Wave 2 Begins		
Wave 2 Ends		
Wave 3 Begins		
Wave 3 Takes out Wave 1 High	Buy the market	Traders are now assured of proper position within wave cycle, since wave 3 can be distinguished by its length and abrupt behavior. Traders know corrective Wave 4 will not out take the beginning of corrective Wave 2.
Wave 3 Ends		
Wave 4 Begins	Buy the downside Enter stop sell order just below beginning of Wave 2	Assures losses are cut if downturn abnormally severe and beginning of wave analysis is wrong
Wave 4 Ends		
Wave 5 Begins	Hold	Wave 5 will increase value of purchases during Wave 4 downside
Wave 5 Takes out Wave 3 High	Sell longs	Downturn to corrective side of cycle is now imminent
Wave 5 Ends		
Wave A Begins		
Wave A Ends		
Wave B Begins	Sell Wave B upside with stop slightly above Wave 5 end	Stop allows holding if Wave B recovery proves unusually strong
Wave B Ends		
Wave C Begins	Cover shorts	This point can be predicted fairly accurately, as Wave C tends to resemble Wave A closely
Wave C Ends		
New Cycle Begins		

*Refer to selected rules given in the previous section.

Trading the S&P 500 Futures Using Elliott Wave Theory

The first example is a daily bar chart of the March 1986 S&P 500 Futures from July 11, 1985 to February 11, 1986, a span of 150 trading days.

Imagine that the traders begin following the market on September 26, 1985. (In retrospect, the S&P 500 bottomed out after a 3-month declining market and began the Wave 1 impulse of a greater impulse-correction cycle.) At that point, however, observers would only see that an uptrend had either begun or was in progress. As such, they would not be able to tell whether they were observing Wave 1 of a 1-2-3-4-5 impulse wave or wave b of an a-b-c correction. Any trading activity would therefore be a sheer gamble.

After this wave had ended, traders might risk the assumption that the market was in a bear impulse and they had just witnessed Wave 1. Then they could further reason, based on this assumption, that Wave 2 would end no lower than the beginning of Wave 1.

For a relatively risky trade, traders could gamble that they were not at the beginning of a larger corrective wave and purchase positions somewhere in Wave 2 with a stop sell order on all positions slightly below the beginning of Wave 1. This would allow them to cut their losses should their hunch prove wrong about where in the wave cycle the market was, because if the stop sell order point were taken out on the downside, it would be highly likely that the market was in a correcting mode.

From hindsight, observers know that Wave 2 ended and Wave 3 began on October 8, 1985. However, traders could not yet have known, based on their limited information since September 26, that the market was beginning a Wave 3 impulse move to the upside. How could traders know that the turning point from Wave 2 to Wave 3 had begun, rather than just some minor wave adjustment within Wave 2, to be followed by further internal correction to the downside?

There was some internal evidence in Wave 2 that gave a clue that this was a definite turn to the upside. Recall from among the rules given in the preceding section that correction waves have the form a-b-c and never take a five-wave format. Since Wave 2 had already completed a down-up-down pattern, traders could safely assume that there would be no further corrective sub-waves within Wave 2. They could then conclude that a new impulse wave was about to start, and bullishly hypothesize that this is a Wave 3 impulse. Bullish, but cautious—for they still need to confirm that this is Wave 3 rather than Wave b. Thus, traders wait until Wave 3 takes out the Wave 1 high before recognizing it as such.

Figure 14-8A Trading 500 Futures Using Elliott Wave Theory

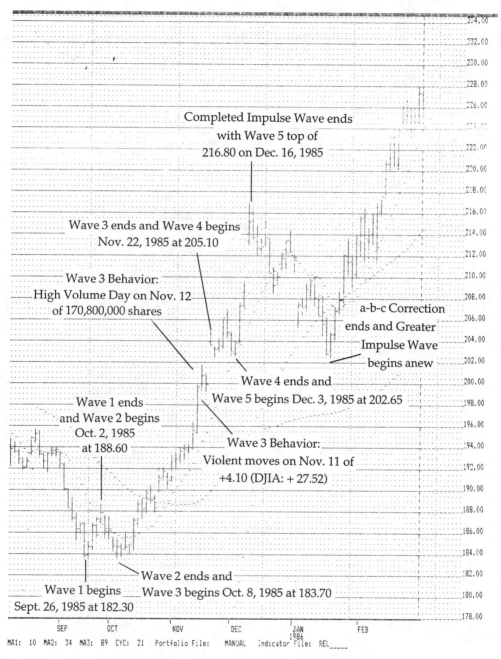

Completed Impulse Wave ends
with Wave 5 top of
216.80 on Dec. 16, 1985

Wave 3 ends and Wave 4 begins
Nov. 22, 1985 at 205.10

Wave 3 Behavior:
High Volume Day on Nov. 12
of 170,800,000 shares

a-b-c Correction
ends and Greater
Impulse Wave
begins anew

Wave 4 ends and
Wave 5 begins Dec. 3, 1985 at 202.65

Wave 1 ends
and Wave 2 begins
Oct. 2, 1985
at 188.60

Wave 3 Behavior:
Violent moves on Nov. 11 of
+4.10 (DJIA: + 27.52)

Wave 2 ends and
Wave 1 begins   Wave 3 begins Oct. 8, 1985 at 183.70
Sept. 26, 1985 at 182.30

SEP   OCT   NOV   DEC   JAN   FEB
1986
MA1: 10 MA2: 34 MA3: 89 CYC: 21 Portfolio File: MANUAL   Indicator File: REL____

Created using Relevance III™ Software

Figure 14-8B

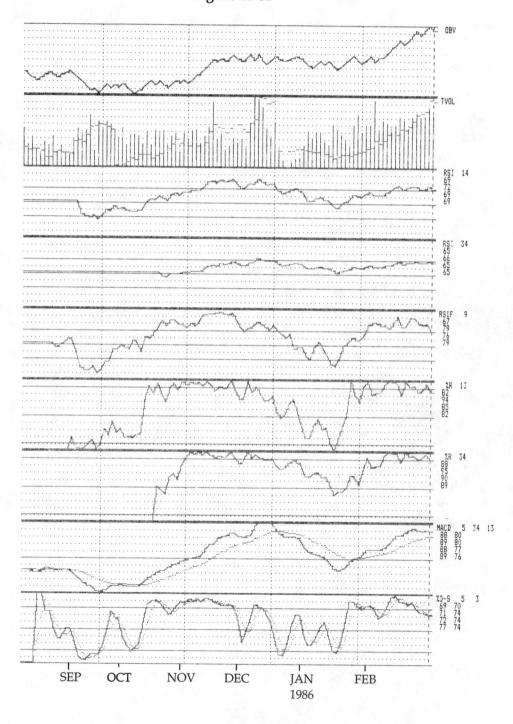

The list of rules in the previous section points out that Wave 3 is often the longest, and never the shortest of the three impulse waves in a five-wave sequence. Furthermore, Wave 3 is more vigorous than Waves 1 or 5. If traders now measure Wave 1, they will find that is is 6.30 points long in price. Therefore, they can assume that Wave 3 will exceed this increase. In this particular case, Wave 1 was 6.30 points long. Since Wave 3 began at 183.70, traders know it must pass 190.00 (= 183.70 + 6.30). Armed with this knowledge, they begin to buy with a vengeance.

Note here that, if they had known Wave 2 to be that for certain, traders could have "picked the bottom" and bought the downside, while buying with the trend during Wave 3. This illustrates how traders can use the Elliott Wave Theory both to trade countertrend and with the trend.

The trading strategy during the Wave 3 impulse wave is to buy and hold. The problem is knowing when Wave 3 is going to end. Elliott did not resolve this problem, and modern-day theorists have employed various means to try to predict the end of Wave 3, including Fibonacci ratios and Pythagorean analysis.

Wave 3 ends on November 22, 1985 at 205.10. Any lingering doubt about where the market was on the cycle would have been cleared up by Wave 3's characteristically violent behavior: a typically high-volume day and a length greatly exceeding that of Wave 1. In this particular example, a high-volume day of 170,800,000 shares was traded on November 12, 1985. The Dow Jones Industrial Average was only up 1.72 points for the day with 101,914,000 shares up and 48,630,000 shares down.

The previous day, November 11, 1985, however, saw the Dow Jones Industrial Average up 27.52 points on a volume of 125,540,000 shares, which, at the time, was a good volume day; further analysis of the volume revealed that 100,730,000 shares traded up and only 16,854,000 shares traded down, or an up volume comprising 79.60 percent of total volume. The March S&P 500 Index was up 4.10 points on November 11, 1985.

There are two kinds of corrections which alternate with one another: zig zag and flat. Since Wave 2 was a zig zag correction, traders can expect Wave 4 to be flat. This is exactly what happens.

Traders could possibly have taken some profits at this level from longs purchased at the 185.00 level. However, the Elliott Wave purist would wait to take profits upon the completion of Wave 4 and the beginning of wave 5.

Wave 5 shows the behavior predicted by Elliott which brings about extensions of the wave, making it longer than Wave 1. One way to observe whether or not extensions are happening is to see the Wave 5 action in greater detail by observing the 15-minute and half-hour charts to see the minor waves developing.

Upon the completion of Wave 5, the a-b-c correction begins. If they had not yet sold their longs, traders certainly must do so now, and even possibly initiate a short position. Having reached its high level of 216.80 on December 16, 1985, the market now begins its a-b-c correction. Trading these corrections as an off-the-floor trader is very difficult. If traders have not made money trading from the long side before the a-b-c Wave correction begins, they would be better off not trading the correction. Corrections, by their nature, are not as predictable using the Elliott Wave Theory.

Traders could use various oversold and overbought oscillators and stochastics to determine buy and sell points both in price and time to trade the corrections. However, they must be very nimble and must not overtrade positions in corrections. In trading from the long side with the impulse Wave 3, traders are assured with a high degree of accuracy that there will be a sustained one-directional move. Therefore, it is not only easy, but required that they pyramid. In corrective waves, however, by the time traders are able to pyramid, that directional move is ended and they would have managed to either sell the last lots at the bottom or buy the last lots at the top.

At the end of Wave 5, traders should stay out of the market and look to buy the market again after the correction is over.

Trading Dow Jones Industrials Using Elliott Wave Theory

This last impulse wave 5 of a larger impluse wave started on September 29, 1986 at the 1733.00 level of the Dow Jones Industrials, and ended on August 25, 1987 at 2746.70, fully 1013.70 points higher and 16 months later.

The first impulse wave ended at 1909.30 on November 12, 1986, or 176.30 points higher from the start of the Wave 1. The correction that ensued turned into an irregular correction that lasted from November 12, 1986 to December 31, 1986 and only covered about 23.90 points to the downside. Irregular corrections are signals that the market is very strong. The fact that the market is not capable of selling off, but internally corrects at higher price levels shows that the price is headed much higher.

At the end of Wave 2 correction to 1885.40, the Dow Jones Industrials started its Wave 3 impulse wave to the upside all the while making new highs. Wave 3 impulse wave lasted 543.00 points and ended on April 7, 1987 at 2428.40. Wave 3 is the longest of the two other impulse Waves, 1 and 5, however, this does not necessarily mean that Wave 3 is the longest of all, i.e. Wave 5 can be the longest, as long as Wave 3 can be longer than Wave 1.

The Wave 4 correction was a brief zig zag correction starting on April 7, 1987 at 2428.40 and ending a full 247.90 points later at 2180.50. This Wave 4

Figure 14-9A Trading Dow Jones Industrial Averages Using Elliott Wave Theory

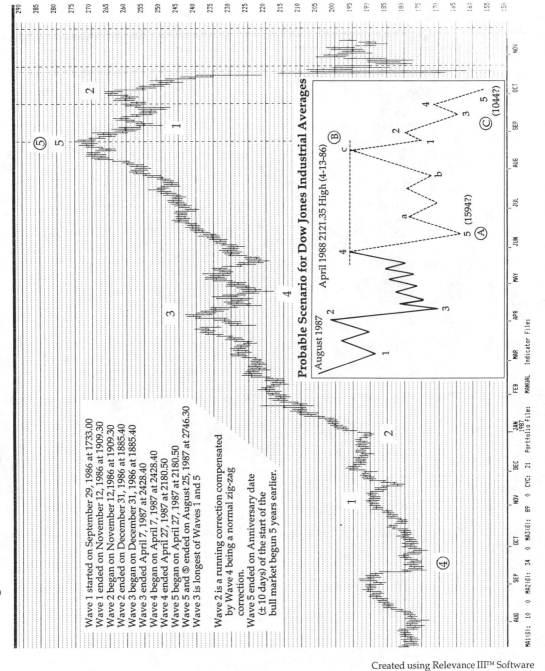

Wave 1 started on September 29, 1986 at 1733.00
Wave 1 ended on November 12, 1986 at 1909.30
Wave 2 began on November 12, 1986 at 1909.30
Wave 2 ended on December 31, 1986 at 1885.40
Wave 3 began on December 31, 1986 at 1885.40
Wave 3 ended April 7, 1987 at 2428.40
Wave 4 began on April 7, 1987 at 2428.40
Wave 4 ended April 27, 1987 at 2180.50
Wave 5 began on April 27, 1987 at 2180.50
Wave 5 and ⑤ ended on August 25, 1987 at 2746.30
Wave 3 is longest of Waves 1 and 5

Wave 2 is a running correction compensated
by Wave 4 being a normal zig-zag
correction.
Wave 5 ended on Anniversary date
(± 10 days) of the start of the
bull market begun 5 years earlier.

Probable Scenario for Dow Jones Industrial Averages

August 1987   April 1988 2121.35 High (4-13-86)

Created using Relevance III™ Software

Figure 14-9B

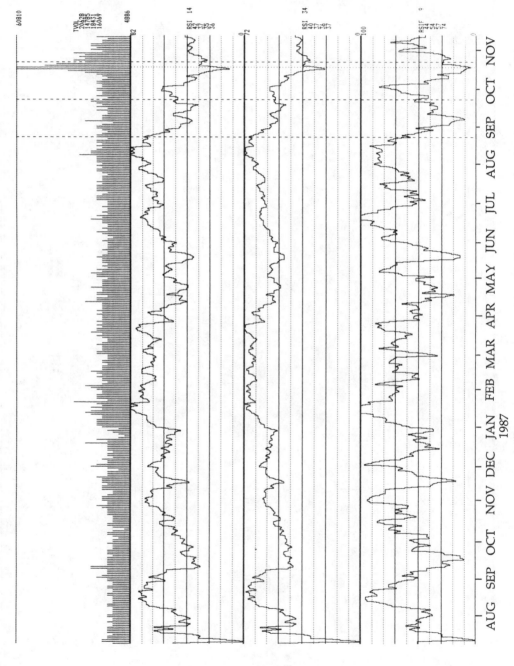

correction type followed the Elliott Wave Theory pattern of alternation: if one corrective wave is a flat correction, then by default the second one must not be a flat. In this case the first is an irregular flat, therefore the second must be a zig zag.

On April 27, 1987, Wave 4 correction ended at 2180.50 and Wave 5, the last of this impulse wave, and the last of many major impulse waves, started it's upward move. Wave 5 lasted four months and ended on August 25, 1987 with a top of 2746.65. Wave 5 travelled 566.20 points, surpassing the Wave 3 impulse wave by 23.20 points.

Within Wave 5 were extensions, thereby allowing the fact that Wave 5 could be longer than Wave 3. The massive corrective cycles follow. The bull market ended exactly 5 years and 13 calendar days from the August 12, 1982 bottom on August 25, 1987. At the writing of this book, one can discern massive correction in store for the Dow Jones Industrials.

The Dow topped out on August 25, 1987 and started an A-B-C correction to the downside. The A correction is a five wave sequence to the downside. The A wave is composed of five waves: three impulse waves to the downside with two intermittent corrective waves. Wave 1 ended in early September 1987 at around the 2500.00 level. Corrective Wave 2 ended at 2662.37 in early October 1987. Impulse Wave 3 sold off dramatically and bottomed at 1616.21, a massive decline of 1046.16 points in less than three weeks.

Impulse Wave 3 ended at 1616.21, intraday low, and rallied into a Corrective Wave 4 back to 2110.90 level on March 18, 1988 which coincided with a gain of 494.69 points. The correction extended over six months. New lows will be made before the end of this first A Wave correction.

The crash from both the 1929 highs and the 1987 highs have certain Fibonacci correlations. The "meltdown day" in 1929 occurred 55 days from the all time highs; the crash in 1987 occurred exactly 55 days from its all time highs also. The second decline in 1929 came on the 154th calendar day. The 154th calendar day from the second decline in 1987 is March 22, 1988. A solar eclipse occurred on March 17, 1988. March 21, 1988 is the vernal equinox. The solar eclipse and vernal equinox were predictable well in advance of the market movements: time can be forecasted; market movements may or may not be predicted.

As of this writing, the Corrective Wave 4 is about to end. This correction recovered 494.69 points. Impulse Wave 5 will begin shortly. As a possible scenario for Wave 5's objectives, traders need to look at how Wave 1 behaved. Impulse Wave 1 sold off from the all time high of 2746.65 to 2465.99, or 280.66 points. If Wave 1 is similar to Wave 5, then the beginning of Wave 5, which is around the 2110.90 level, should sell off at least 280.66 points or some Fibonacci ratio thereof, into new lows surpassing Wave 3's lows of 1616.21. Doubling the 280.66 Wave 1 selloff gives traders 561.32 points. Deducting this from the possible Wave 5 beginning offers a downside objective of 1549.58, which would be a new low and satisfy the requirement the Wave 5 must move into new territory.

If this scenario holds, then the Corrective Wave B will never retrace the gap, and will most likely end at below the 2110.90 level. Once the Wave B ends, then the final C Wave impluse wave will cause the Dow Jones Industrials to go to 800-900, imparting massive equity destruction.

Trading September 1986 Eurodollar Futures Using Elliott Wave

This example of the September 1986 Eurodollar contract lasts from September, 1985 to September, 1986 and spans a move from 90.10 to 94.40.

Observing the chart closely, traders can see a complete impulse wave to the upside which ends with a possible Wave 5 completion on September 2, 1986.

Wave 1 begins on September 9, 1985 at 90.09. Wave 1 ends on December 20, 1985 at 92.09, or a full 2.00 points higher. The correction, Wave 2, started out as a zig-zag correction. on December 20, 1985. Most Elliott Wave technicians would have seen the "a" correction to have been the full Wave 2 correction. From hindsight, the "a" correction was not the full Wave 2 correction, but merely the "a" of an a-b-c correction, which also happened to be an irregular correction which approximates a flat correction. This interpretation of this Wave 2 correction to be an irregular flat correction is due to the existence and formation of Wave 4—which turns into a pure zig-zag. When Wave 4 came into being, there was no doubt as to what type of correction it was. Most Elliott Wave technicians were fooled by the Wave 2 correction. They thought the "a" correction was the complete Wave 2 correction and therefore were expecting Wave 4, when it occurred, to be a flat irregular correction, which it was not.

Wave 2 ended on February 7, 1986 at 91.60 and Wave 3 began. Wave 3 was noted by the abundance of gaps to the upside, one at the 91.90 level, one at the 92.20 level, one at 92.90, and finally one at 93.25. Wave 3 ended on April 16, 1986 at 93.75, or a full 2.15 point higher. Recalling that Wave 1 was 2.00 points in length, traders had to start looking for some top once Wave 3 surpassed the length of Wave 1, or a move greater than 2.00. In this case, it was 2.15.

Wave 4 began on April 15, 1986 and ended, in zig-zag fashion, at 92.57 on June 4, 1986. The correction lasted 1.18 points to the downside.

Wave 4 ended on June 4, 1986 and Wave 5 began to the upside, with an extension, into the September 2, 1986 high of 94.36. This made Wave 5 last 1.79 points, far below the length of Wave 3's 2.15 points upmove and below the length of Wave 1's 2.00 points upmove.

Figure 14-10A Trading September 1986 Eurodollar Futures
Using Elliott Wave Theory

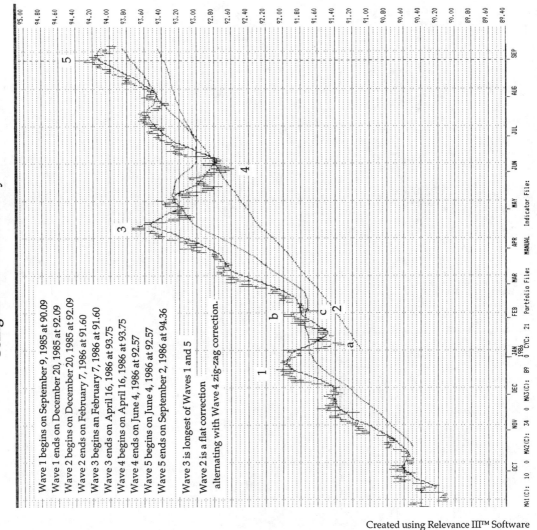

Wave 1 begins on September 9, 1985 at 90.09
Wave 1 ends on December 20, 1985 at 92.09
Wave 2 begins on December 20, 1985 at 92.09
Wave 2 ends on February 7, 1986 at 91.60
Wave 3 begins an February 7, 1986 at 91.60
Wave 3 ends on April 16, 1986 at 93.75
Wave 4 begins on April 16, 1986 at 93.75
Wave 4 ends on June 4, 1986 at 92.57
Wave 5 begins on June 4, 1986 at 92.57
Wave 5 ends on September 2, 1986 at 94.36

Wave 3 is longest of Waves 1 and 5
Wave 2 is a flat correction
alternating with Wave 4 zig-zag correction.

Created using Relevance III™ Software

Figure 14-10B

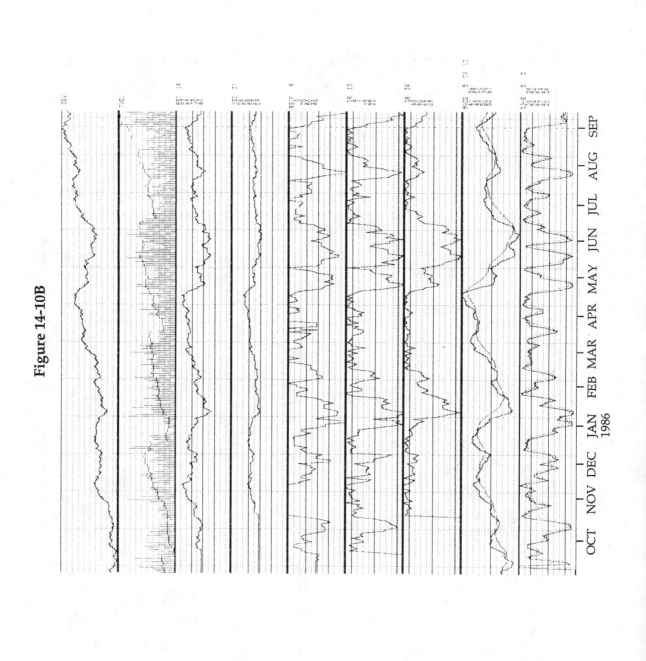

It is possible that this whole series of impulse waves and corrective waves are merely a series of smaller waves and are parts of a much larger wave. Only a longer timed chart can disclose that possible fact, but for now, given what is on record, this is the intepretation that traders can give it.

When to Apply Elliott Wave Techniques

Elliott Wave Theory is probably one of the most profitable techniques devised for the experienced trader in an uptrending market. Not only that, but the theory itself gives signals to indicate when the market is uptrending and when it is downtrending.

Although traders should continue to track the Elliott Wave cycle if they are serious about its long-term use, they will find that the theory has more problems identifying the proper position and turning points within a correction wave. This means that the prudent trader will let the theory take a back seat during corrections.

This chapter's How to Set Up and Maintain section mentions that a short-term moving average can help to identify the third wave in an impulse cycle. Traditional charting techniques can also identify areas of price consolidation and significant tops and bottoms within the individual waves.

The Elliott Wave Theory does not do as good a job on the downside, and therefore it would be best to relegate it to the position of a confirming indicator at these times. During such periods, moving-average, point-and-figure and stochastic indicators might be helpful in revealing more accurate position entry points. Volume-based techniques might also help to pick the bottom of a C wave and tell when accumulation is about to bring on another impulse cycle. Volume-based techniques would disclose accumulation patterns at the beginning of Wave 1 and the ultimate Wave 2 corrections.

Where to Find Out More About Elliott Wave Theory

Books and Periodicals

Beckman, Robert C. *Supertiming: The Unique Elliott Wave System*. Los Angeles: The Library of Investment Study, 1979.

Bolton, A. Hamilton. *A Critical Appraisal of the Elliott Wave Principle*. Toronto: The Bank Credit Analyst; 1960.

Elliott, Ralph N. *The Wave Principle*. Elliott, 1938.

Elliott, Ralph N. *Nature's Law*. Elliott, 1946.

Eng, William. "Stock Price Forecasting Using the Elliott Wave Theory," article prepared for distribution in seminars on the Elliott Wave Theory for Chicago Board of Trade and Chicago Mercantile Exchange members in 1986.

Futures magazine contains frequent short articles and analyses based on Elliott Wave Theory.

Prechter, Robert Rougelot. *The Major Works of R.N. Elliott*. Chappaqua, New York: New Classics Library, 1980.

Prechter, Robert Rougelot and Alfred John Frost. *Elliott Wave Principle: Key to Stock Market Profits*. Chappaqua, New York: New Classics Library,1978.

Supplement to the Bank Credit Analyst. Contributors: A. Hamilton Bolton, A.J. Frost, Russell L. Hall, Walter E. White, et al. Bermuda: The Bank Credit Analyst, 1961, 1962 and addendum 1963, 1965, 1967, 1968.

Consulting Services

Financial Options Consultants, daily Elliott Wave analysis and detailed instructional programs are available to callers on the voice line (312/922-3626.)

Prechter, Robert Rougelot. *The Elliott Wave Theorist*, a monthly newsletter with analysis of interest rates, stock market and gold, Gainesville, GA 30503.

Software to Run on the IBM Personal Computer

Chart Trader Plus—Interday charting package with the following: median lines, Fibonacci lines and spheres, recursion lines, percentage retracements, simple moving averages with bands, oscillators, relative strength index, on-balance Vvlume, %R, cycle intervals, and parallel channels. Investor's Toolkit Ltd., Summit, IL 60501.

Relevance III™—Interday charting package which creates above-average screen graphics and the finest hardcopy chart available using regular computer equipment. Performs many advanced type studies and has the only available Elliott Wave ratio analysis program. Holt Investments, Nashville, TN 37238.

15

Fibonacci Numbers
Cycles Which Build on the Past

Fibonacci Numbers at a Glance

Background and Philosophy of Fibonacci Numbers

Although the Fibonacci numbers were discovered in the Middle Ages, their use in market prediction started with Elliott Wave Theory. This is more a tool to *supplement* other techniques rather than a technique in itself. Its use is based on the idea that future irregular cyclic moves are based on past moves.

Principles of Fibonacci Cycles Analysis

A Fibonacci sequence is a series of numbers where each member is the sum of the two preceding it. As the sequence progresses, the ratio between a number and its predecessor tends toward the value of 1.618..., the famous "golden ratio." Fibonacci numbers can, therefore, be applied to progressions of price support/resistance levels or to the recurrence of certain market phenomena over time by using a first interval as the first number of a Fibonacci series, and then predicting the recurrence of another price support/resistance level at the place where the Fibonacci ratio would predict a successor in the series—more commonly, the recurrence of the market phenomena at a place on the time or price line corresponding to the Fibonacci successor.

How to Set Up and Maintain Fibonacci Cycles Analysis

Traders must first identify which phenomenon they are interested in (market bottoms, tops or price support/resistance levels). Then, on a price chart, using whatever method they find most appropriate, they begin tracking these items until they have identified a first interval. The first identifiable interval is the first term of a Fibonacci series. Traders can then draw a new line which is beyond the first interval by a value equal to that interval's size multiplied by the Fibonacci ratio. This can be done indefinitely, once they've established a first interval.

How to Trade with Fibonacci Cycles

Where Fibonacci cycle lines occur traders should look to other techniques to see if they also predict the reversal phenomenon which is being dealt with. If so, they should consider this as strong confirmation of what the other technique is predicting. The trader must be very cautious when using Fibonacci cycles as a stand-alone time or price reversal forecasting technique.

When to Apply Fibonacci Cycles

Fibonacci cycles are helpful in seemingly irregular markets, especially if traders expect some hidden cyclicity. Traders should not go overboard in trying to find Fibonacci coincident points since a trader can derive any point from any set of calculations if he goes at it long enough. The object of performing these Fibonacci calculations is to find the most obvious points, since the most obvious results will most likely have the best chance of being reduplicated in future calculations. Fibonacci cycles should always be combined with some other method, and complement particularly well such cyclic pattern-recognition techniques as Elliott Wave.

Glossary for Fibonacci Numbers

Fibonacci Cycle—An interval of price between two support/resistance lines, or an interval of time between the recurrence of market phenomena such as breakouts, tops, or bottoms. This interval relates to previous or subsequent similar intervals in some numerical fashion which mimics a Fibonacci Series.

Fibonacci Number—A member of a Fibonacci series.

Fibonacci Series—A series of numbers with the property that each member of the series is the sum of the preceding two members. A proper Fibonacci series starts with the two first terms 0 and 1, so that the first members are 0, 1, 1, 2, 3, 5, 8, 13, 21, 34 and so on.

Golden Ratio—The number 1.618…, which is half the sum of one plus the square root of five. This number was known in ancient times, and has many interesting properties in many fields. In Fibonacci series, the higher one goes in the series, the closer the ratio between a number and its predecessor comes to the Golden Ratio.

Limit, approaching—A property based on a series of numbers is said to approach a number known as a limit if, as the series continues, the property comes ever closer and closer to that number. For Fibonacci series, the Golden Ratio is a limit that the ratio between a number and its predecessor approaches as the series goes on.

Background and Philosophy of Fibonacci Numbers

Fibonacci Cycles are not really a stand-alone technique for trading any type of market. They do, however, constitute a very flexible tool for use as a confirmation signal in numerous other techniques.

The main theoretical cornerstone of Fibonacci Cycle indicators, the Fibonacci series, has been around since the late Middle Ages. Leonardo of Pisa, better known as Fibonacci, was a renowned mathematician of the 13th century who furthered the knowledge of algebra and the use of Arabic numerals in Europe. He also discovered the Fibonacci series, which he used to predict how fast a population of rabbits would multiply. This series, which customarily begins with the numbers 0 and 1, keeps generating successive numbers by adding the last two numbers together to produce the new number. Thus, if the series starts with 0 and 1, the next member of the series will be $0 + 1 = 1$. The member after that will be $1 + 1 = 2$, after that will come $2 + 1 = 3$, after that $2 + 3 = 5$, and so on as far and as long as one may desire.

The whole idea of using Fibonacci sequences or, more abstractly the Fibonacci ratio approximating the Golden Ratio, lies in the notion that market behavior, or any semi-regular, cyclic behavior, must depend in some way on what has gone before.

The Fibonacci sequence is the abstraction of a pattern of events which depends on previous events for their unfolding.

Principles of Fibonacci Cycles Analysis

The First Numbers in a Fibonacci Series

Starting with 0 and 1, the first dozen Fibonacci numbers are: 0, 1, 1, 2, 3, 5, 8, 13, 21, 34, 55, 89, 144, 233, 377.... The "..." indicates that this additive process could go on indefinitely, or, as mathematicians say, "to infinity."

Fibonacci Series and the Golden Ratio

The companion concept for Fibonacci indicators has been known even longer than Fibonacci numbers, since there is proof that it was used in ancient times. It is known as the Golden Ratio and occurs many times in nature and in human perceptual measurements. It is formally defined as

$$\frac{1 + \sqrt{5}}{2}$$

Its main interest in Fibonacci studies is the fact that the ratio between successive members of a Fibonacci series *approaches a limit* (see glossary) if it has continued long enough—and this limit is none other than the Golden Ratio. Thus, the first few numbers in a Fibonacci series approximate the Golden Ratio only very roughly. As it continues, the approximation rapidly approaches the actual value to within a very small difference:

0	
1	
1	1
2	2
3	1.5
5	1.666666
8	1.600000
13	1.625000
21	1.615384
34	1.619047
55	1.617647
89	1.618181
144	1.618977
237	1.618055
377	1.618025

Bear in mind that the Golden Ratio is 1.61803..., so you can see that successive ratios progressively give increasingly better approximations to this Ratio.

Other Properties of the Fibonacci Ratios

The Fibonacci summation series has even more interesting properties. The ratio discussed so far has been the Golden Ratio of 1.618. One can derive the inverse of this ratio, 0.618, if one divided one number with the next adjoining number, instead of by the number preceding it. If one divides or multiplies one number with a number three terms away, one arrives at another ratio. Using various manipulations, ratios such as 2.618, 3.618, 1.23 etc., have been created from this simple set of numbers.

Other interesting properties:

1) The square of any Fibonacci number differs by 1 from the product of the two Fibonacci numbers on each side.
2) Any four consecutive Fibonacci numbers, e.g., A, B, C, D, the following relationship holds: $C \times C - B \times B = A \times D$.
3) Every third Fibonacci number is divisible by 2, every fourth number by 3, every fifth number by 5, every sixth number by 8, etc. These divisors are also Fibonacci numbers also.

4) With the trivial exceptions of 0 and 1, the only square Fibonacci number is 144. John Cohn of the University of London proved that this was the only square Fibonacci number in the whole summation series. Gann relied heavily on the square of 12, or 144, in his cyclic analysis.

Edouard Lucas, a 19th century French number theorist, created the Lucas summation series. Instead of starting with 1, 1, 2, 3, 5, onwards, Lucas started his series with the following sequencing: 1, 3, 4, 7, 11, 18, 29, 47, onwards. This sequencing is subseqently known as the Lucas summation series and this summation series shares similar properties with the Fibonacci summation series.

Extending relationships even further, the Tribonacci summation series was discovered by Mark Feinberg in 1963. In this summation series, 1, 1, 2, 4, 7, 13, 24, 44, 81, one adds the previous three numbers to arrive at the next number in the summation series. The ratio between adjacent numbers, as the sequence grows, converges not to 1.618 nor 0.618, but 0.5436890126. Using the mathematical logic that is inherent in this approach, traders can summate four terms (to create the tetranicci numbers series), five terms, six terms and so forth. In all such sequencing, the ratio of adjacent terms converges on a limit. As the number of terms to be summed increases, the limiting ratio gets smaller and smaller, approaching 0.50 as a limit. This limit 0.50, is found in the markets in the form of halfway retracements of rallies.

Fibonacci Ratios and Timing Predictions

Since there are no hard and fast rules to use in applying Fibonacci numbers, but rather striking occurrences of the Fibonacci numbers and ratios at certain times and prices of market action, one cannot apply ratios with absolute certainty. The problem with using these ratios is that the markets can create a multitude of significant reversal and support points in the course of its movements. How does one know which is the correct one and how can one know for certain if reversal points can be predicted or forecasted by applications of Fibonacci ratios?

One doesn't know! However, one can apply Fibonacci summation series to arrive at the most likely trend reversals in the future. A simple way is to find a major market price bottom or top and then project into the future the second day, the third day, the fifth day, the eighth day, the thirteenth day, etc.

One can expect, with a degree of certainty, to see reversals in price action on one of those Fibonacci significant days from the market bottom or top.

Another way to approach the application of Fibonacci numbers is to see the retracements of bull market moves. One often finds that retracements are

Fibonacci percentages of the previous upmoves, that is, retracements can be 0.618 of the previous bull move. Conversely, one can find that a bull move is 1.618 of the previous down move.

How to Setup and Maintain
Fibonacci Sequences for Trading

Having an Established Price Chart and Technique

To begin using Fibonacci sequences traders need to have two things already set up:

- A price chart that has been running for some time
- One or more main trading techniques already in use

This second ingredient is necessary, because Fibonacci techniques are used exclusively for the confirmation of signals which a trading system generates.

Choosing the Market Event to Predict

Traders then choose the market they want to predict. This can be any necessarily occurring part of a market cycle, usually topside or bottomside reversals or breakouts.

Two Occurrences of the Event

If the chart has already been started, traders will probably already have two occurrences of the phenomenon they are seeking to predict. Otherwise, they should wait until they have two confirmed instances of that phenomenon. It is best to wait four or five days, or whatever interval is necessary so that no amount of hindsight can say the perception of this occurrence was wrong.

Taking the Interval as Base Interval

Once traders have located the two events, they draw vertical lines through the exact time instant on the chart where the events occurred. They then measure the interval between these two lines. This is the base interval. If, for instance, the interval between two market bottoms is 21 days, then 21 days is the base interval length.

Calculating and Plotting the Fibonacci Intervals from that Interval

original interval was 21 days and traders should now multiply it by 1. They would then place a third line (marking the end of the interval thus calculated) Using a table of successive Fibonacci ratios, or their own calculations, traders multiply the next Fibonacci ratio (if they are just starting, this will be simply by the base interval.) Twenty-one days will be the second interval, since the original interval was 21 days and traders should now multiply it by 1. They would then place a third line (marking the end of the interval thus calculated) 21 days beyond the preceding one. The next line will be at 21 × 2 days beyond the previous one (2 is the next ratio number), and the next one 21 × 1.5 days beyond that, etc.

Using the Fibonacci Intervals to Confirm a Main Method

Once traders have plotted a series of interval lines into the reasonable future, they will leave them on their chart. The idea is to wait until their main method has signalled or predicted the phenomenon that their lines predict. A coincidence or near-coincidence between the Fibonacci lines and their other methods' signal should be considered as strong confirmation of the latter.

How To Trade with Fibonacci Cycles

Fibonacci Cycles themselves will not give any trading signals, as their function is to confirm signals given by other methods. Therefore, the most that can be said is that traders can take great confidence in signals which their main method gives and which are confirmed by Fibonacci.

Greater caution would be advisable on signals which are not confirmed by Fibonacci lines. Fibonacci lines alone, without a coincidence with the signals from traders main methods, should be ignored.

Trading Example with Fibonacci Cycles

The following examples were taken from the privately printed newsletter *Turning Point*. It is reprinted here with permission.

The following are strict applications of the Fibonacci ratios to analysis of the Value Line Futures for December 1985, beginning with swings from October 2, 1985 to December 16, 1985.

The quick application for this is the following formula:

$$\text{projection} = (X \times R) + S$$

where

X is the absolute value of distance covered in one swing
R is the Fibonacci ratios (.618, 1.618, 2.618, etc.)
S is the starting point of any major swing

Please note that this formula's variables are also randomly selected within the framework of the parameters and in no way offers a definitive, cast in iron formula to work from.

Projection Formula	*Actual*
$(a \times 1.382) + 188.65 = 195.97$	196.00 (10-17-1985)
$(a \times 6.182) + 196.00 = 192.75$	192.70 (10-28-1985)
$(c \times 4.500) + 192.70 = 207.55$	207.55 (11-12-1985)
$-(d \times 0.382^2) + 207.55 = 205.38$	205.30 (12-03-1985)
$(d \times \sqrt{0.618}) + 188.65 = 207.54$	207.55 (11-12-1985)

Swings of December 1985 Value Line Contract

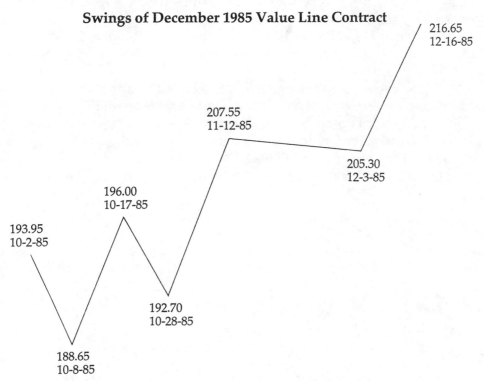

Actual Swing Tops and Bottoms with Absolute Distance Covered

Date	*High*	*Low*	*Distance Covered*
10-02-1985	193.95		start
10-08-1985		188.65	-5.30 (a)
10-17-1985	196.00		+7.35 (b)
10-28-1985		192.70	-3.30 (c)
11-12-1985	207.55		+14.85 (d)
12-03-1985		205.30	-2.25 (e)
12-16-1985	216.65		+11.35 (f)

When to Apply Fibonacci Cycles

Fibonacci cycles work well in markets which seem to have loosely defined but seemingly unpredictable cyclicity. Fibonacci cycles give useless signals in markets with over-pronounced and very regular cyclicity. They also do not work well in very short-cycle markets, as they need time to build up a train of intervals. Fibonacci cycles are an especially good idea to use with pattern-recognition methods, since they attempt to make the kind of predictions which Fibonacci cycles can confirm. Thus, Fibonacci cycles are an appropriate tool for Elliott Wave Theory, where they can be used for local tops and bottoms of the various waves of a cycle (see the Elliott Wave Theory chapter for more details), or Dow/Edwards-McGee, where they can give important confirmation of patterns which predict reversals or breakouts, or of doubtful consolidation patterns.

Fibonacci cycles also have much in common with Gann Anniversary dates and can be used profitably as confirmation tools there as well.

Fibonacci cycles do not work quite as well with methods which rely less on global pattern recognition of price moves, such as point-and-figure, or volume-based techniques, or methods which work more with local breakouts rather than tops and bottoms, such as moving averages or oscillators.

Where to Find Out More About Fibonacci Cycles

Books and Periodicals

Faulconbridge, Albert J. "Fibonacci Summation Economics Part I." *The Fibonacci Quarterly: The Official Journal of the Fibonnacci Association* 2, no. 4, (December 1964): 320-22.

Faulconbridge, Albert J. "Fibonacci Summation Economics Part II." *The Fibonacci Quarterly: The Official Journal of the Fibonacci Association* 3, no. 4, (December 1965): 309-14.

Gardner, Martin. *Mathematical Circus* (1981). A collection of articles from *Scientific American.*

Murphy, John J. *Technical Analysis of the Futures Markets: A Comprehensive Guide to Trading Methods and Applications.* New York: New York Institute of Finance/ Prentice-Hall. 394-98 (principles) and pp. 408-412 (application). Gives some additional, more exotic applications such as "fans" and "arcs" of Fibonacci ratios to price ranges.

Software to Run on the IBM Personal Computer

Chart Trader Plus—Interday charting package with the following: median lines, Fibonacci lines and spheres, recursion lines, percentage retracements, simple moving averages with bands, oscillators, relative strength Index, on-balance volume, %R, cycle intervals, and parallel channels. Investor's Toolkit Ltd., Summit, IL 60501.

Computrac—Interday charting package has the following studies: moving averages, rates of change, oscillators, ratios and spread, RSI, stochastics, on-balance volume, moving average convergence divergence, point-and-figure, etc. Chart zooming, trend lines and parallel channels, cycle analysis with Fourier analysis. Computrac, Inc., New Orleans, LA 70175.

Ganntrader I—Interday charting package for the technician with trading knowledge of William D. Gann's approach. No screen displays but excellent hardcopy charts. Gannsoft Publishing Company, Leavenworth, WA 98826.

Quickplot—Interday charting package creates daily, weekly, or monthly charts, with moving averages of all types, trend lines and parallel channels, oscillators and RSI. This is a basic program without advanced studies. Commodity Systems, Inc., Boca Raton, FL 33432.

Relevance III™—Interday charting package which creates above-average screen graphics and the finest hardcopy charts available using regular computer equipment. Performs many advance type studies and has the only available Elliott Wave ratio analysis program. Holt Investments, Nashville, TN 37238.

16

Gann Trading Techniques
A Compendium
of Techniques

Gann Trading System at a Glance

Background and Philosophy of Gann Techniques

The Gann system is really a collection of several techniques, all tied together by the assumption of an underlying and predictable cyclicity in market phenomena.

Principles of the Gann Techniques

Gann's four main indicators are:

- *Gann Angles*—As a market trends further downward or upward, the trend-line establishes certain significant angles on the chart which define resistance and support.
- *Anniversary Dates*—Major market events are seen to recur on a regular basis, so that future dates of reversals and other market phenomena can be pinpointed.
- *Cardinal Squares*—Traders can put an issue's all-time low price in the middle of a square array of numbers and then spiral progressively greater prices out into larger squares. The lines of numbers formed by significant angles from the central low price then will define future price support and resistance levels.
- *Price-time Squares*—The line between high and low prices in a given time period form the left side of a square. The bottom and top extend along the chart. The right side completes the square and diagonals and other significant lines of the square are Gann angles.

How to Set Up and Maintain Gann Indicators

- *For Angles*—Users determine trendlines on a price chart and draw lines at the significant angles from the origination point of the current trend.
- *For Anniversary Dates*—Users annotate the significant future anniversary dates of major market events on a price chart.
- *For Cardinal Square*—Users check prices against support and resistance levels as predicted by the cardinal square.
- *Price-time Squares*—Users determine the proper unit relation between time and price, then plot squares on the chart.

How to Trade with Gann Indicators

Traders use anniversary dates to predict price reversals and cardinal squares to predict the level at which a price or time reversal will take place. They use these two techniques to confirm angle breakouts. Price-time squares provide a framework for the angles.

When to Apply Gann Techniques

Gann's approach has universal applications, though the anniversay date technique is not as useful in markets without perceived cyclicity. Anniversary date and cardinal square techniques should be heeded only with confirmation from independent indicators. Traders should supplement the Gann System with volume-based techniques and use it to confirm the predictions of price-sensitive indicators.

Glossary for Gann Techniques

Angle—A measure in degrees from the horizontal on a price chart of various key angles (such as 45 degrees) which Gann Theory considers as support/resistance levels for a price trend. When an angle line is broken upside by the trend, the next significant angle line becomes the new resistance level, and the line just broken becomes the new support level.

Anniversary Dates—Significant intervals of days, months or years from the dates of major market events.

Cardinal Square—A square composed of numbers spiraling outward, starting with the lowest all-time price (or the start prices can be used) and increasing by some fixed increment. Significant angles drawn from the center of this square (at, for example, 90 and 45 degrees) are supposed to point out significant support and resistance levels.

Cycle Size—The number of lines in a cardinal square less one, representing twice the number of "coils" in the spiral.

Price-time Square—A square formed on a chart, starting with the high-low range for a given time period, taking that range as being the left side of a square, and then drawing the square over the price fluctuations. Diagonals and other significant lines on the square serve as Gann angles (see definition above).

Step—The number by which successive numbers increase in the cardinal square.

Background and Philosophy of Gann Techniques

These techniques may not at first appear to be logically related, but they have a conceptual relation given them by their inventor, William D. Gann, a famous trader during the first half of the twentieth century. Gann believed that the geometric representation of price through time would reveal important cyclic patterns with predictive value. Based on this assumption, Gann developed several major market-tracking techniques of diverse natures all tied together by the idea that geometric pattern recognition was the key to a greater understanding of market phenomena.

Just as many contemporary technical analysts look to Gann for ideas in developing their approach, so did Gann rely in turn on pioneers before him. Gann's geometrical approach to trading the markets drew heavily on the works of an astrologer, L.J. Jensen. Jensen taught Gann to look at price and time as related phenomena.

Gann observed that price cannot exist outside of time. The price of any stock, future, or bond stops trading as soon as the markets close. However, time continues onward, indifferent to price.

Gann recognized that the standard bar chart shows price as a function of time: the horizontal x-axis is the time line and the vertical y-axis is the price line. Price is plotted against equal time marks on the x-axis.

Gann saw the necessity for consistency in recording data and stipulated that all charts must be created with equal time intervals in the x-axis and equal price intervals in the y-axis. There are no hard and fast rules about what types of incremental units to use in creating these charts. There is a practical consideration: keeping the units constant throughout the chart allows traders to track the price consistently so that they can to apply a variety of tools and techniques to the same information.

Gann relied heavily on Jensen in learning about the factor of time in his analysis. Through his study of astrocycles he realized price is a function of time. Since he systematically recorded seemingly random price movements against a predictable time line on his charts, he could apply mathematical techniques to this geometrical relationship. For example, his charts' geometric balance allowed him to apply the Pythagorean theorem to any triangle created on his charts and so obtain future intersection points of time and price.

One fact helped tremendously in this approach—the total regularity of time. All Gann had to do in order to predict time was to look at planetary movements. Once he could do this, he found that he could solve for the unknown variable—price. There was nothing mysterious with this approach to market analysis. He worked with strict mathematical relationships.

Gann's Anniversary Date analysis considers the repetitiveness of cycles, and so is a primitive application of astronomic timing. The basic method projects some critical price reversal point a full calendar year after a major top. He refined his analysis by further dividing the full calendar year into 12 months, 4 quarters and 52 weeks. He also extrapolated his analysis to two years, three years, and so on into the future. Gann's approach to price prediction is based on the use of the variable of time.

His actual trading techniques were extensions of the accepted trading techniques of his day: swing charts and a series of overbought and oversold indicators. A swing chart by itself is not as valuable as a set of swing charts with different time filters. In Gann's day, there was no was real time market data, hence he started with a daily bar swing chart and extended outwards to weekly and then monthly charts; here this technique is modified by the author by going from the daily bar swing chart to hourly and finally 15-minute swing charts (see the chapter on the swing charting technique).

Gann used a primitive method of tracking overbought and oversold indicators: on his unified charts he drew angle patterns. Since he had made all his charts completely comparable with one another by strict adherence to "one unit of time for one unit of price," he could easily transfer his geometric analysis of price behavior through time to other charts—a concept now applied algebraically with the Relative Strength Index.

Gann's own interpretation of this "road map" approach to prices contains no hocus pocus, just common sense: a steepening line means a trend is intensifying, whereas a flattening line signals an imminent trend change.

Principles of the Gann Techniques

A Price Cycle Predictor—The Cardinal Square

A cardinal square is the geometrically visualized incarnation of the idea that price support/resistance levels occur at predictable price intervals. It is composed of a square array of numbers which are conceived as spiralling outward in a clockwise direction from the central number. The central number represents the all-time low price for the stock or other issue under consideration, and then the progressive numbers along the spiral grow regularly by an arbitrary amount known as the step. Twice the total number of "coils" in the spiral, that is, the number of lines in the square less the central line, is the "cycle" size.

Important directions along the number array from the center define important price support and resistance levels—for instance, the numbers in perpendicular or horizontal lines from the starting central value or the numbers in a 45-degree diagonal, etc.

A Time Cycle Indicator—Anniversary Dates

These are at even fractions and multiples of a year from important market tops and bottoms and can signal either a recurrence of the same event or another significant point in the same cycle that included the original event.

A Framework for Price and Time—Price-Time Squares

This technique bridges the price and time indicators, providing a framework for the angle method described below.

A price-time square chart uses a constant price/time unit (i.e., one which will, on the average, give a 45-degree slope in a trending market). The price-time square for a given market is formed by taking the vertical range of high and low prices for that period and then extending it for the same distance horizontally, thus forming the vertical and horizontal sides of a square. The corners of the square then define the points from which 1-to-1 (45-degree), 1-to-3 (87.5-degree) and other angles can be drawn.

Synthesizing Price and Time Cycles—Gann Angles

The use of price movement angles is based on the idea that there are certain natural levels of support and resistance to price trends, and that these levels are determined by the direction of the trends themselves. Once a level is broken, price will tend to stabilize toward the next level. The steeper a resistance line (that is, the more violent the price move it represents), the less likely

424

it is to get even steeper, and the more likely the trend is to gravitate back to a flatter, less violent trend.

The most important angle is the 45-degree angle, that is, the line drawn on the chart from the beginning of a trend at 45 degrees to the horizontal in whatever direction price is moving. This is called a 1-to-1 line, because it moves one unit of price for every unit of time. Gann considered this 45 degree line to be the "life line" of the chart. If price breaks it on the way down, it is an extremely bearish sign, and if price breaks it on the way up, it would be extremely bullish. A 2-to-1 line moves two units of price for every unit of time, and so represents a 60-degree angle, while a 1-to-2 line represents a 30-degree line, a 1-to-3 line represents an 87.5-degree angle, and so forth.

How to Set Up and Maintain the Gann Indicators

The Cardinal Square

All that is needed for the cardinal square, besides a standard bar chart following price, is historical information on the total range of price fluctuation for the issue traders are studying and some square graph paper. Then they decide on a *step* or interval between each successive price. This should normally be one unit of price.

Traders place the lowest all-time price in the center square of the sheet of paper. To the left, they place the next price up from the bottom, then above that price, the third price, to the right of that, the fourth price and so on until they've described a clockwise square around the original price at the center. Then they jump one square further out and repeat the process, spiraling as many times around the central square as it takes to get a usable range.

Once traders have completed the square, they mark or highlight the rows of numbers extending horizontally and vertically in all four directions from the central square. They also mark the rows which define 45-degree angles to the horizontal and vertical lines.

On the chart where they keep track of price movement, traders mark all the price levels which correspond to the numbers in these significant channels and which appear in the reasonable range of their current chart. These lines should mark important resistance/support levels.

A cardinal square lends itself well to a simple computerized spreadsheet, which has the advantage that traders can change the central number and the step at will, with the entire square recalculating instantaneously, instead of having to re-draw a square every time they want to change markets or change steps on the same issue. The spreadsheet approach means that traders can fine-tune their step value experimentally to give the most useful support-resistance price levels for current markets.

Figure 16-1   Cardinal Square

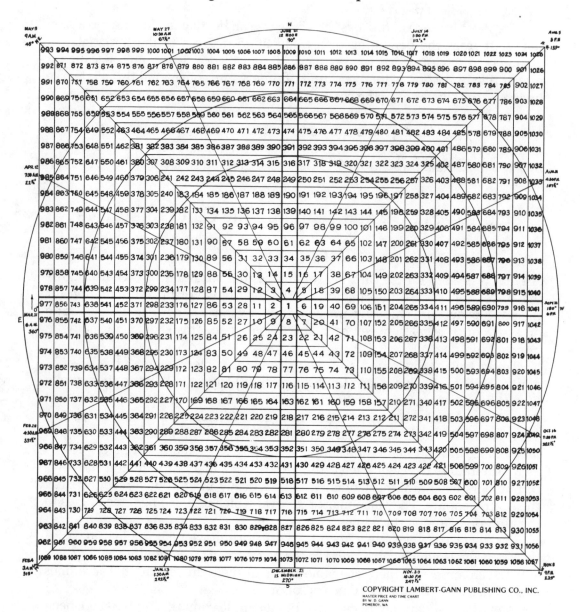

Figure 16-2　Master Time and Price Chart

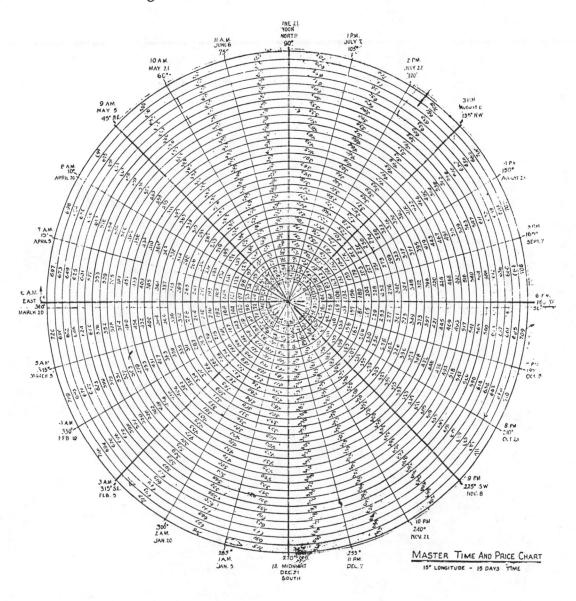

MASTER TIME AND PRICE CHART
15° LONGITUDE – 15 DAYS TIME

Figure 16-3   Price-Time Square Chart

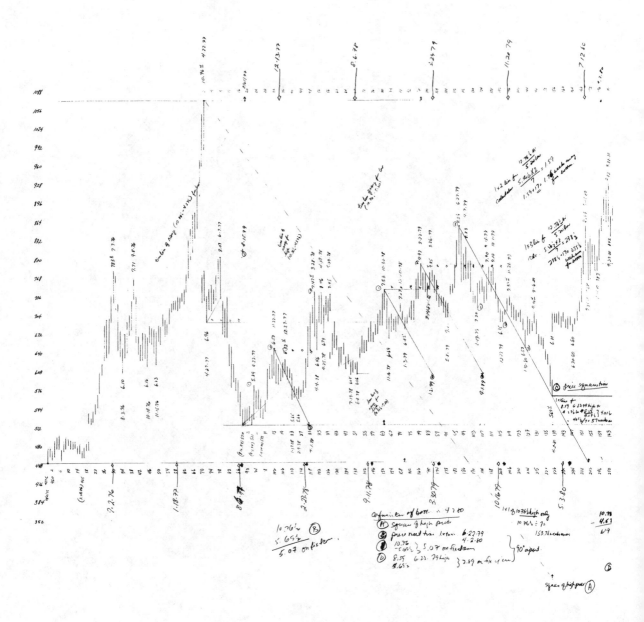

Figure 16-3   Continued

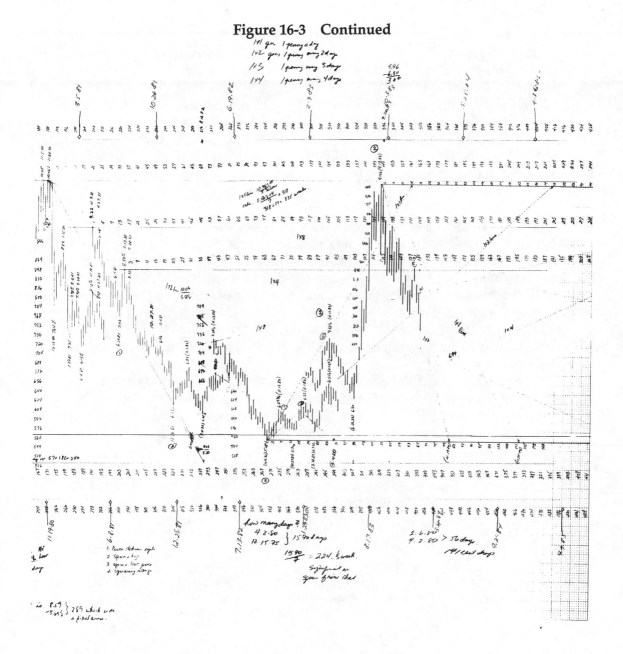

1×1 goes 1 penny a day
1×2 goes 1 penny every 2 days
1×3 1 penny every 3 days
1×4 1 penny every 4 days

Anniversary Dates

To use anniversary dates traders need to do a little historical research into the market or issue they are trading. They need to chart past price on a very wide price graph, leaving plenty of blank space to the right for future price information. Traders pinpoint dates on which significant market events have happened—tops, and bottoms. They mark points at dates which are even multiples and significant fractions of a year into the future from these significant events. The chapter on the use of Fibonacci series, deals with a similar type of cyclic prediction.

Price-Time Squares

First traders define a time period which interests them in the market. Then they find the absolute high and low prices for that period.

They must now determine what scale to use with their particular market, that is, what unit of time will correlate to what unit of price. This is critical to determine the correct angles to draw and what angles will have greatest resistance and support. The idea is to "eyeball" various charts using different scale relationships (for example, 10 cents = one week, .01 points = one day, and so forth) until you find a relation that gives an average price trend at more or less a 45-degree angle.

The Gann-Trader software allows traders to "eyeball" various charts in a relatively painless fashion: a trader picks the scale, and the software then prints out the chart for that scale. Traders can repeat this procedure until they have a chart that looks about right. Then they know that they've hit on the right scale to use.

Traders first go to the beginning of the period on the chart and draw a vertical line between these two levels, then extend two horizontal lines of the same length as the vertical line from the top and bottom of that first line. They connect the ends of these two lines and their square is complete.

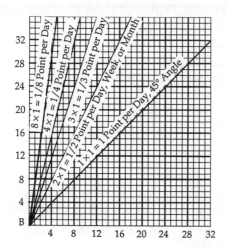

Figure 16-4A
Strong Position Bull Market
Above 45° Angle

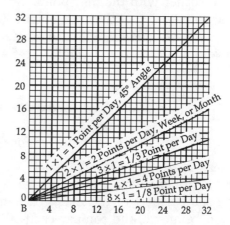

Figure 16-4B
Bear Side Weakest
After Time has Run out
or Squared with Price

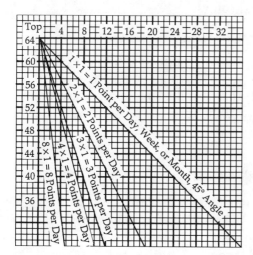

Figure 16-4C
Bear Market Weak Position
Below 45° Angle

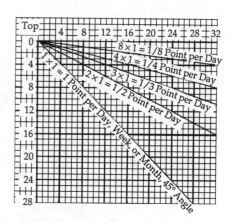

Figure 16-4D
Strongest Position
in Bear Market, 45° Angle

Price Angles

A price-time square is a good basis for keeping track of angles.

Users draw in the diagonals of the price-time square so that you now have eight 45-degree angles, or two in each corner of the square. Then they connect each corner with the mid-points of the two sides of the square not touching that corner, so that they can obtain 30 and 60-degree lines. These are the main lines which traders will use to determine support and resistance for the developing price trend. (Figure 16-5A, 16-5B, 16-5C, 16-5D.)

How to Trade with Gann Indicators

Combining the Four Indicators into a System

These indicators are all related by similar presuppositions of cyclicity in market phenomena. Since they each give very different views of essentially the same aspect of the market's behavior, traders can use them to complement, reinforce, and confirm each other's signals.

Using Angles as the Primary Indicator

Angles follow the actual movement of price at any given moment, so they are the most immediate of the indicators. Users of the basic technique, therefore, watch angles for useful signals and then try to see if what these signals are telling them goes along with the cyclic indicators.

Setting Up a Price-Time Square

Traders should set up the price-time square as described in the previous section, making sure that it takes in enough of the future to be useful.

The parallel and vertical lines drawn through the diagonals of the square give the practical limits of where angles will be formed. This is because price is a function of time, which means that:

1) Price changes with time and
2) No price move can take place without some time elapsing.

Point 1) means that an angle will be unstable at the horizontal or 0-degree position: that is, price cannot continue at the same level for any length of time. Point 2) means that it will be impossible for price movement to ever attain a 90-degree angle that is, to change instantaneously, without some time elapsing. Now, of course, price trend will oscillate between rising and falling, so the large-scale trend must briefly pass through a 0-degree or horizontal

angle—but this static position is fundamentally unstable as well as uninteresting to the investor in and of itself: what is of interest is what it tells traders about where price is going.

Angles in a Bull Market

Traders should be able to see intuitively from this that the stablest angle for a price trend would be somewhere midway between straight up and down and the horizontal: that is, at 45 degrees. Since a trend needs a certain amount of impetus to get going, they do not automatically look for the price to start a 45-degree climb once it moves away from the horizontal line. Rather, they are more cautious, and wait to see if it will pass some intermediate angle—that being the 30-degree angle as determined in the "set-up" section above.

Once the 30-degree angle has been penetrated, traders then look for the trend to rise to the 45-degree resistance line. If it breaks the 45-degree line significantly, then they expect another rise to another resistance line at the 60-degree angle. Such an angle is very steep and represents rapid price change within a short amount of time. It is therefore not very probable that the price will keep up this tendency for long.

Angles in a Bear Market

On the downside, traders wait for the price to break the 30-degree downward-trending angle before assuming that it will fall to the next major angle, the 45-degree downtrend.

Once price penetrates the 30-degree angle, traders then look for the trend to fall to the 45-degree support level. If it breaks the 45-degree line significantly, then they expect another support line at the 60-degree level. Anything beyond 60 degrees is not going to be very stable or sustained.

Determining When the Trend Has Ended

The quick way for traders to determine when a trend has ended and one of another direction has begun is to examine a segment of a longer term bar chart for a given number of days (usually two or three). If, during a downward tendency, two days of successively higher highs (without lower lows) occur, then traders should now begin plotting an upward trend.

Conversely, if two days of successively lower lows without higher highs occur during an upward trend, then traders should switch the trend to falling.

These last two paragraphs are the essence of the Swing-Chart technique, which is discussed in its own chapter.

Trading Signals in a Bull Market

A Gann Angle chart generates buy signals for long positions when price reconfirms its penetration of the 45-degree upward-pointing line (that is, once it crosses, falls below, and recrosses). A signal to liquidate a long position happens when:

1) 60-degree line gets broken to the downside (traders take profits) or

2) The 30-degree line gets broken to the downside (traders cut their losses short).

Trading Signals in a Bear Market

Sell and buy signals for short positions are the inverse on the chart's downside of the signals for a long position.

1) A 60-degree line gets broken to the upside (traders take profits) or

2) The 30-degree line gets broken to the upside (traders cut their losses short).

Improving on Angles with Cardinal Squares and Anniversary Dates

Angles form the core of the Gann trading system. Users can sharpen the signals from angles by supplementing them with the Cardinal Square and Anniversary Date indicators. The following table summarizes trading procedures with the Gann system:

Table of General Trading Procedures with the Gann System

Time-Based Procedures

1) Check to see if the market being analyzed is running correctly with time or not by using a square to draw 1×1, 1×2, 1×3, 2×1, 3×1, lines onto a price chart. If the price action is above an uptrending 1×1 45-degree line, then one can continue to play the market on the long side. If price action is below a downtrending 1×1 45-degree line, one can stay short. If, on the other hand, the market is close to the 45 degree line, watch to see if price squares time (that is, the price reaches the upper or lower right-hand corner of the price-time square) and whether or not a change in trend will ensue.

2) Look over the previous data and perform harmonic cycles analysis on the data by observing to see if there are Anniversary Dates coming up. Square the the number of weeks in the intervals between reversals to pinpoint other reversals.

Price-Time Based Techniques

3) Square the actual price range from the low and high to forecast additional reversal points.

4) Construct an Anniversay Date chart from major swing tops and bottoms of historical data and check projected price reversal points against other important data.

5) Construct a price-time square from the high and low range on the daily bar chart. Do the same for the weekly bar chart.

Price-Based Techniques

6) Check the Cardinal Square chart to determine where the cardinal cross intersects price. This will increase one's ability to track possible reversal points.

7) Construct the mechanical trend indicator, or the swing chart, (see the separate chapter on swing charts) to determine when to enter one's positions.

When to Apply Gann Techniques

This battery of techniques can be used over any market situation, although it is most beneficial in strongly trending markets, or for traders who wish to look at a very long-term picture. Do not use these techniques by themselves when the market goes into a trading situation, for they will generate too many whipsaw signals. The volume-based methods, on-balance volume and tic volume, can confirm or even anticipate breakouts above the 45-degree downward-trending lines. Gann indicators can help greatly to refine the signals generated by price-sensitive indicators in trending markets.

Where to Find out More About Gann's Techniques

Books and Periodicals

Gann, William D. *The Basis of My Forecasting Method for Grains.* 1935 reprint. Pomeroy, Washington: Lambert-Gann, 1976.

Gann, William D. *Forecasting Rules for Grain—Geometric Angles.* Pomeroy, Washington: Lambert-Gann, 1976.

Gann, William D. *Forty-Five Years in Wall Street.* Pomeroy, Washington: Lambert-Gann, 1949.

Gann, William D. *How to Make Profits in Commodities.* 1942 reprint. Pomeroy, Washington: Lambert-Gann, 1976.

Gann, William D. *Speculation: a Profitable Profession (A Course of Instruction in Grains).* 1955 reprint. Pomeroy, Washington: Lambert-Gann, 1976.

Kaufman, Perry J. *Commodity Trading Systems and Methods*, pp. 200-205 New York: John Wiley & Sons, 1978.

The W.D. Gann Technical Review. Lambert-Gann Publishing Company (newsletter.)

Software to Run on the IBM Personal Computer

Chart Trader Plus—Interday charting package with the following: median lines, Fibonacci lines and spheres, recursion lines, percentage retracements, simple moving averages with bands, oscillators, relative strength index, on-balance volume, %R, cycle intervals, and parallel channels. Investor's Toolkit Ltd., Summit, IL 60501.

Computrac—Interday charting package has the following studies: moving averages, rates of change, Oscillators, ratios and spread, RSI, stochastics, on-balance volume, moving average convergence divergence, point-and-figure, etc. Chart zooming, trendlines and parallel channels, cycle analysis with Fourier analysis. Computrac, Inc., New Orleans, LA 70175.

Ganntrader I—Interday charting package for the technician with trading knowledge of William D. Gann's approach. No screen displays but excellent hardcopy charts. Gannsoft Publishing Company, Leavenworth, WA 98826.

Relevance III™—Interday charting package which creates above-average screen graphics and the finest hardcopy chart available using regular computer equipment. Performs many advanced type studies and has the only available Elliott Wave ratio analysis program. Holt Investment, Nashville, TN 37238.

17

Risk Management and Control

Key to Survival

Risk Management and Control at a Glance

Background and Philosophy of Risk Management and Control

Modern risk management techniques have their roots in gambling techniques and probability theory.

Principles of Risk Management and Control

Unless traders wish to avoid any risk by staying completely out of the market, they must learn to manage and control their risks. Rate of return expectations must be reasonable. If traders expect exorbitantly high rates of return they will expose their trading to high risks. Traders can manage risk by spreading it out in one of two ways: over time or over many market opportunities. Risk control and equity control techniques mitigate the risk itself. Traders can do this by improving their success rate (finding better trading methods) and controlling the amount of capital at risk in any one situation (money management). Finally, the traders must learn to combat their own tendencies to take on a gambler's psychology and must learn to analyze and execute trades in a non-emotional, rational manner.

Controlling Risk Across Time or Markets

The floor-trader's traditional techniques are averaging and pyramiding to increase the time window of opportunity. They are discussed at length here because they are not well-known outside of trading circles—and they will ultimately lead traders to ruin. Traders need to diversify into several types of markets and in dissimilar issues to spread risk successfully.

Using Risk Control Techniques to Improve the Success Rate

Success rate depends on traders' own trading expertise and on their choices and applications of correct trading techniques, which is what the rest of this book is about. Also, traders should make sure that they have definite rules for taking profits and cutting losses with whatever technique or combination of techniques they may use.

Controlling Risk with Proper Equity Management

Stop-loss orders will control the maximum amount traders can lose. Traders should consider the worst possible series of runs that could affect them and still not remove them from the trading game: input theory of runs analysis. Then they set aside a specific amount for their trading account, so they always have an idea of their real gains and losses from trading. Then traders determine a small percentage which will be the maximum total percentage of their trading capital to have at risk at any one time. After a loss, the maximum amount to risk is the same percentage of the *reduced* total amount.

Cultivating a Rational Trading Psychology

It is difficult for many traders to avoid the gambler's urge to keep betting in the face of losses or to become greedy after successes and try to "get rich quick." They need to learn to admit when a position is losing and take losses and learn to be mechanical and unemotional in trading. Traders should not ignore the signals of their trading methods because of "hunches."

Background and Philosophy of Risk Management and Control

Risk, in the context of market trading, is the exposure to loss of trading capital. Traders are dealing with degrees of risk when they trade the markets: maximum risk graded all the way down to minimum risk.

All traders know that no situation can engender rewards if there are no risks. They also are led to the belief that in order to make profits they must expose their capital to potential, partial or complete loss, and in certain situations, loss above and beyond their originally intended amount. No trader would argue with those statements, or would they?

Traders have the capital to trade with and they have to sort out the risks that are in the marketplace. What is discomforting about this statement is that oftentimes they don't know what risks are confronting them.

Principles of Risk Management and Control

Rates of Return:
Greater Returns Mean Greater Risks

A subtle fact of normal life is that the greater amount of capital one has at risk the greater one's reward should be.

Some professional traders seek a year in and year out return of 50% of their capital with a 5% risk of their capital. This means that at the end of every year, they have a 100% probability of making 50% of their total trading capital with a 5% risk to their capital. These are proven numbers worked out in actual trading during the past 16 years.

Some traders and speculators look for situations that will return 200% or more on their money . . . monthly, or even better yet, weekly. Do those situations exist? Yes, they do and they exist in this manner: 200% monthly return with 99% risk of loss of capital. When the profits accrue, they accrue tremendously, but when the losses come, they come with surprising frequency.

It is true that those opportunities with exorbitantly high returns on capital with low risk are rarities, but they exist nevertheless. When those opportunities do come, they come for those who are prepared for them, for example, the people who are already in the markets performing their daily trading routines. These high return opportunities do not exist for non-professionals on a continual basis. If non-professionals do happen to get into a high return situation, they should recognize the opportunity and not expect it to happen again. The trading profession is a business and not a speculation.

If traders make a 25% return on their trading capital year after year they should consider it very good. When the rare opportunities present themselves for traders to make 200% on their trading capital they must be around to take advantage of them.

Controlling Risk

There are two ways that traders can control risks. First, they can control market risk and second, they can control equity risk. Whatever traders do, they must control equity risk. If they cannot control market risk they will eventually lose all their equity. If they cannot control equity risk, they will lose everything much sooner.

There are two additional ways to control market risk: spread trades across a time span or spread trades across portfolios of markets.

Spreading Market Risk Across Time

When traders spread market risk across time they track one or two futures or stocks day in and day out. When time or price is right, traders enter their transactions and hope to make their profits. When traders spread risk out over time, they look at only a few commodities or risk situations, then pick a time to enter those markets. Hence, their time is spent waiting for the opportunities to develop. If no opportunities develop, then traders continue to wait while their expenses continue to pile up. If they are tracking only one market, traders may only have two opportunities to make profitable trades in a year. If they miss the two opportunities, they must wait another year. If traders take the opportunities that present themselves, and their analysis is proven incorrect, they not only lose money, but they will also miss out on the opportunities that might present themselves later in those two trading situations!

Within the purview of controlling risk by spreading trading situations out over time appears the technique of averaging. Averaging is an attempt to increase through mechanical means, the limited number of trading opportunities that present themselves in a span of time. What traders do not have, when they average, are real trading opportunities which can make profits without undue risk. By averaging, traders are, in effect, expecting the market to come to their terms: if they buy at the bottom and it goes down more they average because they won't accept the fact that the first low wasn't the low of the move. Implicit in this is that traders are forcing their average position to be closer to the low price. They couldn't pick the bottom, hence somewhere along the line, if traders average enough, they will get to the bottom of all this.

Pyramids and Averaging

There are three ways traders can average their positions: inverted pyramids, conventional pyramids, and averaging to the market. None of these methods is a reliable method. Most people who were using such techniques in October 1987, did not financially survive the great stock market collapse of that month. It does not take such an exaggerated market move to do in the small trader if he or she is using averaging and pyramiding techniques.

Averaging is an action that one performs in relation to the market position. Averaging with specific contracts, whether against or with the trend, is a day-trading technique. There are three variables that traders must know: do they average with or against the trend, do they add greater sized positions or smaller lots and when do they get out.

There are several types of averaging techniques, and all entail market risk. Some traders use the techniques successfully, but others have used these methods to disastrous consquences.

The Conventional Pyramids

Perhaps traders have put on a long position and then see a gratifying climb in price so they wish that they had put in more money. Conventional pyramiding is the answer to that natural desire to try to take the greatest possible advantage of a good thing.

Conventional pyramids are a form of averaging with specific guidelines. The trader buys 30 contracts at $2.00. The market goes in his favor. The market trades higher by a random amount, let's say $2.25. At this point the trader adds 15 contracts to his original 30. Average price for total contracts is $(30 \times 2 + 15 \times 2.25)/(30 + 15)$. The price continues to go up in his favor to $2.48. The trader continues to add, this time about 7 contracts at $2.48 to his now total 45 contracts. The average price is still further away from the current market price of $2.48. This is the conventional pyramid.

The flaw with this technique is that the trader starts to move his total position price closer and closer to the market. The false belief is that if the trader adds fewer and fewer positions to his total commitment as the price goes further in his favor, any reaction or countermove will not reach low enough to cause his total position to be a loser. Well, the later traders get on board a one directional move, the closer they are to a countermove. It is unbelievable that this is considered the safest way to increase the size of one's position without increasing the average price by leaps and bounds!

The Inverted Pyramid

Most traders have tried this pyramid solution. Traders start by buying 30 contracts. The market goes up. Instead of buying less than 30 contracts, they buy more than 30 contracts, thereby bringing the price of their average position closer to the market price. After all, they are trading with profits! That is, money that is not their original capital. Traders may even buy many more than the initial 30 contracts, thereby more than doubling the risks to their trading capital.

The added risk here is twofold: the first risk, that of taking on the first 30 contracts at the market price entails immediate loss if the market turns against them; the second risk: when a second and bigger lot is added to the first lot, it again exposes traders' capital to immediate risk by bringing the total average price closer to the current market price, again exposing their trading capital to a loss if the market reacts ever so slightly.

Traders must remember that the market has gone up so much that the chances of it correcting become even greater!

Averaging to Market

The third way traders can average entails the addition of more and more positions so that their average position is close to the market price. Many floor traders use this technique and it has made them quite a bit of money, but every so often there are such long one-directional moves that occur that they are wiped out! This technique entails averaging against the trend, expecting an imminent reversal of the slightest proportion to show the trader a huge profit the previous pyramids have averaged with the trend. Let's take an example to see how this is done.

Corn is trading at $3.00 per bushel. The trader buys 1 contract at $3.00. It is predetermined by the trader that at every 3 cents down, he will buy a fixed amount of contracts in the following amounts.

Market	Add Number	Average	Away from Market
$3.00	1 contracts	$3.00	at market
$2.97	3 contracts	$2.9775	0.075 cents away
$2.94	6 contracts	$2.955	1.5 cents away
$2.91	9 contracts	$2.934	2.4 cents away

This scheme of position management is used quite frequently. The inherent flaw with this technique is that one increases one's total exposure to market risk by 19 fold—from an initial one lot contract, to an eventual 19 contract position at the last indicated position addition. The one directional move will eventually have to reverse by a minimal amount so that the total position can show a profit. However, when traders deal with managing risks, they are always on the lookout for the one chance in a million, the one chance in a billion, the one chance in a trillion, that will occur. In the futures markets, and now even in the stock market, there are cases which show that corn can go down more than 10 cents in one move and stay down! The unfortunate trader is the one which finds these to be the rule rather than the exception.

If the trader had not averaged down in this manner, this is what it would look like:

Market	Number of Contracts	Average Price	Away from Market
3.00	1 contract	$3.00	at market
2.97	0 contract	$3.00	3 cents on 1 contract
2.94	0 contract	$3.00	6 cents on 1 contract
2.91	0 contract	$3.00	9 cents on 1 contract

if he managed to hold on to one position all the way down. The chances are not great that the market will rally up 9 cents in order for the trader to scratch his trade. In the first example, the trader only has to see the market rally up 2.5 cents in order for him to break even on his total position. If it rallies to 9 cents, he makes profits above and beyond, on a 19 fold increase in positions!

Averaging to the market is a form of pyramiding which is more dangerous than the person who uses it daily in trading knows. The problem with this methodology of trading is that the losses, when they do occur, is great. For traders, the past history that they can present to others as an example of their success is not a valid indication of present and future successes. As traders, they are as successful as only the last trade they made. It is always the last trade.

What happens when the market does not rally and the trader is in a position of having to add more to his total commitment so that he can get the average price of his commitments closer to the last sale of the corn contract? After the trader adds to his position, and finds that the price of corn does not rally, he is faced with the decision of buying more or selling out his total commitment. If the trader chooses the former course of action, the inference is that he has more capital outside of trading account to use to reinforce his position (if not, he is out of the game). If he chooses the latter course of action, that of biting the bullet, and sells out his total commitment at a loss, he also is indicating that he is out of the game, for his originally intended commitment of $1,000 is consumed in reinforcing a commitment which required 19 times the risk.

What if, after the first contract that he bought, instead of showing a loss, it immediately shows a profit and goes straight up? The one, and only one, contract that he is long is showing a profit, but he has $19,000 in his trading account. This $1,000 risk is a gross underutilization of his trading capital. There is nothing wrong with this, but it is a rather backwards utilization of his capital. When the trader is right, he is right for only one contract, and if he averages down when he is wrong, he is wrong for 19 contracts!

Therefore, when the trader who trades this way is taken out of the game using this trading strategy, he is taken out for a lot more money than he had in his account originally.

Spread Market Risk Across Markets

This is the technique that professionals who survive year after year use. Spreading risk across portfolios of stocks, futures or bonds.

When traders spread risk out over many markets, they approach risks as a portfolio of opportunities. Instead of merely looking at a few markets, they track a portfolio of markets. If they track about twenty markets, during the course of a year they may have 40 opportunities to make profitable trades in the portfolio of markets. During the course of a month they will have about 1.5 markets to make profitable trades. Of course, in order to practice this approach traders must have proportionately more risk capital and they must have a great deal of time to spend following the various markets they have chosen. Most beginning traders do not have the capital resources to implement this strategy.

With this approach the trader is looking at more than one market, a portfolio of markets, filtering out all the noise inherent in all markets and then taking the profitable opportunities when they present themselves. With this strategy comes the hard, cold fact that traders cannot enter the markets with less than $5,000 and try to make a full-fledged career out of this business. Instead, the trading capital should be in excess of $50,000, allowing traders to carry more than one position at any one point in time. No markets will consistently offer profit opportunities every day of the year.

As a rule thumb, it is not a good idea to be in more than ten markets at once, as the problems of following more than this number become very great.

Use Risk Control Techniques
to Improve Your Success Rate

The other chapters this book offer traders technical indicators which give them a better than average probability of making profitable trades. Of course, the ideal technique is one in which the trader can make profitable trades 100% of the time.

Even a Highly Favorable System Cannot Guarantee Success

Unfortunately, there are no trading techniques that are at the 100% confidence level. Even with systems that purport to offer 99.9% confidence levels, traders would find ways to lose money on the 0.1% loss side. Proper equity risk management techniques are necessary despite the high accuracy of trading techniques. On winning trades, profits can be relatively small, and on losing trades, losses can be exorbitantly high.

The Stop-loss Order as Equity Management Tool

When a trade is entered, the trader should also enter a stop-loss order at the same time. This is the two order rule. Most traders do not and some even go to the extent of saying to themselves that they have a mental stop placed so that when the price gets to that limit, they enter the order to sell then and there. Such are the mental games that traders play often with ludicrous consequenses.

In a sense, the markets offer less control of risk to traders' trading equity than the race tracks. At the race track people only lose as much as they bet: if they bet $2, they stand to lose only $2. In the markets, if someone buys a stock or futures, they can lose their total up-front equity, and even more. Most traders, when they speculate in the markets, don't realize that they are at total risk for the full amount. It is because of this fact that traders must learn to control their equity risk—the clearing firms won't and the Securities and Exchange won't. If traders don't recognize that controlling risk to their equity is paramount to their survival in the trading profession, then they are letting others control their money.

Stop-loss orders are the simplest and most mechanical way of market techniques to limit traders' losses.

Capital Control Determines How Long Traders Last

This is an area of risk management where traders have total control: the total amount of their dollars risk on each and every trade. Traders alone make the ultimate decision about what amount goes into each trade in each and every trading account. The techniques chapters showed how to assess the market risk to any position that they or anyone else tracking those markets can enter into. The following section details how traders can control the exposure of their equity to loss.

However, many traders are oblivious to how they can control risk until it is too late. If traders start with $10,000 in their accounts and lose it all, they are out of the game. By default they have controlled their risk to the amount of $10,000—but they are unable to come back to trade again, meaning they have lost everything they can afford to lose. (Traders who lose their trading account capital, but come back with more capital are really saying that the amount of money that they originally put up to trade with was only *part of their total* risk capital. Therefore, when they come back to trade again, they come back with fresh funds.)

Putting a Definite Limit on the Total Amount of Trading Capital

Experienced traders who are aware of capital risks manage the amount of capital in their trading account—and never hook up their outside assets to this account. Unlike a businessman who has a line of credit, a good trader, even though he may have funds outside of his trading account, never considers the use of those funds to handle his risk positions, hence the experienced trader positions his account capital into positions of risk capital.

A Trader's Main Goal: Avoid Ruin

The most important fact for traders who want to make their living from the market is for them to always have enough excess capital in reserves to cover obligations, to live on and to be able to make meaningful market plays. If the trader no longer has resources to do these things, then the game is over and the trader will have to either seek employment somewhere else or wait for a large inheritance or a winning lottery ticket to replenish the coffers. Therefore, the bottom line of money and position management is to *avoid ruin*.

If traders find that they have lost all their money, they can no longer trade. It is important that the trader find ways to avoid loss of capital to an extent that would impair their ability to continue trading and support themselves.

One often hears such common-sense tenets of money and position management as the following:

- Don't put a significant amount of resources on the line for a long shot.
- Don't put all your eggs in one basket. Or, even more conservatively, don't put most of your eggs in just a few baskets.
- Have enough reserve back up for a reasonably possible series of bad trades.
- On the other side of the coin, don't be so overcautious that they do not have enough money at risk to be sure of making a decent living in the long run.

These tenets are, in fact, all one really needs to keep in mind for intelligent position management. However, the problem with these tenets is that they are rather vague when it is necessary for a trader to evaluate any given situation. Traders need a precise idea of what such terms as "overcautious," "reasonably possible series of bad trades," "long shot," "enough," "significant amount of your resources," "most of your eggs," and "just a few baskets" really mean in cold numbers.

The rest of this chapter is devoted to giving a mathematically meaningful interpretation of the general dictum:

> Invest the maximum amount of money in those ventures most likely to turn a good profit, and still have enough money left to be able to sustain a reasonably expected run of losses.

There are basically two things that we need to define with mathematical precision here:

- What is a "reasonably expectable run of losses?"
- Once "reasonably expectable run of losses" is defined, what is enough money to have in reserve?

Controlling Risk with Proper Equity Management

There was a professional gambler at the Chicago Open Board of Trade years ago. He said that there was a time period when he followed the horses that he had a series of non-winning bets. During that one season he had a streak of 40 bets on various thoroughbreds which turned into losers. It's mathematically possible to have a streak of 40 losers in a row, but for application in the real world, how possibly is it? Not too probable, but it happens not only to the professional gambler but also to professional traders with alarming frequency.

Traders can determine how much money to risk in any given play, and still have enough capital to come back, by knowing the greatest number of bad trades they can reasonably expect to happen in a row and dividing their total trading capital by the sum of this number plus one. Thus, even if their luck is bad and their run of bad trades happens, traders will still have something left with which to continue. Of course, traders may wish to cushion more by only involving half their trading capital or some other portion in this reckoning. Specific techniques and examples for this kind of management are in the following section.

For those who know how to handle risks this game is simple and a continuous money-maker.

What traders want to determine here is the probability of occurrence for various runs of bad trades, that is two losses in a row, three losses in a row, and so on.

A trader may determine that there is a 30% chance of any given trade turning out bad. Therefore, his chances of the next *two* trades being bad trades will be 30% × 30% or 9%. His chances of the next *three* trades being bad will be 30% × 30% × 30% or 2.7%, and we can see that chances of a run of four bad trades will be 1%, and a run of five's chances of occurring will be 1/3 of 1%. This example illustrates how to determine the probability of a run of a given size ocurring: Take the probability of one bad trade occcurring. Then decide what size run to test for, and simply multiply that probability by itself that many times. As a formula:

Probability of a run of n bad trades =
(probability of any one trade going bad)^n

There is still one thing traders have to do before they can make this computation: they must know the probability that any given trade will go bad. This probability and the amount of trading capital they have are really the two personal variables that traders bring to the whole equation of risk. The amount of capital available is easy to plug into the equation, because traders need only copy it from their bank balance.

Determining Success Rate from Observation

The probability that traders will make bad trades, however, takes a little more work to determine. This is really based on their personal trading records, so of course if they are beginning traders, their problem is to first establish a record before they can use this method of risk management. Thus, traders must keep a statistical record of all their trades and their results.

An Interim Success Rate

What do traders do in the meantime while they are compiling their personal statistics? The most obvious thing is to use some arbitrary (and, hopefully, conservative) estimate of the probability that a particular trade will fail.

This first arbitrary probability can be refined as soon as they have made several trades, though they probably won't want to set their final equations in stone until they have quite a few trades chalked up. A good method for reaching some kind of interim determination of what an overall trading record will be is to use the equation given as follows (a binomial probability):

$$B\,(l\!:p,n)\;=\;\frac{n\,!}{l\,!\times(n\text{-}1)!}\;\;p^l\times(1\text{-}p\,)^{n\text{-}1}$$

where
   l is the number of losses
   n is the total number of trades
   p is the probability of one trade being a loss

The formula is designed to answer the following question: if the trader had made ten trades, and three of them failed, so that his record shows a 30% failure rate, what is the probability that the continuing failure rate will be 30% as the number of trades are increased? As the number of trades increases, given the probability rate per trade to remain unchanged, the trader will find that the total probability of 30% failure will decrease due to the impact of a greater and greater number of trades. Smart traders could then go onto riskier trading strategies (greater probability of one trade being a loss, in this case, the number is 30%) without necessarily jeopardizing their total trading strategy. Traders could be much surer of this statistic after 100 trades had shown them coming in at around 30 failures, and all but the most doubtful would be totally convinced after, say 307 trades out of 1,000 had failed.

How Runs of Profits or Losses Affect Trading Capital

The scenario is as follows:

Trader starts to trade with $15,000.00 in his trading account. The trader can control the risk of losses to his trading account capital in percentage terms. In the same manner, he can control the percentage profits that he can make with each trade.

The trader encounters ten losers in a row, each loss taking a fixed percentage of his remaining capital. These are his numbers:

Percentage Lost on Capital Balance	Capital Remaining After 10 Straight Losses	Percentage Profit on Capital Balance	Capital After Ten Straight Wins	Percentage of Original $15,000
3%	$10,729.52	3%	$14,419.58	96.10
5%	$ 8,532.00	5%	$13,897.73	92.70
8%	$ 5,994.56	8%	$12,941.81	86.30
10%	less than 25%	10%	$12,209.16	81.40
15%	of original	15%	$10,154.95	67.70
20%	capital remains	20%	$ 7,977.99	53.10
25%	—	25%	$ 5,900.18	39.30
30%	—	30%	$ 4,088.37	27.30
35%	—	35%	$ 2,639.22	17.60
40%	—	40%	$ 1,574.11	10.50

What is obviously shown here are two important factors: the string of losses that a trader can encounter which causes adverse results to his ability to survive and secondly, the amount of percentage of total capital to risk also affects the ability of the trader. Even the best ones who are able to recover from ten straight losses in a row with ten straight winners, might never recover their original trading capital.

Given this possible scenario, the trader who knows little about the market would be better off risking no more than 2.5% of his total trading capital if he fully expects to break even after a string of bad trades. This exemplifies how critical it is for the trader to exercise discipline and pick his trades correctly. The numbers already are against his ability to succeed.

Please also note that the above calculations do not take into consideration the cost of commissions.

Determining How Much Capital to Risk at One Time

Suppose that a beginning trader has established a fairly reasonable estimate of his trading failure rate. The next step is to determine what an acceptable level of risk of total ruin would be. In other words, if he knew that his next trade had a certain chance of being the beginning of a run of bad luck that would wipe him out completely, how small would that chance have to be in order for him to comfortably make that trade? A one percent chance? A one-tenth percent chance? Or less?

Perhaps a more useful question would be: Given the amount of capital at risk at any one time, and given a certain failure rate, what are the chances that sometime in his trading career this trader will have a run of bad luck that will completely clean him out?

Of course, once traders recognize a bad trading situation, they don't just keep mechanically "betting" their units of capital until that one fatal run does come along and wipes them out. Traders should maintain their magic percentage of capital, but always over *the remaining balance, not the original balance*. If traders find that risking 20% of their capital in any one transaction gives them a reasonably small degree of risk, and if their capital at a given moment is $100,000, then they will risk no more than $20,000 on a given transaction. If traders lose the $20,000, so that their remaining capital is now $80,000, then they will risk $16,000, or 20% of this total, on the next trade, and not another $20,000. In this way their chances of getting wiped out will remain exceedingly slim (provided, of course, that traders have properly reckoned their failure rate and that the failure rate does not vary over time for some reason). With this approach, traders also manage to increase their risk amount when they run into winners. If the account runs up to $150,000, then their next trade would risk $30,000, not the $20,000 originally started with.

The alternative situation is for traders to continually risk the full $20,000 per trade until they run into a streak of bad trades. This mechanical method would get them out of the trading business if they immediately encountered 5 losing trades in a row.

To summarize, traders need to take the following steps in setting up a risk management program:

1) Find the right mix of trading techniques that they feel comforable with that will give them a better chance of profitable trades and then set up their trading system.

2) Begin their trading by putting very modest experimental amounts in each play for the first two or three dozen trades, that is, a small percentage of their total trading capital.

3) Once traders have a significant number of trades consummated under their trading plan, determine what their failure rate has been.

Find out if the trading system that they have devised is good or not. Not all systems can successfully follow all markets all of the time.

4) Decide on what would be an acceptable risk rate for initiating a series of trades which will lead to total ruin. This can be done by taking into account how many trades they plan over each year and how many years traders plan to be in operation.

5) Determine their observed failure rate as a percentage of total trades (that is, as a number less than 1) and raise this number to as many powers as needed to go under the acceptable risk rate.

6) Take the power to which they raised their failure rate (in step 5) and divide it into their total amount of trading capital. This will give traders the maximum amount of money which they should have at risk for any one trade.

Traders should repeat this procedure every time they initiate a new trading system.

Cultivate a Rational Trading Psychology

Unfortunately for many traders with big egos, the market is very impersonal and is unimpressed by how tough traders are, their past successes or what they think of it. This means that the last thing traders want to do is get emotionally involved with the market. Instead, they should ascertain potentially profitable current situations and input their risk factors and personality makeup into the scenario.

The professional trader is not a compulsive gambler. If a trader has such personality traits, he or she will need to work on them.

Professional traders look continuously to reduce their risk in the markets. Unprofessional traders look to trade the markets for a quick killing, depriving the professionals of their fair share of profits.

When a company offers shares of its stocks for sale, it would be ridiculous for anyone, as potential buyer, to buy it as cheaply as possible. No company, in its right mind, would offer to sell its assets at the lowest prices that the market can offer it; no farmer will sell his crops below what it costs him to produce it. Therefore, traders mustn't think that they can buy at the lowest price and sell at the highest price. That's the role of the insiders and the professionals. What successful traders can do, however, is follow in their footsteps and play the markets the way they do . . . wisely and intelligently.

Where to Find Out More About Risk Management

Epstein, Richard A. *The Theory of Gambling and Statistical Logic.* Academic Press, 1967. A technical, but useful and comprehensive guide to the subject.

Silberstang, Edwin. *How to Gamble and Win.* New York: Franklin Watts, 1979. A good general overview of how to take consistent profits from probabilistic phenomena through educated discipline.

Teweles, Richard J., Charles V. Harlow, and Herbert L. Stone, *The Commodity Futures Game: Who Wins? Who Loses? Why?* New York: McGraw-Hill, 1974. Encapsulates a lot of good knowledge for market technicians about game theory and risk management.

Index

		OB = Overbought OS = Oversold	Trading Markets	Trending Mar**k...** Bull	Bea**r...**
Micro Analysis	Price Sensitive Indicators	Moving Averages	Many false breakouts and whipsaw action	Valid breakouts and continuous confirmation	Vali... and con...
		Relative Strength	OB/OS indication excellent	Skewed number of signals to more overbought	Ske... sign... over...
		Percentage R	OB/OS signals are valid	False OB signals valid. Use modified OS	Fals... vali... OB
		Oscillators	OB/OS signals are valid	False OB signals valid if using modified OS	Fals... vali... mo...
		Stochastics	Crossovers OB and OS are valid	Crossovers from OS only are valid	Cros... OB ...
		Point-and-Figure	False breakouts whipsaw action	Valid breakouts	Vali...
	Hybrid Indicators	Market Profile®	Normal distribution	Can observe and tell upside breakouts	Can... tell ... brea...
	Volume Sensitive Indicators	Tic Volume	Very good accumulation indicator	Can use to possibly pyramid	Vali... beca... har...
		On-Balance Volume	Very good accumulation indicator	Too long to use to pyramid	Vali... imp...
		Bar Charts	Valid, recognizable pattern	Valid, recognizable trend lines, channels	Vali... reco... line...
Macro Analysis	Time Sensitive	Astronomical Cycles	No good	Not applicable	Not...
	Composite	Elliott Wave Theory	Hard to show beginning and end—just that it is occurring	Can project market to take out previous highs	Can... mar... out...
		Gann Analysis	Whipsaws	Long for the upmove	Sho... dow...